T0083630

WALES AND THE SPANISH CIVIL WAR

WALES AND THE SPANISH CIVIL WAR
The Dragon's Dearest Cause?

Robert Stradling

UNIVERSITY OF WALES PRESS
CARDIFF
2004

All rights reserved. No part of this book may be reproduced, stored in a retrieval system, or transmitted, in any form or by any means, electronic, mechanical, photocopying, recording or otherwise, without clearance from the University of Wales Press, 10 Columbus Walk, Brigantine Place, Cardiff, CF10 4UP.
www.wales.ac.uk/press

British Library Cataloguing-in-Publication Data
A catalogue record for this book is available from the British Library.

ISBN 0–7083–1816–9 paperback
0–7083–1817–7 hardback

Printed in Great Britain by Cromwell Press Ltd, Trowbridge

I Meirion, fy nghyfaill,
gyda diolch

Contents

Appendix

Preface and Acknowledgements

To begin with, something long demanded by friends and enemies alike – an *apologia pro vita mea*. I have been active as a historian in Wales for much the greater part of my life, and since 1962 – the year my undergraduate studies began in Cardiff, thanks to a grant from the public purse – as a professional. I am Welsh, and a historian, but not until reaching my seventh decade have I aspired to combine these two accidental yet essential elements of my existence. Whether or not the attempt has been successful, it remains certain that the terrain explored in this book is the only one where it could have been ventured in the first place, because ever since the unforgettable experience of reading Garrett Mattingly's *The Defeat of the Spanish Armada* on its appearance in 1959, my vocation has been the history of Spain. Such was the universal influence and reach of the Spanish monarchy in its days of empire that I sometimes found myself carpet-bagging into the history of other great nations, including France, Belgium, Italy, England, Cardiff and (most recently) Ireland. As such, and in contrast, Wales does not figure in Mattingly's classic text, nor in my own books; but then, so far as I have been able to read, nor does it figure in any other book about the history of Spain. For Wales, and the Welsh, any historical relationship with that great nation has thus far been – honesty bids me report – a remarkably unrequited affair.

Wales has a long history but – at least for extended periods of its course – a two-dimensional one. By this I mean that Wales looks at the Welsh, and they look straight back at Wales. The comprehension is mutual, total and wholly insular – like that of a family of badgers. This is not uncharacteristic of small nations which find themselves, through geographical accident and political evolution, contingently but irretrievably fixed within another which is greater and more powerful. In the early decades of the last century an almost elemental need to supply this missing dimension of communication and identity was the underlying factor leading representative Welsh individuals and institutions towards internationalism. Within this broad, multi-partisan movement, awareness of the similar dilemma of the smaller Iberian nations (perhaps especially the Basque Country) came to play a role. Awareness of the unfolding drama of the Second Spanish Republic was present in Wales in the years after the Bourbon monarchy was overthrown in 1931. Consciousness of the Republic's wide-ranging programme of political and social reform was sharpened by a certain progress towards 'devolution' in its early years. The severe repression, by the colonial army commanded by General Franco, of the Asturias uprising, spearheaded as that movement had been by the coal miners (October 1934) attracted further interest – to some extent, empathy – in different quarters. Down to 1936, therefore, the Republic evoked an attention which was not unlike that displayed towards the more successful Spanish transition to a plural and regionally structured democracy half-a-century later, in the 1980s; more intense in some quarters than others, but widely apparent, and often apprehensive.

For thirty years, I taught twentieth-century European history to under-graduates as a member of staff at (what is now) Cardiff University. In particular, I offered an option on 'The Spanish Republic and the Civil War', which ran perennially through most of the epoch during which Spain was managing the difficult but exemplary development of a mature (and monar-chical) democracy. The present book draws on the challenging experience of teaching this subject to successive generations of students, of all ages and from all walks of life – and many of them from Wales. I set out to write it in the belief that interest in the Spanish Civil War and the International Brigades remains stronger and more widespread in Wales than in any other country which became involved. However, its main *raison d'être* is not simply to record this phenomenon but to provide a critical exploration of it. Working towards this latter objective has produced a somewhat different reading from that which I had expected. This was as much of a surprise to me as it may prove to be for some of my readers.

As usual, my indebtedness to many who have assisted my work is chronic – to the extent that I am relieved to have worked in the present record era of minimal interest rates. Not for the first time, foremost among my creditors is Meirion Hughes, cherished friend and collaborator. Without his superb translations, by turns graphic and poetic, of dozens of reports and articles in the Welsh-language press, these richly meaningful texts would have stayed locked away, not only from this one, miserably monoglot, Cardiffian but also from public enquiry in general. In offering Meirion the book's dedication, I recognize not only this present contribution, but also past decades of fruit-ful intellectual association and stimulating companionship. It is a pleasure to record my debt to Bill Jones, who likewise reversed his original relation-ship with the author and acted as my unpaid tutor in the history of inter-war Wales. The world of scholarship sometimes brings home its consolations as well as its contentions. Substantial enrichments of the book's contents were also donated by Sidney Robinson, who loaned me his personal archive as one-time secretary of the Newport Spanish Aid Committee; by John and Gillian Mehta, who provided copies of valuable unpublished letters of Gilbert Taylor and Alec Cummings; and by Mary and Jonathan Thomas, who allowed me to read the unpublished correspondence of Frank Thomas. Mr Jeffery Robinson, of the Gwyn Thomas Estate, responded readily to my request for access to the relevant papers held in the National Library of Wales.

In the more public sphere, Elizabeth Bennet (university archivist) and Sue Marsh were unfailingly helpful during my labours in the rich seams of the Coalfield Collection at Swansea. Steve Thomas of the Welsh Centre for International Affairs kindly allowed me access to the archive of the Welsh United Nations Association. Pat West, director of the Gwynedd Museum, drew my attention to various memorabilia deposited there by John Williams-Hughes after his sojourn in Spain. Lona Jones and her colleagues in the Printed Books and Archive sections at the National Library of Wales gave sympathetic help to a novice researcher in that excellent institution. At UCNW Bangor, Shan Robinson facilitated access to the newspaper collection in short order, and kindly made and dispatched copies of press materials. As always, Tish Collins and her volunteer helpers at the Marx Memorial Library made it a pleasure to work there. At Cardiff University's Information Services Centre, Peter Keelan of the Salisbury Library, and his colleague, Tom Dawkes, were (as always) ready with problem-solving suggestions and general assistance. It seems appropriate here to state anew my general sense of obligation to many other librarians and archivists in Britain, Spain and Russia – a feeling already expressed in detail in earlier books.

If rather belatedly, I wish to record my sense of thankfulness to Dr Susanne Marten-Finnis, of the Queen's University, Belfast, who 'smuggled' an important reel of archival microfilm out of Russia on behalf of a fellow scholar whom she had never met. I am deeply grateful to Jim Carmody and Richard Baxell, who once again placed their impressive knowledge of the British Battalion at my disposal. Several other kind contributions and interventions are acknowledged *en passant* in the relevant reference notes. The following also deserve thanks for support, material, intellectual and spiritual: the families Collier, Hearder and Stradling; Lala Isla, Tom Buchanan, Alan Davies, Terry Hawkes, Alun and Lynne Hutchings, Gwynfor Jones, Scott Newton, Arnold Owen, Richard Griffiths and Keith Robbins.

I remain obliged to the committee of the International Brigade Fund, administered by the Welsh Centre for International Affairs, Cardiff, for a travel grant which greatly facilitated my research in Spain in June, 2001; and to the trustees of the T. E. Ellis fund of the University of Wales, who awarded me a welcome research grant. At the University of Wales Press, I am especially mindful of the keen interest and enthusiasm of Duncan Campbell, which much enlivened and lightened the practical labour of producing the two books of mine on which he has acted as commissioning editor. Duncan's colleagues, Liz Powell and Ceinwen Jones, have also been immensely supportive throughout these processes.

Two volunteers, one on each side, offered me encouragement and friendship in the last years of their lives. Though neither regretted their decision to go to Spain, nor changed their minds about the rightness of the causes for which they fought and suffered, Frank Thomas and Lance Rogers had both grown more understanding of the ethical position occupied by the other side. It is an example that all should follow.

Finally, I wish to pay tribute to Hywel Francis, who read and approved the original synopsis of this book. It was never my intention to attempt the task – both impossible and gratuitous – of replacing his superb book *Miners Against Fascism*. The present offering, I hope, will merely complement Francis's indispensable study, providing a more comprehensive context for the reader's approach to its general subject. Our interpretations differ at basic levels of instinct, emphasis, methodology and hermeneutics: and there are places in this book where failure to explain this in candid terms would have disingenuously confused the reader and may (perhaps) have appeared mealy-mouthed. Yet my admiration for the rigorous, unsentimental scholarship Hywel Francis brought to bear on a subject on many aspects of which – as inherent elements of his own life and culture – he must have felt so deeply and strongly, has remained undiminished on each of the numberless occasions when I have consulted his writings. There can be no greater praise of a work of history than to recognize its fundamental influence on the intellectual culture of its own time. Indeed, in this case I would go further, for *Miners Against Fascism* both created the history of Wales and the Spanish Civil War and at once became part of that history. Remarkably, the book provides the only (partial) exception I know to the statement made in my opening paragraph. In his analysis of international reponses to the Spanish Civil War (though in practice about England and France rather than Spain), Juan Avilés Farré pays tribute to the Welsh International Brigaders and to the 'excelente estudio monográfico' of their historian (1994: 64).

The author and publisher gratefully acknowledge the permission granted by the following to reprint extracts from:

Sean Burke, *Deadwater*, published by Serpent's Tail
Reprinted by permission of Serpent's Tail

Robert Goddard, *Hand in Glove*, published by Bantam Press
Used by permission of Transworld Publishers, a division of The Random House Group Ltd

Lewis Jones, *We Live*, published by Lawrence & Wishart, ([1939] 1978)
Reprinted by permission of Lawrence & Wishart, London

Jan Morris, *The Matter of Wales: Epic Views of A Small Country*, published by Penguin (1984)
Copyright © 1984, Jan Morris
Reprinted by permission of Oxford University Press

T. E. Nicholas, 'In Remembrance of a Son of Wales (Who Fell in Spain)', first published in *The Daily Worker* (1938)
Reproduced by permission of *The Morning Star*

Alan Perry, 'Spain (1975)', first appeared in *Planet*, vol. 30 (1975)
Copyright © Alan Perry
Reprinted by permission of Alan Perry

Dai Smith, 'Back to the Future', first appeared in *Planet*, vol. 56 (1985)
Copyright © Dai Smith
Reproduced by permission of Dai Smith

Dylan Thomas, 'O Make Me a Mask', *Collected Poems*, published by Dent
Reproduced by permission of David Higham Associates

Gwyn Thomas, 'GT in Spain – his experiences there: 2nd Part. Man of action', MS in Thomas Collection NLW/E46'; 'The Spanish Flavour', MS in NLW/E127; *The Alone to the Alone* (1947); 'Gazooka' (1957)
Reproduced by permission of the Estate

Rosie Thomas, *The White Dove*, published by William Heinemann
Copyright © 1986, Rosie Thomas
Reprinted by permission of The Random House Group Ltd; also Curtis Brown on behalf of Rosie Thomas

Gwyn A. Williams, 'Defending the USSR', first appeared in *Planet*, vol. 62 (1987); *When Was Wales?* (1985)
Reprinted by permission of Penguin

Every effort has been made to trace the copyright holders of material reproduced in this volume. In the case of any query, please contact the publisher.

Abbreviations

The author apologizes that the promiscuous mix of Welsh and Spanish politics has produced the following prodigious offspring.

BUF	British Union of Fascists
CNT	Confederación Nacional de Trabajo (Spanish anarchist syndicate)
CPGB	Communist Party of Great Britain
CPSU	Communist Party of the Soviet Union
CPUSA	Communist Party of the USA
FAI	Federación Anarquista Ibérica (elite anarchist directorate)
FET/JONS	Spanish Fascist party
IB	International Brigades
ILP	Independent Labour Party
LONU	League of Nations' Union
MFGB	Miners' Federation of Great Britain
NUM	National Union of Mineworkers
NUWM	National Unemployed Workers' Movement
OC	Officer Commanding
PCE	Partido Comunista de España
PNV	Partido Nacional Vasco (Basque Nationalists)
POUM	Partido Obrero de Unificación Marxista (Spanish Revolutionary Party)
PSOE	Partido Socialista de Obreros Españoles (Spanish Socialist Party)
SIM	Servicio de Investigación Militar (Republican Military Intelligence)
SWMF	South Wales Miners' Federation ('The Fed')
SWRC	South Wales Regional Council of Labour
TGWU	Transport and General Workers' Union
TUC	Trades Union Council
UCNW	University College of North Wales (Bangor)

UCSWM	University College of South Wales and Monmouthshire (Cardiff)
UCW	University College of Wales (Aberystwyth)
UDC	Union of Democratic Control
UNA	United Nations' Association
WEA	Workers' Educational Association
YCL	Young Communists' League

PART I: INTRODUCTION

1 Prologue: Castles in Wales

Teruel, Tetuán – and Tenby

On 18 July 1936, a group of senior army officers began an uprising in certain towns of mainland Spain (for example, Teruel) and in the Spanish colony of Morocco (Tetuán and elsewhere). Their aim was to overthrow the democratically elected government of the Second Republic. Because of the unexpectedly stubborn resistance to the *pronunciamiento* by proletarian organizations in the big cities – a resistance belatedly endorsed by the left-liberal cabinet in Madrid – it proved to be the beginning of the Spanish Civil War. Within a week the Spanish people, even unto the tiniest and remotest village, were engulfed in a chaotic internecine struggle, an outbreak of mutual slaughter. It resembled, perhaps, a Russian pogrom, except that it covered the whole of a large country and was actually unique in modern European history. As this ghastly tragedy unfolded a thousand miles away – indeed, within a week of the rebellion's outbreak – the thirty brethren of a Cistercian monastery, on the Welsh island of Caldey in Pembrokeshire, were addressed by the renowned Catholic thinker, Mgr Ronald Knox, and 'exhorted to pray for Spain, caught up in a civil war'.[1] As it happened, at that very moment, the community's basic function of private prayer was felt to be under threat. The monks, it was claimed, had too frequently been disturbed in both their working and spiritual lives by the noise and intrusive curiosity of tourists. Soon afterwards, the abbot provoked a bitter local dispute by issuing an 'ordinance' which restricted public access to the island and imposed new rules of comportment for all visitors.[2]

Caldey was understandably a curiosity on the Welsh landscape of the 1930s. The lease of the island had been acquired by the order of Anglican Benedictines early in the century, during a late flowering of the Anglo-Catholic revival. But not long after the new abbey building was completed the whole community decided to convert to Rome. In 1926 they sold the monastery to the Cistercians, who were keen to revive the medieval traditions of Welsh monasticism.[3] The site was isolated, a choice perhaps not wholly attributable to earlier precedent, but also made in recognition of the fact that the region was one of deeply rooted Protestant Nonconformity, and thus generally unsympathetic to the Roman persuasion.[4] Moreover, in the 1920s, the number of vocations in Wales for the Cistercian (or 'Trappist') life was limited. The community was composed largely of Belgian and French priests, in 1936 the abbot (Fr Lefèvre) and many of his charges being still, undeniably, foreigners. Indeed – according to a local historian – around that time 'there was so much talk of spies' that 'Father Abbot urged upon all to become as English [*sic*] as possible using every means to live according to the customs and ways of their adopted country'.[5]

All the same, the abbot was within his legal rights in imposing the new regulations. Though one correspondent to the local weekly, the *Tenby Observer*, pointed this out, the offended vested interests of boatmen and other tourism-dependent citizens were exacerbated by chauvinism, local pride and religious suspicion. Then as now, as has often been noted, Tenby itself was not a typical Welsh town – any more than Caldey was a typical Welsh island.[6] Though communities similar in certain socio-economic aspects existed along the north Wales coastline, Tenby was a uniquely English (as distinct from 'anglicized') place, historic centre of 'little England beyond Wales'. It was a bizarre fact that this dubious status originated in the deliberate plantation, by the eleventh-century Norman monarchy, of hundreds of Walloon (that is, French-speaking) families from the Netherlands. However, potential awareness of some distant genealogical relationship with the Caldey fraternity failed to ameliorate the hostility of many citizens.

After several weeks of lively controversy, into the core of the furore strode Gladys Horner, to whom the modern (if sexist) term 'feisty' can be confidently applied. The monks of Caldey, asserted Mrs Horner, were clearly engaged on conspiracy. 'The object of Rome', she proclaimed, 'is to prepare the ground behind closed doors for revolution in all countries, and to stamp out religion, as, for example [is happening] in "Most Catholic Spain"'.[7] The editor of the *Tenby Observer* was taken aback, more by the apparent lack of empirical logic in Mrs Horner's letter than by surprise at the irruption of conspiracy theory into the debate. It is true that, even in late August, few British newspapers had made much progress in accurately describing the causes of the Spanish War, far less in identifying its various competing power-blocs, and the differences at issue between them. But some elements seemed axiomatic to him: though 'holding no brief for the Caldey community', the editor nonetheless dismissed allegations of plots as misplaced, even as puerile.[8] He was soon to regret his imprudent arbitration. Mrs Horner reacted as though the last letter of her surname was a 't', not an 'r'.

What is happening [on Caldey] is part of a great plot by Rome to take advantage of the hospitality so foolishly and freely accorded to her by a tolerant and forgetful people. It is common knowledge that hundreds of priests belonging to Rome are sent out daily, in all countries, to distribute communist literature. I often wonder how many of these leaflets are printed at Caldey . . . All the commotion that Rome is making about the evils of communism is only a smoke screen to cover up her own work.

The editor – now obliged to reassert his authority – pointed out that 'the Pope in his recent address to Spanish refugees spoke in unequivocal language against the evils of communism'.[9] He also queried Mrs Horner's claim that scripture identified and condemned the Popish Church as the Beast of the Apocalypse. This was the rock on which the editor perished, for though his grasp of international politics may have been more logocentric than his adversary's, when it came to biblical exegesis he simply was not in the same class. Over the next few issues he was battered into submission, and in the end he not only retreated from the ring but gave up writing editorials altogether.

Thankfully, Mrs Horner seems to have been right about the 'tolerant and forgetful' nature of her fellow citizens. The affair was soon settled amicably and, when the Remembrance Day season came along, the retiring priest of the local RC parish was invited to speak at the annual British Legion dinner. Fr March 'recalled a recent visit to the border of Spain' made with one of his parishioners during a break from a pilgrimage to Lourdes. 'They did not get over the border [the *Observer* reported] as the authorities evidently did not like the look of them.' Indeed, it was just as well that Fr March's intentions were frustrated. As it happens, Republican border guards were members of a militia organization – the anarchist FAI – which was currently acquiring a reputation for an attitude to Catholic priests which made that of Mrs Horner or any other Welsh Protestant, seem positively obsequious. Fr March could well have become the first Welsh Catholic martyr since the seventeenth century. At any rate, the Legion president, in his own speech, sympathized with Fr March. 'What is happening in Spain is anything but nice', he observed. 'Germany and Italy have openly declared for the Fascists and Russia has practically openly declared for the Communists . . . Whichever way it goes it is going to be very serious for England, because we may be forced into it.' It seems that none of his auditors objected to this assumption of their collective concern for the well-being of fellow Englishmen in the event of a decision by the British government officially to involve itself in the war in Spain.[10]

One locally resident celebrity was apparently preparing for a decisive involvement in European affairs. For some time the 85-year-old Charles Geard had been holding meetings in a farmhouse near Pentlepoir. Calling himself 'Shiloh – The Ruler', Mr Geard had attracted a large following of country folk. The *Observer* reported (not without some sceptical innuendo) that 'Mr James Williams of Holborn Farm is one of his closest followers, and believes that Mr Geard, who visits his disciples in a large chauffeur-driven saloon car, will ultimately overthrow both Hitler and Mussolini during the impending millennium.'[11]

The continental dictators certainly seemed to be in need of intervention from a higher power. With the intrepid aid of another opportunist with his head in the clouds – daredevil Welsh pilot, Cecil Bebb – General Franco had meanwhile been flown from his base in the Canary Islands to Tetuán, where he took command of the elite Army of Africa, Spain's only experienced professional division. Another airlift, the first such operation in history, then saw much of this army moved to the mainland, courtesy of aircraft and pilots sent to Franco's aid by Hitler and Mussolini. By the end of the year, rebel Teruel had rebuffed an assault by government forces which included a battalion of foreign volunteers; at the same time, loyal Madrid – also with the help of the International Brigade – had resisted the onslaught of the Army of Africa.

A Historian's Journey

My opening section is (perhaps) a somewhat anecdotal overture to what is intended as an earnestly analytical study of Wales and the Spanish Civil War. All the same, the Horner versus Lefèvre affair vividly illustrates the complexities of twentieth-century politics – both at parish and global levels – along with the kaleidoscopic possibilities for misgiving and confusion among people who were, in the solid centre of their daily existence, *believers*. In the 1930s, nearly every adult Welsh person occupied a fortress of absolute belief. If an Englishman's home is his castle (even when that castle was in Wales) the Welshman's being *and* belonging was his interior castle – the spiritual site described by Spain's greatest writer-theologian, St Teresa of Avila. Gladys Horner would, of course, have been outraged at such a reference – and the reader may note that I have taken care not to mention her name in the same sentence. Yet we cannot doubt that Mrs Horner's philosophical world was one she shared with many, perhaps even still a majority, of people in Wales – a fundamentalist City of God, which felt itself under siege simultaneously by the ancient enemy, the Papist Whore of

Babylon, and by a new and fearful adversary, Atheistic Communism. So intensely committed was Mrs Horner to the survival of her Old Testament culture and its vital witness to truth, that these two self-proclaimed destroyers of such truth were imperatively united in evil alliance. How could it be otherwise?

Like the hapless editor of the *Tenby Observer* – more so, given the dubious gift of hindsight – we scratch our scalps in bemusement. But was Mrs Horner's conspiracy theory, for all its unquestioned originality, quite so eccentric as it seems? After all, even as she wrote, the leader of the Soviet Union was embarking on a bloody purge of his personal friends, the surviving Bolsheviks who had created that utopian state in the first place. For the most part eminent intellectuals, they were arrested, tortured and murdered after publicly confessing to being agents of the fascist-imperialist powers – a revelation which was taken at face value by hundreds of intellectuals in Britain. Meanwhile, the leader of the Welsh Nationalist Party, intellectual to his core, firmly believed that communism and capitalism, both of which equally threatened the soul of our nation in the 1930s, 'were two sides of the same coin'.[12] Bereft of hindsight, like the editor of 1936, what would we have said if Mrs Horner, assuming some hypothetical but minor adjustments to her angle of vision, had divined an evil alliance of communism and fascism? – in August 1936 a logical and historical absurdity, a truly farcical proposition, which exactly three years later became catastrophic reality.

In any event – as we shall see – there were many others in Wales who, if not precisely of Mrs Horner's opinion, responded to the situation in Spain according to the interests of their own religious persuasion. In so doing, many drew on a populist, even atavistic, history of communal hostility between supporters of Rome and Geneva (or, which amounted to the same thing, those of Spain and England).[13] On the other hand, a large and growing segment of Wales's population had more recently embraced a different rationale of political belief and action, along with a contrasting explanation of history. This creed wished a plague on all religious houses, Cistercian and Calvinist alike, subscribing instead to a revolutionary materialist determinism of class struggle and the dictatorship of the proletariat. In all these cases and others, the issues which erupted with the Spanish War confronted belief-systems and truth-claims, strongly confirming popular commitment to them on one level whilst threatening them with destruction on another. The news from Spain, mass slaughter of workers and peasants, militarist overthrow of democratic freedoms, proscription of the rich as 'fascists', widespread slaughter of priests and nuns, all struck painfully on the exposed nerves of Welsh believers. Even the British Legion president, with his fears that 'England' might be dragged into a war which was 'anything but nice', seemed to give voice to a feeling akin to pacifism, mindful as he doubtless was of the holocaust of heroes who died not many years earlier for King and Country, the commemoration of which was the occasion of his remarks.

The issues which were at stake in 1930s Spain, which still concern and fascinate modern historians, are serious, profound, complex, above all in the present context emotional. They remain (or perhaps better expressed, they ought to remain) fundamental to the ethical concerns of society. More immediately, this book will attempt to illustrate the ways in which they impinged on Welsh society by throwing into intense relief the cultural absolutes mentioned above. The Spanish War – I use the oxymoron deliberately – was an acid test of the intangible realities of Welsh life. Thus, perhaps, we may better understand our ancestors, appreciate their values and empathize with the decisions they based upon them. It is in this sense above all – whatever the dialectical and scholarly conclusions my book may arrive at – that the Spanish Civil War represents a significant event in the history of Wales.

If the reader, for her/his part, can appreciate why the Spanish Civil War demands constant study and alert refocusing, it is equally true that no historian can expect readers to be familiar with the constantly elusive historical background to the struggle. Confronted by its myriad shades of detail the present writer frequently finds himself uncertain of the ground, needing to seek guidance in the magisterial reference books. (However, ethical uncertainties, also pervasive in this subject, are never quite so easy to resolve.) In many years of teaching the subject at degree level, it was rare to find a student immune to occasional confusion: and (I regret to report) rather less rare to encounter one who after a 36-hour course and much opportunity for private study, exhibited in the final exams a level of misapprehension which – if not aspiring to Mrs Horner's surrealist realm – was often daunting. Nevertheless, one of the most rewarding aspects of the present writer's teaching life was the appetite of young people from the sixth forms and further education colleges of what is his native land and once was his academic constituency for learning (and even arguing) about the Spanish Civil War.

Partly for this reason, when incubating the idea for this book, I was convinced that its major justification would be the existence of a 'special relationship' between its two subjects. After all, the project developed pragmatically as an extension to the research and writing of my books on *Cardiff and the Spanish Civil War* and *The Irish and the Spanish Civil War* in the mid-1990s. The reality of a 'special relationship' was indicated by much of my own reading and experience, so much so that it became deeply rooted: a salient and 'natural' feature of my mental landscape. References to the Spanish Civil War in the printed and audio-visual media of Wales – especially of south Wales – seemed to be regular, even routine, rather than occasional. Such reportage nearly always concerned the Welsh volunteers who went to Spain and fought on the Republican side, overwhelmingly as members of the British Battalion. Media treatment of the theme was always positive, and often reverential. The political establishment of the Principality in the post-Second World War era honoured these men in all the seasonal ritual of trade union and party conferences, Gala Days, May Days and so on. No major industrial dispute, especially if involving the traditional heavy industries of south Wales, passed without some invocation of the Welsh response to the plight of the Spanish Republic in the 1930s. 'Spain' was a sort of mantra which endowed any Welsh worker with a spiritual advantage in his or her struggle: our working communities and their leaders, heirs of the heroes of the Spanish Civil War, were eternally, in some unspecified but palpable way, confronted by the reactionary successors of 'Franco-Fascism' and Non-Intervention. In moral terms, at least, it was no-contest.

The collective memory sought to place upon these veterans, and especially those who had died for the cause in Spain, a heroically transcendental status. They came to represent symbolically the innately beneficent qualities of our nation, the imperishable commitment of the people of Wales to the eternal virtues of liberal politics – democracy, social justice and an active compassion for other minorities that was both altruistic and international. Perhaps there was, comparatively, too little concentration upon other relevant aspects of these qualities. Though often recalled at the grass roots, less public recognition was given to the sustained material sacrifice of poverty-stricken communities who willingly contributed their pennies, and/or simple possessions which were held as surplus to the normal subsistence standards of their domestic economies to the relief of human suffering in the Republican zone of the conflict. Above all, the emotional and material damage imposed arbitrarily upon surviving parents, widows, orphans of the dead heroes was often ignored or elided. Nonetheless, the identification of south Wales with the cause of 'Spain' remained a noteworthy feature of its public life fully sixty years after the war itself had ended.[14]

At the same time, the writings of experts on the history and culture of Wales seemed both to complement and explain this feature. Nearly all scholarly and other professionally informed studies of twentieth-century Wales draw attention to the Spanish Civil War as an event which encapsulated the crisis of the 1930s. This, it is often argued, was uniquely the case for Wales. In Wales as a whole the negative socio-economic consequences of laissez-faire capitalism were more deeply and painfully established than in any comparable region in Europe. In particular, in the age of Hitler and Mussolini, the politics of labour, and their specifically antifascist trajectory, predisposed south Wales to a highly committed antifascist profile. Further, this profile was not simply ethnocentric, but had both an ideological and an internationalist dimension. All the unacceptable injustices of existence under the laws of capitalism came to be summed up in the name of 'Franco'. What could be more voluble on this subject than the fact that when coalminers, metalworkers and merchant seamen signed up for the International Brigades, the sons of Spanish immigrants who had settled in Dowlais and Abercrave went to fight alongside them?

Since this aura of 'correspondence' between Wales and Spain formed a coherent part of my personal intellectual heritage, it seemed 'natural' to give this book the working title of 'The Dragon's Dearest Cause'. Some time before starting to write, I was visited by a German academic colleague, an expert on the Spanish Civil War, and we went out for a meal in Penarth. On our way to the restaurant, I explained some aspects of the 'special relationship' characterized above. During the meal we exchanged relevant experiences and information. Suddenly, from behind, we heard a voice raised in strident objection to the tenor of our conversation. 'That's a stupid thing to say! Do you know how many young Spanish boys were killed fighting with the maquis against the Nazis in France?' A man was on his feet and approaching us. A lively exchange of views – thankfully, no more than that – took place. However, our interlocutor refused an offer to join our discussion on a more sociable basis, and shortly afterwards left the restaurant. So demonstrable seemed this evidence of the 'special relationship' that my visitor could have been forgiven for suspecting it had been arranged in advance.[15]

Every work of history is predicated upon an evolving process of research amongst an ever-widening and ever-deepening pool of resources; upon countless little exercises of corroboration, contrast and comparison, constant internalized questioning and externalized debate. Every historian selects a subject, and with this initial act inevitably begins a journey towards its assumed location. But the nature and logistics of the journey itself cannot be accurately predicted. It always leads to unforeseen, even radical, changes in direction. If one is unlucky or ill-prepared it can often go in ever-decreasing circles, and not infrequently has to be abandoned altogether. Not until the last line of a book is written, until (in the case of the present publishers) the second proofs are corrected and returned, is the place one envisioned finally discovered – in all its difference from the original – and properly described. In the mean time, the more thought is given to the subject, the more it becomes historicized and relativized. 'Thus conscience doth make cowards of us all'. And as I worked, my convictions about the assumption implicit in my title began to display evidence of erosion. At first appearing as a mere shadow, an imagined interrogative against the phrase 'The Dragon's Dearest Cause' assumed gradually denser substance.

The Dragon's Dearest?

The general interrogative – of course – eventually came to comprise several particular lines of enquiry. Was the Welsh response to the Spanish Civil War actually 'greater' (in all the nuances of that word) than that of any other region of Great Britain, or that of any comparable region of the western world? Or was it that, in a small and relatively obscure nation with a long but comparatively uneventful history, our encounter with the universal tragedy of a nation-state of much greater historical influence assumed an artificially magnified importance? Following on conversely from this, I asked myself why it was that during dozens of research visits to Spain spread over a working lifetime, I had failed to encounter any recognition that Wales had ever impinged on the consciousness of the mass of Spaniards, no more in 1136 or 1536 than 1936. (This in marked contrast to the case of Ireland.[16]) Indeed, the only reference to Wales I ever found in the Spanish (national) press in all that time was a rather patronizing editorial comment on Welsh voters' almost grudging acceptance of the principle of regional autonomy in the referendum of 1997, a principle which had been resoundingly endorsed by the Spanish electorate some twenty years earlier.[17]

In any case, was my subject actually of greater significance to the history of Wales than other causes which had been at various times espoused by Welsh opinion? Several historians of Wales make reference to a sequence of world events – conjunctures of vast historical influence, generating ideas of radical change in politics and society, above all of revolution – which evoked notable interest in Wales. Thus writers from Gwyn Alf Williams to Jan Morris apostrophize an internationalist tradition which includes empathetic responses to both the Reformation and the Counter-Reformation, the Great Rebellion in England, the American and French Revolutions – even theHungarian 'revolution' of 1848 – all in terms of a 'just cause'. The Dragon (it is implied) may have been plunged in millennial slumber, but his dreams were many and always utopian.[18] Few treatments of modern Wales fail to dwell, if only for a few phrases, on the phenomenon of its response to the Spanish Civil War. 'It stirred deep feelings', comments John Davies, writing (laconically in the circumstances) of the south Wales valleys; whilst K. O. Morgan writes more expansively of

> socialists or radicals responding, as men had done in 1789, to the cause of oppressed liberty overseas, in this case in the face of insurgent and increasingly well-armed Fascism. The Spanish Civil War was a major landmark, not only for poets, but also for the maturing political and industrial consciousness of the coalfield.[19]

It is Jan Morris – better known as travel writer and novelist than historian – who lines up the elements which lay at the core of memory and history. For her, the people of Wales

> saw their own struggle for fairness as a microcosm of a much greater campaign. When the Spanish Civil War broke out 174 Welshmen went off to fight in the Republican cause, 122 of them miners – the largest regional group in the International Brigade. Welsh sea-captains, long familiar with the iron-ore route to Bilbao, repeatedly defied the Nationalist blockade to take food to beleaguered Basque republicans, and two of them, Captains 'Potato' Jones and 'Ham-and-Eggs' Jones, have gone into the folklore. Asked why he was going to Spain, one volunteer replied, pithily 'The Powell Duffryn Coal Company is Fascism!', and at home whole Welsh communities really did feel, as they faced the great coal combines, that they were standing up to just the same enemies as their men with the Brigade in Spain.[20]

The most recent general study of Britain's role in the Spanish War places south Wales alongside London and industrial Scotland as the regions where activity on behalf of (Republican) Spain was most intense, but notes also a tremendous spirit of sacrifice amongst equally deprived communities in the more patchily industrialized north of the country.[21] An underlying explanation for the special quality of the Welsh response was (it seems) that the south Wales valleys possessed 'a remarkably cultured, enquiring generation in the 1930s', with a 'continuing sense of a shared historical heritage'.[22] Most of these writers, and to some extent the sentiments they express, are reliant upon the work of Hywel Francis, the outstanding historian of Wales and the Spanish Civil War.[23] Although the overt focus of its research is on the proletarian masses of the coalfield, Professor Francis's book acknowledges that communities all over Wales shared in the enthusiasm for 'Spain', and that to that extent it is valid to regard it as a truly national, or at any rate *nationwide*, movement. He claims, nonetheless, that it was south Wales which adumbrated the direct action of the world proletariat in forging a united front on behalf of the Republic, and that here, 'the depth of solidarity for Republican Spain [was] probably unrivalled elsewhere in Britain'.[24] A recent examination expresses scepticism over certain aspects of the Francis hypothesis. It regards as too sentimental the view that the mining valleys took 'Spain' and the Means Test as synonymous, providing the agglutinate for a united front of Welsh workers and writers. Further, Dr Lyne points out that the rush of miners to the republican colours was not a spontaneous expression of Welsh egalitarian feeling. It was rather that

> most of the members who embraced this new cause from its inception seem to have been the hard-core [Communist] Party activists, some of whom had been trained in Russia, and whose loyalties were to the Party rather than to the Spanish Republic. A desire to throw themselves into the Spanish struggle does not seem to have had such an overwhelming appeal for less committed, less, perhaps, indoctrinated, members.[25]

Inevitably, it will be one concern of the present book to register differences of perspective and interpretation between itself and the earlier study, the main title of which was – it should be recalled – *Miners Against Fascism*. Yet it must be said that Professor Francis, himself hailing from a background dominated by the Communist Party, rather proclaimed than obfuscated his conviction that, without the work of the CPGB, there would never have been any 'special' quality in the Welsh response to the plight of the Republic. He clearly explained that, in particular, volunteering for the International Brigades was 'completely directed' by the Comintern.[26] Indeed, that this was the case all over the world is well established. To take a roughly comparable example, exiles from the industrial regions of Lombardy were organized by the Comintern agent, Vittorio Vidali (known in Spain as 'Carlos Contreras').[27] Moreover, in a later contribution, Francis returned to some implied reservations made in his book, firmly renouncing the residual tendency to a 'romantic' or sentimental approach to his theme, and bringing out its darker aspects – particularly the personal suffering imposed by Party priorities upon wives and children, in what was a remarkable – if somehow rather Soviet – exercise in self-criticism.[28]

Yet Dr Lyne's reservations retain some point. Professor Francis's monograph is a model of meticulous research and scholarly moderation. There are many important areas in which the present study cannot hope to improve on its treatment, and its very existence has been indispensable to my project – not merely (I would emphasize) in the passive dimension of rendering so much basic fieldwork unnecessary. Yet there is a sense in which *Miners Against Fascism* is not mainly about Wales at all – let alone about Spain. Once you stand outside its terms of reference it can be seen as a study in political solidarity and the role of the CP in south Wales. It pays lip service – or perhaps slightly more than that – to other communities of Wales: but in essence (and certainly as regards 85 per cent of its subject matter) it concerns a minority of Welsh people living in the coalfield zone, an elliptical geographical-geological enclave stretching between Ammanford in the west and Pontypool in the east.[29] The population of this area was less than 750,000 in 1936, that is to say, hardly even 33 per cent of the principality's total. Taken together, the number of citizens inhabiting the maritime-industrial ports of Cardiff, Swansea, Newport and Barry was not far short of this figure.[30] A further indication of the book's selective criteria is that Aberystwyth and Bangor do not even appear in its index – likewise Cardigan, Brecon, Llandovery and so on. This degree of exclusivity has inevitably led to corresponding textbook glosses of Francis's monograph. In the most recent example, D. Gareth Evans has seen the influence of the Spanish War as a phenomenon limited purely to the industrial south-east. He concludes that 'enthusiasm for the Republican cause reflected the maturing political consciousness of Wales in the mid-1930s'.[31]

And indeed, *Miners Against Fascism* is overwhelmingly dedicated to charting the reaction to the war of one homogeneous community and its culture – the labour force of the coalmining industry and (to a much lesser extent) the heavy metallurgical plants to be found on its westward and eastward fringes (at Llanelli and Merthyr-Dowlais). It is, *par excellence*, a study of one episode of the class struggle in the context of its times, of a kind which could be largely replicated by looking at (say) Teesside or Lothian. Its dominating concern in terms of content, sources and interpretation is not to inform us about Spain and its Civil War, or even to contribute to the history of Wales, but rather about the role of the crisis in mobilizing the revolutionary spirit and antifascist feeling in the Valleys. That is to say, its real subject is the victory of the mining valleys, in the van of the British proletariat as a whole, over domestic fascism in all its forms. The tragic fate of Spain and the defeat of the Second Republic are, in the last analysis, subordinate, even in a sense incidental, to the heroic success of the workers' struggle. It is not surprising, therefore, that the result is a picture of a singularity, not a composite – a society in which 'Spain' was a given, necessary and for a period even sufficient, as a cultural definition of identity and interpellation. It did what all the 'Popular Front' and 'Unity Campaigns' signally failed to do. As Francis rightly argues, 'Spain' equalled the Popular Front in Wales, but that movement (for him) was driven by the coalfields, just as the coalfields were driven by the CPGB.[32]

Could it be, then, that Jan Morris's casual use of the word 'folklore' might provide a key to historical analysis of the Dragon's Dearest Cause? Shortly after the final collapse of the Spanish Republic, writing in his new *Welsh Review* – which had quickly become the flagship vessel of Welsh intellectuals – Gwyn Jones confessed that 'General Franco's reputation as a great Christian Gentleman is forever blasted in my eyes by memories of maimed babies carried because they had no legs to walk on over the Pyrenees in winter'.[33] Jones was specifically referring to the exodus into France from defeated Catalonia of more than half-a-million Republican supporters and their families, fearful of the fate that the victorious Nationalist regime had promised them. This tragic and prophetic event had taken place in January, and Gwyn Jones was not the only observer to be moved. Yet in the very week that Barcelona fell to Franco, around the time that Lewis Jones – according to legend – collapsed and died after a day on which he made no fewer than thirty speeches appealing for aid to the Republic, the *Caernarvonshire and Denbigh Herald* carried the following cynical and deeply ironic advertisement.

SPAIN
for the SPANIARDS
but the Red Garages
for USED CARS
Standard – Wolseley – Austin
Morris – Rover – Hillman
THE RED GARAGES
Caernarvon
also at Llandudno, Old Colwyn[34]

It may be considered that such exploitation was typical of a businessman on the make. However, the editor who accepted this copy had himself displayed a consistent level of indifference to the Spanish War. As the miserable refugees struggled and died in the snow, he composed his first – and last – leader comment on the whole unfortunate episode. 'With the end of the civil war in Spain, which, according to well-informed political correspondents, is not likely to be long delayed, it is generally hoped that Europe will enjoy a long period of peace.'[35] Should we dismiss these sour and dissident voices because merely characteristic of uncharacteristic north Wales, a region which, unlike the rest of the nation, felt no 'natural' affinity with the cause of 'Spain'? Before doing so, we pause: because even *Welsh Review* – now seen as the first banner of 'Anglo-Welsh' literature, and descried streaming in a breeze somewhere south and east of Aberystwyth – had made no previous mention of the Spanish War, despite including a regular feature on international affairs, which was grandly titled 'Beyond our Frontiers'.

PART II: LANDSCAPES AND SEASCAPES
2 Bible and Babel: Rural and Industrial Wales

Wales is one of the world's smaller nations, but the millennial interaction of its complex geophysical and human history has ground out many differing communities. These shades of difference, as various as the greens of Wales's countryside, allow apparently infinite possibilities for argument about which people and which places might fit possible categories of functional description. For example, in the 1930s, was the cathedral city of Bangor, which a century earlier had been 'the heart of rural Wales',[1] still part of a 'north Wales' thought of traditionally (at least in the south) as 'rural' in essence? Or rather, had it become an urban complex that had flourished more by a typical nineteenth-century 'industrial' conjuncture? Its proximity to the slate-mining industry of Snowdonia, which – if by then in serious decline – had dominated the local economy since the mid-nineteenth century, was a strong element in its growth, and was fortuitously complemented by the contemporary creation of a main-line railway link. In other words, is Bangor better regarded as comparable to Pontypridd rather than to Caernarfon? Conversely, was Pontypool part of a 'south Wales' usually considered as 'industrial' in essence: or is it more properly seen as a 'semi-rural' settlement, with strong links to its eastern agricultural hinterland? Thus, should we relate it to Merthyr or to Abergavenny? In the north, Wrexham stood in the middle of its own coalfield, and had many characteristics of an industrial zone, both economic and social. In the deep south, the market town of Cowbridge in the Vale of Glamorgan, though surrounded – admittedly at a respectful distance – by an industrial envelope, nonetheless basked in rural tranquillity.[2]

The extent of urban alienation experienced by the huddled proletarian masses can easily be exaggerated today. Despite – or partly because of – the intense contemporary concern over the gulf between the countryside and the town, we tend to forget that there was no able-bodied adult denizen of any part of Wales in 1936 who could not walk out of (or up from) any given conurbation of mean terraced streets into pure air and green fields in the course of thirty minutes at most. And all this is only to refer to the material infrastructure and environmental ambience of the places mentioned, leaving aside all cultural and political factors – which are of equal importance and may well further compound the difficulties of a working taxonomy.

Yet if we wish to examine the proposition that different geographical regions of Wales responded differently to the Spanish Civil War, it must perforce be managed by drawing lines of division, however tentative and provisional. My *modus operandi*, adopted mainly as a convenient strategic ploy, has been that of a geographical anatomist. I propose to flay Wales of its skin, or to use a simile which is less uncomfortable because less animal, to peel it like an apple of its long and complex coastline. This operation produces two subject areas (or zones) of study. On the one hand, interior Wales, a landscape of many differing communities but having in common a life in which the sea is physically out of sight and/or effectively out of the reckoning (that is, not part of the local fabric). Exterior Wales, on the other, is a landscape-cum-seascape of maritime communities, historically dependent on seaborne commerce and/or the fishing industry. Its settlements are dotted around the whole of the coastline, all different in detail, but all the same in that they tended to gaze away from the mountains behind them to the great oceanic plain. For both zones, out of sight is, for much of the time, out of mind. This chapter deals with the first of these areas, the landscape.

The Common Ground

In *Miners Against Fascism*, Hywel Francis advances the view that, whilst all of Wales responded in some fashion to the urgent claims of Spain for attention, there was little uniformity or consistency in the pattern of this response. It was in the coalfields (he argues) that the earliest popular response was felt, and where it was best sustained throughout the course of the conflict. Here, the overwhelming majority of the population nurtured a fellowship solidarity based on shared economic circumstances and class experience, which predisposed them to support for the oppressed masses of Spain. In the course of the previous generation this majority had constructed by democratic means a near-monopoly of local political influence.[3] Thus, the movement was both spontaneous in grass-roots inspiration and organized in terms of leadership and policy. Moreover (and finally) it was a movement deeply committed to the succour of the Second Republic. Here, Francis maintains, is the homogeneous exemplar – not only to Wales but to the world. This, his subtitle inescapably implies, stands for Wales.[4]

The pro-Republican *locus classicus* of the southern coalfield may be fairly contrasted with another relatively uncomplicated region which falls within my 'landscape' – this time one of apparent indifference. In terms of physical extent, it is, in fact, nearly a half of geographical Wales. Mid-Wales, for present purposes defined as the great ellipsis of land with settlements punctuating a rough perimeter (going, as it were, clockwise) at Carmarthen, |Lampeter, Machynlleth, Llangollen, Welshpool, Brecon and Llandovery, none of them places of more than 15,000 people. This area was an economic monolith of hill-farms and rural townships, an area in which the twentieth century had made a distinctly limited impact by 1936. True, the towns had their sprinklings of professional middle-class families – solicitors, teachers, accountants, auctioneers, land-agents, local government officers, shopkeepers and other small businesses. Moreover, in the countryside itself, the squire and the vicar no longer shared a hegemony of socio-political influence. It was not the lineaments of traditional Welsh Toryism which held back the wheels of progress, but rather agricultural depression, which had set in simultaneously with substantial (if piecemeal) land redistributions, and persisted grimly and almost unremittingly for two generations. The sheer tenacity of the inhabitants' belief in a promised land, quite literally arising from the example and prophecy of scripture, had brought them religious and economic freedom, but in both cases it proved a freedom only to achieve a new bondage. Here dwelt the 'my people' excoriated in vitriol by Caradoc Evans, and who – understandably – cursed him (and his fellow intellectuals) for his pains. Small farmers were, of course, small-minded by the standards of societies which they knew – and could know – nothing about. Their families and their neighbour-labourers, working with land which was amongst the least productive and most difficult in the British Isles, lived a tense and rigorous regime just above subsistence, in which there was often little time to take an interest in local politics, leave alone in issues of an international character. Their children, for the most part, abandoned the area as soon as they were (theoretically) capable of earning a living, and mid-Wales was slowly being emptied of human society. Here was not, on the whole, a Wales throbbing with the fever of internationalism.[5]

Thus, within the present 'zone', Francis's case for the homogeneous and representative character of the coalfield experience *vis-à-vis* the Spanish War is a strong one. Indeed, it may be conceded that reactions in the rest of the nation as a whole were more mixed, sending a less steady and clear signal to posterity. The earliest newspaper editorials to make comment on the situation in Spain, for example, expressed contrasting views. In Cardiff, the *Western Mail* at first recommended careful consideration of the issues. But it rushed to support the government's policy of non-intervention as soon it became clear (during August) that this offered the most convenient vehicle for a strictly ethnocentric – indeed, in material terms, frankly selfish – indifference. In the north the editors of *Seren Cymru* ('The Welsh Star'), weekly Welsh-language voice of Wales's Baptists, adopted quite a different attitude. A week into the war, in a commentary apparently composed at sight of the first press cables from Madrid reporting the generals' uprising, they denounced the role of corrupt landowners and other conservatives in inspiring the military coup. The writer had no doubt that the aim was to install a fascist regime in Spain, and that the Republican government was right to arm the workers as the only method of preventing this outcome. Indeed (the leader concluded) it already seemed that the rebellion had failed – 'and a good thing too!' (Da gwybod i'r gwrthryfel fethu).[6]

But in this we detect a note which is strikingly discordant with the smooth and broad diapason, comparing an enthusiastically pro-Republican south, with a cooler, less committed north. Though the *Western Mail* claimed a national circulation, it may be doubted that it was widely read in the non-industrial and (especially) the non-maritime districts. It can be more confidently asserted that the paper was not part of the mental diet of the poor and deprived in any part of Wales. Published in Cardiff, it spoke above all for coal-, iron- and shipowners, along with the professional, business and managerial classes of the south-eastern littoral. Still, the broadly political interest and readership base of *Seren Cymru* was not radically different from that of the *Mail*. Though evidently supported by Baptists all over Wales, and to that extent arguably more 'national', it reflected (to use contemporary social usage) a solidly 'respectable' constituency, a largely non-proletarian readership, composed of independent farmers on the one hand and small-town professional families – above all, teachers, ministers of religion and shopowners – on the other. The paper was as close as one might expect to approach to 'rural Wales', yet at the same time was read by people whose concern for stability, property and international order was not notably less strong than that of grander compatriots in their Penarth mansions. On the face of things, then, it may seem surprising that, even when news of social revolution, property expropriation and mass murder in the Republican zone began to hit the headlines – confirming, at least to its own satisfaction, the sober moderation of the *Western Mail* – the organ of Welsh Baptism held fast to its discordant ostinato pedal. *Seren Cymru* roundly dismissed as 'lies' the claim that the Spanish government was responsible for any violence against civilians and their property. At the end of 1936, the General Secretary of the Baptist World Alliance announced that in Spain, religious liberty – apparently upheld by the Republic – was in peril from 'the fanaticism of masses of ignorant Roman Catholics'.[7] For the rest of the war, *Seren*

Cymru's support for the Republic, though never rantingly antifascist, remained unflinching.

The nuances at work here were (of course) to do with religion and ethics. The *Western Mail*'s editor was hardly able to write with complete freedom in either mode.[8] His employers, the Bute family, who were Catholic and thus highly suspicious of the pre-war Republic, enjoyed a controlling interest in the newspaper. His pragmatism, at once austere and shabby, nonetheless reflected not simply thoughts of his own job security but also a widely accepted rationale based on the morbid fear of another European war. It is hard to dismiss as lacking in ethical substance an opinion which sought to avoid – in empathy with the survivors of 1914–18, at almost any cost – another armageddon, another holocaust of young lives. In contrast to many subscribers to the *Mail*, few readers of *Seren Cymru* had property or profit to lose over the Spanish imbroglio. This enabled a more straightforward ethical response when it came to material issues. Baptists, in general, could afford the conscientious luxury of putting mammon behind them. They held to the solid principles of Liberal Wales, of Gladstonian democracy and its Welsh tribunes such as T. E. Ellis, far from moribund in many corners of the land: social progress, institutional reform, anti-militarism, international law and order based on ethical axioms. These were ideas which had become established – if still, largely, in the representative sense, by what are now called 'non-governmental organizations' – in a process led by the western European proto-democracies, lately joined by the United States of America, during 'the long nineteenth century'. All this indicated a need for decent and firm support for a sovereign democratic republic under attack from its own army, aided and abetted by the international fascist gangster, Mussolini.[9] At the same time, *Seren Cymru*'s enthusiasm for the Republic was underpinned by its prior commitment to Protestant Nonconformity. In explaining away the anticlerical violence then raging in Spain (and, it must be said, frequently sensationalized in the 'London Press') it could not forbear to inform its congregation that 'hostility to the priesthood – which keeps the minds and persons of its tenants in thrall – is very strong in parts of Spain'.[10] The remark betrayed a prejudice hardly less vitiating in ethical terms – if also less hidden from the casual observer – than any imposed by the Bute dynasty on the editor of the *Western Mail*.

The attitudes touched on above provided fertile common ground between north Wales and the southern coalfields. The work of religious revival in eighteenth-century Wales, along with the contemporary European enlightenment, the legacy of the French Revolution and the steady evolution of English law, had laid down a firm basis of principle from which few thinking citizens would dissent. In the north, these feelings were expressed in ways which were essentially 'civic', via institutions which were broadly a product of the venerable Liberal–Nonconformist ascendancy. They were not only led by, but overwhelmingly composed of, middle-class people – especially by politically conscious women endowed with the requisite amount of leisure time. The proceedings of such groups, several of them set up in response to the Great War and its international aftermath, were transparent and deeply 'respectable'. Above all, the organizers of 'Aid Spain' movements in the late 1930s were primarily conscious of the suffering object of their charity, and much less concerned with a subjective, domestic or local political agenda. In the coalfield valleys, broadly similar ideological mainsprings produced a tradition of personal and collective action which was far more dynamic and overtly interventionist. Francis, for example, argues that the spirit of the campaign was essentially an anarcho-syndicalist one, emanating from the miners' lodges with their 'constitutional' privilege of local responsibility and decision-making. The democratic proceedings of the community were here, however, much less public and certainly less transparent. Rather, they were the business of closed shops of union members, and secretive cadres of dedicated communists. Thus they endorsed a procedure which was less 'civic' – direct action up to and beyond the point of extra-parliamentary activity, and mass illegality up to and beyond the point of violence. The ultimate and symbolic step along this road led to outright defiance of government and Labour Party, and ultimately to taking up arms in Spain. In contrast to the situation in the north, 'Spain' was a matter of urgency in the coalfield, a matter of self-defence. For leaders and led of the Fed, the trenches of Madrid and the barricades of Barcelona ran across every valley and every street.

Yet by 1936, warnings of war and of predatory international fascism had been heard well outside the Valleys, and for some time past. Far from the lodges and the party executive committees, many other (and prior) voices drew attention to the potential dangers of the rise of the dictatorships. Indeed, whilst the CPGB, including its Welsh membership of around 3,500, had been emphasizing the need for common action in this area only since 1934 in line with the Comintern's general *volte-face* in favour of left unity, many other Welsh people had been drawn since 1918 into an epic struggle for international order and peace. Veteran leftists of the 1930s – especially in Wales – often write and speak as though they alone descried the threat of Mussolini and Hitler, that only the insights of their Marxist-Leninist faith vouchsafed the correct 'international' perspective. Hywel Francis's book begins with a chapter entitled 'Internationalism – A Welsh Tradition?' in which the Miners' Federation and its leadership of the drive for a 'People's

Front' occupy centre stage. Less than a page is devoted to the phenomenal contemporary movement centred on the League of Nations and its perceived remit for International Peace and Order. Yet the latter, vast and complex in nature, not only provided the immediate historical context for the supposedly 'international' orientation of politics in the coalfield, but also flourished and peaked at exactly the same time.[11]

From the mid-1920s at the latest, the Welsh branch of the League of Nations Union (an organization with over one million members in Britain) was issuing constant warnings of the dangers of 'international anarchy'. Such perceptions were widely disseminated via an ongoing programme of public meetings and a plethora of published literature. Dozens of affiliated groups, and many distinguished figures of inter-war Wales, were involved at some stage of the campaign for peace. After all, what were people to make of the long sequence of disarmament conferences in 1923–33 – most of which failed miserably of any achievement – if not a repeating alarm signal that world war was a real threat to civilization? Not surprisingly, far from such activities being confined to socialist and working-class organizations, thousands (perhaps even millions) of middle-class and business people were involved in a broad, populist 'peace movement'. Churches, chapels, rotary clubs, business and professional associations of all kinds, were involved in 'internationalism', in Wales as elsewhere. In 1933, for example, 'a series of mass demonstrations' were addressed by Lord Davies of Llandinam, and aimed at persuading the League of Nations to adopt sanctions against Japan over its invasion of Manchuria. In the same year the Welsh Baptist Union endorsed a strictly pacifist resolution: 'only in Wales', comments one historian, 'had pacifism struck deep root' amongst Baptists.[12] More than thirty discrete organizations took part in the 1935 Peace Ballot. This event itself registered a phenomenal 11.5 million votes, within which figure (moreover) the Welsh contribution was well in excess of the nation's proportional parliamentary franchise.[13]

There was much common ground here between the people of Wales, whatever corner of the principality they hailed from and on whichever side of the class struggle they aligned themselves. A subliminal sense of internationalism in Protestant Wales perhaps originated in a certain affinity with 'small nations' which was instilled at home and in Sunday School. Many children learned from their catechistical copies of 'Rhodd Mam' ('Mother's Gift') that Wales resembled the Holy Land of Canaan, and with it the feeling that the same was true of other poor and insular communities in distant lands.[14]

Determined to put this elemental impulse into ideal practice, Lord Davies himself nurtured a desire – amounting to an obsession – to convince the world of the need for an international police force which could be deployed by the League to deter or suffocate military aggression of the large against the small. Such thinking was surely not wholly out of kilter with that of the SWMF and of the Comintern leadership in the aftermath of Hitler's accession to power in Germany? After all, Lord Davies's pet notion infringes the precepts of conventional pacifism in a way analogous to that in which the idea – occasionally advanced by coalfield tribunes – of a defensive militia or 'brigade' of coalminers organized to fight fascism offends against those of constitutional politics.[15] Is it wholly inconceivable that the prior existence of such a force may have precluded the deaths of some thirty Welshmen in Spain, not to mention the prolonged suffering and sacrifices of the loved ones of so many of the volunteers? Moving to another corner of the common ground, it is easily conceivable that the views of many involved in the peace movement could with equal ethical validity lead to support for the official government policy of non-intervention. By extension, support for non-intervention did not necessarily mean an absolute divorce of principle – or even, in the broadest sense, of ideology – between the colliers of the Rhondda and the crofters of Merioneth.

There was certainly some moral equivocation at work here. Little more than a month before the Nationalist victory, and after thirty-one months of war, a north Wales newspaper ventured for the first time a leader comment on the war. Its last-gasp expression of sympathy for the Republic was wrung out of it by the sheer enormity of Franco's 'Law of Political Responsibilities', proscribing his defeated enemies for their ante-bellum political allegiances. 'The savagery and injustice of this position is terrifying, and those on the government side may be excused for thinking that what they will suffer by continued resistance will hardly be worse than their fate if they surrender.' From this, however, the editor, feeling pharisaically that his paper had done its duty, went on to criticize the British government for 'belatedly trying to exert their influence in Spain' on this issue![16] The feelings of communities all over Wales on the Spanish issue were mixed, the predominant or active factor varying with a variety of local cultures and personal experiences. But mixed only up to a point. If it seems true that the southern coalfields made a response to 'Spain' which was both rapid and demonstrably popular, in one respect it seems less clear that only in 'the Valleys' was the response a monolateral one. Though at times, indifference, neutrality or even criticism of the Republic were not lacking, no person resident in the whole of the landscape I have defined – it seems – ever gave public voice to a feeling in favour of General Franco.[17]

The Broad Church

General Franco was the self-proclaimed and, not long afterwards, explicitly recognized champion of the Catholic Church in Spain. His cause was characterized as a Crusade ('La Cruzada') to extirpate the ideological left – not only Muscovite Communists but native anarchists, socialists and liberals too – reconquering Spain for the Faith, just as the Muslim invaders of the peninsula had been defeated and expelled in the Middle Ages.[18] Now if there was one residual notion which in this decade provided a common denominator to all denizens of the landscape of rural and industrial Wales, it was their suspicion, more often than not amounting to hatred, of Roman Catholicism. To a majority of Welsh people whether or not Franco was actually a fascist was immaterial: beyond dispute was his role as the champion of Rome, the harbinger of absolutism, Inquisition and Index, the representative of an irresponsible monarchy, an obscurantist clergy and a feudal aristocracy. As *Seren Cymru* so instantaneously and perfectly expressed it, the Roman priesthood 'kept the mind and the persons of its tenants in thrall'.[19]

The historical Protestantism of this Wales was, if hardly fanatical, still severe and unforgetting. In line with the 'Whig Interpretation' of British history established in state education from its very inception, Welsh schoolchildren were frightened by the fires of Bloody Mary, alarmed by the Spanish Armada, warned about Gunpowder, Treason and Popish Plot, and assured of the utter dependence of British freedoms upon their common constitutional Protestantism. It was a lesson taught on a weekday basis by secular school-teachers, which thousands of Sunday school teachers enthusiastically elaborated via biblical exegesis about chosen people on the Sabbath. Even outside Wales's classic 'Bible Belt', in the cosmopolitan streets of Dowlais and in such a middle-class home as that of Glanmor Williams, the parishioners of St Illtyd's were known as 'Plant Mari' – 'Mary's Children'.[20] Furthermore, for thousands of denizens of the more 'industrial' districts of the defined landscape, their political lives and altered ideological convictions merely overlaid and confirmed a prejudice which has for a century been known in Hispanic scholarship as 'The Black Legend of Spanish History'.[21]

In the last week of July 1936, two men returned from Spain to Clydach, close to the anthracite centre of the Swansea valley. Raymond Hopkin and Matthew Cullen had been in Barcelona as members of the British athletic team sponsored by various left-front organizations to take part in the 'Workers' Olympiad'. This event had been arranged as a protest against – and ideological alternative to – the orthodox Olympic Games which were being held concurrently in Nazi Berlin. The military uprising began the day before the Barcelona games were due to open, and as a result the whole programme was cancelled. The two men witnessed fighting in the streets and the first stages of the popular revolution which George Orwell was later to apostrophize. They told a local reporter that in Barcelona

> the churches, in fact, were the most difficult strongholds of the Fascists which the government had to overcome. To get rid of them, the government decided that all the churches, except the Cathedral, should be 'opened' either by fire or shelling – and cleaned out . . . The general impression throughout the city, and we spoke to many people, was that the chief danger had been created by Fascist priests . . . One horrible sight which we saw was the burned body of a Fascist priest who had absolutely refused to surrender and who was finally shot at bay at the top of a church tower . . . All reports we have read [about atrocities against clergy] have been greatly exaggerated.[22]

The 'Fascist priest' soon became a turnip-ghost of Welsh Nonconformity. The following spring, the council of the English(-speaking) congregations of the Presbyterian Church in Wales was held in Swansea. It debated a resolution proposed by the East Glamorgan Presbytery 'urging the Council by speech and pamphlet to combat the opportunistic combination of Fascism and Roman Catholicism as movements opposed to freedom of religious thought and practice'. In debate, the Revd Watcyn Williams (Merthyr) stated 'there was today a strange combination of Fascism, Nazism and Roman Catholicism seeking to impose upon others a particular way of life'. Another speaker took the case further: 'Roman Catholicism was commending Fascism to the people of this country and the Pope had expressed gratitude for the steps which had been taken [by the 'Fascist' side] in Spain.'[23]

Within the coalfield, Nonconformist ministers often sermonized and lectured against fascism, many adopting a strong pro-Republican profile. Among the latter was the Aberdare Unitarian minister, Revd James whose lecture on 'Current Events in Spain', denouncing non-intervention and bombing atrocities carried out by the fascist powers, was reported in the local newspaper.[24] Another prominent figure of coalfield origin was D. R. Davies, whose tortured journey on a radical switchback of belief and doubt had led him via Unitarianism, the Maesteg Miners' Lodge executive, and membership of the ILP, into the Congregationalist ministry by 1917. Becoming overtly empathetic with communism in the 1930s, he left the ministry (for a second time) and worked tirelessly in the 'Aid Spain' movement, speaking at many Welsh meetings and on similar platforms in other parts of

Britain. After an official tour of the embattled northern front of Spain in 1937, during which he noticed burnt-out churches in Santander, he asked himself why Spaniards had turned so violently against their religion. 'A study of the history of the Catholic Church in Spain provides the answer: it has always been against the people. Were I a Spaniard living under the harrow of an exploiting Church, I should hurl the faggots with the best of them.'

Accordingly, Davies blithely accepted his hosts' explanation that the churches of Santander had been burned out as a 'spontaneous popular act . . . for the safety of the realm and that of the priests themselves . . . My impression [he added] was that there was certainly no Government persecution'.[25] Some characteristics of a rather more substantial figure in contemporary Welsh life, the poet and pacifist T. E. Nicholas ('Niclas y Glais'), closely resembled those of Davies. Born in north Pembrokeshire and dying in Aberystwyth, Nicholas spent two of the intervening nine decades in the Swansea valley, mainly at Glais, a few miles from Clydach, where he was Congregationalist minister. He too was an ILP-er and an active pacifist campaigner in both world wars. (Shortly after the First War Armistice he was physically attacked by members of a female audience, and in the Second War he served a term of imprisonment for 'sedition'.) In 1922, Nicholas abandoned his ministry and became a founder member of the CPGB. By common repute, this self-consciously prophetic icon 'had three bugbears – capitalism, the Catholic Church and the English monarchy'.[26] A voluble supporter of the Spanish Republic in the 1930s, of all Welsh writers he remains the most plausible candidate for official bard of the Welsh 'Volunteers for Liberty'. As a poet of some distinction, his heritage is today worth claiming and is therefore disputed between his two allegiances. More plausibly, they may be seen as not two, but twin: as Francis rightly argues, both were 'firmly in the Welsh Christian–Communist tradition'.[27]

This dual secular and religious influence was reflected in the letters and later reminiscences of several Welsh members of the British Battalion of the International Brigades. It was reliably reported, for example, that priests who had been killed by the people deserved their fate, if not for actually taking up arms in the insurgents' favour and firing on their own parishioners, then at least for long collaboration with the forces of economic exploitation. A number of volunteers expressed grim satisfaction that village churches had been destroyed or were being dedicated to more socially useful purposes. 'The Spanish people have been for many years in bondage to the landlord and the Priest', Sam Morris of Ammanford informed his mother. Jim Brewer, an alumnus of Coleg Harlech, wrote to the college principal from the British Battalion's training base in Madrigueras:

Did I tell you in my last letter that we go to church twice a day? We eat there. Last summer the chief priest fired on the people with a machine gun and killed thirty. That's the sort of atrocity you never hear of in England. The church was built in 1520 and this is the first time its been put to decent use.[28]

Brewer's story was confirmed – down to the detail and almost to the phraseology – by another Welsh volunteer, Harry Stratton, many years later.

The church . . . was now being used as a dining hall. 'The best service that had ever been given there', they said. They told us that the local priest had hidden arms in the church ready for the Fascist uprising, and that on the appointed day, 18th July . . . the priest had barricaded himself in the church tower with a machine gun.[29]

Even Lloyd Edmunds, an Australian lorry driver of Welsh parentage – who was apparently not a Christian and had never been to Wales – was prone to remarks about the Spanish Church which bore the authentic stamp of his ancestral Nonconformity. 'If we win', he wrote home to his 'Pop' on one occasion, 'it will be a terrific blow to world Catholicism'.[30] He also wrote at times to his ex-Sunday School teacher, who belonged to a *Socialist* Sunday School established in Melbourne. As the editor of his letters explains,

Anti-Catholicism was part of the mental baggage carried by the men and women who founded the Socialist Sunday School and sent their children to it. To them the Pope and hierarchy of the Catholic Church . . . had in all countries been reactionary and in Spain, where the Inquisition had flourished, particularly so. The support of the Spanish church for Franco confirmed the anti-Catholic convictions which Lloyd had inherited both from his atheist socialist father and his Welsh Methodist mother.[31]

A large majority of Welsh International Brigaders were – as Francis puts it – 'lapsed Christians', but even among those who had ostensibly turned from Protestantism to communism, many nurtured irremediable reservations about 'dialectical materialism' and its atheistic sanctions. *Miners Against Fascism* argues that, as far as the 'Aid Spain' movement was concerned, 'the prominent role Nonconformist chapels were now playing revealed not necessarily a theological response (that is, an anti-Catholic response) but more a demonstration of their continuing radical outlook'. Later, however, it acknowledges that in north Wales 'strong anti-Catholic feeling' was often in evidence. But it seems to the present writer that the culture of anti-Catholic (even in some respects, anti-Spanish) feeling was profoundly involved right across alleged geographical and class divisions in Wales. In the last analysis, Francis's assertion that 'the Welsh response was in no way religious' is simply untenable.[32]

It is surely no accident, in the present context, that several generations of the Welsh socialist leadership were lapsed or passive Christians. Not only Noah Ablett, most admired theorist of south Wales syndicalism in the inter-war years, but also two of his disciples, Arthur Horner and S. O. Davies, had been intended Nonconformist ministers. K. O. Morgan goes so far as to claim that the Labour Party in Wales was 'an essential product of the Sunday School'.[33] In some parts of the coalfield this joint hegemony could produce tensions. For example, in the steel-making town of Dowlais, and in Abercrave — a tiny anthracite village at the top of the Swansea valley — dozens of Spanish immigrant families were to be found.[34] Again in Dowlais, as well as Mountain Ash and Aberdare, somewhat larger colonies of south-ern Irish expatriates had thrived, in some cases, for generations.[35] In 1936–9, the *Welsh Catholic Times* showed itself consistently concerned to deny the sympathies of these communities to the 'Aid Spain' movement. In October 1938 an anonymous 'Welsh Miner' complained to the news-paper that

> I belong to an affiliated Union, and as a Catholic I consider it monstrous that money subscribed by me and paid to the Union should be used to support Red Spain. The Miners' President during his visit to the Reds was evidently shown everything except the dead bodies of the bishops, priests and nuns.[36]

By the 1930s, the sons of the Spanish ironworkers who had come to south Wales around the turn of the nineteenth–twentieth centuries had often left the faith. One study of Dowlais reaches the sweeping (and unconvincing) conclusion that 'sympathy for the Spanish Republic and its Popular Front Government amongst Spanish families was total and unequivocal'. In Abercrave, where the colony boasted several miners, the process of assimilation was so fervent that whole families in 'Spanish Row' learned Welsh — though elder members (especially women) still insisted on the rosary being said in the household.[37]

Further north, Welsh Catholics found themselves potentially under suspi-cion. Most of the surviving British volunteers who had served in Spain arrived home in late 1938, having been officially demobilized and repatriated. Their return went relatively unnoticed, and certainly uncelebrated, by the press and population in general. In contrast, Tom Jones of Rhosllannerchrugog (hereafter, simply 'Rhos'), one of the last POWs to be released by the Franco regime, arrived back in Wrexham to a hero's welcome.[38] This was in April 1940, by which time Britain was at war with Nazi Germany, once Franco's ally, but now – by a breathtaking *volte-face* – allied to the USSR. Jones was a coalminer, employed in the Bersham colliery outside the town, and a member of the CPGB. He told a reporter that

> The prison authorities would not give him the two Bibles that his mother had sent him. But at one prison, 3,000 prisoners were forced to take the Sacrament in an exercise-yard, at an altar flanked by pictures of the Virgin and of General Franco, for the benefit of press photographers, while covered by machine guns.

This was a story calculated to inspire local outrage, as well as the disapproval of the broader Liberal constituency of the *Manchester Guardian*.[39] Much nearer the beginning of the Spanish War, in November 1936, as the outcome of the furious battle for Madrid hung in the balance, the Women's Peace Council held a meeting in Bangor. They debated the issue of whether 'it was a crime to disband a priesthood [in Spain] identified with vested interests and opposed to reform'. Miss Sheepshanks, whose speech in other respects had a neutral tone, was nonetheless happy to stoke up the local prejudice. 'Spain has not thrown over its religion, but it resented the political work of the priests; in fact the churches were used for the convenience of the insurgents and for the secret storage of arms.'[40] Nearly a year later John McGrath, Catholic bishop of Menevia, reported in a pastoral letter that his diocese was in good shape, expressing particular satisfaction at the large number of conversions. A lecturer at Llandudno Town Hall promptly warned citizens of papistical plans 'for the conquest of Wales'. A plot for the seduction of the whole nation by the Whore of Babylon was well in hand. Moreover, 'Roman Catholicism is absolutely Fascist, and pro-Italian'. Mussolini – the speaker insisted – had donated £16 million to the Vatican which was to be drawn upon 'for the intensive R.C. propaganda in this country'.[41]

A prominent scourge of papism, the distinguished academic W. J. Gruffydd, also objected to Welsh Catholics' support for the Nationalist side in Spain. He argued that the Civil War was intended 'in its planning and its financing and its aim, to restore the power and wealth of the [Catholic] Church'.[42] In 1937, Bishop McGrath, in a speech made at Rhyl, had declared that 'Communism is a diabolical movement . . . ready to wade through blood and tears to its Utopia. Unless Britain checked subversive efforts we might expect to hear bullets and hand-grenades as in Spain.' The press report provoked a comment from a reader, who pointed out that 'these phrases would make an excellent broadcast for General Franco', adding that 'communism' had played no part in the instigation of the Spanish War.[43] This episode occurred as part of a vigorous debate in the pages of the *Wrexham Leader*, sparked off by the ruthless bombing of Guernica by the Condor Legion in the last week of April. The issue of Spain, which dominated the letters page for the whole of that summer, was infused with religious feeling. The prematurely plural nature of the Anglican communion was illustrated by the vicar of Gwersyllt, who agreed with McGrath on the question of subversive communism. In this he begged to differ from his own spiritual leader, the archbishop of Canterbury, who had expressed sympathy for 'suffering Madrid', implying that the Spanish Church had brought disaster upon itself.[44] One reader concurred with the vicar in distinctly non-Anglican language, asserting that Spain would always be in chaos 'until a National Abbatoir is provided to which all Spanish Communists are consigned'.[45] The BUF picked up on some of these local debates, and professional agents in their London HQ often intervened. A long exchange of fire in the pages of one newspaper ended when 'Labour Party Member' replied to a Mosleyite spokesperson's account of the Republic's religious intolerance by pointing out that in Franco's Spain 'we have the shooting of priests favourable to the government and the banning of all the Catholic services in the Basque Language'.[46]

The 'Aid Spain' movement began to gather impetus in mid and north Wales in the spring of 1937. This process was undoubtedly and fundamentally inspired by feelings of common humanity. People empathized with the sufferings (above all) of the ordinary people of Madrid, besieged by the Nationalist rebels and subjected during the previous winter to aerial bombing and artillery bombardment, along with desperate fuel and food shortages. In April 1937, a meeting in aid of 'Spain' was arranged under the auspices of the Church in Wales at Church House, Wrexham. The vicar of Rhos, presiding, defended the principle of non-intervention but also acknowledged the duty of Christians to relieve human suffering.[47] However, whilst representatives of the Welsh Anglican communion were often equivocal, it is notable that ministers of every Nonconformist denomination mobilized enthusiastically for the cause. The local CPGB agent, Douglas Hyde, was able to exploit the services of such men with cynical thoroughness for the tasks of disseminating propaganda, of fund-raising and (more surreptitiously) of recruiting for the British Battalion. Members of the ministry helped him by providing the locations for meetings, solving transport problems and appearing as speakers.[48] As he later recalled, 'the platform at the first meeting was solidly lined with clerical collars and it had been announced from pulpits all over the district'.[49] On this actual occasion (at Caernarfon), the Revd Oswy Davies of the Free Church Council spoke, and the Revd S. O. Tudor moved the vote of thanks.[50] At Penrhyn Hall a week later, a 'sympathetic address' on 'Spain' was given to the meeting by the Revd Curig Davies.[51] In Aberystwyth, the Revd Dan Jones and the Revd O. H. Jones served on the Spain-orientated Union of Democratic Control's foreign affairs group.[52] In short, the hymns of the Hebrons of Pontypridd and the Tabernacles of Bangor harmonized perfectly with the arias issuing from the Miner's Institutes – whether in the Rhondda or in Wrexham.

In sharp contrast to all this, one newspaper was resolute enough to carry news about a Nationalist air ace who had been partly brought up in Wales. Flight Commander Alvaro Matamoros was the grandson of a lady from Abergele, and a former pupil of the celebrated Friar's School in Bangor. He returned to Spain, and began training for the airforce, some time before the beginning of the Civil War. In August 1936, he wrote to his former Welsh guardian, relating his escape from the 'Reds' after two weeks in hiding in Madrid.

> The government forces were looking for me to fly for them. I saw people being taken from their houses and shot like dogs. When I left Madrid every church had been burned down. In the train from Madrid to Valencia I was accompanied by nine priests, and when we arrived at Valencia to get the boat the nine priests were shot dead in my presence.[53]

Matamoros went on to fly many missions for the Francoist airforce, doubtless including sorties in which innocent civilians were killed or wounded. He was later shot down and himself seriously crippled.[54] By a curious irony, he had spent part of his youth living only a few miles from Old Colwyn, where some of the children who fled from 'the bombs of Bilbao' were to be hosted a year later. Hardly less ironically, a dramatic dimension of north Wales's encounter with the Spanish War was strongly related to the controversial debate over aviation bombing of civilian targets.

The commonality of Protestant culture had a dragonfly even more exotic than Matamoros stuck in the ointment of its consistency. The leaders of the Welsh Nationalist Party (Plaid Genedlaethol Cymru) – most of them distinctly unexotic men of middle age – who had founded the movement over a decade earlier, were largely out of sympathy with the Nonconformist tradition. Saunders Lewis, J. E. Daniel, T. C. Edwards and W. A. Bebb were intellectuals who derived their politics from a European dynamic and eschewed what they saw as the cultural poverty of chapel-centred Wales.[55]

Though only Lewis, party president since 1925, actually embraced the Roman Catholic faith, all regarded France as the historic centre of western civilization. W. Ambrose Bebb, for example, had studied in Paris and became a teacher of Welsh at the Sorbonne in the early 1920s. According to one writer, 'he fell in love with the doctrine, liturgy and architecture of the Catholic Church and came to regard it as one of the main pillars of civilization'.[56] This group shared a perspective which was a radical, even revolutionary one in the context of its time and place. It represented a reversion (or reaction) to even more ancient traditions of Welsh history, deriving ultimately (perhaps) from the neo-Gothic revival which has already featured in this book.[57] But, more dangerously, it also flirted with more recent francophone political philosophy, in particular the labour-syndicalism of Georges Sorel and the authoritarianism of Charles Maurras; combining these affections with an admiration of the corporate state patented by Benito Mussolini.[58] The sum of all these ideas was little less than heretical in the Welsh context of the 1930s, representing a kind of national apostasy on the part – precisely, but anomalously – of the party which called itself 'nationalist'.

Amongst Bombing Schoolchildren

In Emyr Humphreys's novel *An Absolute Hero*, the central character (and real heroine) Amy Roberts, is a young school-teacher living in the normally tranquil land of Llyn. The coming of the Spanish Civil War sees her emotionally torn by various allegiances – her serious interest in politics, a deeply feminine concern for friends and family values, her introspective Welsh-speaking culture and her love-life. She and her husband, a chaired bard, support 'the cause' by assisting the relevant work of a minister of religion and a landed family with coalmining connections. On one level, this conjunction accurately depicts the collaboration of Nonconformism with the local patriarchate which seems to characterize the 'Aid Spain' movement in the more northerly regions of the principality. Yet the content of the novel hardly bears out the publisher's blurb that north Wales in the 1930s was a society 'entirely obsessed by the Spanish Civil War, which holds a mythic significance for Amy's generation'. Indeed, it takes repeated incursions across the cultural frontier by Amy's lover, Pen Lewis – a leader of south Wales miners – to bring the urgency of Spain's plight home to his more indifferent northern compatriots. His targets are carefully chosen. On one occasion he leads a deputation of rude anglophone mechanicals onto the holy field of the National Eisteddfod; on another he literally floats across the mock-baroque scenery of a country house draped in an 'Aid For Spain Now' banner. Pen later joins the British Battalion and is killed on the Jarama. Ultimately, the novel seems to argue, his sacrifice might help the Dragon to speak with one voice in its two tongues. But in another, more domestic scene, Amy's beloved but delicate stepchild, Bedwyr – symbol of the hoped-for spiritual renewal of the Cymru – is recovering from illness. Suddenly he recalls an incident in his playing with a friend, and asks 'what's a bomb, Mam? . . . Clemmie says they hang down from the sky. And drop in the storm'.[59]

Bedwyr's panic was vicariously inspired not by the atrocities of the German Condor Legion in Spain, but by the contemporary and more local scandal of the government's decision to build a school for RAF pilots – to be situated on the Llyn peninsula. In a watershed event in the history of Wales, on 7 September 1936, three leading members of the Welsh Nationalist Party set fire to a number of partly completed, empty buildings at Porth Neigwl near Penyberth. It was intended as a symbolic act of illegal political protest, the first made on behalf of an indigenous Welsh policy since the fifteenth century. The perpetrators, Messrs Saunders Lewis, D. J. Williams and Lewis Valentine, drove immediately from the crime scene to the nearest police station in order to hand themselves (and a written confession-cum-manifesto) over. Their decision to act had been preceded not only by an intense campaign of lawful protest in which Plaid's was by no means the only voice, but also by similar campaigns, which had – crucially – succeeded in changing Whitehall's mind over several other proposed sites for the training school *in England*. At the same time, however, the protest involved the use of a potentially dangerous – arguably even 'violent' – medium, and this aggravated the dilemma of many respectable citizens over the question of support for 'The Three'.[60]

At any rate, the scandal caused by the event and the subsequent trials aroused intense feelings of pro and contra. It dominated the political ambience of all Wales (outside the south-east) for a year or more, and it was this issue, rather than the Spanish War, which obsessed these regions. Indeed, it had a similar effect to that which the anti-Means Test campaign and the associated hunger marches exercised in south-east Wales. For, coming as both did shortly after the beginning of the war in Spain, and before the deeper implications of this distant event had had time to register with a wider constituency, these issues acted as a sort of prophylactic, limiting the extent of public interest and individual commitment to the cause of 'Spain'.[61] Yet, at the same time, the target of the Penyberth protest had obvious links with the Spanish situation. As Saunders Lewis and his confederates were planning their action, Franco was negotiating with Nazi Germany for a great increase in aviation support for the armies advancing towards Madrid, while the

Republic's application for identical modes of assistance from the Soviet Union was equally advanced. Both sides had already been responsible for incidents – if relatively minor by later standards – which the other was able to characterize as the deliberate bombing of civilians. As the first (abortive) trial of 'The Three' at Caernarfon was in progress, a period of intensive aerial bombardment of Madrid began. Over the next six months, a series of attacks took place against largely defenceless urban targets. Intensive Republican propaganda exaggerated (and perhaps even invented) some of these events, associating them with the Nazi Condor Legion and alleging that women and children, along with hospitals and other medical units, were the enemy's explicit targets.[62] Later on, such propositions seemed demonstrably confirmed by the dreadful and epoch-making attack upon the Basque town of Guernica, not far from Bilbao, on 26 April 1937. It was an atrocity which (for the first time) combined all the features which were to become familiar in the Luftwaffe's vocabulary of terror. Repeated waves of bombers attacked an open town, first of all to drop incendiaries, which were duly followed by impact explosives and the merciless strafing of civilian refugees.[63]

During this period most political parties of Wales – eventually, and to some extent – mobilized themselves to organize protest at the horrors of fascism and (specifically) to provide assistance to the Spanish Republican peoples. But in areas where Plaid Genedlaethol Cymru enjoyed greatest popularity, such was the obsession with the Penyberth case that it had the effect of diverting attention from the specific international context in which the meaning of the protest was set. Even in places where the Peace Movement and its various constituents were well-established, where distaste for both the general heritage of the military and suspicion for the particular issue of rearmament were entrenched, awareness of the Spanish cockpit itself was slow to spread. However, in some ways, Plaid Cymru had staked out the ground even before its protest at Porth Neigwl. In February, 1936, the party's English-language monthly asserted that 'the English Government have already begun to prepare a camp for the official practice of murder . . . for the mangling of the helpless bodies of little children, for the dropping of poison-gas bombs on innocent and helpless people'.[64] Well over two years later, in a period when the almost daily bombing of Barcelona and Valencia by Italian aviation based in Majorca dominated the foreign pages of the British press, the Porth Neigwl 'bombing school' was officially opened. Saunders Lewis returned to the subject which had occasioned his recent gaol sentence. The large crowd which attended the opening, he claimed, 'were much more impressed by . . . the Welsh Nationalist [protestors] than by the demonstrations of the baby-murderers of the English government'.[65]

Lewis's remark seems to have been directly influenced by the vocabulary of pro-Republican propaganda. In response to incidents such as the alleged bombing of Getafe, air attacks on refugees fleeing the city of Málaga, and finally the Guernica atrocity, appropriate propaganda copy was circulated amongst British volunteers in the International Brigades by their commissars. Amongst others, men like Tom Jones of Rhos and Frank Owen of Maerdy wrote home to their families and local newspapers of their hatred for the 'Fascist baby-murderers' against whom they were fighting.[66] But, of course, Saunders Lewis's own position was much more equivocal. Whilst the party retained an official neutrality over Spain, his stance was both dictated and (at times) threatened by the party's internal divisions over contemporary politics and ideology. In the 1930s, as for much of its history, Plaid membership incorporated those of both left- and right-wing allegiance – even to the extremes. The same newspaper issue in which Lewis condemned English militarism carried a feature article by Cathrin Huws. Her article 'We Are The Workers' Party' lamented that 'our message has not touched the workers to any great extent', despite the fact that 'our doctrine . . . is a song of hope for those who have no possessions. It is a belief for which the workers of Wales should fight and perhaps die.'[67] Elements amongst the leadership had powerful reservations about the motives behind such writing. At times both the *Welsh Nationalist* and its Welsh-language equivalent *Y Ddraig Goch* ('The Red Dragon') implicitly attacked conventional left-wing assumptions about international fascism and – by implication – its role in Spain. Some younger members were deeply embarrassed. One of them, Dafydd Jenkins, later described how, during the campaign on behalf of the Penyberth 'Three', the party made attempts to open up new fields of support in south Wales. He was sent to canvass subscriptions for the party press in areas of the coalfield located promisingly close to Welsh-speaking Carmarthenshire. Despite some success, he 'secretly hoped that the subscribers would not read the papers too diligently. Among much that was commendable and much that was innocuous, they contained comments sympathetic to Franco and at least a tinge of antisemitism.'[68]

Here and there, it seems clear, the published opinions of Plaid mandarins reflected ideas not strikingly dissimilar to those of Nationalist Spain. In September 1936, J. E. Daniel quoted approvingly from the Spanish scholar Salvador de Madariaga. Some years earlier, Madariaga had given a historical analysis of Spain's innate tendency to disorder and wrote of the prevailing need for 'an exceptional man who "pronounces" a new order'. Such saviours, he added 'almost without exception, having been leaders of men, often generals in the army'. Daniel chose – at least by implication – to look on this observation as having prophetic force. Whilst fully recognizing its indigenous causes, Daniel also added his own gloss that the Spanish War was 'a symbol of the most important struggle of our time, that being the conflict between Communism and the European tradition'.[69] At the same time, Saunders Lewis too emitted a powerful indication of where his sympathies lay, with a leader comment in praise of Dr Oliveira Salazar and the 'New State' of Portugal.[70] Daniel was taken to task by Cyril Cule, a young teacher who had recently returned from Spain.

> Very few people in Wales see things in the same way as J. E. Daniel. Let there be freedom for them to voice their opinion. The impression must not be given that [the editor's] views are at one with the principles of the party. There is room in the party for people like us, who are prepared eagerly to accept Communism if we have to choose between it and Fascism.[71]

In his turn, Saunders Lewis was sternly criticized by Walter Dowding of Hafod-y-Bryn, who took exception to the 'continual cheap sneers at the parties of the Left, and the continued evidence of sympathy with Fascist Governments in Europe'. As the latter pointed out, Salazar's regime was hardly one which should be admired as 'a bright spot in the European darkness'. Composing his letter only a matter of days after the Penyberth incident, Dowding warned that party unity was the paramount consideration.[72] Though both leaders defended themselves stoutly, the critical response to their remarks thereafter obliged them to rein in what – probably, if not patently – was indeed a pro-Franco inclination. In subsequent issues of *Y Ddraig Goch*, the more moderate figure of Ambrose Bebb was – as the appropriate Spanish phrase puts it – 'given the word'. Even Bebb's articles failed to tread the pure path of neutrality with a sure footing, but at least succeeded in conveying a sense of empathy with the suffering masses on both sides. In the event, Plaid's prominent spokesmen consistently drew back from outright endorsement of either side, whether in general terms or when treating of a specific item of controversy over the conduct of the war.[73]

The Welsh Ambulance: Vehicle of Hope

In September 1937, 15,000 enthusiastic nationalists packed into and around Caernarfon Town Hall to welcome home 'The Three' on their release from an English gaol, in a triumph which the ex-prisoners must have felt justified their deeds and their sufferings. The attendance on this occasion probably exceeded the aggregate total of all those who attended public meetings called by the 'Aid Spain' movement, within the 'landscape' of this chapter, but out-side the coalfields, during the whole of the year 1937. Yet the International Red Cross Committee had become aware of the plight of Spanish children at an early stage of the war. As early as September 1936, the Labour ex-minister Lord Noel-Buxton wrote on behalf of the committee to various Welsh news-papers appealing for funds to help evacuate children from Spain. He informed readers that 300 such refugees had already been taken to France by the Save the Children Fund.[74] Yet it was not until nearly six months later that any measurable action in response to the accumulating human disasters of the war can be observed in north Wales. The situation of apparent torpor and indifference was altered by the resolution of two dynamic and dedicated personalities.

The first of these was Douglas Hyde, a Bristolian who had recently become the CPGB organizer for north Wales. On arrival in 1935 he had nothing to organize, being – in his own estimation – 'the only communist between Chester and Holyhead'.[75] Within a few months the situation began to alter. In particular, the foundation of the Left Book Club, one of the more successful 'front organizations' of the period, and which the party sponsored in alliance with the publisher Victor Gollancz, brought in recruits.[76] Hyde's job as assistant in a dental surgery also helped to put him in touch with sym-pathizers and fellow-travellers inside the medical profession around the region.[77] By autumn 1936 he was able to arrange small, local protest meet-ings about the government policy of non-intervention in Spain. Sessions became more popular once he began to show documentary film footage from the Madrid fronts, supplied by the London HQ. With the irresistible help of what was in two senses the moving image of suffering, Hyde raised regular small sums for 'Spanish Aid' and, occasionally at least, recruiting young men for the International Brigades.

> Often the sacrifices were so huge as almost to appal me. At a meeting in a village near Bethesda, for example, I had an audience composed entirely of working folk, to whom I made my speech, showed the film and then made an appeal during the course of which I 'Dutch-auctioned' a Spanish militia man's hat and a militia girl's scarf. Two men made the final bids for the first. When I knocked it down to the purchaser, he passed up an unopened pay packet. The same happened when I followed with the militia girl's scarf. Both went to quarrymen earning pitifully little. Similar sacrifices were later made at our later meetings by miners, agricultural workers, railwaymen and other low-paid workers.[78]

The second human catalyst, John Williams-Hughes, was a writer from

Marianglas in Anglesey. In the mid-1930s he was earning a living – or augmenting a modest private income – by contributing articles and columns to local newspapers.[79] What precipitated his interest in 'Spain' can only be guessed at.[80] At any rate, Williams-Hughes had contacts with the Lloyd George interest and knew the great man's daughter Megan, his local MP. According to his own account, however, the process of aiding 'Spain' began when he got in touch with Robert Richards, Labour MP for Wrexham, who subsequently persuaded all Welsh members to combine in a non-partisan appeal.[81] Williams-Hughes probably met Hyde via the medium of the Left Book Club.[82] At this point, the policy of the central Spanish Medical Aid Committee in London (a body strongly influenced by the CPGB) was to send custom-built, fully equipped ambulances to Spain, preferably with a dedicated driver and full medical team. In Scotland, civilian response to the Spanish War had largely taken the form of raising money for a 'Scottish Ambulance Corps'. With the aid of a prominent businessman, this group was sent to Madrid with enormous expedition in the summer of 1936 – actually arriving before the main Spanish Medical Aid Committee in London had been able to organize such assistance.[83] In the early weeks of 1937, Williams-Hughes was appointed secretary of the Welsh section of the SMAC (Megan Lloyd George having graciously accepted the chair) and emerged as the main protagonist of pro-Republican action.[84] Clearly, the idea of sending a 'Welsh Ambulance' to Spain was not original, but it was well-suited to the quasi-pacifist temper of north Walian politics. Furthermore, the specific anti-military context of the Penyberth protest campaign, some fervour of which might be tapped for the use of 'Spain', also exerted an influence. Its further usefulness lay in providing a finite target of £500 needed in order to purchase a vehicle installed with state-of-the-art equipment.[85]

Fund- and consciousness-raising meetings were arranged for Caernarfon and Wrexham to take place in the first weekend in March. The timing proved hugely unfortunate, for a fierce blizzard developed during that week over the whole of the region, leaving much of north Wales snow-bound. Understandably in these circumstances, the audience at the Institute, Caernarfon, on Saturday 6 March was not impressive. In addition to Williams-Hughes, another speaker was provided by the Liberal Party, while the CPGB sent Roy Poole who had recently returned from serving in the British Medical Unit (by now incorporated into the International Brigades) in Spain. Poole made an effect by producing a dum-dum bullet which had allegedly been found on a wounded German officer brought in to a British dressing-station. At the end of the meeting, however, only £15 was collected from the audience.[86] This was not an auspicious start, but the next day in

Wrexham the same platform produced a somewhat better result. Williams-Hughes proclaimed that 'the democracies of Europe are sheltering behind the wall of human flesh which the people of Spain have set up to guard us'. Poole demonstrated that his colleague's metaphor was no hyperbole by describing several incidents in which enemy aviation (usually German or Italian) had attacked hospitals and ambulances. The audience contributed £40 towards a new ambulance.[87]

Then, on Saturday 14 March, the documentary film *The Defence of Madrid* was screened in Bangor. Such was the already growing dominance of the visual over the oral that the third member of the media trinity gave this event much more prominent treatment. 'Aid Spain Meeting – A Bangor Demonstration' headlined a local newspaper report of a large paying audience at the Penrhyn Hall. After the film, speakers with a wide variety of affiliations supported an appeal by Señora Camps of Barcelona University, and a further £40 was raised. Moreover, 'following a proposition from the body of the hall, it was decided to form an "Aid Spain" Committee in Bangor [for] the provision of comforts for the defenders' of Madrid.[88] Shortly afterwards, the committee duly held its inaugural meeting. 'All present voiced the feeling that widespread sympathy exists for the people of Spain' in Bangor and resolved on a campaign to collect goods and money.[89]

Meanwhile Douglas Hyde, backed by the resources of the CPGB and the sympathy of many clergy, went into overdrive. He organized meetings and film shows in parish and memorial halls, cinemas and dance palaces in the remotest villages of the wintry landscape.[90] A further Wrexham meeting, sponsored by the Church in Wales, but doubtlessly inspired by Hyde, was addressed by another returned ambulance man, armed like his predecessor with a dum-dum bullet and stories of air attacks on medical units. Gordon Davies also emphasized the concern for education of both children and sol-diers in the government zone, in the face of what 'was not [really] a civil war but an invasion' by international fascism.[91] Williams-Hughes worked closely with Hyde. A film show, he reported, was to be organized in Holyhead by John Bellis, the local Liberal Party agent. Another was to be mounted at Llangefni by the Lloyd George interest. Liberals in Brecon were busily arranging meetings for Spanish medical aid.[92] The ambulance was duly pur-chased, and displayed in Westminster Palace Yard for the satisfied perusal of Welsh MPs. Megan Lloyd George, whose only involvement in the campaign seems to have been as a passive enabler, made the most of a photo-opportunity.

Regarded as the most up-to-date ambulance yet sent to that ill-fated country, it is painted in blue, brown and green camouflage . . . On the bonnet is a Welsh Dragon Flag and at the back a Union Jack . . . Mr. John Williams-Hughes, the secretary of the Welsh Committee . . . will drive the ambulance in Spain.[93]

Williams-Hughes, in command of several other north Wales volunteers, duly left for Spain on 6 April. Hyde, however, had no intention of resting on his laurels. 'We are contemplating sending two more [ambulances]', he told a reporter. 'We have scheduled seventeen meetings in the next twenty-one days for North Wales. The collection at each meeting averages £20.'[94] In fact, Hyde and his London controllers were less interested in the collection plate than in the converts, along with the publicity and political prestige, which accrued to the Party. For this was the era of the 'Popular Front' in which the Communist Parties of 'democratic' Europe, on the Comintern's instructions, emerged from a semi-clandestine state of isolation in order to help create a cross-party core of public resistance to fascism – whether in its domestic or international manifestation.

The Basque Children: Wales's Popular Front?

On the issue of fascism's domestic profile – that is, in effect, the attempts by the BUF to proselytize in Wales – that section of the principality's population treated in this chapter was virtually unanimous. The numbers who wanted anything to do with Mosley, his satraps, imitators or defectors were statistically insignificant. In the southern coalfield, Mosleyite meetings had been met with a rebarbative, at times violent, resistance which led to a widely publicized sequence of protests, arrests, trials and punitive convictions. Here, without question, a populist and dominant antifascism was already firmly established before the Spanish War broke out.[95] In other places, occasional published expressions of hostility to communism or the Soviet Union rarely or never seemed to emit any positive vibes towards fascism. On the other hand, in the case of any given individual, such a position did not seem, necessarily, to indicate an interest in obstructing the progress of fascism abroad, far less in providing assistance to the Spanish Republic – mainly, of course, since both stratagems were apprehended as involving the risk of war. The correspondence page of the *Wrexham Leader*, for example, evinced a lively local interest in the international scene during the autumn of 1936. A debate on fascism and communism was sparked off by the communist miner, Tom Jones, who portrayed an 'insidious Fascist octopus, planning to capture the whole of Europe' – starting with Spain. The only answer, stated

Jones, was a 'popular front' of all parties opposed to the National Government.[96] It was a lively exchange, featuring about a dozen contributors, and which ran for several months – but the issue of Spain was in practice largely ignored. Meanwhile, a 'crowded' mass meeting, jointly sponsored by the TUC and the Labour Party, was held to 'Protest against Fascism and Dictatorship'. But the many speeches by local MPs and Wrexham councillors made – at most – merely passing references to Spain.[97]

Indeed, the trade union movement in Wales was divided against itself. In Wrexham, Walter Monslow, local leader of the Locomotive Engines and Firemen's Union, was a vociferous spokesman for the cause. At the TUC Congress of 1936 he announced – not without bathos – that 'if Fascism triumphs in Spain I predict that in the near future this Trade Union Congress will be dispensed with'.[98] In Caernarfon, however, the TGWU secretary, J. P. Jones, dissociated himself from the 'Aid Spain' meeting recently held in the town. His branch had been asked by the local Labour Party to make a collection for the Welsh ambulance, but he

> had resolved to have nothing at all to do with it, firmly believing in non-intervention which is the only solution for that misguided country. Although the suffering must be terrible in Spain, the dispatching of an ambulance is not enough to alleviate same. Our own burdens are enough for us.[99]

If Labour Party stalwarts were uncertainly so on this issue, the Liberal Party was, predictably, even shakier. Cardigan Women Liberals held their annual conference at Tregaron in 1938. Miss Winstanley, the president, argued that if the legal government of Spain had been given its rights by the international community, the war would have ended quickly with a victory for democracy. The guest speaker, Mr D. O. Evans, begged to differ, urging the meeting to adhere to the principles of strict neutrality. In his view 'the trouble was that [the Republic] had allowed the Communists and Anarchists to run amok'.[100]

Various groups struggled to counter these dichotomies and disparities by collaborating across party lines. It cannot be disputed that the atmosphere of the 1930s – apparently endless economic depression, the rise of the European dictatorships, and increasing despair at the National Government's attitude to both – encouraged a spontaneous groundswell of feeling for unity. Without this it seems inconceivable that the CPGB could have been able to operate in the way it did. At the same time, had it failed to operate, it seems unlikely that the movement for unity would have become any sort of force in British politics.[101] Despite the enormous enthusiasm it generated, the Unity Campaign soon ran into the sands which sundered the competing constitutional elements of British politics. The distinguished Labour Party 'Three' (Cripps, Bevan and Mellor) who had initiated and fronted the campaign were suspended from party membership, and forced into a smouldering silence. These disincentives and events in Spain itself rendered any further collaboration of the parties – especially between the ILP and the CPGB – out of the question.[102] Of course, at the grass roots, especially in the mining valleys, intensive volunteer labour of collecting, speaking and writing for 'Spain' went on apace and often involved unofficially combined operations. But at official level, mutual suspicion and even jealousy – in a word, disunity – soon returned. No more than the Spanish Republic itself, it seemed, could the leaders of the people of Wales allow political self-interest and ideological belief to stand aside, even temporarily, even for the defeat of fascism, and ultimately even for the sake of suffering Spain. It was to take the horror of Guernica and the plight of the Basque children to bombard some genuine and focused 'unity' into this situation.

Concern about children exposed to the hazards of internecine warfare in Spain was expressed from an early stage. Speakers at 'Aid Spain' meetings, newspaper coverage and newsreel footage, provided apparent evidence that women and children were not only innocent victims of, but also participants in, acts of violence. In November 1936, there was a widespread emotional reaction to the deaths of around forty children whose school was bombed in the township of Getafe, near Madrid. As we have seen, concerns were commonly linked to the wider question of aerial bombing of civilian targets. The 'siege of Madrid' that winter sustained the world's concern for the fate of thousands of refugee orphans trapped in a city which – it seemed to many – was being relentlessly reduced to rubble. When further attempts to isolate and capture Madrid failed, Franco's attention turned to the northern provinces, whose resistance was headed and coordinated by the autonomous Basque government in Bilbao. The Nationalist army made full use of the air power of its Nazi and Fascist allies, in particular the Condor Legion, to soften up key targets behind the front lines. Within a few weeks of the campaign's opening, various Basque towns had been bombed, a tactic culminating on 26 April in the systematic destruction of Guernica.

A month before this event, Cardiff City Council had been asked 'to raise funds for the relief of the children of Spain, who are suffering as a result of the Spanish War'.[103] A few days before the Guernica atrocity, the North Wales Women's Peace Council presented the results of a series of events and collections in aid of child refugees.[104] At the same time the intervention of Lloyd George raised the matter to a new level of public interest in this region. Via speeches in the House of Commons and various statements to the press, the grand old man of British politics – still the tribal chieftain of their north Welsh province – identified his people with those of the Basque Country. In March 1937 he contributed £250 to a food ship bound for Bilbao and told its skipper 'I too am a Basque, as also was General Foch. The Welsh and the Basques are of the same race.'[105] The idea of offering domestic succour to young victims of the war had already been discussed in circles linked to the National Joint Committee for Spanish Relief, and in May the Basque Children's Committee was formed for this purpose. Leah Manning and a team of doctors went to Bilbao to supervise the evacuation of children to be transported to Britain on a liner provided by the Basque government. On 23 May, nearly 3,900 children and over 200 Spanish carers disembarked at Southampton. So began a difficult and courageous humanitarian venture which remains unique in British history.[106]

Unique as the event also was in Wales, the evidence, both quantitative and qualitative, suggests little to distinguish its history from that recorded elsewhere in these islands. Their arrival at Southampton prompted one editor to claim that they 'have so much in common with the Welsh', and the next two months were full of feverish activity.[107] The National Committee proposed to allocate 400 children to be hosted in Wales. At that time it was assumed that they would be staying for three months only, but the effort needed was still considerable. Political and charitable organizations all over Wales struggled to pool their resources and energies. Lord Davies's Welsh Fund for Basque Children – primed by donations totalling £1,500 from his own family – put the financial situation on a sound footing.[108] The resulting regional committees, many of them *ad hoc* and others somewhat ephemeral, incorporated representatives from a wide range of groups prepared to put ideological differences aside. Indeed, the urgency of the situation created a real sense of collective purpose amongst philanthropic workers of all political colours, to the extent that at last – and for once – it made the concept of 'Unity' a working reality. Hywel Francis is surely correct to emphasize the extent of interest and involvement in an aspect which literally came home to the public as a tangible and visible epitome of 'suffering Spain'. 'We had conservatives, labour, communist, a bit of everything', recalled Mrs Fernandez, the Spanish-born, Dowlais-reared immigrant who was later placed in charge of the main centre in Caerleon.[109] Indeed, so powerful was the wave of empathy which swept across the country, reaching its peak in the wake of the children's arrival in mid-July, that even Plaid Cymru would not be seen to stand aside. Cyril Cule gave a consciousness-raising radio talk about the Basques in June, and in August the party's annual conference at Bala 'proceeded to consider a resolution asking the conference to send the President of the

Basques an official message from the Welsh Nationalist party, expressing sympathy with them in their terrible plight. The resolution was carried amid cheers.'[110]

The most besetting problem was locating suitable accommodation premises for the children, who it was agreed were to be distributed to different areas of Wales.[111] In the event only one settlement – or 'colony' as they came to be known – was established in north Wales, but three of the original four were sited in rural areas. Offers received of urban locations (including one from the Cardiff sand-dredging company of F. Bowles and Son) were considered but usually rejected. None of the children had any English, many were already bemused and withdrawn, and most – despite the popular impression that they were all from Bilbao – had no experience of life in big cities. Local committees arranged the distribution of children, often in pairs, to the homes of suitable guardians. A disused army training camp in west Wales was earmarked for use – at Brechfa (in the Carmarthenshire forest). A large house was found in Swansea, and another – recently used for a Montessori school – in Old Conwy. But by far the largest group of children was destined for a large communal residence in Caerleon, 'Cambria House', donated on extended loan by Monmouthshire County Council.

Two of the 'colonies' were not destined to last long. A notorious outbreak of violence in Brechfa, which evoked much unfavourable national attention, led to the premature repatriation of several teenage delinquents, and the camp was closed by the autumn. Similar problems in Swansea led to an even more rapid redistribution of its inmates. The small fellowship of twenty-one children in Old Conwy, despite warm local sympathy and involvement – including free weekly shows at the local cinema – was also dispersed during 1938.[112] Within a year of the children's arrival, only Cambria House remained as a collective centre. Fifty-two children disembarked at Newport Railway Station on 10 July 1937. They must have felt specially welcome from the start, though as it turned out the abundance of bunting and other public decoration on display was meant for the newly crowned King and Queen, who were due in the town to begin their first visit to Wales four days later. Among the reception committee were Christopher Hill and Gwen Jones – both stalwarts of the Cardiff Aid Spain Committee and the Communist Party. Victoriano Esteban, from Abercrave, acted as interpreter – an experience which moved him, later that year, to volunteer for Spain, where he was to be killed in operations around Teruel.[113] The funds raised for the home permitted a paid administrative structure to be set up, with Cyril Cule as head of education and Gwen Jones as warden.[114]

These events met with a national (and local) opposition which cannot be dismissed as merely mean-spirited or reactionary. Many who did not share an outright commitment to the Republican cause felt, not without some reason, that the whole affair was a propaganda exercise. In Newport, a Conservative town councillor, C. T. Clissit, voiced this suspicion, quoting the Catholic paper *The Universe* as evidence that the children were in no danger from the Nationalist conquerors of their homeland.[115] A series of unruly outbursts amongst the older refugees provided ammunition for both the Catholic Church and more overt pro-Franco interests to stoke up the pressure for rapid repatriation. Particularly damaging (in both senses) was the near-riot by the boys sent to Brechfa, which caused much local fear and resentment, shortly after their arrival.[116] By the end of 1937, several hundred children in Britain as a whole had already been returned to their parents. Leo Abse was sent by Jim Henson of the International Transport Federation on a potentially dangerous undercover mission to conquered Bilbao, in order to gather information on whether it was safe for children to be sent home to parents who might be actually or potentially at risk from Francoist reprisals.[117] Though this initiative reached sceptical conclusions, large numbers of parental messages were regarded by a special bi-partisan committee as authentic, while many children simply elected to return, the older often speaking for younger siblings. Thus 1938 witnessed a constant dribble of repatriation. At the same time, the income source of places like Cambria House began to dry up. As the initial impact of the 'orphans of the storm' on the public mind wore off, aid organizations began to redirect attention to the primary aim of helping the civilian population of the rest of Republican Spain, whose need increased after the start of the great Nationalist offensive in Aragon in March 1938.

By then, however, the children had learned how to sing for their supper. Of course, fund-raising was also fun-raising for most, but the effort put into self-help at Cambria House was surely impressive. Within a week of their arrival in Caerleon, a press photographer snapped some of the boys playing soccer. Soon the Basque boys team garnered a busy fixture-list for the approaching season and in the autumn began a hugely successful run of matches against Welsh school teams. Meanwhile, the concert party was invited to perform far and wide. A typical programme would include songs and dances from the Basque lands as well as other regions of north-central Spain, selected 'Welsh' items (including the national anthem) along with songs from the Republican *cancionero*, such as the famous 'March of the 5th Regiment'.[118] In addition, pictures and poems by the children were auctioned, and the Cambria House magazine achieved a wide circulation.

The success of the Caerleon settlement – surely a lasting credit to all concerned – meant that children were often transferred to it from other colonies when the repatriation process inevitably brought their closures.[119] In early 1939 there were fifty-four children left in the whole of Wales, but six months later fifty-five, a higher number than the original intake, were resident at Cambria House.[120] However, the outbreak of war a few weeks later brought further uncertainty. Many thousands of local children were immediately perceived as needing shelter in rural Wales from the hail of bombs expected daily to cascade upon the south Wales ports. In contrast, Spain was now at peace (if peace of a discriminate kind, yet to be fatal for many). That winter, many Cambria House children left for Spain. By 1945, just over 10 per cent of the original party of 3,900 refugees remained in Britain. In the end, Wales gained perhaps thirty-five new denizens of Spanish descent.

3   Armadas and Alcázars: Urban and Maritime Wales

In 1982, the BBC Wales producer John Ormond advertised in the *Western Mail* asking for Welsh veterans of the Spanish Civil War to get in touch. He was engaged on a TV project, *The Colliers' Crusade* – a documentary series intended to tell the story of the Welsh volunteers, as far as possible in their own words, via extended interviews with survivors. It was taken for granted amongst the production staff that any response would come exclusively from International Brigaders, if not necessarily always from colliers *per se*. Indeed, this assumption was so instilled and instinctive that the newspaper notice neglected to spell out the basic requirements. Mr Ormond was, therefore, somewhat nonplussed when he turned up to interview Frank Thomas in Rhiwbina, Cardiff. As he quickly discovered, Thomas was certainly an authentic volunteer of the war, but had fought for 'the other side', for the Nationalist cause; and, as a rifleman in the 6th Bandera of the Spanish Foreign Legion, had seen more action in the fighting than any other Welshman. Worse still, it was only the temporary contingency of acting as his commanding officer's batman which had precluded him (much to his disappointment) from being in the front line of fire *against* the British Battalion of the International Brigade at the battle of Jarama. For Ormond, the occasion must have been like attending a reunion of a Welsh Armoured Brigade from the Second World War only to meet a grizzled but articulate veteran of a crack Panzer division – in other words, a culture shock.[1]

Frank Thomas's experience of the Spanish War was – so far as can be judged – unique for a Welshman.[2] Yet this young commercial salesman, brought up in Cardiff after his family business had moved from Pontypridd in 1921, was not unrepresentative of a certain strain of opinion to be found in the 'seascape' zone of Wales, as defined above.[3] A survey of attitudes towards the Spanish Civil War, as expressed in the English-language newspapers based in the south-eastern littoral, has found evidence to suggest that a large minority of readers held views which were out of sympathy with the Republic.

Given that South Wales is usually considered to have been very much a pro-Republican area, one of the most notable features of the Anglo-Welsh press coverage of the Civil War was the large amount of pro-Franco correspondence in the readers' columns. It is perhaps the case that support in Wales for the Nationalists was greater than has hitherto been acknowledged . . .[4]

It may be presumed that the backbone of this apparently 'heretical' section of the population was the commercial middle classes and white-collar workers, domiciled in these areas on a scale vastly greater than elsewhere in Wales. The coastal strip of south-east Wales was the centre of capital and business, the physical location of the domestic and office premises of many wealthy families. Office employment was of huge importance in all three of its main ports, and in an epoch when business premises qualified an occupier for a second vote, when office workers had no job security to speak of, and when (in any case) a genuine sense of personal loyalty was often present in the workplace, the political opinions of businessmen were commensurately influential with employees. This is not to say that the management echelons of the dozens of companies which still traded in the Cardiff Coal Exchange, and/or owned, chartered, berthed, maintained or supplied the city's still impressive merchant marine, were necessarily pro-Franco in elemental sympathy. Rather – as we shall see – they covered a range of allegiances and sympathies which often shifted during the course of the conflict and in reaction to some of its more notorious episodes.

Frank Thomas himself, a strong supporter of the British monarchy and empire, had developed a distaste for fascism as a result of Mussolini's imperialist ambitions. His job with the family wholesale foods firm often took him down to Cardiff's docklands where his retailer customers included dozens of small concerns run by immigrant families. In late 1935 he wrote an extraordinary letter to the *Western Mail* on behalf of the Somali residents of Tiger Bay, which gave an account of their feelings over Italy's brutal invasion of Abyssinia.[5] His support for freedom took no account of the ideological imperatives which dominated the thought-processes of so many contemporaries. Ten days after the military rising in Spain he told *Echo* readers that: 'Liberty is the cornerstone of democracy and if priests (or mullahs or rabbis for that matter) are not permitted to carry out their holy offices and are murdered simply because of their calling, then liberty – and, therefore, democracy – does not exist.'[6] Elsewhere, anxieties about the Republican government were not so much concerned with abstract philosophical issues. The political history of Spain's fledgling democracy had never inspired an underlying confidence in the Second Republic's commitment either to domestic property rights or to an international market economy. A prevailing unease affected shipowners and maritime communities all over Wales, such as companies who exported slates to northern Spain, or trawlermen who helped satisfy the Spanish appetite for fish and seafood. Moreover, since 1931, Spanish customers for Welsh coal had increasingly defaulted on payments, and figures for relevant exports had declined accordingly by mid-decade.[7] Unpaid bills in an era of depression meant that the experiences of industry and the maritime sector tended to deter them from support of the Republic. This provides the context of mildly pro-insurgent opinion, at least during the opening phase of the Civil War. Alongside these elements may be placed the traditional 'Tory' interest – farmers and landowners of some of the richest countryside in Wales, especially in the Vale of Glamorgan and rural Monmouthshire. They and their dependants were to evince perhaps the least complicated disbelief in the 'cause' of Republican Spain. Such inclinations were considerably buttressed by the horror-stories of violent social revolution in the peninsula which poured from the international press syndicates in the summer and autumn of 1936.

But business interests (broadly understood) were by no means the only factor involved, and it would certainly be ill-advised to attribute a lack of solidarity with 'Spain' in the major ports of Llanelli, Newport, Swansea and Cardiff, along with the satellite towns of the two latter (Port Talbot, Aberavon, Barry, Penarth), simply to traditional class or economic distinctions. The politics of the situation were complicated by the presence of a large and emphatically working-class population of families who saw themselves as Irish (despite, in many cases, being third-generation descendants of immigrant ancestors) and, more to the point, were devout Catholics. In 1936 there were perhaps as many as 20,000 families of this description distributed amongst the relevant communities, often concentrated in unofficial ghettoes such as Newtown in Cardiff and Greenhill in Swansea.[8] If less important numerically, of at least equal significance in terms of active concern over the Civil War in Spain, was the fact that this region boasted the presence of a Spanish immigrant 'colony' comprising something over one hundred discrete (if interrelated) families, perhaps totalling 600 members in all. In the mid-1930s a high proportion of this community lived in the docklands districts of Cardiff. Within both Irish and Spanish communities, the coming of the Spanish conflict triggered radically opposed, and often emotional, responses. These situations might be characterized metaphorically as 'Reflections of the Civil War', vividly illustrating the fact that events in Spain in 1936–9 were truly international in resonance. Amongst its multitudinous echoes were those heard on the very street-corners where the *South Wales Echo* was stentoriously sold.

Welsh Armadas: Exploitation or Compassion?[9]

Nothing more typifies the divided character of Wales's attitude to Spain than the mixed motives behind the involvement of its business–maritime community. The latter, after all, represented an element of conventionally 'civilized' leadership in the nation's affairs, men who were educated, experienced, knowledgeable, wealthy, well-travelled – and thus influential both inside and outside its borders. Was this not another face of 'internationalist' Wales? Its very fabric was international, and to the extent that Welsh capitalism was built around and depended upon seaborne commerce, it was bound to be interested in world peace. Yet self-interest was not the only spur to feelings which might be called 'liberal', aspirations tending towards support for international order and justice. The deeply humanitarian culture of nineteenth-century liberalism and the enlightened self-interest of the business section were inseparable and intermingled motives for most individuals involved. Many business families of maritime Wales – large and small – were traditional (and often munificent) supporters of the Liberal Party. Although this may not have inspired consistent opposition to the National Governments of the 1930s – even in respect of 'Spain' – it nevertheless endowed a certain level of understanding of, and even empathy with, minority causes and peoples perceived as 'oppressed'. Even where such virtues were not prominent in a given individual, the influence of his womenfolk – wives and daughters more often than not fully engaged in works of humanitarian purpose – might well have come into play.[10]

Undoubtedly the most celebrated single character in the minor mabinogion of Wales and 'Spain' (indeed, more so than any of its 'volunteers for liberty') is Captain David Jones of Swansea, known universally as 'Potato Jones'. He is a symbolic figure in fact as well as in legend. Although he was *not* 'the skipper who called Franco's bluff' – as so many contemporary newspaper stories claimed – he was thoroughly involved in trade with the Spanish Republic. According to well-established, if perhaps cynical, local belief, these activities extended to gun-running, in defiance of international agreements. Thus the avuncular and media-ready Jones may have been working for a cause in which he believed, but was also (with rather more empirical certainty) paid handsomely for the risks he ran in so doing.[11] In any case, the 'Potato Jones' episode caught the imagination of the whole world in April 1937, bringing Wales to world attention in a way which is perhaps difficult to understand today. Even the editor of the heavyweight intellectual magazine *Left Review* was sold on his story, giving Jones a starring role in one of the best-known English poems about the war.

> Restive, our sailors watched the shore
> Whilst hundreds drowned who'd starved before,
> Victims of Franco's sham blockade –
> Though in the way of honest trade
> Potato Jones and his brave lass
> Had proved this husband knave or ass.[12]

The publicity circus which surrounded Franco's attempt to blockade the Republican-held ports of northern Spain came about as the fortuitous result of large numbers of newspapermen being holed up in the French seaside towns close to the Nationalist-held borders of Pyrenean Spain.[13] As their land forces closed in on centres of resistance further west, the Nationalists declared that their naval forces would forcibly prevent ships attempting to enter Bilbao – capital of the Basque (autonomous) Republic. Despite the proximity of the Royal Navy, merchant steamers were indeed fired upon, if only by way of warning. Meanwhile, it was also asserted that the approaches to Bilbao had been heavily mined. On Admiralty orders, British vessels bound for the blockaded ports diverted in order to await the development of portentous international events in the small French harbour of St Jean de Luz. Story-starved pressmen, well aware of the diplomatic crisis now afoot – a crisis counterpointed by a fortnight of frenzy in the British Parliament – made a bee-line for this port. The fact that three of the four vessels sheltering there were skippered by men with a surname in common precipitated them and their country of origin to international celebrity. The Joneses of St Jean became the protagonists of adventure stories which made headlines on a global scale. Whilst his namesake colleagues tended to keep their counsel, David Jones gave a series of interviews which provided perfect copy. The barnacled physical presence and briny character of a veteran sailor whose very name evoked the eternal myths of the sea came across vividly to millions of readers. Combined with portrait shots of him on the bridge of his cockleshell steamer, the *Marie Llewellyn*, all this arguably created the first-ever 'stage Welshman' of the modern media. *Inter alia*, Jones's comments showed that like so many compatriots (already touched upon above) he was aware of the mutually hostile history of Britain and Spain, especially on the sea; and in so doing, unmistakably proclaimed his intention to take on the Don. 'Spanish Navy? Never heard of it since the

Armada. It makes me sick to think of these Spanish Dons strutting about the quarter-decks of their miserable ships intimidating the Royal Navy and interfering with shipping.'[14] Such sentiments so well encapsulated the feelings of the House of Commons, whose members were similarly outraged by the prospect of Britannia's rule being defied by tinpot Iberian dictators, that Jones seemed to appear as a sort of sea-monster, rising from the deep to terrify Stanley Baldwin and his harassed cabinet. Not surprisingly, Jones's subsequent attempt to challenge the contemptible Spaniards – so literally well-telegraphed – was brusquely frustrated by the Royal Navy, and the *Marie Llewellyn* sent back to St Jean in humiliating circumstances. Shortly afterwards, another Welsh steamer, the *Seven Seas Spray*, left St Jean and after a few hours' sailing made it safely into the estuary of the Nervión and Bilbao docks on 20 April. Commanded by William Roberts, a more taciturn skipper who had cleverly taken advantage (in more than one sense) of the diversion caused by 'El Patatero', its cargo of mixed food supplies was certainly welcome to the hungry population. However, the razzmatazz reception it received in Bilbao was as least equally due to the Basque government's determination to exploit the propaganda value of what they saw as nothing less than a victory.[15] The lionizing of Captain Roberts and his teenage daughter Florence (ex-denizens of Penarth) was given saturation coverage both in the local and international press, partly in order to humiliate the Franco government, but also as a way of encouraging other owners and skippers to brave any remaining risks perceived to stand in the way of supplying the beleaguered Basques. Accordingly, in the second half of April alone, some twenty merchantmen followed in the wake of the *Seven Seas Spray*. Though still exposed to the enemy's bombers, the citizens of Bilbao at least had no further need to fear starvation – that is, until the city eventually fell to the Nationalists on 19 June.[16]

By far the greater proportion of foreign businesses and seamen who risked their livelihoods and their lives in the task of supplying the Republican side during the Spanish Civil War were British. This fact usually fails to gain recognition in both Spanish and British accounts of the war's international dimensions, perhaps because it fails to conform with the required impression of a Britain – especially the Britain of the City of London and the stuff of 'finance-imperialism' – so fundamentally out of sympathy with 'Spain' that it is often saddled with a share of the moral obloquy for the victory of 'Franco-Fascism'.[17] Within this substantial British contribution to the 'cause', the role of the Welsh merchant marine was prominent.[18] The presence of Welsh vessels and skippers in St Jean de Luz in April 1937 was therefore not surprising or unusual in the general context of the war's maritime history.[19]

Whilst the aid to 'Spain' involved in this trade was – officially at least – wholly made up from food, fuel and medical supplies, it seems likely that men like David Jones also contributed in a more direct manner to the Republican war-effort. During the six-month period before the network of international conventions which constituted the Non-Intervention Agreement came into force (November 1936–April 1937), British firms traded arms and other war-related materials into Spain. This traffic was from the start mostly with the Republican side and, although severely discouraged by the British authorities, remained for the time being a lawful undertaking.[20] David Jones was one of several Welsh skippers who ran arms supplies from continental sources to Bilbao, Alicante and other ports during the later months of 1936.[21] In this context, it is worthy of note that the *Marie Llewellyn* was only one of a remarkable flotilla of steamships which were queueing up to run into the Republic's northern ports, preferably under the protection of the Royal Navy's guns, in precisely the period just before the new regulations, forbidding traffic in military materials, were to be imposed. Another of these demanded that an official agent of the Non-Intervention Committee must sail aboard any ship trading to Spain with goods laden at any port of the High Contracting Parties, in order to ensure conformity. Ships of the participating navies (Britain, France, Germany and Italy) were authorized to intercept and examine any suspicious vessel within the zones to which they were allocated. It can hardly be a coincidence, then, that David Jones again left St Jean de Luz on 19 April, the day before D-day, this time bound not for Bilbao but for Alicante in the Mediterranean; nor, perhaps, that Captain Roberts timed his own short but epic voyage on D-day itself, before any non-intervention agent could arrive in St Jean. What was really in Davy Jones's locker? In contrast to the unequivocal calumny of some historians, I merely report the long-lived local rumour that Jones's potatoes – already starting to sprout – provided the crust on a pie filling which his customers would find rather more meaty.[22]

Be these issues as they may, the Spanish War clearly offered an opportunity to the commercial interests of south Wales ports. Following a decade of decline and contraction, many businessmen were quick to take advantage of the situation in which the legal government of Spain was prepared to offer much-enhanced rates of contract. Some shipowners, having sold or laid up vessels in recent years, now discarded the mothballs and even purchased vessels specifically in order to enter the trade. P. M. Heaton, a leading expert on the history of south Wales shipping in this period, mentions almost forty different companies engaged in the ownership, contracting or managing of trade with the Republic.[23] One or two firms were actually set up, and new steamers commissioned, specifically for this purpose, while in addition there were a number of adaptations and considerable restructuring in various departments – in short, an all-round expansion – of the shipping business. The great majority of companies involved were based in Cardiff, though a large number of voyages were out of Swansea, Port Talbot, Barry and Newport. In the years 1936–9, the Spanish trade therefore provided a source of limited revival in profits and employment in these communities – since, of course, shipping is a matrix industry with spin-offs in a wide variety of contingent occupations.[24]

During 1937, commerce with the Republic centred upon two outstanding cargoes – on the one hand, general food supplies, almost entirely loaded at ports in continental Europe (Scandinavia, the Low Countries and the French Mediterranean) and on the other, the miserable human by-product of modern war, refugees. Not long after the Biscay events described above, the latter emergency rose to critical proportions. The Nationalist military offensive in northern Spain was pursued relentlessly throughout the spring and summer. The Valencia government's almost total inability to assist its geographically isolated Basque allies – a major logistical problem which had never been seriously tackled – limited the latter's powers of resistance. In particular, the enemy's use of air attack against undefended towns was gradually escalated, a tactic culminating in the unprecedented outrage of the saturation bombing of Guernica on 26 April. As was partly the intention, this horror stimulated large-scale panic flight from settlements in the wider vicinity of Bilbao, and the city quickly became overcrowded with refugees. The Basque government contracted dozens of ships and voyages in order to evacuate not only those persons and families most at risk from potential Francoist reprisals, but also as much of its own material apparatus as could be salvaged (especially its residual financial assets).[25] The ensuing refugee crisis lasted well into the autumn, as successively the provinces of Vizcaya, Cantabria and Asturias, and thus the chief ports (respectively) of Bilbao, Santander and Gijón, along with many smaller harbours, fell one by one into Nationalist hands. As Heaton chronicles in detail, Welsh steamers were to the fore in attempting to ferry thousands of terrified evacuees across to France. As things reached a climax in October, modest armadas of five or more such vessels were frequently to be found in waters adjacent to Santander and Gijón, in what became an increasingly frenzied operation, and often a horrendous experience for the sailors involved.[26]

Indeed, not only were the refugees' sufferings a heart-rending sight, but their would-be saviours themselves were also at serious risk. The smaller the enclave of resistance became, the more effective was the Nationalist naval blockade, and for the Welsh mariners, the success of each individual mission depended on the timing and speed of their dashes back and forth across three dangerous miles of territorial waters. Though it seems that Franco's commanders had orders to avoid the actual sinking of refugee ships – if for no other reason, because in the aftermath of Guernica such an atrocity would have represented a publicity disaster for Burgos – the risk of death or injury was ever-present. During these operations, many Welsh steamers were fired on and several were captured and impounded by the Nationalists.[27] Meanwhile, time and again, small craft laden to the gunnels with refugees made the hazardous voyage across the moody waters of the Bay of Biscay and returned for more of the same. It seems likely that Welsh ships alone rescued as many as 25,000 people from the harsh imprisonment or worse they faced if left to the tender mercies of Francoism victorious. Doubtless, the experiences of hundreds of Welsh mariners in Spanish Biscay were deeply influential in confirming (or sometimes changing) popular attitudes to the Civil War in maritime and urban Wales. As is the custom of seafarers, they went home to share them, suitably elaborated and encrusted, with all and sundry, a generosity often displayed in public watering-holes where expanding eddies of wider distribution were guaranteed. It may be speculated that it was this real if obscure phenomenon, as much as the headline-occupying horrors of Guernica, Durango and of the refugee Basque children, which led to a widespread reappraisal of feelings over the Spanish War in south Wales during the summer of 1937.[28]

All this enterprise had its profits, which (of course) ran higher commensurately with the dangers. Substantial premiums were available in the contracts negotiated by Cardiff's shipping agents and managers with their Spanish customers. Crews received extra wage rates, and often bonuses, for time spent in any war-zone. While companies had to meet these wage-bills as well as hefty extra insurance costs, the trade was evidently lucrative enough to justify risks taken. Against this, it must be said that, in the final stages of the refugee crisis, many businessmen must have been dubious over what was the most serious of these gambles – at least in a fiduciary sense. Amidst the anarchy of military collapse and political chaos, the chances that settlements would ultimately be fully honoured by a doomed authority were bound to decrease. Yet any such apprehension did not, it seems, cause them to hold ships back when confronted with the sheer desperation of the refugees who crammed the quaysides of Gijón and Avilés.[29]

In the spring of 1938, the Nationalists, having weathered the storm of great Republican offensives in central war-zones, battles which dominated the military scene in the second half of 1937, themselves developed a determined onslaught in Aragon.[30] Within a few weeks the whole Republican defence line was shattered. Franco's troops made rapid progress towards the Mediterranean, once again pushing in front of them a great tide of refugees. Having reached the sea at Viñaroz on 19 April, thus dividing the Republic into two zones, Franco's Army of the North dug in for a period of consolidation, hemming in Catalonia, whilst that of the Centre continued the offensive against the southern sector, that is, towards the city of Valencia. Once again, but this time with ever-mounting urgency and for the rest of the war's duration, the coastal cities of the Republic relied on the services of international commerce. Unmanageably swollen with refugees, their makeshift hospitals crowded with wounded men from the fronts, their towns open to enemy bombing sorties from east and west, they needed all the food and medical supplies they could get. In addition, however, and especially once a great counter-offensive in the region of the lower Ebro valley had been decided upon, the war-related industries of Barcelona and Tarragona had to be stoked up with fuel as a matter of urgency. Welsh shipping was to deliver a disproportionate fraction of the former, while both providing and delivering the lion's share of the latter.[31]

One of the areas of Welsh business to benefit from the war was the staple industry of coalmining. This sector, however, was slower off the mark than others dealt with so far. Partly because of persisting apprehensions arising from the non-payment for contracts fulfilled earlier in the decade, exports of coal to Spain had slumped in 1935 and decreased still further during 1936, a fact doubtless attributable to the parlous domestic prospects of Spanish capitalism. Slow recovery marked 1937, but in the following year, exports soared, a phenomenon, as the *Western Mail* pointed out, 'almost entirely due to the [Republican] government purchases'.[32] Following the catastrophic defeats of the Republic in Aragon, a constant procession of steamers left the coal ports of south Wales, chartered to deliver fuel to Cartagena, Valencia, Tarragona and above all Barcelona. Indeed it was the Welsh merchant marine which continued doggedly to pay homage to Catalonia, making an outstanding contribution to the region's resistance, particularly in the later stages of the bitter and prolonged battle of the Ebro, from August to October of 1938. Nationalist intelligence sources provide us with data concerning some forty voyages in this period, which unloaded a total of over 150,000 tons of coal and coke, mostly in Barcelona.[33] These deliveries were particularly intense in the months when the Republic was gearing up to mount its greatest campaign of the war, the do-or-die Ebro offensive. Data in the main source-document for Table B, for example, indicate that deliveries from Welsh ports represented nearly 60 per cent of all British coal fuel reaching the Republic. Some ships made repeated return voyages into waters which had become infested with enemy submarines and surface warships, following a route lined with hostile shore batteries and aerodromes. In many respects – as we shall see – they were to pay dearly for their determination and daring.[34]

In addition to the direct Wales–Spain trade, other vessels with Welsh connections were engaged in the shorter span carriage of supplies from Marseilles and Toulon. This route was notoriously that which military munitions importers (mainly though not exclusively from private enterprisers) were by now obliged to take, and it thus attracted extreme Nationalist attention. It seems clear that both Burgos and Whitehall suspected one or two Welsh businesses of being involved in 'gun-running' despite the tough quarantine obstacles in place.[35] Meanwhile, the manifest dangers of running supplies into the Mediterranean ports had forced Stalin to order the gradual withdrawal of Soviet-registered ships from the traffic. Though Soviet aid was, in any case, being reduced, it now reached Spain (if at all) in the holds of British ships.[36] The long and hazardous voyage from Odessa in the Black Sea to Barcelona was now undertaken by small steamers such as the *African Mariner*, crewed by sailors like Tom Williams, Humphrey Roberts, Gwynfor Jones and Robin Williams – all hailing from Pwllheli, and under the command of Captain Manley from Penarth. The Royal Navy took special interest in voyages from Russia, calculating not unreasonably that they would hardly be undertaken at all without the Soviets insisting on an arms payload – which, in any case, offered tempting extra profits to all concerned. The *Mariner* completed one round trip, sailing right through the Mediterranean under the noses of the Italian Navy and over the eyebrows of its submarines, going on to defy Mussolini's airforce and Franco's own war-fleet as it approached Barcelona. On a second attempt, late in 1938, it was intercepted by HMS *Repulse* and taken to Malta. Having no non-intervention agent on board (and perhaps as a result of a tip-off from Burgos) the ship was held in Valetta for ten days while exhaustive investigation of her holds was conducted. When found to be clear, the innocent vessel was given special protection to continue its voyage, and came safely again into Barcelona with its cargo of grain and salt fish.[37]

Like other ports on that coast, Barcelona was now seething with would-be evacuees frantic for a passage to France. One Cardiff veteran recalls several return voyages to Marseilles in which refugees were the only cargo.[38] Tom Williams told a north Wales reporter that in Cartagena 'mangled corpses strewed the streets', whilst

I have seen a crowd of women and children begging for crusts on the quays by the ships, deliberately bombed and blown to atoms. The fight for democracy in Europe is carried on by British ships carrying predominantly Welsh crews, and we are known on the continent as the 'Welsh Navy'. The Spanish people bear a close resemblance to the Welsh – and they are winning![39]

The ubiquitous presence of maritime Wales in the humanitarian relief of the Republic's death throes also came to the notice of a wider audience through the press, if not on the scale of the earlier Biscay voyages. An American journalist whose supercharged style matched his scoop-conscious enterprise interviewed the 'redoubtable Caernarvon sailor', Captain Llewelyn Davies, in the early days of 1939. This skipper was evidently marked for media promotion as a kind of Potato Jones with angel's wings:

> Throughout the whole duration of hostilities, Captain Davies has been consistently pumping nourishment into Loyalist Spain . . . How much longer must he play his part in winning freedom for these always-cheerful Spaniards? Without him and his colleagues the plight of the Spanish people must be infinitely worse . . . He has kept a steady course with all the tenacity that distinguishes the service he represents, and even as I interview him here in Barcelona his light still flashes unquenchably through the penumbra of Spain's Civil War.[40]

In December 1938, Captain Manley, hero of the *African Mariner*, was arrested by the police in Barcelona on a charge of aiding the passage of illicit persons to France.[41] This matter seems to have had its sinister side. The lengthening lists of people desperate to escape from Spain were by now not limited to those fleeing from Franco. They included members of revolutionary parties proscribed in the Republic, victims of the Soviet-inspired persecution of Stalin's perceived enemies – soul-mates of Eric Blair, who had managed to extricate himself from the jaws of the Republican secret police in 1937 – along with large numbers of International Brigaders who had deserted from units on the Aragon front. Many skippers were sympathetic to the plight of the latter, especially since it was widely believed that they ran the risk of execution if captured. The secret police had long suspected that a covert operation was being run by subversive elements, which involved deserters being smuggled on board British vessels.[42] Not long before he himself disappeared from the ranks, a Neath volunteer, Alwyn Skinner, was recovering from illness in a coastal convalescent home. In a local hotel bar he encountered a group of Welsh merchant navy officers. Being himself a survivor of a submarine attack on a ship carrying hundreds of International Brigade volunteers from France to Spain, he keenly appreciated their daring and determination. He enjoyed the company in particular of 'Captain Roberts of Newport, a comparatively young man. For all their main impetus is money making', he added, 'still they show amazing pluck.'[43]

The 'Welsh Navy' in Spain was skippered and crewed by a good many sailors whose seafaring lives had begun on tramps and trawlers operating out of the small harbour towns of west and north Wales. At this level, the response of the maritime community in my 'seascape' section of Wales was all of a piece. Dozens, perhaps hundreds, of the men involved were members of the National Union of Seamen, an organization which (if not, at that time, in its central leadership) included powerful cells of CPGB and other radical groups. However, the ownership and management elements which employed them had a different agenda. As suggested above, the latter were concentrated in south-east Wales, and above all in Cardiff. And of course – other things being equal – the profit motive is politically (and often morally) neutral.[44] Indeed, the evidence suggests that the individuals and companies concerned in the Wales–Spain trade set out with the natural assumption that profits would be best maximized by doing business with both sides. This was the case even with firms which were later looked upon as basically pro-Republican, such as the shipping companies owned or managed by Jack Billmeier in London, and in Wales those of Claude Angel, Alfred Pope and Percy Barnett. Like Billmeier's, the interests of Claude Angel were identified as hostile by the Nationalists at an early stage of the war, when his ships were involved in running guns into the loyalist ports of Bilbao and Alicante.[45] The latter of these two voyages – from Hamburg – was a seemingly daring operation which caused embarrassment to both Burgos and Berlin.[46] On the other hand, the Bilbao expeditions – as recent research has revealed – represented one of the more outrageous and cynical acts of deceit practised against the much-abused Republican arms purchasers.

> The *Yorkbrook* made three trips from the Baltic to Bilbao and on two of them nearly all the arms were found, when unloaded, to be useless or sabotaged: cartridges without percussion-caps or the wrong size for the rifles, machine guns without firing pins, aircraft-bombs without fuses, shell-cases filled with rags instead of explosives and field-guns with their carriage-axles broken.[47]

Because the Republic controlled the Spanish treasury and had exclusive legal access to its worldwide financial assets, it was a much more reliable customer than the Nationalists. Though it may have been – partly for the same reason – easier to defraud, the former's assets were probably the main factor in moulding events. However, underlying the financial rationale was the pressing consideration that almost from the start it was the Republic which lacked strategic materials of all kinds. By the end of 1936, most of Spain's great food-producing regions had fallen to the enemy, and less than a year later, Franco's reduction of the entire northern enclave meant the loss of a large fraction of its heavy industry and mineral production – the ironworks of Vizcaya and León, the coalfield of Asturias. On top of these factors must be placed the proactive approach of the Nationalist navy and the arrogant tactlessness of its diplomacy, which soon alienated much of the international business community. Lastly, following the fall of Bilbao, all vessels known to have traded with the Basques were banned from the ports of the Nationalist zone, a punitive measure which further reduced the options of many shipping companies.

One company which succeeded in maintaining good relations with Burgos despite all these obstacles was Constant Brothers of Cardiff. Their business had flourished by supplying coal to Spain, returning with iron ore from Bilbao, along with pyrites and mercury from the western Andalusian port of Huelva, for the metallurgical industries of south-east Wales. Constants owned one of the largest mercantile fleets in Wales, a total of sixteen vessels. This enabled them to carry on trading with both sides, even after the fall of Bilbao, simply by switching the steamers which had been used for the latter run for others in their fleet. However, when Franco decided to award this company the lucrative contract to supply Basque ore to Britain, he was not aware that they were also supplying much of the mortgage capital for Jack Billmeier, the London shipowner who was amongst the Republic's most significant commercial associates.[48] Another firm which proved able to resume their business in Spain not too long after the start of the war was Gibbs & Co., the Cardiff-based cork import company with estates and wide contacts in the regions known as Extremadura on both sides of the Portuguese border. Doubtless because of their one-dimensional dependence upon an existing dictatorship – that of Salazar – they were seen as trustworthy by the new Francoist state. For the same reason they worked actively (if covertly) for a Nationalist victory and came to be regarded by many in their home town of Penarth as 'fascists', along with another wealthy Catholic family who lived nearby. Their active support for Franco seems nonetheless to have been unique amongst the relevant trading companies of maritime Wales.[49]

More surprising is the fact that on the other side, too, only one prominent shipman was actively engaged. This was John Emlyn Jones, a former Liberal

MP, who campaigned tirelessly throughout the war, making anti-Franco speeches on many a public platform. Deeply influenced by his regard for the Basque people, fluent in French and Spanish, his experience and contact network as a ship's broker was put at the disposal of the Valencia government. Though on a more private basis, Percy Barnett, an energetic entrepreneur with a finger in many commercial pies, also made himself exceptionally useful to the Republic. Most of his operations were undertaken on behalf of the PNV, the governing party of the Basque Autonomous Republic, but in addition his links with the Baltic seem to have provided an avenue of contact for Valencia with the USSR, and his vessels were prominent in the Odessa–Barcelona trade during 1938.[50] Two shipmen of more conservative inclinations, Frederick Jones of the Abbey Line (a Tory councillor in Cardiff) and Lord Glanely of Tatem & Co., also came to develop some sympathy for the Republican cause; but this was strictly limited to its Basque – essentially non-revolutionary – aspect, and inspired wholly by humanitarian response to the plight of a conquered people. Much the same applied to Alfred Pope, charismatic owner of the *Seven Seas Spray* and one of the Republic's most loyal and determined suppliers. On the whole, it seems, their historian is judicious in his general conclusion that

> no one would pretend that the shipowners were motivated by any ideological ideals, but having been involved in many cases with supplying the Republican side from the start of the conflict, albeit for handsome returns, it is surely to their credit that they didn't desert them when the going got rough.[51]

Though it would be difficult to argue that Wales's coalowners were any more inspired by altruism than the shipmen, the liberal-philanthropic tradition was by no means entirely absent. The activities of Lord Davies of Llandinam have already been mentioned. When the case of the Basque 'orphans of the war' focused the sufferings of civilians in the Republican zone more intensely than ever before, Davies took a leading role in the campaign, whilst the names of several coalowner colleagues were present in the lists of donations.

Two Aspects of the Catholic Cause

However, the greatest of all the dynastic businesses of south Wales was inclined powerfully in the opposite direction. The marquess of Bute, whose grandfather had been the bitterest commercial rival of the Llandinam dynasty's great founder, belonged to a family which had sensationally converted to Catholicism in 1868. Since that time the Butes had developed various links with Spain, amongst other things building up interests in the holiday market of Andalusia and Spanish Morocco. In early 1937, Stephen Spender and T. C. Worsley were sent on a Comintern mission to Spain. They scoured the bars of Gibraltar looking for the Soviet weapons ship *Komsomol*, which had disappeared at sea en route to Cartagena. Nothing useful to the Kremlin was unearthed, but Worsley – brought up in Llandaff, where his father was Cathedral dean – overheard some fascinating tittle-tattle about Cardiff Castle's connections with Franco. It appeared that the marquis of Bute, owner of their hotel, employed a prominent local Falangist as his secretary.[52] Indeed, though the marquis himself stayed in the political background, his wife was an outspoken Franco supporter. In 1938, Lady Bute published an article in a Nationalist propaganda magazine which gushingly described the conditions of peace and plenty which 'liberation from the reds' had brought to the Franco zone. 'Everywhere', claimed the marchioness, there was 'the same spirit – that of a Crusade'.[53] When the article was reprinted in the *Western Mail* – in which her husband held a majority interest – it sparked a strongly disapproving reaction from readers. Amongst others, the secretary of the 'Heath Co-operative Women's Guild' wrote on behalf of a unanimous committee to protest at the line taken by the lady of the Cardiff manor.[54]

The marchioness defended herself with vigour.[55] None of her critics had apparently suggested any religious or economic reasons for her commitment. Yet it was widely rumoured in Cardiff that the Butes had contributed generously to the financing of Franco's war-effort. Many years later, the veteran International Brigader, Pat Murphy, told Jack Klugmann, then editor of *Marxism Today*, that 'the Marquis of Bute sold £10,000,000 worth of Cardiff and loaned it to Franco'.[56] Faulty memory and perfect enthusiasm had augmented the figure Murphy quoted to an extent of which interest rates have rarely been capable, but other evidence seems to corroborate at least the gravamen of his indictment. A few weeks before the publication of Lady Bute's article, the British consul in Tangiers reported that 'the [Nationalist] High Commissioner told me confidentially that Lord Bute had recently approached the Nationalist Government with a view to purchasing the docks of Cadiz, Malaga and Algeciras, presumably out of the profits of the Cardiff sale'.[57] In the months before the outbreak of war, the marquess had been in dispute with the Republican government, which had prevented him from exporting some original paintings purchased in the country. The collection had been stored in Algeciras while legal proceedings were initiated.[58] But things were apparently not as straightforward as these bare facts might imply. The consul's report continued:

> General Franco turned down [Bute's] proposal . . . primarily on strategic grounds . . . especially in the present case when they had considerable doubts as to the political sympathies of the purchaser. I can hardly think that this applies to Bute himself, though he is a very curious character, but you will remember that his lawyer here, Mr Palma, has always been one of the leaders of the Communist Party, and many of his other employés are very much inclined to the left. Lady Bute evidently wishes to correct this impression and now appears wearing numerous Nationalist emblems . . .[59]

As with his fellow-businessmen, and given the fundamental uncertainties of Spanish politics, it was clearly in Bute's interest to have contacts with both sides, with an eye not only to present opportunities but also upon more long-term prospects. However, in consequence, the Burgos authorities – obsessed with security – regarded Bute as too risky. In Franco's eyes, one was either with 'the movement' or against it. By the summer of 1938, however, no serious doubts can have remained amongst well-informed circles as to which side was on its way to victory. The marchioness's comportment was evidently a strong signal that (if indeed it was ever thus perched) the dynasty had climbed down off the fence.

Cardiff Castle – the manor house itself – stands in the very centre of the city. Just across the River Taff, passage of which it was originally constructed (by the Romans) to defend, are the districts of Riverside and Canton, densely populated with working-class immigrant families in those days, as they still are in our own. In the 1930s, the area was home to many Jews, but also to a much larger and fast-growing population of 'Irish' Catholics. The latter were also strongly represented in Grangetown and other dockland districts, in addition to their domination of Newtown, which likewise abutted onto the city centre. Yet although situated cheek-by-jowl, and in theory co-religionists with the Butes, the gulf between Catholic Canton and the Castle was unimaginably vast. Whilst on the one hand the Castle patronized Catholic institutions and organizations in the city, a charitable commitment from which many hundreds of deserving cases benefited, on the other the Bute family were still, in a quite literal sense, the owners of Cardiff. Not only did they still control the various docks (which they had constructed in the previous century), most of its associated railway companies and many other businesses, they also owned many of the houses and possessed the very land which most Irish families lived on. Thousands of them thus paid property rent and/or ground rent to the Castle, and one suspects that the resentment of the squirearchy that these circumstances inevitably engendered played its part in producing feelings such as that evinced by Pat Murphy. Moreover, the religion of the Butes and that of their urban Catholic tenants, ostensibly identical, was very different in cultural texture. The former belonged to an essentially aristocratic English order of neo-Gothic Romantics, an elite club to which many intellectually refined Jesuits were attached and by means of which many upper-class teachers and artists were converted to Rome. The latter practised the intensely ethnic – and socially alienated – religion of their homeland. It was a crude and puritanical spiritual environment, perfectly reflecting their socio-economic circumstances, organized in tightly knit parishes which were so many little Irelands.[60]

Upper-class 'English' Catholics had little experience of discrimination and no memory of religious hatred. Little else divided them from any aspect of the British socio-economic establishment. Their support for the Spanish Nationalists – such as it was – called for little particular comment in this context. In Cardiff (as in Swansea, Newport, or for that matter, Liverpool and Glasgow) Irish communities were ruled, politically as well as morally – and in both autocratically – by secular priests who were normally citizens of the Irish Free State, men who were deeply mindful of past eras of religious persecution presided over by what was (in Wales until 1920) an officially Protestant Britain. It was this exemplary history of persecution which commanded their feelings in the summer months of 1936, when the Church came under savage attack in every part of Spain – except the Basque Country – where the military rebellion had not succeeded. As we have seen, saturation press coverage of this phenomenon inspired outright denunciation of the 'Communists' (and by clear association, the Republic itself) by the senior clergy. As their catechism told them, the word 'Catholic' meant 'universal', and real (if neither obsessive nor overwhelming) concern was felt in Catholic homes for the fate of Spanish Catholics.

In other parts of Wales, reaction to anticlerical violence in Spain took place mostly on religious-historical grounds, whereas Irish communities were inescapably part of the urban texture of the south-east, and tensions were more significantly explained by current socio-economic apprehensions. Many Irish families belonged to the most economically deprived sections of the population, which in the mid-1930s could often mean near-penury and daily distress. There were exceptions, of course: like the Purnell family whose undertaking business thrived to the extent that they produced Cardiff's third Catholic – and Tory – lord mayor in 1937. Nevertheless the Irish of the south Wales ports were, under normal circumstances, firmly behind the Labour Party and strong in their support of the trade unions. Indeed, because of their perceived historic grievances, they were a radical breed, if ever there was one. But the onset of the Spanish Civil War – a conflict one historian has called 'a religious tragedy' – meant that circumstances were no longer normal.[61] Over Spain, the poverty of working-class Catholics failed to make them commensurately solid with the cause of antifascism and unity. As another expert has shown, a vocal minority of working-class Catholics all over Britain began to manifest a sense of identification with General Franco – only by whose leadership, they believed, could the persecution of their religion in Spain be brought to an end.[62]

In a leader at the end of July, a fortnight after the uprising in Spain, the *Welsh Catholic Times* warned the faithful against giving money for schemes to aid Spanish workers, since it might be spent 'on petrol to burn churches'. The editorial added that, 'for ourselves we do not regard the rebels as necessarily proved defenders of the Catholic Church . . . but it is quite clear that the Government of Spain and its main supporters are venomous haters of the Church'.[63] The archbishop of Cardiff, the Revd John Mostyn, issued a carefully worded pastoral letter on 13 August, asking God 'to grant that this hatred of religion may cease in Spain'.[64] Shortly afterwards a special service was held in St David's pro-cathedral, attended by many members of Cardiff's Spanish colony.[65] Fr James Hannon preached in English and Spanish: 'Today, Spain is an immense blazing conflagration. Our immediate task is to smother the outbreak. Later, when the danger is past, the day of reckoning for the guilty will come . . . I don't ask you to take up arms, but to join your hands together . . .'[66] Only a few weeks later, Fr Hannon, despite qualifications in Spanish and experience as parish priest of St Cuthbert's in the Cardiff docklands, was transferred to Aberavon. In his choice of phrase, and for the tastes of some of the congregation, he had evidently moved too close to the Francoist side, and too far from the necessary spirit of forgiveness. Even in his new posting, Fr Hannon seems to have transgressed the spirit of his own advice about taking up arms. In November, a young man wrote to offer his services to General Franco, on paper headed 'Port Talbot Hotel, Aberavon':

> My reasons for writing are; first of all I am a Catholic, in fact a daily communicant, a statement my parish priest will endorse. Second . . . for seven years I was at a famous Welsh public school, Christ College, Brecon, before proceeding to Sandhurst . . . My age is 21 and I am willing to accept any position . . . to act as a spy, or perhaps you need an English wireless announcer.[67]

Fr Dalton, parish priest of St Illtyd's in Dowlais, identified a more useful and practical way of aiding the Spanish faithful. He called on Catholic members of the Labour Party and working-class organizations, not only to disavow but also to resist 'publicly and emphatically' any attempt to provide aid for 'Red Spain'. 'Only thus', he maintained, 'can they acquit themselves of the guilt of sharing in another's sin'.[68] Dowlais, though having many Irish and Spanish denizens, was a major centre of 'Aid Spain' activity. But the public response to Fr Dalton came from an Irish docker in Cardiff:

> As a member of the Labour Party and a Trade Unionist let me assure him that we are fully alive to the danger, and we have not all been silent . . . There are a few thousand Catholic men fighting for a living on Cardiff Docks . . . It is absolutely necessary for us to be members of a Trade Union to protect ourselves, and at all times ever since I have worked on the Docks, we have had to fight the anti-Catholic element . . . In regard to the money that has been sent to Spain . . . Catholics like myself in the three Trade Unions – that is the coal trimmers, railwaymen and transport workers – have protested and although we have been beaten, because we are in a minority, our presence is felt.[69]

Mr Daly's letter illustrated the delicate difficulties faced. The struggle against 'the anti-Catholic element', and the folk-culture through which they often militantly identified with the cause of Irish nationalism, imparted a sense of empathy with victims of persecution in Spain, which was probably exceeded only among the nationalist community in Northern Ireland.[70] Even further splits could be caused within the family circle when (typically) the father hesitated to take any action which might divide him from his workmates, and unmarried sons were strong for 'Spain', while mothers and daughters seethed with anger about the desecration of churches and the rape of nuns. A majority of breadwinners amongst Irish in the port towns were, as Daly suggested, unskilled or semi-skilled dockers, at the mercy of the fluctuating demands of the job market and the daily whim of foreman 'butties'. Though some of the new generation were filtering into better jobs – including skilled jobs – in heavy industry, many more were ordinary seamen in the trawler and tramp sections. Unemployment among them was higher than the average. One working-class Protestant, who grew up in Canton, Cardiff, recalled that local Catholics 'had strange names that all began with "O" or "Mac", they belonged to large families, they tended to be poorly dressed, and were dangerous if provoked. Their homes were a rent-collector's nightmare.'[71]

After 1936, problems of paying the rent were gradually reduced by the employment opportunities offered by increased exports to Spain. So long as this meant loading or crewing ships destined for Republican Spain, the Irish had only the concomitant problem of avoiding – if conscience so dictated – the collecting tin for 'Spanish Aid' which was rattled insistently around the areas of the dock gates and in nearby pubs. But when – for example – ships of the so-called 'Inge Line' (Constant Brothers of Cardiff) offered rates for lading cargoes for Franco's Spain, another and keener difficulty arose. Attempts were sometimes made to 'black' such vessels, which might lead to offers of premium piece-rates, in turn increasing the temptation for Irish stevedores with large, young families to join the 'scabs'. In this way, though we can never access their history in any intimate detail, a whole seething complex of minor civil wars in the homes, streets, pubs and clubs of urban south Wales was unravelled by the Civil War in Spain. Tensions between Catholics and others within working-class districts and organizations were of course religious-cultural in origin rather than political. But some clergy were aware of potential political complications and were concerned to defuse the situation. In the event, in terms of political action – even at the ballot-box – the results of the Spanish War were limited. Whilst it seems established among historians that, nationwide, Catholics were more likely to join fascist movements than others – in Leeds, for example, Oswald Mosley's nickname was 'The Pope' – only a tiny minority of Welsh Catholics could see him as a crusading saviour of Rome.[72]

Aiding 'Spain': A Cause Divided

Thus, despite the fears of Mrs Horner in Tenby, and various other conspiracy hunters who feared for Protestant Wales, there was little sign in the ranks of its potential popular armies that Roman Catholicism in Wales was preparing to back either a communist or a fascist takeover. All the same, in many of the busy port towns of south Wales – not just in Cardiff – there were obsessive, perhaps even fanatical, men and women at work, people who were 'doing their bit', sometimes in social contexts which were both covert and bizarre, to bring about final victory in Spain for one side or the other. These *dévots* ranged from CPGB officials engaged in the recruitment and organization of volunteer levies for the International Brigades to full-time agents of the Spanish Fascist Party (Falange Española) whose task was to gather and relay information concerning these and other pro-Republican activities to Franco's government.

Throughout virtually the whole duration of the war, political parties and other organizations struggled to unite their efforts to 'Aid Spain'. For much of that time the yearning for 'unity' met only frustration. The left in Wales was, if anything, more divided than elsewhere in Britain over the key issues of neutrality and non-intervention. This arose mainly from the fact of CPGB influence – which fell short of outright control – within the single most powerful labour interest, the South Wales Miners' Federation. 'The Fed' was committed at an early stage to the 'defence of democracy in Spain', a commitment formally pledged at a Cardiff meeting in October 1936. It was not until very late in the year that the Cardiff Provisional Committee for Spanish Aid was set up as an umbrella organization for the motley spectrum of lobbies which it was hoped to incorporate. This, too, was mainly the result of the communist dynamic, being stimulated into existence by the local party branch.[73]

The decision of three prominent Labour left-wingers, Stafford Cripps, Aneurin Bevan and William Mellor, to challenge their party's policy on Spain by heading up a 'Unity Campaign', was an index of the desperate need felt in many thousands of hearts.[74] On Monday 1 February 1937, the *Daily Worker* banner-headlined the story that 'WALES CHEERS UNITY CAMPAIGN', a report of 'six great meetings' held the previous weekend in Merthyr Tydfil, Dowlais, Newport, Swansea, Llanelli and Cardiff. At Swansea, Bevan and Mellor spoke on the same platform as Fenner Brockway of the ILP and Harry Pollitt of the CPGB. 'Resolutions were passed pledging aid to the people of Spain, fighting in the trenches of Madrid against the onslaught of Fascism.' A quarter of the 1,200 in the audience filled in and passed up 'pledge cards', vowing to work in person for the campaign. At Cardiff, the communist miners' leader Arthur Horner himself pledged that the SWMF 'will place the needs of the Spanish people in their heroic fight above all else'.[75] All the same, attempts to coordinate action, to create (that is) an integrated 'Aid Spain Movement', were dogged by dissension. Only days after it was made, for example, Horner's pledge was proved to be empty and meaningless. The SWMF refused to collaborate with the South Wales Regional Council of Labour, set up by the Labour Party and the TUC in the midst of the fervour of Unity, to supervise all 'Spanish Aid' in the region. Since the function of the SWRC was so obviously to compete with – and if possible render redundant – the existing Provisional Committee which they backed, the Fed's attitude was predictable. In its turn the SWRC dissociated itself from meetings at which CPGB leaders addressed the audience, and soon developed its own imperialist policy, brusquely informing the Provisional Committee 'that the Regional Council is the appropriate body for co-ordinating efforts in South Wales on behalf of Spain'.[76] Official Labour

Party organizations were alive to the dangers of 'entryism' by the CPGB, and though both the Cardiff Trades Council and local Labour affiliated to the Provisional Committee, it was with a wary eye. In the winter of 1936–7, sub-committees were painstakingly established in every electoral ward of the city. Though rather desultory compared to the campaign developing in the Rhondda, street collections and street-corner speeches got under way.[77]

'Entryism' was indeed one of the tactics being developed by a cell of young communist professionals and students in Cardiff. Shortly after graduating from Oxford in 1936, Helen Smith (not her real name) was sent by the party to organize a youth movement (YCL) in the city while training as a teacher at the University College. She liaised with another agent, Alec Cummings – a former sergeant in the Welsh Guards – and, after carefully prospecting the meetings of the Left Book Club branches, they gathered a group of about a dozen, including the daughter of a university lecturer, a law student, a publisher's printer and a left bookshop manager. They were soon joined by another student, Sid Hamm, a Labour Party member friendly with Wilfred and Leo Abse. Earlier that year, Hamm, Leo, Ted Edwards and others had founded the Cardiff United Youth, an expression of the keen desire amongst left-thinking young people to support a 'united people's front' over pressing issues like the Means Test at home and 'Spain' abroad. Hamm neither left the Labour Party, despite its ban on dual membership, nor informed Leo, his best friend, of his CPGB affiliation. Inside the communist cell he was able to assess the chances of converting other young Labour supporters. In April 1937, however, he abandoned his studies and volunteered to fight in Spain, joining a large group which gathered in Cardiff en route to the International Brigade HQ in Albacete.

In any case, the cell he belonged to was already internally riven by sexual rivalry and betrayal. Influenced by their reading about the USSR, and in some cases the habits of their elders in the party, the group were eager to practise the communist theories of free love.[78] The relevant activities of two members, Gwen Jones and Gilbert Taylor, had particularly disruptive consequences. Indeed, the latter's behaviour (involving misuse of 'Aid Spain' funds) was scandalous enough to attract the attention of party HQ. Later in 1937, Taylor was ordered by Harry Pollitt to expiate his sins in Spain – with the alternative of being exposed to the rigour of the law. But it was too late to save the YCL cell from effective paralysis.[79] In contrast, the Cardiff United Youth group flourished. In early 1937 the City Council granted permission for it to hold meetings in a public park, and a dynamic programme of speeches, debates and (above all) collecting for 'Spain' was initiated.[80] A much-publicized memorial meeting was held for Sid Hamm after his death at Brunete in July 1937. A 'Unity' platform of speakers was assembled, but the young hero's family turned up and his mother stridently accused the CPGB representatives of responsibility for her son's death. At her request, the police intervened to prevent the meeting proceeding, and it took the forceful personality of Isabel Brown (known as 'the English Pasionaria') to persuade them otherwise.[81]

The local trade unionist most active in working for unity was Jim Henson of the International Transport Federation. Henson was keen to deny port facilities and dock services in Cardiff to all shipping bound for destinations in Nationalist Spain. But he confessed to his London office that

> I think it would be useless for you to ask any assistance officially in the fight from the N.U.S. or T.G.W.U . . . It seems a great pity over here to see the attitude of some unions and the Labour Party on this question, especially as, on the other hand, the Communist Party are working in all ways to help Spain. On the Cardiff Spanish Medical Aid Society we are all working together at assisting and have no time to fall out politically, whilst it seems that our leaders, with a few exceptions . . . seem to be waiting . . . until Franco, Hitler and Mussolini arrive in London.[82]

As Henson's letter illustrates, the sanctions of non-intervention had obliged the 'Provisional Committee' to adapt its banner to something more in accord with what was now – in effect – international law. But Henson's experience also suggests that opposition was entrenched within the official labour movement. After initial doubts, the local Trades Council was persuaded to endorse the Provisional Committee. Later, however, its secretary told Walter Citrine, the TUC leader, that they had been misled into believing that the committee had backing from Congress. They withdrew support again on receiving a pamphlet from the committee which attacked both the TUC and the Labour Party![83]

In political terms, though without being aware of it, the pro-Republican campaign in Cardiff had come to resemble the situation inside the Spanish Republican government itself. Having moved from besieged Madrid to Valencia, the latter became more and more dependent on Soviet military aid, along with the ruthless commitment of the Spanish Communist Party to ultimate victory. Stalin's grip on affairs in the government zone thus tightened steadily, and soon the PCE, under Comintern direction, was cohering and controlling the whole Republican war-effort. This focused leadership, however, involved the gradual suppression of the views and influence of other constituent parties of the Popular Front.[84] Though the problem in south Wales never approached the danger of an open or serious contest of allegiance, far less that of 'a civil war within the civil war' – as happened in Spain with the bloody uprising of the dissident revolutionary parties in Barcelona (May 1937) – it was nonetheless a situation which meant disappointment and depression for many people of goodwill.

Thus the great south Wales campaign for a Unity Front – despite the jubilant headlines of the *Daily Worker* – failed to achieve its objective. The situation in Cardiff proved especially recalcitrant. The SWRC noted that 'although well-advertised the meetings were not crowded. Collections had not reached the amounts hoped for.' The council asked Cardiff Labour Party to organize a meeting at which three prominent MPs (Noel Baker, Ellen Wilkinson and James Griffiths) were to speak, but got no response, and instead the platform was moved to Newport.[85] In the Monmouthshire port, greater success attended efforts to combine, at least at first. A young Newportonian, Sidney Robinson, was appointed secretary of a local 'Aid Spain' committee formed as a result of the MPs' meeting.[86] As a member of the ILP, Robinson was an enthusiast for the revolution in Spain, and attended an open-air meeting in August 1936, called to raise working-class consciousness. A few days later he helped take up a collection for the Spanish workers at Somerton Park, during a Newport County game. For several months, his energy at the helm of a scratch, voluntary body was rewarded with success, and he managed to bring most relevant organizations on board.[87] Robinson and his comrade Edwin Williams (who later volunteered to fight) visited several Spanish ships in Newport docks, invited their crews home for tea, and arranged other social events designed to spread the spirit of solidarity with 'Spain'. From Albacete, Bill Morrisey, an ex-seaman from Cardiff, provided a Newport comrade with propaganda material about the International Brigades and the Republican war-effort for circulation to press and party sources.[88] It helped the cause that the local newspaper, the *South Wales Argus*, had been consistently pro-Republican in editorial sympathy since the start of the conflict.[89] In addition, the prospective Labour parliamentary candidate, Peter Freeman, had declared both his commitment to 'Spain' and a willingness to cooperate with other interests.[90] In March, a large audience attended a showing of the film *Defence of Madrid*. However, alerted to the growing CPGB influence this and other events implied, the local Trades Council moved to take over the management of the committee 'on constitutional lines'.[91] A renewed phase of enthusiasm was generated by the arrival in the town of some fifty Basque refugee children in July 1937, but during the prolonged period of Republican defeats and retreats throughout the following year, popular interest slowly subsided.[92] Despite the terrible

'May Events' in Barcelona, and the ruthless communist persecution of the POUM (the ILP's affiliate party) Robinson – like his fellow-ILPer, Lance Rogers – remained convinced that the cause of unity in the face of fascism and war was greater than what could be viewed as minor divisions over tactics. In the winter of 1938–9 he threw himself with new vigour into the struggle to supply the Republic during its last major campaign in Catalonia.[93]

Thus, though a multiplicity of interest- and lobby-groups worked in their own ways for the cause, suspicion of communist motives on both right and left (perhaps abetted by the temperamental British dislike of monopoly) constantly frustrated unity. Arthur Horner, communist leader of the 'Fed', was careful to praise organizations which 'had the courage to associate with communists, members of the Socialist League and the ILP and other progressive people'.[94] But his words were not enough to change attitudes. The fact was that most 'progressive people' were not inclined even to privately condemn, leave alone to demonstrate publicly against, the government's policy of non-intervention. A majority of people in the labour movement respected the reasons for the Labour Party's action against the founders of the Socialist League, despite the disgust that one fellow-traveller expressed in a letter to the British Battalion fighting in Spain.[95] Some communists were determined to expend their last ounce of energy on the struggle for 'Spain' and unity. Perhaps supreme amongst them was Lewis Jones, successful novelist and SWMF-sponsored Rhondda councillor, who worked exhaustively in speaking, persuading and organizing for unity over 'Spain'. Jones increasingly spent time in Cardiff and other port-towns where support was lukewarm compared to that in his home patch. In October 1937 he attended another (presumably more decorous) memorial meeting for Sid Hamm at the University College, and was also guest speaker at the Cardiff United Youth dinner.[96] As the Republic entered its final agony in the winter of 1938–9, Jones increased his already taxing schedule in order to raise money for food ships destined for Barcelona. Again, Cardiff, where indifference seemed to rule amidst a mixture of relative affluence and nerveless poverty, was his main target.[97] One January morning, the day after he had toured the mean streets with his soap- and collecting-boxes, he was found dead of a heart attack in a house in one of the city's working-class districts.[98]

Meanwhile, the SWRC struggled on, reporting forlornly in June 1938 that 'the sum of £127. 13s. 5d. passed through our funds . . . we are of the opinion that a great deal of energy and effort has been dissipated as a result of the establishment of a variety of organisations endeavouring to deal with this work'.[99] The committee decided to make another effort to galvanize opinion by arranging a conference in Cardiff to discuss 'an embargo on cargoes from the South Wales ports to Franco Spain'. When representatives gathered in late August, the motion (moved by Jim Griffiths) was attacked, adapted and diluted until it became meaningless. In a last effort, the SWRC announced a 'Welsh Spain Week' programme of activities for a week in December. When the chosen week arrived, virtually nothing happened.[100]

Nonetheless, the understandably deflated tone of the SWRC minutes must not lead us to dismiss the effort made in the urban contexts of maritime Wales, and the contributions that because not mainly motivated by political commitment was not for that reason any less – indeed could be argued as more – charitable and worthwhile. In Swansea and Llanelli as well as Cardiff and Newport, such work went on uninterruptedly in assembly halls, committee-rooms and private dwellings. Most people, whether or not disposing of leisure time, believed that every little helped. The Newport Women's Liberal Association sent Sidney Robinson a 'parcel of bandages . . . in the hope that it will bind some aching wound. We also pray that the need for such articles will soon cease and that peace will prevail throughout the whole world.'[101] But the aching wound of disunity on the left could not be bound up; and soon the whole world would be in need of bandages.

Franco's Cardiff Alcázar[102]

For all his efforts, Jim Henson was unable to persuade local union executives to sanction the 'blacking' of ships bound for Nationalist Spain. Nevertheless, in the winter of 1936–7, Henson was able to work with the Norwegian seaman's union branch in Cardiff, and the Spanish consul, Señor Clemente Cebada, to prevent the departure of several vessels for Francoist Spain, while also lobbying effectively against recruitment of blackleg crews. Opposition to such moves was not limited to sources within the broad labour movement. The established political and legal authorities also were anxious to discourage action which may have aggravated feeling and adversely affected business interests. At various times in these years, fears for public order in the city may well have come to the fore. By the very nature of the investigative exercise, discretion was the order of the day. On one occasion Steffen Greve, an official of the Norwegian Seamen's Union, was visited by two suspicious characters. The men

> sought to point out to him the unacceptability of the seamen joining the boy-cott and pressed him to persuade – or order – them to rescind their decision and honour their obligations to their employers. Greve pointed out that such

decisions were made on board ship by the crew themselves and not by the union as such. Moreover, it was outside the power of the unions to order its members to carry out actions – policy was made by the members. Apparently, the plain clothes visitors then began to indicate the vulnerability of Greve's position as a foreigner involved in a politically motivated dispute. At this point, Greve asked the men to wait for a moment while he got his hat and coat, and invited the men to accompany him to repeat their statements in front of a magistrate. The visitors protested that his reaction was quite excessive and uncalled for and, as the conversation quickly petered out, they left the office.[103]

Greve clearly believed his visitors to be Special Branch detectives. It seems from this account that Cardiff's Norwegians were solid enough when it came to 'Spain'. The same did not always apply to the many Spanish sailors who frequented the south Wales ports, nor to the resident Spanish community of Cardiff. Indeed, both were split down the middle over their country's Civil War, a gulf which opened along the fault lines of class and religion. At first dash this may seem a predictable observation, but – as with the Irish – in each individual concerned these two factors often interacted in quite unpredictable ways.

With a population as large as its three greatest port competitors put together, Cardiff offered a much wider variety of opportunities for immigrants than any other town or region of Wales. In the prosperous decades prior to the First World War, this created a colony of Spanish families, unique in Wales, and almost certainly the largest outside London. When harder conditions supervened after 1918, others who had originally come to work in the Dowlais iron mills, upped sticks and resettled in the still relatively busy metropolis. Here, contraction in one employment area could always be compensated by expansion in another, while a large service sector was coming into being. As the Spanish-speaking community augmented in size, it brought a range of economic and social advantages for its members. Families helped each other out financially, and as they grew better off, established formal business relationships, and intermarried. Long-established commercial links between Cardiff and Spain – especially with Bilbao and Huelva – encouraged the growth of trades which provided services for Spanish ships and seamen, and by the 1920s no fewer than four ships' chandlers firms of Spanish ownership were well-established. For good business reasons most Spanish families lived in the narrow terraced streets leading off towards the sea from the main docks drag, James Street. Extended family relations and employees of the business firms lived close to their places of employment. In

1937 the Cardiff Directory recorded that eighteen out of forty-four houses in George Street alone were occupied by persons with Spanish surnames. Little wonder that one writer refers to the area as 'Cardiff's Latin Quarter', while another recalled:

> We had a Japanese family, we had Portuguese, Irish, English, Greeks, North Walians and a lot of the Spanish Armada, who were mostly living in George Street, but we were all boys and girls, no different to each other and playing happily together. When Frankie Mayo's granny shouted to him 'Ven Aqui' we all knew that the answer in Spanish was 'Que Quieres?'[104]

Given the terrible recession in Cardiff-based maritime commerce in the 1920s, the fact that so many enterprising families continued to derive a living, mainly from services to Spanish ships and sailors, is in itself a testament to the robustness of the links between Cardiff and Spain.

Indeed, so important was the Spanish colony that its problems and opportunities came to the attention of Franco himself. In the winter of 1937–8 the duke of Alba, head of the Nationalist diplomatic office in London, sent a professional agent to Cardiff. Amongst other things, Alba was fearful that Cardiff, with its unique mixture of left-wing activists and pro-Basque sympathizers, was becoming a dangerous focus for anti-Franco activity. His man, Eduardo María Danís, was lodged secretly in the homes of various sympathizers, and began to observe the situation in the south Wales ports with an interest at least equal to that of his Special Branch colleagues in the espionage trade. He was soon able to enlist the collaboration of a number of well-connected individuals. Prominent among these were members of a branch of Falange Española which already existed in the city.[105] The group was patronized and provided with office accommodation by local businessmen. Some, like Señor Munitiz, were well aware of the contrary sympathies of his own and (doubtless) of other firms' employees. Others, it seems, had access to details of shipping contracts and forthcoming sailings. Both were of great interest to Danís.

The immediate issue was the fate of a number of Spanish ships which had been berthed in Welsh harbours for some time. Following the loss of Bilbao, the Republican government, anxious to protect its industrial–commercial stock from being grabbed by the enemy, proclaimed the expropriation of Spain's entire merchant marine. The majority of these vessels were at sea or already berthed in British ports when this happened – including many which had recently left Bilbao and other Basque venues. Valencia's decree had the effect of dividing most crews into mutually hostile factions. The usual pattern was that officers (skippers, mates, engineers) quietly resolved to sur-render their ships to Franco as soon as the current contract was completed, while ordinary seamen, perhaps led by a syndicalist steward, and with equal secrecy, determined otherwise. By the time Danís arrived, around a dozen ships' officers were being sheltered in the homes of Spanish expatriates, after having suffered physical ejection by their own crews from vessels berthed in Aberavon and Milford Haven, and as far away as Immingham (Hull), as well as in Cardiff itself. These were angry and humiliated men, eager to give Alba's agent all the help they could.[106] On the other hand, a group of Basque fishermen who had abandoned their home ports with a flotilla of trawlers, ended up in south Wales, where they gained the help of the 'Spanish Aid' activists.[107] At Milford Docks, six men absconded from Nationalist trawlers and joined a Republican steamer which was leaving for Spain the same night. The two Francoist boats were stranded at Milford Haven 'with skeleton crews, consisting of the two skippers and chief engineers'.[108]

A struggle ensued between the two sides, focusing on Cardiff where Republican sailors remained defiantly in occupation of four Spanish steamers. This further genetic microcosm of the Spanish Civil War involved a complex legal dispute which dragged through the local and London courts, providing the long-term context for much bitter hostility. Consul Cebada, with the aid of left-wing dockers and others, kept the sit-in sailors supplied with food and propaganda. His Francoist rival, with the benefit of surreptitious advice from Cardiff's immigration officer, B. E. Reeve-Jones – 'an officer [who] is very well disposed towards us' as Danís eagerly reported to London – worked behind the scenes to repossess the vessels and obtain the arrest and deportation of the 'mutineers'.[109] While Cardiff's Spaniards divided accord-ing to taste, the affair also attracted attention in the press and many others also took sides.[110] The most remarkable incidents, in the spring of 1938, involved attempts by squads of Brownshirts to take forcible possession of Spanish vessels in Cardiff, Aberavon and Port Talbot with the aim of sailing them to Nationalist Spain.[111] In all cases the boarders were repelled with little (if any) shedding of blood.[112]

Alongside this work, Danís also needed to feed intelligence information back to London. Alba himself needed to know which Spanish families could be relied on, and (doubtless) which – in any opposite case – had relatives in the Nationalist zone in whose continued well-being they might be interested. In addition, Burgos was becoming increasingly anxious over supplies reaching the enemy from the south Wales ports. In April 1938, an official reported to Franco's foreign minister, General Jordana:

The Spanish representative in London has passed on to me a communication from our sub-agent in Cardiff, accompanied by reports concerning the activities of certain Basque nationalist elements, along with others about the personalities of various Spanish persons who, on the contrary, have shown themselves favourable to our cause.[113]

By September 1938, Danís had cracked the telegram codes used by Clemente Cebada, so that the latter's messages could be intercepted in London.[114] It may have been Danís's presence in Cardiff which encouraged many Spanish seamen who were holed up in the docks for various reasons to resist – on more than one occasion at risk of their lives – attempts, in which Reeve-Jones was prominent, to return them to Spain.[115] It also seems a reasonable surmise that details obtained by Burgos of coal and food supply ships which sailed for Republican Spain with mounting frequency during 1938 originated from Danís and his informants inside various Cardiff business offices.[116] At the end of the war, the man who had commanded this Francoist outpost in the midst of the largely hostile political atmosphere of Cardiff docklands – a modest and much less percussive version of the famous siege of the Toledo Alcázar – was able to succeed his defeated rival as consul of Spain.

PART III: CHORUSES

4 The Academy: Education and the Press

The Legend of Harlech

> It is regrettable that there are so few young men left in South Wales, Wales as a whole for that matter. But what cares capitalism for such things. I guess the College will have to take a strong anti-capitalist line. Impartiality of investigation leads to that anyway . . . Faced with a world as ours we have soon or later to decide where we stand, with reaction or against it. Reaction is a swinish thing anyway and not for men of intelligence.[1]

Jim Brewer was an ex-miner from Rhymney who had spent a memorable year studying at Coleg Harlech. He volunteered for the International Brigades in the spring of 1937, and kept in touch with college warden, Ben Bowen Thomas, from Spain – writing this letter, for example, during a lengthy rest period which the British Battalion enjoyed after vicious fighting in the battles of Brunete (near Madrid) and Belchite (in Aragon). It seems likely, however, that Brewer's appeal to the 'intelligence' of a man whom he clearly valued as a tutor was largely wasted. Though by no means a 'swinish reactionary', Thomas was not a man of the ideological left, and indeed the entire mission of the college which he headed was one which strove to rise above the ephemeral seductions of politics. Coleg Harlech had been opened a decade earlier as a result of the work of Thomas J. Jones, Lloyd George's personal secretary during his government career. Its establishment in a harsh and remote corner of north Wales was the result of charitable investment by a group of Liberal Party mandarins, amongst whom Lord Davies of Llandinam was prominent. The notion was to provide free further education for suitably deserving single young men from deprived backgrounds. The nature and content of the curriculum was designed to counter 'alienation' by acculturating students to the real, pragmatic world. Far from taking a 'strong anti-capitalist line', its emphasis on economics and 'civics' as well as history and English literature was intended precisely to encourage a mature and enlightened understanding of capitalism, along with bourgeois culture and constitutional politics. It was no accident that its foundation followed close on the heels of the General Strike, along with the much more prolonged and bitter miners' dispute which chronologically enclosed that unique and better-known event.[2] Harlech's ethos was firmly in contrast – not to say opposed – to that which (in the 1920s) had moved the Central Labour College in London, where politically committed students like Brewer's local acquaintance, Aneurin Bevan, studied in an atmosphere of socialist-radical thinking and (often) action.

Brewer's remarks – we may infer – indicated a relationship with his ex-tutor which was warm enough to encompass the use of deliberate irony. In an earlier letter he complained of 'a shocking shortage of Harlech and Ruskin men out here', expressing the hope that 'the newly disbanded body of students did something more than the passing of resolutions in support of Spain. Maybe they're coming out here in a body.'[3] The overwhelming majority of these students were from industrial south Wales, an imbalance which the warden himself lamented. In 1936 this trend became 'disquieting' since only four out of thirty-six students were from north Wales.[4] For all this, there was a remarkable absence of radical action to be found amongst them in this most radical of all decades in Wales's recent political experience. At this time, Thomas was intent upon raising a fresh round of subscriptions to build a purpose-built library on the college site. In November 1936, as Madrid's defenders struggled amidst the ruins of its university city to repel the attacks of the 'Fascist Invaders' of Spain, he wrote to his powerful patron: 'your heart will be gladdened to know that the students have decided with great enthusiasm to clear the site for the new library'.[5] The following spring, after the epic resistance of Madrid with the concomitant suffering of its people had enabled the Republic to win a first clear victory in battle – that of Guadalajara – Thomas reported that 'in Harlech, folk want to celebrate the Coronation [and] are anxious to do so in style'.[6]

All this seems curious if meant to apply to the student body, even when due allowances for academic enthusiasm and loyalty to the crown are made. In fact, it is difficult to be sure what the students themselves were feeling or doing about the Spanish issue (or anything else). The warden's reports and correspondence never seem concerned with student matters – a strange lacuna, but one faithfully reflected in the college's 'biography' by Peter Stead. During the 1937–8 session, the students arranged no fewer than twenty-nine guest lectures. One of them (by Labour MP, A. V. Alexander) was entitled 'Spain', and another (by the Cardiff communist, Idris Cox) professed 'The Faith of a Communist'. All the remaining twenty-seven had, on the face of things, politically innocuous titles.[7] This was not a programme likely to give the warden much anxiety about simmering student revolution. On the other hand, at the end of that year, the staff tutor in philosophy, D. James Jones, who had been at Harlech from the beginning, left to take up a chair at UCNW. His farewell report, though carefully worded, gives us a striking insight into the tensions which had developed in the classroom atmosphere. Jones noted about his students that

> the social temper of their times may be inferred without much difficulty from the issues which they regard as central and to which their discussions inevitably gravitate. Pride of place has been occupied of late by Fascism and Communism and by industrial, political and international relationships. One of our major problems in this respect is set by the fact that the zeal of the reformer is not tempered by the patience of the student. Many who are drawn from industrial areas tend to speak the language of a new orthodoxy and *the spirit of the Inquisition* is never far from orthodoxy in any intellectual creed. If belief in the inerrancy of scripture has been abandoned belief in the inerrancy of Marx, Engels and Lenin has sometimes been substituted for it. Not unexpectedly, therefore, there may be observed in the early stages of the discipline a tendency to rely on the emotional satisfaction which results when propensities for aggressive action find expression in the declamation of a ready tongue . . . Criticisms of cherished beliefs have occasionally been taken as personal affronts and . . . the process usually entails considerable pain and misgiving.[8]

Evidently Jones felt long-suffering as well as long-serving, and was relieved to escape to the more sedate academic surroundings of Bangor. At any rate, there is perhaps enough here to allow the legend to survive; the legend being that Harlech's students at one point voted – just as Brewer hoped – to join the International Brigades 'in a body'.[9]

Moreover, although Jim Brewer was destined not to enjoy a reunion in Spanish trenches, unknown to him at the time, two of his Harlech contemporaries had also joined up.[10] And they were not the only Welsh students who volunteered. As we have seen, Sid Hamm, a student of Cardiff Technical College, was killed at Brunete, and in the spring of 1938, an undergraduate from the English Department at the UCSWM, Morien Morgan, followed him to Spain.[11] Hamm had been a member of the Cardiff reception committee when in the spring of 1936 a deputation of students from Nazi Germany toured Wales on a so-called 'goodwill visit'. Along with his friends Leo Abse and Ted Edwards, he formed a debating team which took on the visitors in a Students' Union meeting.[12] In Cardiff, it was said that the event 'caused bad feelings' rather than goodwill, but in Swansea, the deputation's next stop, they received a more civilized welcome: 'Given the highly-charged political atmosphere of the time, it seems surprising how tolerant the students were . . . [The Germans] lost the debate – "That Communism is a menace to Europe" – but the behaviour of the audience was exemplary.'[13] According to one report, this group of no fewer than sixteen representatives of the Third Reich had come in order 'to study social and economic conditions in South Wales, by arrangement of the Anglo-German Fellowship'.[14] It may be wondered whether this was the whole truth of the matter.

Meanwhile, in the previous January, a leader of the Federation of Student Societies came to Cardiff to attend a conference of the University Labour Federation. This was John Cornford, who was to become perhaps the best known of all the 'martyrs' of the British left in Spain. His main mission at the 1936 conference was to push for the adoption of the CPGB's 'popular front' policy via unification of the two main student unions. At the time, Cornford had recently left his Welsh girlfriend, Ray Peters, in favour of a new love, Margot Heinemann. His affair with Peters – a miner's daughter from Bargoed – had seen him become so fascinated by her background that he had written poetry (published in the BBC magazine *The Listener*) using the pseudonym 'Dai Barton'.[15] He and Heinemann, along with Philip Toynbee, later organized visits to the Rhondda by what was hardly less of a foreign delegation of students, this time from Oxbridge.[16] The exotic young gentlemen and ladies were billeted upon miners' families during their vacations in order to study 'social and economic conditions in South Wales'. It would not be surprising if this arrangement was the cause of some bad feelings among some members of the host community. Most of the (one hopes, paying) guests were members of the Young Communist League. They may not have been 'a menace to Europe', but their purpose was hardly less innocent than that of the German 'debaters'.

Morien Morgan was apparently due to be accompanied to Spain by two fellow students. One of these – possibly Ted Edwards – was dissuaded from his intention by history lecturer, Christopher Hill, while the other was unwise enough to tell his parents, who threatened to pass the information on to the police.[17] Morgan himself was clearly physically unfitted for the vocation, and nearly died of exhaustion during the hazardous Pyrenees crossing which formed a suitably testing introduction for many volunteers.[18]

Brewer and Hamm were, of course, among those who coolly accepted what Auden called 'the chances of death' by volunteering for 'Spain'. Other students were inadvertently trapped in Spain at the time of the outbreak of war in July 1936. Their consequent discomforts were compensated by the fact that local newspapers were eagerly seeking stories of adventure and danger, which might be inexpensively acquired, yet provide an attractive seasoning to the normal diurnal fare. As we have already seen in the case of the two Clydach athletes, the results highlighted the macabre and ghastly aspects of eyewitness reportage.[19] Clare Kols was the daughter of Wrexham parents, and on a study trip to San Sebastian from Liverpool University. Before being rescued dramatically by HMS *Verity* (a name which left readers with small room for scepticism) she found it 'difficult to know what to believe. Some said one thing, some said another.' Friends claimed to have seen the bodies of 'two Fascists riddled with bullets . . . It was said that several rebel officers shot themselves when the soldiers surrendered to the government.'[20] From the British Embassy in Madrid, Rhodri Evans, a recent graduate then in training for the diplomatic corps, wrote home to his father – whose status of vicar of Mold again provided a kind of auto-authentication – about the street battles in the capital against insurgent groups sniping from rooftops. With a prescience which seems to justify his choice of career, young Evans added that 'the rebels have arrived at the mountains . . . as far as I can see they are just going to hold on there until troops arrive from the south and it is only a matter of time'.[21]

Also in Madrid at this time was another recent Welsh graduate, Cyril Cule. A member of Plaid Cymru, but also radically left-wing in sympathy, Cule (in his own words) 'drifted to Spain' after failing to find work in Wales.[22] He was eventually promised a full-time post teaching English in a government secondary 'institution' which he expected to take up that autumn. He shared in the popular rejoicing after the left victory in the 'Popular Front' election in February 1936, and was later granted membership of the celebrated intellectuals' club, the Ateneo. Perhaps because so immersed in his studies in the marvellous library thus placed at his disposal, he apparently remained unaware of the growing atmosphere of mutual political violence and destruction – including huge demonstrations and running gunfights – which disturbed the capital during the spring and early summer. Cule himself later claimed that 'I do not remember seeing anything unusual until July 18th when war broke out.'[23] Once he woke up to the situation, his first intention was to stay and work for the struggle, but a hair-raising encounter with a militia security patrol, and the advice of Rhodri Evans's colleagues in the embassy, persuaded him otherwise. Like hundreds of other foreigners stranded in Spain, Cule was eventually rescued by the Royal Navy, in his case by HMS *Devonshire*, from Valencia. He returned to Wales and threw himself with energy and dedication into the cause of campaigning for 'Spain'.[24]

Undoubtedly the best-known of Welsh persons who nurtured a lifetime association with Spain was the writer and broadcaster Gwyn Thomas. Like Cule, Thomas had recently graduated in 1936, and was looking for work as a teacher – indeed his fondest hope was of landing a post at Coleg Harlech. In the second year of his language degree at Oxford, and with little enthusiasm, he had been sent on secondment to Madrid's Universidad Complutense. Also like Cule, he seems to have made little rewarding contact with social and political life amongst the Madrileños. He, too, was preoccupied with his own intellectual development, and later recalled being 'closely interested in the attempts of Ramón Pidal and his associates to break down illiteracy and introduce elements of communal education into areas of Spain where nothing comparable had been attempted before'.[25] In a published retrospective account he deprecates his naive and backward response to the political upheavals of 1934, which culminated in an attempted socialist *golpe de estado* in the capital and social revolution in Asturias that autumn, yet simultaneously seems to claim a small part in the action of student comradeship and street demonstrations.[26] In fact, in this quite unlike Cyril Cule, Thomas was never particularly 'political', and he resisted being drawn into the culture of 'Spain', both in the 1930s and subsequently. He developed instead a defence mechanism of denigration, an almost studied aloofness from the multifarious foibles of his people, in which such commitment sometimes figured. Though often uniquely funny, it seems in essence much more Oxford than Valleys – or even Coleg Harlech.[27]

Yr Academi Gymraeg[28]

Sometime in the mid-1930s, the mischievous undergraduates of University College of Wales, Aberystwyth, had elected Ivan Maisky – the Soviet Ambassador, close personal friend and drinking-companion of Stalin – as honorary president of their union. In February 1938, he came to give his annual speech – which proved a fairly predictable idyll about life in the USSR.[29] A few months later, Ben Davies, university lecturer and writer, who (one might deduce) was a guest at Maisky's occasion, wrote to the local press in order to clear Stalin of charges of tyranny: 'all he does and all he speaks must be within the framework of the constitution and in alignment with decisions already arrived at in Parliament. Our retrograde press calls him a dictator, no doubt with a purpose. He is not.'[30] Not long after the war in Spain began, Davies was contacted by the radically orientated but (ostensibly) non-partisan pressure group, the Union of Democratic Control, to which he belonged. The UDC had decided to form local 'Foreign Affairs Groups [in order] to support the struggle which the Spanish people are making for democracy and peace [and] to counteract the strongly pro-fascist line of the popular press like the *Daily Mail* and the government press like the

Times and the *Daily Telegraph*.[31] Although he felt 'it is a poor time to begin because of the holidays', Davies immediately responded by forming such a group. The college's Sydney Herbert, prominent in the League of Nations Union, became its president, and Davies roped in at least four other academics for the committee.[32]

In this instance, academics comfortably outnumbered ministers of religion. In overall terms, however, the mortarboard only managed a respectable second to dog collars on the platform parades of 'Aid Spain' meetings throughout Wales. Professor Archer (UCNW), a Liberal Party member, presided at what the local press called the 'Bangor Demonstration' in March 1937, which kicked off the Welsh ambulance campaign. His colleague, Dr Gwenno Williams, became treasurer of the 'Aid Spain' committee set up in its wake.[33] In a parallel effort, the North Wales Women's Peace Council raised the sum of £33. 15s. 9d. towards refugee children from the Republican zone, to which various academic sources contributed – including the UCNW professors of philosophy and history. In Cardiff, Principal Frederick Rees and his wife were keen supporters of the Spanish Republic and helped enable many fund-raising events organized by staff and students within the UCSWM. Christopher Hill, appointed to the Cardiff History Department in October 1936, immediately took a leading role in 'Aid Spain' campaigning in the city.[34] His colleague, J. H. Shaxby, a member of the Botany Department, was among the reception committee which welcomed speaker Sir Peter Chalmers-Mitchell, one of the most dedicated British propagandists for the Republic, to speak at the League of Nations Union.[35] Back in Aberystwyth, T. A. Levi, professor of law, addressed the local branch of the same organization in April 1937, to proclaim that

> the real enemy of peace is Fascism, and a spiritual war had been declared between democracy and Fascism which would know no quarter and would have to be fought to a finish. That was the fight now going on in Spain. All the non-intervention pacts in the world would not stop them helping the Spanish people in their fight for liberty. As Drake's men chased the Spanish Armada and 'drummed them down the Channel' so Captain David Jones and his men would defy Franco's phantom fleet and dodge them in the Bay of Biscay.[36]

Aberystwyth was certainly the spiritual home of the Welsh LONU. Pacifist action in the town had been stimulated above all by Professor Charles Webster who had succeeded Alfred Zimmern as head of the international politics department.[37] However, Webster left the post in 1935, and the UCW soon became embroiled in its own civil war over the appointment of E. H. Carr to replace him. The latter decision was vehemently opposed by Lord Davies, college president, whose fortune patronized the Aberystwyth chair and who was also the most influential leader of the LONU in Wales. The ostensible reason for the quarrel was that his Lordship's preferred candidate had been passed over. However, since Carr made no secret of his Marxist allegiance, political discrimination was widely suspected.[38] In true Snovian fashion, sides were taken and many a hard word exchanged in corridors and common rooms. Though Carr's appointment was eventually confirmed, its circumstances seem to have encouraged him to hold back from any overt commitment to the cause of 'Spain'.[39]

Many of these scholars were deeply concerned for the long-term future of democracy, an anxiety that in these years was expressed in projects for educational reform. In early 1937, Professor Morgan Rees of UCNW – perhaps speaking circumspectly because in the educational rather than the political context – told the north Wales council of the Workers' Educational Association that democracy was under threat from both communism and Nazism, above all in Spain.[40] Rees, along with professorial colleagues like Archer, Lloyd and Fleure, agreed on the importance of a new syllabus for history in schools, designed to encourage democracy and pacifism, taught in a spirit which might counter the romantic and patriotic attractions of war – almost, that is, as a prophylactic for the belligerent tendencies of pupils.[41] Another powerful educational institution, which at this time threatened to eclipse the WEA, was the communist-inspired Left Book Club which flourished in many parts of Wales. This organization was less dedicated to pacifist and neutralist thinking.[42] On the contrary, if anything, its hidden agenda encouraged pre-emptive action against the threat of fascism. All the same, teachers and academics (not all of them fellow-travellers) subscribed to the reading list, and attended focused discussions in groups to which working-class and unemployed men also belonged. The club thus provided an underground transmission link across class and cultural boundaries. Though its influence is largely impalpable – concrete instances involving issues, persons or places are always elusive – it was like a turbulent but silent meeting of the waters, in which electrical currents of empathy with the Spanish Republic spread far and wide through British society.[43]

Some of this intellectual and educational ferment found a sympathetic response inside the ranks of Plaid Cymru, including ideas on which both its opposed ideological 'wings' might agree.[44] But, in general, the nationalists, for all their efforts and anxieties, remained outside (or perhaps better, *above*) the political mainstream, on 'Spain' as on other issues. More than any other political party in British history, Plaid was a society of elite intellectuals. Led and guided by writers and academics, its commitment to the higher reaches of philosophical and literary expression was epitomized in its regular publications, *The Welsh Nationalist* and (particularly) *Y Ddraig Goch*. When 'The Three' launched their attack upon the RAF installation at Porth Neigwl, they were consciously seeking to add the character of 'martyrs' to an existing status as prophets of a spiritual revolution in Welsh history. The figure of Saunders Lewis is, of course, central to this profile. Lewis's controversial reluctance to condemn European fascism and his readiness to accept at least part of the Spanish Nationalists' case were derived largely from his intellectual and spiritual background. The former was focused upon an intense involvement with the history and culture of France, the latter – hardly unconnected – upon his profession of the Roman Catholic faith. In France itself, particularly during the opening phase of the struggle, Catholic intellectuals extended their support and understanding to the Francoist side.[45] Though Lewis never (at least in his writings or other public utterances) went as far as to endorse this cause, his proclivities linked him potentially with some strange bedfellows amongst the people of Wales. In reality, however, neither in his spiritual nor in his social life did he have any more in common with the Bute dynasty, or with the south Wales Irish, than they had with each other. The bizarre fact, and one which governed his political destiny, was that it was only within the rarified ranks of the society he himself had founded a decade earlier that Lewis was able to subsist.

Here were Lewis's only soulmates. Friends like Ambrose Bebb, with whom he had founded the original 'Welsh Movement' (Y Mudiad Cymraeg) in Penarth in 1925, along with J. E. Daniel and others, saw themselves as Christians rooted in a powerful – and perhaps above all, cosmopolitan – European tradition. Such men partook of the anti-modernist flavour of the French Catholic revival of the post-1870 era, founded upon reaction against the horrors of the Paris Commune and the secular agenda of the Third Republic. They admired the right-wing thinker Charles Maurras and the proto-fascist movement (Action Française) which he inspired – though (it must be said) consistently refusing to follow Maurras down the path of anti-semitism. Likewise, although Bebb nurtured an admiration for Mussolini, as did Lewis for Portugal's dictator, Salazar, none of the Plaid leadership was much attracted to the cause of extreme Catholic nationalism in Spain. Here, it seems, their approval of men and movements which had decisively revived and advanced 'national' programmes, while yet remaining alert against the threat of Bolshevism, was severely tempered by apprehension over their distasteful by-products, militarism, despotism and an imperialist ethic.[46]

Almost the whole of this middle-aged and middle-class leadership was intellectual and academic in character. Yet they did not share the instinctive sympathy for the Spanish Republic felt in academic circles, instead forming their own micro-academic clique. They assumed the mantle of what in Welsh is sometimes called the 'Llenorion' – a bench of magisterial minds appointed (informally, and by providence) to guide the people ('gwerin'). Several were employed in university lectureships or enjoyed close affiliation with scholarly institutions – amongst them, for example, Lewis's comrades at Porth Neigwl, J. H. Williams and Lewis Valentine. The two latter, however, shared his stormy pacifism but not his 'Catholic-European' perspective. They were, of course, representative of the majority Nonconformist tradition of Welsh-speaking Wales. It may be seen as bizarre that their constituency comprised many who strenuously rejected (often to the point of contempt) the religion of their party president and the 'continental' culture of some colleagues. But at the same time, the virtues of liberalism – of plurality and mutual tolerance – within Plaid were further buttressed by the intellectual, even scholarly, atmosphere of its proceedings. The dramatic gesture at Penyberth – and more so the heavy-handed reaction to it – had the effect of uniting the party as never before during the lead-up to the Second World War. This unity was strengthened when Saunders Lewis's own university college (Swansea) seemed to act more in conformity with the 'English' establishment than its commitment to the universal values of liberal humanism by sacking him because of his illegal act of sabotage and sedition. The intense interplay of all of these issues contributed to the ferment of Welsh politics and academic life in the late 1930s.[47]

The Editorial Chair

According to the census of 1931, some 910,000 or 42 per cent of the population of Wales was Welsh-speaking.[48] Given the history of the nation, and especially its religious aspect, since the mid-seventeenth century, it is not surprising that it produced an emphatically – even obsessively – education-centred and literate community. Nowhere else in Britain was the local press so firmly established, so widely utilized and so sincerely respected as in Welsh-speaking Wales. And nowhere else than in its pages was the Spanish Civil War so much the subject of debate and analysis. Indeed, both in nature and quality, Welsh-language coverage of the issue seems to occupy a rarified sphere which is markedly distinct even from that to be found in the so-called 'quality' press of Fleet Street. This is perhaps especially true of Plaid Cymru's monthly newspaper Y Ddraig Goch.

Of course, having no staff of professional reporters (if no less so in Madrid than in Cardiff) the paper depended as much as its most isolated or ignorant reader upon stories printed in the 'English Press'. Partly for this reason it was keen to display a scepticism about the general reliability of information over Spain, at the same time adopting a contextual-analytical approach to the war, an attitude which was characteristically responsible and pedagogical. Indeed, it was an overriding concern for the latter task which led one contributor to produce a lengthy exposure of the former – press propaganda. The specific item of offence was an elaborately confected story concerning a German military takeover of Spanish Morocco – allegedly conceded to Hitler by a grateful Franco. The writer's careful examination of French press coverage of the issue led him to conclusions and warnings which may be regarded, at least in some degree, as Orwellian *avant la lettre*.

> The nastiest aspect of this whole affair is the prominence given to falsified news and the subsequent lack of corrected reports in the French and English newspapers. We have to accept the simple fact that there are elements in Europe resolved to plunge the continent into war, and not just to secure victory for one side or the other in Spain.[49]

In his first editorial comment on the Spanish War, J. E. Daniel showed similar acumen, and partly anticipated an interpretation that specialist historians have arrived at only comparatively recently. He argued that 'Spain's problems have their roots in the country's history', while also positing a duality of causation, in that contemporary European problems were bound to interact with this deeper cause. Daniel looked in particular to ideological divisions: 'the war is also a European Event since it is a symbol of the most important struggle of our time, the conflict between Communism and the European Tradition'. Having established this point, Daniel went one step further, reaching a conclusion which could only be interpreted as basically pro-Franco:

> But the Spanish Civil War is not merely an interesting arena for the great international confrontation. It is a turning-point for several loyalties. Either way, if the Communists win, the ancient civilization of Spain will be destroyed . . . Though the Communists are not part of the government they are a strong and organized party which has been armed by the government, and it is they who have been responsible for many of the atrocities which are recounted by refugees . . . On the other hand if Franco and his army win, then it is likely that some kind of Fascist regime will emerge under Italian influence . . . Little wonder that England is so keen to steer clear of the mess . . .[50]

As we have seen, Daniel had stepped into the lion's den and needed all the fiery breath at his command in order to fight his way out again. In response to the swingeing attack by Cyril Cule, he confessed that 'not every Daniel is a faultless prophet' but also asserted that 'it is high time to protest against the tendency to stigmatize anti-communists as fascists, as if there were no other choice'.[51] All the same, Daniel felt it politic to hand over the leash to another, at least when it came to taking the Dragon on its regular extramural exercise. Even before the reply to Cule was published, Ambrose Bebb had begun what was to become a regular foreign affairs column which soon adopted the by-line 'Through the Telescope'. Bebb at first proceeded cautiously, agreeing with Daniel that 'Spain is the classic land of civil war' and speculating (soundly, as it turned out) that the war 'will not end as soon as we would like, and not even a wizard can know what will follow'.[52] With Cule's intervention, however, Bebb sought a more even-handed line in terms of balance and roundly disavowed the ideological interpretation advanced by Daniel. Indeed, he announced, in a carefully emphasized sentence, that *'it is not in such handy, simplistic and narrow terms that the Spanish Civil War should be genuinely understood'*.[53]

The point to be made here arises from the last phrase of this sentence. The priority concern for Bebb and his colleagues was the sincere struggle for and communication of *understanding*. Since they were faced in immediate terms and 'real time' with what scholars from various disciplines now consider to be the most elusively complex and explosive of all the twentieth century's multitudinous conflicts, this determination is surely impressive.[54] It is not surprising, too, given the environment of pulpit and lectern, of scripture and history, in which most of them existed, that they saw the struggle as being a religious (or at least *spiritual*) one and reached instinctively for appropriate metaphors.[55] Indeed, Bebb's known (or, at any rate, insufficiently disguised) personal prejudices, along with his headmasterly approach, evoked a murmuring amongst party malcontents. He complained about being 'branded a Papist' and 'a militarist of the worst stripe' for his attempts 'to explain' Mussolini's invasion of Abyssinia: 'and every time you are a Fascist! There's an end to you for ever . . . And if you dare to question Russia's policy towards Spain, then you are an anti-proletarian and guilty of the worst sin in the world . . . Whilst we argue, Spain is in agony and running red with blood.'[56] Bebb's punctured skin reveals – if only in negative image – a seething mess of bitter disagreement within Plaid's ranks.[57] Earnest and thoughtful as the effort to explain and interpret was, the issues involved were so delicate that the Red Dragon's fire and claws proved instruments too crude to dissect them clinically. When the flak rose, he seemed almost tempted to turn these weapons upon its sources, the internal malcontents themselves. In the next issue, Bebb offered a sop to his critics by condemning the aid given to Franco by the Axis powers, which in his view was 'a grave injustice to Spain' – using the denomination, this time, almost in the sense (used throughout this book) of 'Spain'.[58] Yet he also lamented that

> It is a strange thing to think and hateful to announce that if we had had our own government during the last year many of us would have been desperate to hurl ourselves into the Spanish Civil War. When will we, in the name of goodness, learn to discuss the misfortunes of others with a modicum of calm and restraint, instead of rushing like mad hotheads into a battle which is not ours to fight. This is exactly what Italy and Germany have done. And we are hoarse in our condemnation. Yes, this is precisely what Russia did – before them . . . We extend our condolences to the whole of Spain, to both sides, to both armies.[59]

The party leader stood shoulder to shoulder with his old comrade, rejecting any accusation of support for a Franco victory. 'The truth is', wrote Lewis, 'that we seek to obstruct the creation of enthusiasm in Wales for an English war in Spain that pretends to be for the defence of democracy but that in reality would be to defend Gibraltar and Malta and Aden and Suez.'[60] An overview of *Y Ddraig Goch*'s discourse on the Spanish War can only conclude that the staff contributors were essentially of one mind. Bebb announced as early as July 1937 that 'Franco will win'. A year later he foretold – with an approbation bordering on relish – that 'when Spain lifts its head again, we believe it will be as a nation cleansed and purified by the present woes; a country whose life will be built on new foundations . . . which can only leave Spain the better'.[61]

The net effect of all this placed the Plaid mandarins in an embarrassing state of conformity with the British government's actual (and consistent) position – a recommendation in favour of non-intervention. Needless to say, this policy was quite unacceptable to the left of the party. But such 'hotheads' could also forge an alliance with those who wished to support the effort of Basques and Catalans to achieve some degree of national fulfilment – aspirations which a Franco victory was bound to asphixiate. Of course, Plaid's interest in the two leading minority linguistic cultures within the nation-state of Spain was well-established prior to the war's outbreak.[62] But Ambrose Bebb stoutly resisted sentimentalism in this area, deriding, for example 'the fanciful revelations of Mr Lloyd George' that the Welsh and the Basques were ethnic cousins. 'We sympathize with them because they are suffering, because they have been defeated . . . not because they are the opposite side to Franco.'[63] In a similar spirit an article on Catalonia, though identifying a certain commonality, and expressing sympathy for the anarchist emphasis on local self-government, warned that Plaid could never agree with its full revolutionary programme.[64]

In contrast and opposition to the nationalist newspapers stood *Seren Cymru*, organ of the Welsh Baptist Union. Having the advantage of weekly publication and a wider readership, it also more faithfully reflected opinion amongst the great majority of Welsh speakers.[65] Though the writing staff shared the analytical and didactic mission of *Y Ddraig Goch*, and attempted to follow a neutralist path, their fundamental commitment to liberal – for many Baptists, Liberal – principles surfaced irremediably and constantly. A negative reflection of these beliefs shone out in liberal doses of 'The Black Legend of Spanish History'.

The history of the Spaniards shews that their cruel nature has been aggravated by an Asian sovereignty[66] . . .

The Spaniards, like the Prussians, are a cruel people, in this respect they are also close relatives of the Moors; and so we, in 20th-century Christian Europe, find ourselves back in a barbaric age which brutalises humanity . . .[67]

In the 16th century the King of Spain gave the Inquisition powers to censor all writing which was inconsistent with the teaching of the Papacy . . . It is this spirit – of concealing the truth from the people – which has thwarted the coming of freedom and justice to the religious, social and economic life of the country.[68]

Identifying the figure of General Franco as the modern symbol of these atavistic tendencies, *Seren Cymru* conversely praised the resistance of Madrid, whose citizens suffered under the shells and bombs of his 'inhuman rage'.[69] The editor also directly challenged J. E. Daniel – his colleague at *Y Ddraig Goch* – over the role of Russia; in his view, 'although Russia is more ready for war than any other country, there isn't a nation with less appetite for conflict than the USSR'.[70]

The Wrexham-based weekly *Y Cymro* was even more inclined to the left discourse. Here, too, the conventional Liberal allegiances of its constituency, rather than any empathy with revolution or even socialism, underpinned the attitudes expressed. An emphasis on 'British' loyalty and respectability which would not have deformed the pages of the *Daily Mail* was also evidenced in distaste for Welsh nationalism and a sincere sympathy for the troubles of the royal family during 1936–7. Yet a powerful admiration for learning, and a concern for education, particularly in their religious (that is, Nonconformist) dimensions, also influenced the newspaper's approach. In the early months of the war, *Y Cymro* printed several reports and letters by Cyril Cule, the Plaid intellectual and teacher who returned from Spain in the summer of 1936. Cule became a prominent publicist for the Republic and a tireless advocate of 'unity' over the issue in Welsh politics. Apparently denied sufficient access to his own party press, Cule warned against Francoist propaganda and asserted that the Communists 'are our best friends in the struggle . . . only Russia is behaving honourably towards the government of Spain'.[71] Several readers agreed that a government enjoying the support of a majority of Spaniards had been foully attacked by 'the enemy of freedom and the working class'.[72] These themes provided a *basso ostinato* of contributions by various correspondents throughout the autumn and winter of 1936–7. Another long unsigned article early in the new year – probably also by Cule – ended by proclaiming that 'as the Spaniards say today "Madrid will become the grave of Fascism", and not only of Spanish Fascism, but of European Fascism'.[73]

The destruction of Guernica in April 1937, an event which was critical in altering perception in other editorial offices, served only to confirm the policy of *Y Cymro*. A letter from Cule argued that the Basque cause and that of the Welsh was the same, equating the British government's desecration of the 'national site' at Penyberth with 'the work of Mr Baldwin's friends in bombing that sacred city'.

It should be remembered that the people of Guernica's only sin was to stand up for the same principles as those espoused by the Welsh Nationalist Party. All honour to the three martyrs who are rotting in jail for their faith in these same principles . . . The struggle is the same the world over, the enemy too is the same. After Abyssinia we now have Spain and Euzkadi as sacrifices to international Fascism. Can we not see the plague is coming ever nearer?[74]

Later that year, J. Williams-Hughes, the leader of the Welsh ambulance campaign, now working for the Red Cross in Spain, contributed a piece about his experiences. Even more exciting for many readers was the prospect that Williams-Hughes might broadcast Republican propaganda from Madrid *in Welsh*.[75] Though anticipated in more than one source, and apparently commissioned by the Valencia government, it seems that in the event no such material ever reached Wales across the airwaves.[76] However, a compensating excitement was generated not long afterwards when *Y Cymro* asked the eminent 'Christian Communist', T. E. Nicholas, to contribute a regular column on the international situation. 'Niclas y Glais' – to give him his bardic name – was a senior and much more eminent version of Cyril Cule; and a founder-member of the CPGB as distinct from a mere stripling fellow-traveller. One reader rather neatly dubbed him as 'Apostol Lenin yng Nghymru', and his remarks sparked off a vitriolic squabble in the correspondence columns.[77] In what represented the paper's first concession to a voice from the other side, A. F. Peake asserted that 'the Soviets have planted their new religion very successfully in Spain . . . with the result that thousands of monks, nuns and priests have been shot there and hundreds of churches of the "old" religion have been destroyed by the Bolsheviks'.[78] In reply, Nicholas blamed the Spanish clergy themselves for 'the great slaughter': '[Spanish] priests are offering special places in Paradise for Moors who murder women and children . . . Moors are given communion before they begin to massacre defenceless girls and children – a captive white girl is sometimes given to twenty Moors.'[79] These lurid and ludicrous tales evoked the outrage of the (Anglican) bishop of Monmouth, who challenged Nicholas to justify his 'extremely serious accusations against priests in Catholic Spain'. Rather relishing than deterred by the *odium theologicum*, the intrepid reverend dentist cited a pamphlet by the ILP propagandist, John McGovern: 'it costs two pence . . . Has the Pope prohibited Catholics to read it? After all, he has already banned the majority of the world's best books on philosophy, economics, science, etc. . . . The Papacy is anti-Christ and anti-worker.'[80]

Though this last example hardly qualifies for such an encomium, the level of commentary often found in the Welsh-language press was frequently thoughtful and perceptive. Similar qualities can only rarely be encountered in their English equivalents – inside or outside Wales's borders. Most of the regional/local papers in the principality, regardless of linguistic allegiance, or of the actual political slant of their content, shared a reluctance to state a clear commitment, to explicitly adopt a consistent position on the Spanish War. Partial exceptions to this were the Plaid press and *Seren Cymru* whose opposed stances were obvious if not, perhaps, strident. Not until very late in the day did the editor of *Y Cymro* give any indication of support for the Republic, whereas others (for example, the *Caernarvon and Denbigh Herald*, or the *Wrexham Leader*) remained congenitally coy.[81] In south-east Wales, however, if only because its much larger and wider readership base allowed the luxury, the daily press were somewhat less backward. The

Western Mail, which saw itself as a 'national' daily, and the *South Wales Echo* acidly criticized the Republican government and made noises supportive of the Nationalist rebels, as did the *Swansea Evening Post*.[82] These voices were apparently worried by the collapse of order and stability within Spain, yet they also quickly espoused the government's policy of non-intervention. In Newport, the *South Wales Argus* (and its stablemate, the more county-orientated *Weekly Argus*) were firmly pro-Republican and opposed non-intervention on moral and legal grounds. By the end of the war, the daily *Argus* was giving voice to the 'popular front' interpretation that the Spanish War was the result of an international fascist conspiracy. 'Our leaders are blind if they do not see that this Franco rebellion is part of the great scheme of totalitarian states to destroy the democracies and to dominate Europe as a preliminary to dominating the world.'[83]

Yet, if the correspondence pages are to be regarded as an accurate guide to public opinion, 'this Franco rebellion' actually registered a majority vote in the popular reckoning of the Welsh.[84] According to one survey, it was the widespread fear of communism which led many letter-writers to perceive a Comintern and not an Axis plot behind events in Spain. Typically succinct comments along these lines were 'Spain will be the first European country to go Bolshevik' and 'This war is an issue between Christ and Lenin'.[85] In the spring of 1937, the *Western Mail* published a syndicated series of reports by the writer C. S. Forester – author of the Hornblower novels – a detail which seems to corroborate the maritime interests and romantic inclinations of much of the paper's readership. Forester praised the 'efficient and capable government' set up by General Franco, and assured all concerned that any donations sent to this recipient would be devoted to medical and other humanitarian purposes.[86] It was strikingly ironical that the first of these encomia appeared in the issue of 26 April 1937 – the very day that the Condor Legion attacked and destroyed the town of Guernica with the massacre of some 1,000 civilians. This atrocity was to cause an epiphanal alteration in public opinion and in press attitudes throughout Britain. For the rest of the war, praise of Franco's leadership, and expression of support for the Nationalist cause as a whole was a rare occurrence.[87] The most that the *Western Mail* could manage, for example, was an occasional grudging acknowledgement that 'the point of view of those who are opposed to the government is well put'.[88] On the other hand, the precise significance of this sea-change should be understood. Its main beneficiary was not the main Republican government located in Valencia (from the autumn of 1937, in Barcelona) but rather the autonomous Basque government in Bilbao (and later, in its French exile). This tendency was especially marked in

Wales, where sympathy for 'suffering Madrid' was almost bodily transferred to the 'suffering Basques'; and again, once Franco turned his attention eastwards following the defeat of the Basque-led northern provinces, to the 'suffering Catalans'. In contrast, the Valencia authorities, whose close dependence on Moscow became increasingly evident, evoked support only from those committed to the 'popular front' take on the issues.[89]

5   The Miners: Little Moscows, Big Moscow

Internationalism I: The Coalfield and Asturias

The village of Maerdy is situated at the top of the Rhondda Fach, nestling in a small valley (in Welsh, *cwm*) almost fully enclosed by steep hillsides. The description sounds at once idyllically pastoral and characteristically ethnic, perhaps even to ears unfamiliar with the strains of 'Cwm Rhondda'. In the 1930s, the reality was somewhat different. Hardly any other community in Wales was more depressed by the great depression or more crushed by the great crash. It was a fate felt all the more keenly, since Maerdy's fall had been from heights of material production, relative prosperity and political influence. Five decades earlier, the original speculators had hit rich steam-coal deposits and within a generation 2,500 miners were employed at four busy pits. The infrastructure of municipal civic life was rapidly constructed, with great emphasis on providing the means of social intercourse, religious expression and secular education. Crucially, workers and bosses alike contributed to and participated in these creative processes.[1]

It was at the end of the First World War that the village emerged from obscure contentment to an almost national notoriety. The miners of Maerdy were radicalized by a series of contentious political issues in 1916–22; first by the struggle over wartime conscription, then successively by the Bolshevik revolution in Russia, the debate over the peace with Germany, the war of independence in Ireland, and finally by the first sharp recession in the coal industry. Each of these besetting concerns had an international significance and resonance – though, arguably except the last, having no special relevance to Maerdy. The attraction of widespread attention to the village came about partly through the accident that Noah Ablett, a local checkweigher, was the main author of the strategic programme *The Miners' Next Step* (1912) which was widely credited with (or blamed for) the significant gains made by mineworkers' unions during the war. Ablett's protégé, Arthur Horner (who was to become president of the SWMF in 1936, the year of the Spanish Civil War), along with other prominent local leaders, soon came to dominate the local miners' lodge. Horner was a working-class warrior born in Merthyr, the town associated in folklore with the first

Welsh workers' uprising. He served gaol sentences in 1918–20 for avoiding conscription and (worse) for leaving Wales to join the cause of armed resistance to the British Empire in Ireland. On his release he was re-elected as miners' agent in Maerdy and soon joined the fledgling CPGB. Thus it was that even before the General Strike of 1926, Maerdy 'came to stand for south Wales along with the "red villages" of Durham and Scotland, and that attracted as its nickname "Little Moscow"'.

The appellation certainly had a point. By 1926 the lodge dominated the community. Its forceful intervention in cases of perceived social as well as industrial injustice at times had extra-legal and even violent aspects. Its pro-Soviet tendencies were to be seen even in bizarre details of funeral obsequies – rites so deeply redolent of spiritual commitment – where there were 'red ribbons in place of black ties, with wreaths in the shape of the hammer and sickle, not the cross, and rendition of the "Red Flag" or the "Internationale" instead of Welsh hymnology'.[2] In the bitter years following the strike and lock-out of 1926–7, both below and above ground the revolutionary solidarity and discipline of the Maerdy colliers – often under extreme pressure from mine-owners and Cardiff-based media – became a byword. Its commitment seemed to sum up the mission of the CPGB and (what was now becoming) its main Welsh medium, the Fed (SWMF). In 1927, there was 75 per cent unemployment and this was to get even worse by 1936. In 1930, the lodge, determined to brook no compromise in its militancy, was banned by the MFGB and in effect broke away even from the Fed. For a few years, it was Maerdy against the world, when the way the community – and its leaders – had always wanted things was exactly the other way round. Thanks to Horner's single-minded and often inspirational leadership (which brought him yet another gaol sentence in 1931) the village was able to rejoin the 'gradualist' and 'defensive' mainstream of the working-class fellowship supervised by the Fed. Accordingly, when the era of antifascism and its most evocative cause, the Spanish Civil War, arrived, Maerdy was able to play a full part in the fights for Moscow and Madrid. Nowhere was the consciousness of unity and the belief in 'one struggle for all working people' more profoundly entrenched.

In this twenty years, Maerdy came to occupy the core of the folk-memory of the Welsh coalminers' century-long struggle against the bonds of the bosses and the iron whim of capitalism. Poverty-stricken, tiny in population, geographically isolated, ignored by an indifferent world – except, that is, for the regular negative press attention given to its struggle[3] – it reacted to oppression on an international scale and with boundless concern. By the 1960s, the place had become not just another site of industrial archaeology, more a place of mythic significance, a monument to Wales's endless, morbid fascination with its own decline, struggle and defeat. After Jan Morris paid a visit in the course of her researches for a travel book on Wales, she chose to attempt a reconstruction of its life in the 1930s as an epitome of the Rhondda experience.

Things are hard in Maerdy in the 1930s, in the depths of the depression. The main street badly needs some paint. The women standing at their doors in flowered aprons and slippers, babies wrapped in shawls, looked pinched and anxious. They call Maerdy 'Little Moscow' because of its militant trade unionism, *and God knows, it seems a proper place for revolution.* The tuberculosis rate is terrible, diseases of lungs and eyes are rife, many a Maerdy miner suffers from permanent and unremitting back pains. Half the children go barefoot, nearly all are undernourished, and infant mortality rate runs at about seventy deaths per thousand.

But wait! down the road from the pits above there comes marching in cheerful disunity the Maerdy Kazoo Band on its way to the Sunday afternoon meeting in the square! And suddenly, for all its miseries, Maerdy comes alive. The women rush indoors for their coats, small boys come whistling and dancing down the steep wide streets. Mr Evans the grocer looks benignly out from his poster-plastered door . . .[4]

In this miraculous scenario it takes no revolution but only a song in your heart to make a utopia out of dystopia. Barefoot children racked with TB blow like lusty cherubs on their trumpets and gambol like spring kids along the steep cobbles. My valley grows as green as ever it was, the sylvan Rhondda of the simple light is restored, and all seems more like lovely Llaregyb than a plague-ridden wasteland.[5]

It was not only in its resemblance to a contemporary Warner Brothers film set – Gold Diggers rather than Coal Miners – that Maerdy, along with the Rhondda as a whole, 'represented the cause of internationalism' in Wales.[6] As the Oxford Welshman and (covert) communist, Goronwy Rees, protested in 1938

We are not a backward, a remote, or an uncivilized people . . . Indeed, we have a strong sense of belonging to an international community, as may be seen in the annual message sent by the children of Wales to the children of the world, or, in more remarkable forms, in the attempts of the Welsh miners to relieve the distress of their comrades in the Asturias.[7]

The sacrifices made by miserable places like Maerdy to alleviate the suffering of the coalmining villages in Spain's Asturias – perceived as the result of an oppression even worse than their own – is seen by Welsh historians of the labour movement not only as the essence of their own subject, but also of the history of world support for the Spanish Republic. It was, so their story goes, a link which was forged in the years before the Civil War began, in a manner which demonstrates how the Rhondda provided both prophecy and example to the world.[8]

Asturias is one of Spain's smaller provinces, occupying approximately the same land-area as the South Wales Coalfield, strikingly similar in its topographical outlines, and with an economy in those days largely dependent on coalmining. In October 1934, the region witnessed a popular uprising against the centre-right government in Madrid, led by an alliance of syndicalist (that is, trade union) committees. From the provincial capital, Oviedo, this insurrection spread out to most of the regional mining villages, quickly developing both violent and expropriatory characteristics. It was nothing less than *la révolution à l'outrance*, red in tooth and claw. Pits and other workplaces were occupied. Dozens of priests, hundreds of local businessmen and leaders of government parties were murdered. Unfortunately for the rebels, theirs was the only part of the country which actually went through with a planned nationwide uprising, which had been organized by the Spanish Socialist Party (PSOE) with the aim of overthrowing a government elected by a large majority less than a year before. The ostensible occasion for the rebellion was that recently, and for the first time, two leaders of the party which was the largest in the Cortes, but which happened to be a right-wing coalition, had been given ministerial portfolios. Whilst the plan misfired elsewhere, or was easily thwarted, the leaders in Asturias perpetrated the hard business of revolution too enthusiastically to permit any secure retreat. The government called in the army, and General Franco was appointed to command. Spain's youngest and most energetic general brought units of the Foreign Legion and Moroccan auxiliaries to spearhead his assault on the mountain fastnesses of revolution. Many hundreds of miners, particularly members of the anarchist CNT, died in the fighting or during subsequent 'mopping up' operations. Thousands more were physically maltreated and/or imprisoned in harsh conditions. It was in many ways a prelude to or even a dress rehearsal for the main tragedy which was to ensue within twenty months.[9]

Only a few weeks before the Asturias uprising, an underground explosion occurred in the Gresford colliery, near Wrexham. Encouraged by the coincidence in time, and despite the huge differences in terms of moral responsibility, sheer scale, and essential character, opinion in the Welsh coalfields equated this accident – which cost some 250 lives – with what subsequently happened in Asturias.[10] An empathetic feeling for their Spanish co-religionists apparently took root in the villages of 'Red Rhondda', a sentiment which became more firmly established with the attempts of the BUF, protected by the police, to 'invade' their mountain fastnesses in 1935–6.[11] As Francis and Smith have shown, in the 1920s, the political influence of Spanish immigrant workers in places like Dowlais and Dulais was out of all proportion to their actual numbers. In the former, a branch of the PSOE was established, whilst 'the more "advanced" ideas of socialism and particularly syndicalism did not arrive in the upper Swansea Valley with the publication of *The Miners' Next Step* but with the coming of the Spaniards'.[12] Even during the 'Angry Summer' of 1926 – as its bard has recorded – young miners still managed an occasional night out

> And across the moor at midnight
> We'll walk back home again,
> And arm in arm sing catches
> From America and Spain.[13]

It was at the suggestion of Abercrave and other anthracite villages where exiled Spaniards worked that, following 1934, the Fed contributed financial relief to Asturian miners' families, who suffered while breadwinners languished in gaol as 'political prisoners'. By the time Civil War in Spain began, one expert asserts, there had already been

> a long-standing interest in Spanish working class affairs . . . the action of the Cambrian Lodge was symptomatic of a growing sympathy for the harsh struggles of the Spanish miners. A letter sent to the Spanish ambassador in 1935 demanded 'the unconditional release of Gonzales Pena and all other heroic miners and socialists now held in the prisons of Spain under danger of execution.'[14]

Despite all this, on a visit to London in July 1936, no less a figure than Largo Caballero, PSOE leader – soon to be chief of a republic at war – complained of the lack of support given over Asturias by the British labour movement. 'Did this mean [he asked] that they were only to make speeches and write articles . . . If Fascism should again attempt to take power . . . was it to be only a verbal fight?'[15] Yet it is difficult to see how – in practice – local mining communities could have reacted to any degree or with any effect to the insurrection itself. In October 1934, no British newspaper reported the outbreak or the development of events taking place in a region both notoriously inaccessible and forbiddingly distant from any major city in Spain. Even in *The Times*, no official report of the fighting or its consequences appeared before the end of the year. What reached the offices of the *Daily Worker* were merely vague rumours of troubles in northern Spain – which nonetheless precipitated a headline appeal for the faithful to 'Help the Spanish Workers'.[16] It was not until the TUC sent Leah Manning to Oviedo the following year that any details of the revolt and its repression emerged in Britain.[17]

Once the Civil War itself had begun, recollections of events in Asturias precipitated powerful disagreement in the Welsh press. When Franco's troops conquered the region for a second time in 1937, one north Walian implored the government to act to prevent 'a new horror . . . the wholesale massacre of thousands of Asturians . . . Three years ago [he explained] hundreds of Asturians were shot down by troops.' In reply, an irate correspondent, who had recently returned from Spain after being imprisoned by the government, argued that in 1934 it had been the 'Reds', not the military, who engaged in massacres.[18] In Cardiff, pro-Republican businessman John Emlyn Jones cited the Asturias incident as an example of how the Spanish right traditionally practised the 'brutal repression of legitimate opposition'. An Aberystwyth reader objected that the insurrection of 1934 hardly qualified as 'legitimate opposition', asking (rhetorically but not inaptly) 'was an armed uprising like this ever treated with gentleness?'[19]

In the last analysis, the 'special affinity' which (it is claimed) existed between the Welsh and Spanish coalfields has little substance under examination. Over the years there was, of course, much talk of the heroism of 'La Pasionaria' – the Basque-born communist, Dolores Ibárruri, who represented Asturias in the Cortes, and whose slogan 'No Pasarán' (taken from the French army's slogan of resistance at Verdun in 1916) became the international mantra of antifascism. In 1970, there was '*an intention* . . . to smuggle money into the Asturias for the miners who were on strike'.[20] But the only act of complementary recognition from the Asturian side came in 1978, when the local UGT reciprocated an earlier visit to Wales by inviting the Welsh NUM to send a delegation to Oviedo.[21] Worthy of remark for its exotic uniqueness, the 1930s connection between the Welsh and Asturian miners seems too flimsy to bear the grand hypothesis of a pioneering south Wales version of 'internationalism' which has been placed upon it. To some extent, a parallel conclusion drawn by Francis seems valid – up to a point; viz., that the politics of local decision-making and direct action in response to 'fascism' (however identified), a tendency reaching its peak precisely in the summer of 1936, was something the coalfield lodges shared with the 'workers alliance' groups in the Asturias, inspired as they were by the anarchists.[22]

Internationalism II: Coal Brigades and the Comintern

In the years following the end of the Spanish Civil War, the surviving leaders and men of the International Brigades' British Battalion worked to set up a domestic organization which would maintain its memory and ideals.[23] One suggestion current at the time was that the Welshmen who had died for democracy should be celebrated as members of 'the coal brigade'. Indeed, at the very outset of the twentieth-century miners' struggle, one prescient Welsh politician had threatened the coal-owners with the prospect of 'fighting brigades of miners' unless they and their police allies put an end to aggressive strike-breaking tactics.[24] In 1911, motive and organization for such physical resistance were both too recent in origin and too localized in grasp. By the mid-1930s, things had changed. If not to the same degree or in the identical time-span, all over Wales the social fabric was painfully ruptured by the consequences of prolonged economic depression. Men from the mining valleys went in groups to London on hunger marches or individually to help defend the Jewish streets of Hackney against the incursions of the BUF. Violent resistance to 'fascism' in all its forms saw many determined individuals committed to the gaols of Swansea, Cardiff and London for aggressive disturbances of the public peace. The minds of many became focused on the class struggle – and on social revolution itself – as the only way out: or, in an even more desperate construction, as some *ex post facto* justification for the collective life-sentence of unemployment and helplessness which the crisis of the capitalist system had already passed upon the Welsh proletariat.

Above all, the Communist Party, whose influence in Wales had grown substantially since the trauma of the General Strike, had imparted belief, organization and discipline to the situation. The extent of their success can be gauged by events which indicate the growing apprehensions of Whitehall in 1936. In the November weeks following the Welsh hunger march – a period coinciding exactly with Franco's great assault upon Madrid – the government reacted not only by ameliorating the harsh terms of the Means Test, but also by sending the popular new monarch, Edward VIII, to placate the anger of the Valleys and (as it were) to seduce its women and children away from revolution. The proles were softened up by press announcements that 'something must be done', 'something should be done' and finally 'something *will* be done for South Wales'.[25] But by now, a leader whose writ ran more electrically in the coalfield valleys had spoken of an imperative way forward. Comrade Stalin had agreed to the establishment of a Soviet-backed international army of intervention in the Spanish War, and the way to getting something done was seen to lie through Madrid and Albacete rather than through Westminster.

Although probably no more than 3,500 strong in terms of membership – with a cadre of around 500 providing active, sustained leadership – the Wales District Branch of the CPGB came to act as a kind of underground resistance movement in the 1930s. Their greatest success was the gradual penetration of the SWMF, which gave them the loudest voice in the policy-making of an organization of some 100,000 members.[26] Via the influence of many lodges on the local community, 'resistance' became almost institutionalized – literally so in the miners' institutes, where common rooms and libraries were utilized for formal meetings and impromptu debates, Left Book Club discussions and intensive private reading of Bolshevik history and Marxist theory. All this connected the coalfield to a different species of 'internationalism' – the worldwide apparatus of the Soviet-run Third International, or Comintern.[27] Maerdy – 'Little Moscow' – and 'Red Rhondda' as a whole were connected not so much to the 'international community' in the universal sense intended by Goronwy Rees as to 'Big Moscow' and to Russia, unchallenged source of wisdom and authority for the party faithful. From the offices run by Gyorgy Dmitrov in the Kremlin, via the central committee of the CPGB in London, orders went out to the regional branches and local cells – Wales, like Hungary or Canada or Spain, heard and obeyed. In the early 1930s, men like Will Paynter, Jack Roberts and Harry Dobson, all three later to be stalwarts of the British Battalion in Spain, were sent to Moscow to 'study' for a year in the Lenin School – an elite training centre for the party cadres in revolutionary tactics, propaganda and (above all) disciplined obedience.[28] None of the British veterans ever recorded what they observed of life in Moscow during those horrific years of forced urbanization, systematic privation and the Stalinist terror, though a large number left the party soon after returning home.[29] Of course, the commitment of hardened loyalists to the Soviet Union arose out of and was driven by a fierce concern for the working classes in general and for their own communities in particular. Nevertheless, in the last analysis, such men, and many other party members who never made it to Moscow, were emissaries of the Comintern and thus (in effect) not so much 'internationalists' as single-minded agents of the totalitarian Stalinist state.

The extent of such influence should not be overestimated. In terms of representative politics, at least, the sustained communist 'offensive' in the wake of the 1926–7 strike had only limited success. The Labour Party never lost a parliamentary election in the coalfields, even during the most intense period of 'antifascist' agitation, and hardly more than a handful of communists ever entered municipal councils.[30] Moreover, Victorian notions of self-help persisted stubbornly and widely in a variety of altered forms. This phenomenon was adventitiously assisted by the communist obsession with national and international issues – often seen as abstract by the voters – and their dogmatic habit of addressing even the local socio-economic crisis in explicitly political ways. The obvious lacunae in terms of the empty daily lives of the out-of-work majority was filled to some extent by Labour Party initiatives, but more importantly (perhaps) by the Quakers, who by 1936 had established a powerful presence in the Rhondda.[31]

The crisis of 1926 had attracted the attention of the Friends to south Wales. Indeed, their mission to the suffering poor was exactly contemporary with that of the CPGB, though differing strongly in tactics and motivation, and it was arguably even more successful. The Quakers set up a network of unemployed clubs, centred on a home institution ('Maes y Haf') in Trealaw, which provided daytime shelter and soup kitchens, craft training and adult education. In 1932 they established a thriving holiday home for unemployed miners and their families near the Ogmore beaches in the Vale of Glamorgan. In August 1936, the CPGB failed to lobby Stanley Baldwin – later seen as the godfather of non-intervention – in an attempt made by a flying column from south Wales sent to Gregynog, the country home of Lord Davies.[32] In contrast, a few weeks later, a group of colliers from the Friends' holiday home at Wick gained admission to St Donat's Castle, where Randolph Hearst was entertaining a galaxy of plutocratic guests. In a Hollywood scene set somewhere beyond the imagination of John Ford, they entertained the robber baron whose enormous press empire was active in the cause of General Franco to an impromptu rendition of 'Cwm Rhondda', and walked off with the multimillionaire's cheque for $250 towards the amelioration of distress in the Valleys.[33]

These anecdotes illustrate (to my mind) the differing essences of the communist and Quaker vocations. The former demanded that the presently suffering individual devote a significant aspect of daily life to working towards a solution which was both universal and distant – whether or not through actual revolution is of relevance only as regards the element of personal hazard it might involve. The latter also required work and commitment, but in a more intimate, domestic context, and one which brought almost immediate and direct relief. Moreover, the ideological commitment was – and this is strikingly paradoxical – of a less total kind, asking for little more than a respect towards conventional (to most, familiar) religious beliefs. Though it was professedly apolitical in temper, several of the leaders of the Friends' campaign were in fact Liberals and pacifists.[34] But more to the present point, they were partly inspired by the decline of religious practice in the Valleys, and what they saw as the concomitant spiritual dangers of atheistic communism. In the mid-1930s a clearly competitive tension existed between the two interests.[35] Indeed, it may be speculated that the alternative culture offered by the Quakers may have adversely affected the communist drive to recruit volunteers for the International Brigades. By 1938, they had 9,000 members of their clubs working and learning productively, in pacifist/quietist environments, *in the Rhondda alone*. They had a notable influence inside many homes gained through the widespread generation of 'women's-work' societies.[36] The opportunities provided by the Friends, along with the personal counselling which doubtless accompanied them, surely provided a prophylactic deterrent for many – especially for men who might have been attracted to Spain by material desperation or spiritual emptiness.[37]

For this and similar reasons, the overwhelming majority of miners recruited by the communists to fight in Spain were already members of the Party. Of the 110 or so pitworkers from the South Wales Coalfield – in itself some 70 per cent of the overall total – some ninety-five were communists before they went to Spain, and several others joined the Party – usually the PCE – whilst serving with the Brigades. In theory, given this concentration of locality and ideology, they should have been a very cohesive group, but (as we shall see) experience was to run counter to this expectation.[38] The claim that they represented the greatest sacrifice offered by any one region and occupation to the cause of 'Spain' is, on one level, valid enough, yet this achievement must be put in context. In the first place, it should be noted that the overall Welsh contribution was less impressive than that made by the Irish and the Scots, and not just in quantitative terms. Put at its maximum allowable, volunteers from Wales numbered 160, compared with some 200 Irishmen and over 500 from Scotland.[39] The last of these figures represents easily the highest return of the home nations in pro rata population terms. By the same token, the Irish contribution is no greater than the Welsh, but is surely a more remarkable phenomenon, given that the great majority were from Nationalist/Catholic backgrounds, and were thus volunteering from within a culture as hostile to the Republic as any in Europe.[40]

Moreover, as Hywel Francis demonstrates, the Welsh effort was produced almost entirely by the machinery of the Party and (at least in its later stages) was in effect the result of a 'membership quota' of 'volunteers' imposed from the central committee on local Party cells. There was never any spontaneous rush of workers into the arms of Party recruiting agents, even in the Rhondda. This was not simply because of the effort already being put into the indigenous antifascist struggle, the Means Test campaign and the Welsh hunger march to London, which was being planned in the summer of 1936, and took place that October. It was not until that same month that orders came through from Moscow indicating that Stalin had decided to support (in effect, to take over) the unofficial 'international column' – that is, a number of genuinely spontaneous 'popular front' militia units which were already fighting in Madrid and various parts of Aragon – and that the CPGB should begin the organization of recruitment.[41] On 7 November the French Communist Party was ordered: 'il faut redoubler efforts pour récrutement des volontaires non seulement en France mais en Europe'.[42] But even thereafter, the process was painfully slow. By January, the British Central Committee was receiving complaints from Albacete, HQ of the brigades in south-eastern Spain, that very few men had arrived from Wales. Dave Springhall, British Battalion commissar was driven to make a specific and heartfelt plea:

> Why such an incredibly small percentage of comrades from South Wales. We could do with a group of 20–30 or more of Welsh miner comrades. They, with their particular unity, singing and fighting qualities, would help to balance our battalion . . . Let us have some more of these in preference to the sort with no background at all.[43]

Springhall's references to 'comrades', 'unity' and 'background' show that from a very early stage spontaneous recruitment from non-Party elements was not to be seriously envisaged. In many ways, therefore, the whole phenomenon, more acutely in south Wales than elsewhere, resembled 'conscription' rather more closely than 'volunteering'. At any rate, no more than a dribble of this Welsh elite arrived in Spain before the battle of Jarama in February 1937.[44] Shortly thereafter, strenuous efforts produced a party of around fifty men – some thirty-five of them from the coalfield. They arrived in two or three groups during the spring, while the battalion was still quartered in the Jarama valley, occupying the positions it had successfully defended during the battle. Another draft of about thirty Welshmen reached Albacete that autumn, and a further contingent of around forty went out in the early spring of 1938. These three gobbets together represented two-thirds of the total who went to Spain from Wales.[45]

The most extensive and reliable account of any Welshman who went to fight for Republican Spain was that written in the 1970s by W. D. ('Billy') Griffiths.[46] Bred in Llwynypia in Rhondda Fawr, Griffiths joined the Party at eighteen and soon became hyperactive in its ranks. A full-time official by 1936, he was then acting as secretary to no fewer than eleven branches in the Valleys. His memoir illustrates the difficulties of canvassing for volunteers, a feature which was in evidence even before details of the dreadful casualties amongst the British Battalion at the battles of Jarama and Brunete filtered back. Sometime in 1937 Griffiths was allocated primary responsibility for the fulfilment of 'quotas', and early in 1938 he was ordered to volunteer in person. At first, he recalled,

> I resented being asked to go to Spain. Why me? . . . It was only [later] that I began to look at the problem with open eyes . . . What one believed in one must be prepared to die for . . . At the same time, within the Party there was a growing opposition to what was known as inner party conscription. Recruiting was not easy. There was a reluctance among leading comrades to volunteer . . . In the early days one was victimised and lost ones job. Later the struggle became sharper and one went to prison. Now it was expected that one should die for the Party . . . Only after long discussion was it possible to find a volunteer. J. Jones, 40 years old, the least robust and physically the most ill-fitted. It was 'Hobson's Choice'.

In the spring of 1937, Will Paynter of Maerdy became the first official to be explicitly 'conscripted' by the Party for important work in Spain. His position there was additionally endorsed by the SWMF, a fact which was to endow him with unique authority amongst his compatriots.[47] After mid-February 1937, recruiting for Spain was illegal (under the terms of Non-Intervention Agreements) so that all concerned had to act 'underground'. The coordinating centre for recruitment was set up in Cardiff, and it was to a secret location in the city that the vast majority of men bound for Albacete came for interview and registration. But even with these precautions, and a further sifting-out process in London, an uncomfortably large fraction of the men who left Victoria Station – usually with weekend return tickets for France – still proved unsuitable. Many were overcome by the attractions of 'internationalism', some disappearing in Paris (in one case for good), several others getting drunk and frisky and – after arrest and detention – being deported back to Britain.[48] Some Welshmen were full of astonished admiration at receiving lectures from Charlotte Haldane, who was in charge of the reception, instruction and onward dispatch of British comrades in Paris, on the need to resist the brothels and the risks of venereal disease.[49] For her part, Haldane had poignantly mixed feelings about her charges. 'They were mostly unemployed lads, miners, often from the valleys of South Wales or the mining villages of Scotland. Years of depression and the dole had forced them into enlistment . . . They were fine, honest, healthy, and bitter.'[50]

The Valleys Mobilize for 'Spain'

In early October 1936, just when the massed ranks of the hunger march were about to set out for London, the young nationalist Cyril Cule attended a great antifascist meeting in the Rhondda. Fluent in Spanish, he was able to interview 'a teacher from Barcelona' who came to address the gathering. The Spaniard consistently emphasized the invasive and barbaric nature of the uprising.

> I am ashamed to admit that they are Spaniards . . . Although they have not used gas up to now, it is surely a horror yet to come. Men of the Foreign Legion and African barbarians predominate . . . Small children have had their hands amputated for giving the anti-fascist salute [. . . but still] hordes of children flock to the authorities to ask for weapons. They are not issued with guns, nevertheless they are sometimes found alongside the men on the front lines. A boy will follow a soldier until he is cut down, then he will take the adult's gun and join the fray. We are not appealing for men [as] we have more than enough. But we do need weapons. We can fight our own battles if we have the guns.[51]

Despite – or perhaps because of – the manifest exaggerations and internal inconsistencies of such propaganda, 'workers in the Rhondda, many of them on unemployment assistance, have contributed their scarce pennies to the fund in aid of the Spanish workers'.[52] Though the sums of money contributed from such sources were relatively small, from the beginning to the end of the war in Spain the coalfield communities collected and dispatched tons of old clothing and tinned food, never failing to respond to any appeal sponsored by the Fed.[53] In Abertridwr, recalled Jack Roberts, 'we loaded the shop with tinned stuffs and clothes that people had given us out of their poverty, and then sent them down to Cardiff for them to be sent to Spain'.[54] At the other end of the scale, in May 1938 the Male Voice Choir of the Fed joined with the chorus of the London Philharmonic Orchestra to perform at a meeting in the Royal Albert Hall, with 8,000 people crowded inside and over 2,000 more outside. In ten minutes, it was reported, £1,400 was collected for 'Spain'.[55]

In the mean time, in Clydach Vale, Lewis Jones, county councillor and novelist, geared himself up for a unique personal effort. In the early months of 1937 his routine (after signing on for the dole) was to attend council committees in the morning, make open-air loudspeaker tours in the afternoon, give lectures in the evening, then to go home and work on his novels through the night. Prominence in the Communist Party and the County Council gave this intensely local but charismatic personality a truly international dimension. In the spring, for example, he met 'Field the composer' and Paul Nizam, the French communist novelist. May was exceptionally busy with 'Spain' work, especially speaking at documentary film- and slide-shows. Later in the year, his activities, in which fund-raising as such played a secondary role to the stimulation of a political consciousness over 'unity' and 'Spain', became more concentrated on Cardiff. In October he attended a party conference in the city called to discuss the crisis in recruitment for the International Brigades, which had fallen to virtually zero in the wake of the dreadful disaster of Brunete. Around this time, after consulting with Will Paynter, who had recently returned from a tour of duty, he expressed a willingness in principle to 'volunteer'. Little wonder that in December he confided to his diary that he had experienced a 'seizure' at his home.[56] Jones's fellow writer and miner from the Rhymney valley coalfield, Bert Coombes, began his own diary at the outset of the Second World War. He could not resist pointing out how Wales had warned the world of the coming of this event.

> In this area we miners contributed our coppers every week to help the Spanish Government and held demonstrations and meetings appealing in aid of them because we realised they fought our battle . . . Over Spain it seems that the wishes of the whole Principality were ignored. Yet we are to fight for Poland, a country that is further away from the mind and knowledge of most of us . . .[57]

Whilst Coombes, unlike Jones, remained politically inactive (even uncommitted), another product of the Rhymney valley coalfield became the country's most outstanding opponent of the National Government on the question of Spain. In a life in politics as the stormy petrel of the Labour movement, Aneurin Bevan was arguably never more intensely dedicated to any cause than that of the Spanish Republic. Elected as MP for Ebbw Vale in 1929, Bevan had found himself two years later as one of the leading members of the Labour rump left in the Commons after the disastrous split and general election rout of 1931. Since the official opposition was not measurably stronger by 1936, Bevan was faced with an intensely difficult crisis of conscience over Spain. Having spent his honeymoon with Jennie Lee in Andalusia, Bevan had formed a personal impression of the historical condition of the unprivileged labouring masses in Spain.[58] In October 1936, they were both crushed by the party conference's decision to endorse the government's policy of non-intervention. That winter (as we have seen) along with Stafford Cripps and others he stomped the platform of 'unity' and 'Spain' up and down the country, a campaign which, even if only subliminally, was intended to test the possibility of an entirely new socialist party made up of Labour, ILP and Communist elements. In successive crises Bevan suffered suspension from the House and expulsion from his own party, accompanied by the occasional execration of erstwhile colleagues and frequent ostracism from their social ranks.[59] Early in 1938, he was amongst a group of Labour MPs who spent a week in Republican Spain. Although, of course, the delegation saw only what their hosts wanted them to see, the visit took place amidst the rare euphoria of military success which attended the Popular Army's capture of Teruel in the last week of 1937. He returned with renewed commitment to and confidence in the path he had set for himself. Though he was never to convince the Labour leadership – or, more significantly, the trade union mandarins – of the full rectitude or practicality of his cause, some progress was made. The party abandoned its support for non-intervention, and in autumn 1937, Labour Party leader Clement Attlee not only visited the British Battalion's billets in the Tajuña valley, but consented to its No. 1 Company being decorated with his own name – complete with military rank.[60]

James Griffiths, Labour MP for Llanelli, was also a member of Bevan's delegation. He wrote to his wife from Barcelona that he could see how Britain's neutrality had adversely affected the Republican war-effort and that 'they attach considerable importance to [a change in] our British attitude particularly at the Non-Intervention Committee'. He described the International Brigade, rather curiously, as 'a new kind of Foreign Legion'.[61] Like Bevan, he was infected with the confidence inspired by the heroic (but as it proved, temporary) success of Teruel.

> It is a wonderful experience – there are scores of indelible impressions on my mind. I have seen War – nearly at first hand and it is terrible and yet the marvellous thing is Life goes on . . . They will not give way – their spirit is indomitable. Their confidence grows every day. The morale of the soldiers and people is truly marvellous and this will carry them through.[62]

But Griffiths knew the people of the western coal valleys of south Wales as well as Bevan – his colleague and fellow ex-miner – knew those of the east. Though he went to Spain, and threw himself energetically into campaigning at home for the relief of the Republic's suffering masses, Griffiths was not of Bevan's camp when it came to defying the party line. His consistent refusal to break ranks on Spain suggests an underlying consensus within his constituency, and perhaps also in its hinterland anthracite coalfield generally, that the issue should never be allowed to risk a potentially fatal division of the labour movement.[63]

By 1938, in contrast, many Fed stalwarts had come to believe that pennies and tins of milk, on the one hand, and human sacrifices on the other, were neither of them enough to make the government listen to the case for ending non-intervention and 'saving Spain'. They were convinced that only a strike of all members could bring home the urgency of the matter. The campaign for a strike in support of miners fighting in Spain was led by the joint lodges of the Dulais Valley, who fought it with hard-jawed determination through the absorbingly complex levels of union democracy. The torch of resistance, it seems, had finally passed from Maerdy. Eventually, with Will Paynter's support, the motion was put to the SWMF executive council recommending a strike 'to enforce the release of arms to the Spanish Government, to prevent the supply of any material to the fascist powers who were supporting the fascist rebels, and also to bring about the downfall of the present pro-fascist British Government'. Given that the motion seemed to represent a programme for immediate revolution rather than a token strike, it was not surprising that Horner soon let it be known that the CPGB did not approve, and the motion effectively lapsed.[64] In any case, and ironically, by the time this stage had been reached, the south Wales coalfield was delivering crucial supplies of coal directly to the war-industries of the Republic. One wonders what well-informed commissars of the International Brigades, who read of the pro-strike campaign in their regular magazine, made of its two incompatible elements.[65]

6   The Word was God: Writers and Heretics

All indigenous sources agree that in their recent history – say, until the later decades of the last century – the Welsh people cherished a culture which placed a premium on education and literacy above all other individual and collective accomplishments. Regardless of linguistic or regional background, the Welsh person traditionally placed a high value on these outward accidentals of inner (spiritual or soulful) essentials. We were, we used to assure ourselves, not only a musical, but likewise a poetical and artistical nation. This key element of Welsh life, which was, surely, at its florescent peak in the 1930s, also (as it happened) reflected a culture which was associated with the 'organic' ideological left. Nevertheless, the ways in which all its (otherwise differing and competing) political allegiances privileged the bard – preacher, prophet, poet, philosopher, even by that decade, economist – have already been amply illustrated in this book. It was nothing less than an entrenched value-system, and one which guaranteed that, even as coalmines and steelworks melted into air, the production of teachers should persist to become the nation's premier export in the last quarter of the twentieth century.

Given the consensual elevation of the writer's role in its society, it is passing strange that no International Brigader from Wales has ever produced a full published memoir of his experiences in Spain. Moreover, this lacuna stands in sharp contrast to efforts made by veterans of other nationalities, including hundreds of examples from other anglophone countries, to put things on record, to construct in book form their testaments and narratives. Such testaments explain, justify, document and above all perpetuate, the ideals for which they fought. Ultimately, only in this way can the cause be consummated, endowed with eternal meaning, given both scripture and exegesis. It seems all the more bizarre, therefore, that the first extensive memoir by a Welsh veteran of the Spanish War ever to be published should so diametrically contradict this orthodoxy. It was written not by a 'volunteer for liberty' but by a man who went to Spain avowedly to fight against communism, and whose explicit desire to engage the International Brigades in battle was amply fulfilled. How odd, too, that Frank Thomas, a man who many in Wales would instinctively dismiss as a 'Fascist', should make off with the palm so coveted in the culture of his enemies.[1]

Perhaps less surprising is that Frank Thomas had to wait for over sixty years to see the results of his work appear in hard covers. Yet he dearly hoped to become a writer as well as a soldier – both of them aspirations which his book repeatedly justifies. Though equipped with a solid foundation for the former profession by his education in a typical Welsh grammar school, Thomas did not boast a background which in the 1930s would have been considered 'literary' or 'intellectual'. Many Welshmen of similar socioeconomic derivation were to be found in the ranks of the British Battalion, not only students, but also teachers and men of 'cultural' or 'refined' sensibilities. Although the issue was a contentious one during the 1930s, working-class persons were still hardly expected to nurture the seeds of 'bourgeois culture'. All the same, Pat Murphy – who left Cardiff for Spain only a few weeks after Thomas – was another who experienced the desire to write which was so characteristic of this era. Murphy was a hard-drinking, riotously anarchist seaman, who as a young man made Cardiff his base, after being born to Irish immigrant teachers in Workington. After spending an eventful six months with the British Battalion – he went into action with John Cornford at Lopera and with Jack Roberts at Brunete – Murphy was invalided home with a serious wound. When his ship was mined off the east coast early in the Second World War, he finally decided to retire and write. He became an agent for distribution of the International Brigade Association magazine, the *Volunteer for Liberty*, and bombarded this, the *Daily Worker* and various other publications with stories of the sea and the Spanish War. Even in the 1970s, shortly before his death, he was still sending reams of recollections to James Klugman, one-time Cambridge associate of Cornford and then editor of *Marxism Today*.[2]

Despite the presence of a large number of autodidacts, typical of their time and place, amongst the Welsh contingent of the brigades, and leaving aside their private letters home, I have been unable to find fresh relics in any literary form or genre which refer to their feelings about or experiences in Spain.[3] The absolute nature of this void, at the centre of an apparently deeply valued heritage, makes it all the more astonishing that a carapace of literary reference has grown over it, giving it an external appearance of reality, and one as toughly armoured as it is resplendent. The brilliant image is the work of many hands in many kinds of writing, ranging from documentary reportage to 'fictional' film script, from the work of engaged contemporaries to that of more objective observers of later generations. The only thing they have in common is that all operate vicariously, indirectly,

Sid Hamm snapped by a girlfriend in Llandaff Fields, Cardiff, shortly before he left for Spain. See p. 68.
(The author is grateful to Mrs K Doyle for this portrait)

DEFENCE of MADRID

has been produced by the Progressive Film Institute and is distributed by Kino Films (1935), Ltd., solely to encourage aid for the people of Spain. It is on 16mm. silent, non-inflammable stock, on three reels, running time about 50 minutes. The film is classified as a newsreel and does not require a censor's certificate. It can be shown in any hall or meeting room without special precautions or permission.

Terms for 16mm. showing on application to:

KINO FILMS (1935) LTD.
84 Gray's Inn Road,
London, W.C. 1

Telephone: HOLBORN 1760

KINO FILMS (1935) LTD.
(By arrangement with Progressive Film Institute)

Presents

DEFENCE
OF
MADRID

A FILM IN AID OF THE SPANISH PEOPLE

The propaganda film Defence of Madrid *was shot around Madrid by the aristocratic British communist, Ivor Montagu, in the autumn of 1936 and became a staple feature of 'Aid Spain' meetings all over Britain. See pp. 38, 70. (Sidney Robinson Collection)*

Balance Sheet of Film to March 12th

Sale of Tickets   4- 17 9
(= 39?)
Collection   1- 3- 0

Film & Operator   2- 0-
Rent of Hall   1- 17-
Printing Tkts   8-
Posters   3-
Advertising}
Argus   }   4
Profit   1- 6-

          6- 0- 9   6- 0-

Tickets taken at door 3?
   "   sold at door   14.

A/c Spanish News 15/-
 " Lawrence & Wishart 12/8.

Sidney Robinson's accounts for the showing of the film Defence of Madrid *in Newport in February, 1937. See p. 70. (Sidney Robinson Collection)*

The Cardiff Trades Council and Labour Party

Secretary : E. ALLAN ROBSON, 51, Charles Street, Cardiff.

SPANISH AID COMMITTEE

Chairman :	*Secretary :*	*Treasurer :*
ALLEN POPE.	J. C. HARRIES.	H. O'CONNELL.
	Tel. : 7079	

---

*To all Working-Class Organisations and sympathisers with
the Spanish People's struggle for Democracy and Liberty.*

"COME TO OUR AID"

DEAR FRIENDS,

This appeal was recently issued by the Executive Committee of the General Trade Union Movement of Spain, to democrats, socialists, co-operators and trade unionists the world over. The appeal asked for supplies of foodstuffs, clothing, medical supplies and money to help secure victory for the democratic forces, led by the elected Spanish Government, in the shortest possible time.

A highly successful local conference was held in Cardiff, on Saturday, January 9th, at which 33 organisations were represented. It was resolved unanimously to call an all-in Conference for South Wales. The Conference will be held on Saturday, February 13th, at the Cory Hall, Cardiff, beginning at 3 p.m. sharp. The Conference is assured already of the full support of the Monmouthshire Federation of Trades and Labour Councils.

The Cardiff Committee believe that the appeal of the Spanish people will receive a hearty response from all socialists, democrats and humanitarians, anxious as they must be to mitigate the horrors of the civil war, the burdens of which fall most heavily upon those completely innocent of its creation—the Spanish women and children.

The Cardiff Committee feel that not only would this Conference assist materially in facilitating the collection of goods and money for the Spanish people and in reducing the cost of transport, but also that only by such a mass demonstration of solidarity with the Spanish workers in their struggle against international fascism can pressure be brought to bear upon the National Government to revise their policy towards affairs in Spain.

The Spanish people, enthusiastic but often unskilled, assisted only by volunteers of all nations, are putting up a magnificent fight against the conscript troops of fascist powers. It is up to us to render all possible assistance to these heroic workers, both men and women, and to their innocent children. Make the Cardiff conference a gesture of working-class solidarity. Let us make it quite clear that we stand by the side of our comrades in all lands.

All efforts will be made to secure a good speaker for the Conference. Organisations are invited to send 2 delegates. A form for notification of your intention to send delegates is attached. Please return this, together with delegation fees of 1/- per delegate, to the Secretary of the Spanish Aid Committee as soon as possible. Credential papers will then be sent to the delegates.

The fight in Spain is our fight ; we must do all in our power to ensure that it is brought to a speedy and successful conclusion.

Yours fraternally,

E. ALLAN ROBSON, *Secretary, Cardiff Trades and Labour Council.*

ALLEN POPE, *Chairman, Spanish Aid Committee.*

J. C. HARRIES, *Secretary, Spanish Aid Committee.*

*Call for delegates to the conference intended to establish a 'platform of unity'
over the 'Aid Spain' campaign in the local south Wales context. See p. 66.
(Sidney Robinson Collection)*

Cardiff 19 de Julio de 1938.

III Año Triunfal.

ESTADO ESPAÑOL
SUB-AGENCIA EN CARDIFF   Asunto: s/ Fiesta Nacional en Cardiff.

Europa.

No 17.

E:cmo Señor.

Publici

Entrado...
...

Hecho el 1-8-38

Tengo la honra de confirmar a V.E. el telegra-
ma elevado ayer a esa Superioridad con motivo del segundo
aniversario del Glorioso Movimiento Nacional liberador de
España, remitiendo al mismo tiempo adjunto una copia dupli-
cada de aquel mensaje.

En dicha ocasion fue izado en la Casa donde se
hallan instaladas las oficinas de esta Sub-Agencia el vene-
rado Pabellon de España y obsequie, como era debido, dentro
de mis medios y de la austeridad del momento, a los elementos nacionales españoles residentes en esta Ciudad, concu-
rriendo tambien a la reunion algunos subditos britanicos
simpatizantes.

Entre estos he de citar especialmente al Jefe
local de la F.E.T. Sr Richard Gordon Parsley, sobre quien
ya he informado con anterioridad,-Despacho No 14- y el cual
en toda ocasion se halla siempre dispuesto a servir a España prestando valiosos servicios a la Causa.

Los Oficiales de la Marina Mercante española, per
tenecientes a los barcos que se encuentran en estas aguas,
tambien estuvieron en esta Sub-Agencia, debiendo mencionar
por su categoria a los Capitanes D. Isidoro Urgelles del va-
por Hercules y quien es tambien Delegado Maritimo de Falan-
je, a D. Faustino Frias del "Cristina", a D. Jose Fradua del
"Marques de Urquijo" y a D. Luis Isusi del "Arinda-Mendi".

De entre los subditos españoles que se encuentran en Cardiff y mantienen su adhesion constante y entusias
ta por la Causa Nacional, he de señalar de un modo particu-

*Franco's agent reports the names of prominent Cardiff Falangistas and
guests present at festivities to celebrate the second anniversary of the Nationalist
uprising. See p. 74. (Archivo del Ministerio de Asuntos Exteriores, Madrid)*

ESTADO ESPAÑOL
SUB-AGENCIA EN CARDIFF

MINISTERIO DE ASUNTOS 7 de Julio de 1938.
EXTERIORES
ENTRADA II Año Triunfal.
N.º 76
2 0 JUL 1938

Europa.

No 16.

Asunto: remite recorte prensa acerca tripulacion
casi toda extranjera en un barco ingles
destinado a España.

Politica

curso a Propaganda
para de fecha
N.-

Hecho el 1-8-38.

Excmo Señor.

A titulo de informacion adjunto tengo la
honra de pasar a manos de V.E. un recorte de esta prensa donde se da cuenta del juicio seguido en contra de
un marinero ingles por no haber salido en el barco don
de estaba contratado el cual se dirigia a la España ro-
ja.

El asunto en si mismo tiene poca importan-
cia pero he considerado son de interes las declaracio-
nes del encartado quien ha manifestado en su descargo,
como se consigna en la referencia periodistica aludida,
que no permanecio a bordo por haberse encontrado con
que todos los tripulantes eran españoles o griegos.

Esto es una prueba mas de la clase de barcos que se dirigen a los puertos rojos los cuales no
tienen de britanicos mas que el nombre en la mayoria de
los casos , aunque para ellos se lleven a cabo las re-
clamaciones oficiales y campañas de prensa publicamente
conocidas.

Dios guarde a V.E. muchos años.

El Sub-Agente, Encargado del

Consulado de España.

Eduardo Ma Danis.

*Another of Eduardo Danís's reports, claiming that vessels sailing from Cardiff
with cargoes for 'Red Spain' were crewed mostly by Spanish and Greek
communist sailors rather than British sailors. The implication was that it would
do no diplomatic damage to sink them!*
(Archivo del Ministerio de Asuntos Exteriores, Madrid)

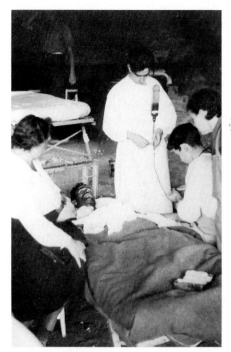

The death of Harry Dobson in the cave of La Bisbal during the Ebro Battle, as described on pp. 140–1. Leah Manning sits on the left; Dr Reg Saxton adjusts the blood transfusion bottle on the right. Here we have a superb example of the propagandist's art, through which the war in Spain and the struggle at home in Wales are brilliantly rendered synonymous. Dobson himself looks for all the world as though he has just been brought up from Blaenclydach pit after an explosion. (By permission of the Marx Memorial Library)

The forbidding façade of the Monastery of Puig, near Sagunto, used as a prison for International Brigade deserters. See p. 156. (Author's photograph)

THE NEXT STEP

Communists on Caerphilly District Council have asked that body to make a grant to widows and orphans of men killed while serving in the International Brigade in Spain.

The Caerphilly Leader protests against any prescribed contribution to 'Aid Spain' being imposed on local ratepayers. See p. 159. (By permission of Swansea University Library) outside the authentic guild of actual membership of the brigades. Whilst drawing on all of these, the present chapter seeks to achieve analytical focus by attempting a discourse based on themes rather than canonically established genres. The most ubiquitous of these tropes is covered first.

The Welsh *Brigadista*

In 1939, Lewis Jones's novel *We Live* was published posthumously. It was intended as a sequel to his first book, *Cwmardy*, which narrated the early life of Len Roberts through his own eyes, but always in the context of his family and his community.[4] The story is punctuated by the successive crises of the early twentieth-century south Wales coalfield, culminating in the rise of fascism and the Spanish Civil War. Though evidently produced with a propaganda purpose, the novels have no overt ideological content – after all, they were written to be read by Jones's workmates as well as his Party colleagues. Indeed, on the contrary, they contain aspects of sentimental (what would today be called soap-opera) stereotyping in both character and plot. More by happenstance than overt design, the approach represents a felicitous example of the technique of 'socialist realism' adopted by the CPSU as its main artistic medium in the 1930s.[5] On almost every page, and particularly after the watershed of the 1926 strike is reached, the indispensable role of the Communist Party in leading the Chosen People out of the Land of Egypt is demonstrated and affirmed. Once *Cwmardy* was published in June 1937, a copy was sent to Albacete and circulated rapidly amongst Welsh members of the British Battalion.[6] At this point, it seemed that the novelist himself might be going to Spain to join his enthusiastic readers on the front line of antifascism. But after developing signs of heart trouble he withdrew his name from the conscription list. Later, he told Billy Griffiths, who was desperate to fulfil the quota of volunteers imposed by London, that he had no right to demand such sacrifices.[7] *We Live* remained unfinished at its author's sudden death in January 1939, and – according to Hywel Francis – the final chapters were almost certainly added by Jones's lover, Mavis Llewellyn.[8] It was she, it seems, who decided to send Len Roberts, Jones's fictional hero, to Spain as an imaginary substitute for the real thing. In these pages, Len Roberts is 'chosen' by the local branch as one of its 'volunteers', and thus becomes the earliest representative in fiction of the standard Welsh Brigader. As such, he was to have many followers.

Both Llewellyn and Jones held prominent positions in the Welsh CP leadership. They had the opportunity to speak privately to Will Paynter, who returned to Wales in October 1937, knowing as much as any of its leaders of the detail of the infernal and often sordid sufferings undergone by members of the British Battalion. In spite or perhaps because of this the novel sets out to create a myth of selfless sacrifice and eternal reputation. After stoically accepting the party call, Len tells his wife, Mary,

> I was thinking of all the little kiddies who think so much of us when they come from school and shout 'Hallo, Len. How be, comrade' before asking for fag photos. They are so true. They follow us into our meetings and on our demonstrations . . . When they look back upon their youth, they'll be able to say 'We knew Len. He fought for us in Spain and Mary helped him' . . . Who knows? Perhaps, when they look back on the past, they'll be able to brag to each other: 'Our Len died in Spain'.[9]

But the ruthless reality of war on Spanish battlefields was sharply encapsulated by Len's real-life namesake, Jack 'Russia' Roberts of Abertridwr. Surrounded by noise and horror, pain and death, crouched under a bush at Brunete, Roberts scribbled a few lines of verse which have come to rival W. H. Auden's ode 'Spain' as the most famous English-language poem of the Spanish Civil War.

> Eyes of men running, falling, screaming
> Eyes of men shouting, sweating, bleeding
> The eyes of the fearful, those of the sad
> The eyes of exhaustion and those of the mad.
>
> Eyes of men thinking, hoping, waiting
> Eyes of men loving, cursing, hating
> The eyes of the wounded sodden in red
> The eyes of the dying, and those of the dead.[10]

This bitter and uniquely immediate testament may be compared with the lines written by Cardiff brigader, Tony Hyndman – in this case after some lapse of time – following his experiences in the battle of Jarama.

> He was dying
> And the blanket sagged.
> 'God bless you comrades,
> He will thank you.'
> That was all.
> No slogan,
> No clenched fist
> Except in pain.[11]

Such agonized effusions – emphatically not the kind of sentiment wished for by the commissars – may be contrasted with the poetic apostrophe to a Welsh Brigader written by T. E. Nicholas, immersed in the cocooned security of his study and the certain faith of his Party. 'In Remembrance of a Son of Wales (Who Fell in Spain)' represents an official version of the moment of martyrdom.

> Far from the hills he loved, he faced the night,
> Bearing, for freedom's sake, an alien yoke;
> He fell exalting brotherhood and right,
> His bleeding visage scorched by fire and smoke.[12]

Before the end of 1937 'Jack Russia' had apparently come to share the official Moscow line as reflected in the work of comrades like Jones and Nicholas. He wrote home to his children's carer: 'I bet that Junior isn't half swanking about his father fighting in Spain killing fascists and Franco.'[13] Meanwhile, Len Roberts dies in battle. In another powerful innovation, the emotional-ideological peroration of *We Live* is reached when Mary reads Len's last letter, brought back to Wales by a comrade, who testifies that 'we found him lying among a group of fascists and we brought him away from them to bury him with his own people'.[14] Thus Len had indeed died 'killing fascists and Franco' – for the tale is a metaphor of final victory-in-death as surely as the crucifixion of any Messiah. Cwmardy – Len asserts, before setting off up the line to death – 'Cwmardy and our people are worth going to Spain for, Mary.' In his last letter he tells her

> I could swear sometimes I was still in Cwmardy and that the Fascists are not far away in a strange land, but are actually destroying our birth-place and all it means to us . . . The same old hills are somewhere around here, and I know the same old smokestack and pit is not far away. The faces I see about me are the same faces as those in Cwmardy . . . Yes, my comrade, this is not a foreign land on which we are fighting. It is home. Those are not strangers who are dying. They are our butties . . . Fascism may kill us, Mary, but it can never kill what we die for. No, never! Our very death is creation, our destruction new life and energy and action . . . Give my love to all the comrades at home. Throw your whole weight into the Party . . . Sleep happy in the knowledge that our lives have been class lives, and our love something buried so deep in the Party that it can never die.[15]

Politically speaking, which to Jones and his comrades in the class struggle was the discourse of all human existence, the world had become Cwmardy – or Cwm Mardy, and even (a word not as clichéd in 1937 as it was to become in 1984) Cwm-unity. The community, in the innate oxymoron of its meaning, is a veritable apotheosis of internationalism.

Fifty years later, during a renewed period of representative right-wing assault on the coalfield, no fewer than three novels appeared which consciously referred back to the traditions and techniques of Lewis Jones's epic romance. In Emyr Humphreys's *An Absolute Hero*, indeed, the eponymous Pen Lewis is clearly based upon Lewis Jones himself. He writes to his lover, Amy, from Spain: 'The whole world has got to understand that we must win the anti-Fascist struggle. We've got to give Franco, Hitler and Mussolini and their capitalist chums one-way tickets to Hell. Keep your chin up and do what you can for the Cause.'[16] But Amy Roberts is a different sort of woman from Mavis or Mary – recognizably an adumbration of a later generation. She is relatively underwhelmed by Pen's death in battle, and by her poet-husband's hero-worship of the working-class martyr. Her concern is rather for the fatherless child in her womb and the future of a Wales which is remarkably distinct from Cwmardy. Despite his debt to Lewis Jones, and despite the contemporary struggle against 'Thatcher-fascism' during which his book was written, Humphreys's treatment of 'the Cause' seems in line with the more objective attitudes which are to be found in the greater bulk of relevant fiction published since 1939. Indeed, this relative objectivity is present also in a novel by Rose Thomas which appeared in the same year as that of Humphreys and which shares several characteristics of nomenclature and plot.[17] Here, too, there is a gulf of class, culture and geography between the romantic protagonists; a hero from the south Wales valleys (the pit village of 'Nantlas') who goes to Spain and whose name is Nick Penry; even – can this have been mere coincidence? – a heroine called Amy! In contrast to her Welsh equivalent, this English Amy follows her lover to Spain as a nurse, and helps to save his life during an operation behind the battle zone at Jarama. Like Lewis Jones's couple, they are both Party members, but in contrast to Len Roberts, Nick's loyalty is put to a test which it fails to pass. Soon after arriving in Spain, Nick wonders, in a letter to Amy, 'is this the right thing, being here? God knows. There is an element of Party manipulation in this that seems to have nothing to do with Spain. I hope I'm wrong.'[18] His agony culminates when, having disobeyed an order during an attack, he is punished by being put in charge of a firing squad for two deserters the Party has condemned to be executed. The moment of truth arrives for Nick as he is recovering from his wounds in Amy's care.

'It's finished,' he said wearily.
'What's finished?'
'All that. The Party.'
'Why?' Her voice was very gentle.
He heard the violent bitterness of his own as he answered her.
'Fuck the Party. Everyone's dead, aren't they?'[19]

The last novel we must consider in this section embodies the most complex and purely political text, and is quite avowedly a product of the ultimate and most miserably tragic of the great miners' strikes of the last century. Raymond Williams's *Loyalties*, published in 1985, is, above all, a deeply confessional document about the leadership of the British working class in a revolutionary class struggle by middle-class intellectuals.[20] The novel begins with a re-enactment of the Oxbridge students' vacation visits to the Valleys in the 1930s. The brilliant Cambridge science undergraduate and student Party leader, Norman Braose, meets and seduces Nesta, a miner's daughter from Danycapel. She gets pregnant, he abandons her. Later, she marries Bert Lewis, a local coalminer who has been to Spain with the British Battalion, and (thus) is the real hero of the novel, politically pure and morally perfect. However, during an action against the Germans in France during the Second World War, Bert is wounded and left horribly disfigured. His subsequent life is nothing other than a prolonged and tortured testament to antifascism. His fiendish features are a living monument to the sacrifices of the coalfield on behalf of freedom and democracy, and to the unblemished ethical rightness of the Popular Front. The handsome and well-connected Braose, on the other hand, is the real fiend. His unflinching loyalty to the Soviet Union dictates a sequential betrayal of everything in the cause which is really worthwhile. Braose goes to Spain – not to fight, but to take part in the Comintern witch-hunt of International Brigaders suspected of 'Trotskyist tendencies'. He thus compromises 'Spain' and the working class as foully as he compromised Nesta. In later life, as a prominent academic and government adviser, he provides Moscow with key data about western advances in strategic applications in his special field, computer technology. Cornford, Guest, Burgess, Blunt and Philby combined into one, Braose – whose very name recalls the Norman invaders and plunderers of south Wales – has recognized nothing as sacred except the twentieth-century's central Lucifer, Stalin.[21]

Whilst in the imaginative fiction produced by Welsh writers the International Brigader seems to play a complex and even contradictory role, in the work of 'outsiders', the Welsh 'volunteer for liberty' is often pictured in ways which do little more than confirm his mythic status as hero and martyr.

Here – even where the overall tone of authorial response to the abstract issues of the Spanish Civil War is neutral – the miner himself becomes an honorific stereotype. Indeed, this stereotype is, in itself, a generic feature of such stories. One example boasts not one but two brigaders based on Welsh originals.[22] The first is a black fighter ('Sergeant Vallee') from the Rhondda, evidently intended to evoke associations with Paul Robeson. The Spanish comrades call him Blanco, but 'I been called worse than that, boy. I been called a Taffy before now.' Vallee is killed during the opening assault of the battle of Brunete.[23] The whole incident used in the novel is taken from the memoirs of a Nottingham brigader, in which he writes about marching into action at Brunete with a Welsh comrade – whose name he cannot now recall.

He had rabbitted on interminably about how when the war was over I had to go and visit him and how he would take me to a pub which he knew in a green Welsh valley. He eulogized over this pub and described it so vividly that, in the dreadful heat and dust and plagued almost beyond endurance by the flies, I too came to see his favourite hostelry. I could clearly visualize the dark-haired barmaid plonking the pints of beer on to the counter and the foam easing its way over the top of the glass, creeping slowly down the sides and soaking into the towelling which lay along the top of the bar. Taffy had nearly driven me frantic with thoughts of such delights. When I had dived for the safety of the roadside ditch he had been right behind me and now, safe from the fire of the machine guns, I turned to look for him . . .

I worked my way back along the ditch and saw him lying on his face. I rolled him on to his side. He was dead. A bullet had gone through his forehead. His mouth hung open and was full of flies. His tongue, which had swollen from thirst, was protruding. His eyes were still open and covered with those blasted flies which were also working their way into his ears. It is a picture which has stayed with me for forty-five years and one which I am certain will never leave my consciousness.[24]

Betty Burton's novel also features a more central character, Ozz Lavender, loosely based upon the real-life Lloyd Edmunds, an Australian of Welsh descent who drove a supply lorry in Spain. 'He smiled as he mimicked the Welsh tongue. "Mam's a Thomas, you see . . . From Welsh Wales. Her da was a miner." ' Like Sergeant Vallee, Ozz Lavender dies in Spain fighting 'for an ideal that had emigrated with them from Welsh Wales'.[25] But in the alleged honesty of art, and *pace* Len Roberts, the ideal itself rarely survives the battle intact. In a novel by thriller-writer Robert Goddard, the villains of the piece are tracked to their lair with the aid of Frank Griffiths, a Swansea valley veteran of Spain. Frank is a recluse but also an autodidact, the shelves of whose cottage near Llandovery groan under the weight of books on history and politics by 'Hill, Hobsbawm, Orwell, Symonds on the General Strike, Thomas on the Spanish Civil War'. Fifty years earlier, as he saw it,

> A stand had to be taken. Against capitalism. Against fascism. Against the entire class system. That's why I went to Spain. And that's why I was sickened by what I found there. Because it was no more a class war than any other. Because settling old scores and winning internecine squabbles mattered more . . . than ensuring the defeat of fascism.[26]

In a novel by the Irish film director Neil Jordan, the central character is a Dublin volunteer who is captured by the Nationalists and imprisoned in a hellish POW camp. His cell-mate is a Welsh miner, wheezy with 'the dust' but defiant and inspirational. It takes six guards to haul him off to arbitrary execution by firing squad against a wall of the prison.[27] Lastly, in the film of Alistair McLean's best-seller *The Guns of Navarone*, one of the sabotage team, the engineer, Casey Brown, is transmogrified into a Welshman – if only by virtue of being played by Stanley Baker. The screenplay casting was evidently regarded as adding authenticity of ethnic detail to Brown's altered history as a veteran International Brigader, a man known in the trade as 'The Butcher of Barcelona', who (in his own words) has 'been killing Germans since 1937'. This example illustrates how casting Welshmen – above all, miners from the south Wales valleys – in the role of 'premature antifascist' became an item of verisimilitude within the relevant narratology in the years after 1939.[28]

Flocks of Iron Eagles

Second only to the theme of the antifascist Welsh warrior in the relevant textual accumulation is that of the bombing of helpless civilians by the ruthless enemy – usually, if not exclusively, by the Condor Legion, appropriate symbol of the alliance between Nationalists and Nazis. In the autumn of 1936, images of Madrid – both literary and visual – crowded with refugees, lying helpless under the waves of enemy aircraft, were transmitted ubiquitously to the outside world via Republican propaganda sources. Here, victims are invariably children and mothers, and the chivalric male instinct to protect the weak is summoned up and celebrated. T. E. Nicholas's hero has gone to Spain (his sonnet implies) since

> There, death-charged missiles blazed a trail of woe,
> Leaving each shattered hearth a vain defence
> While flocks of iron eagles, swooping low,
> Clawed out the life of cradled innocence.[29]

For some, it was the vicarious reaction of the oppressed which even more than the primary injustice inspired a further reaction of commitment. In Burton's novel, an upper-class British film-maker whose work incorporates footage of Madrid's agony, widely distributed in Britain to raise money, considers that this is not enough.

> I heard about an extremely small mining village in Wales – no work, no hope of it, kids half-starved, no money for food – yet apparently they made a collection and raised two pounds. That's a lot of money in farthings and ha'pennies. I think about that when I wonder if I should take up a rifle.[30]

Letters home by International Brigaders almost more often than not contain some reference to the enemy's bombing atrocities.[31] The theme of mass destruction, of the slaughter of the innocents, an intense awareness of a world in which the whole concept of the non-combatant civilian was slipping away, was a catharsis which moved many people who are now forgotten to writing, and especially to poetry. In December 1936, a single verse titled 'Madrid' was submitted by a reader and appeared (in Welsh) in the Baptist monthly, *Seren Cymru*. It pictures the city in the aftermath of an air raid.

> In the exhaustion of filth, I imagine
> I see persecuted ruins:
> And hear plaintive groans in wrathful debris,
> This is to survey Madrid.[32]

A south Wales man who had worked for nineteen years in a steel foundry left to seek his fortune in London in the early 1930s. William Glynne-Jones was primarily in search of literary success and fame, a typical aspirant artist of the 1930s. This was the decade *par excellence* when writing offered a rewarding, even exciting, living to thousands. Thousands more responded to the temptation, since a majority of the population regularly read books, most people had been given a firm (if often basic) literary education and a fair minority wrote something nearly every day to be read by others. Amongst Glynne-Jones's literary effects is a poem dedicated to '1936 – Spanish War, Local boy'.

I hear the distant throb
Of planes on their errand of hate.
It is war! . . .
The German beast shambles from the dark caves
To stalk his prey.
Children of Madrid, count your blessings,
Prepare to receive your crown of thorns.

Weep not, dear mother,
Though your child be but a bloody splotch
Upon the sun-drenched road . . .[33]

A good illustration of the literary education referred to above could evidently be found at the Intermediate Boys' School in Pontypridd, at the gateway to the Rhondda valleys. In 1938, a copy of a new poem published in Barcelona came into the hands of the school's Spanish teacher, Lawrence Londesborough. The work, entitled *A Europa*, was written in Catalan rather than Spanish, but one of the sixth-form pupils, H. G. A. Hughes, undertook to translate it into English, and permission was duly obtained from the author, Alfons Maseras. The poem addresses a reified concept of Europe as the historical matrix of civilization, the beneficent and eternal entity imagined by all its peoples from their first encounter with history and philosophy. But Maseras goes on to construct a rhetorical case for Europe's betrayal of Spain, not only of standing by impassively whilst its positivist legacy is destroyed, but in imminent danger of being itself terminally corrupted by complicity in the act.

Oh Europe! Stop this cataclysm!
See how the fields of Spain are burning,
desolate, and the towns
where flourishes so much heroism!
See the mothers and their tender children
stark beneath the ashes;
see those bewildered faces
which multiply in the trenches day by day.
. . .
Be not weak to combat evil;
do not return to barbarity now.

In the last year of the conflict, the young translator was often asked to read his work aloud at 'Aid Spain' meetings in the Rhondda, where it made a profound impression. In 1991, after more than fifty years, it was published 'in memory of those Welshmen who fought and died in defence of the Spanish Republic'.[34]

At an earlier stage (spring 1937) John Williams-Hughes, the Anglesey writer who had driven the Welsh ambulance to Spain, was working in Valencia for the International Red Cross. He was deeply troubled by the results – which he had dealt with at first hand – of the bombing of civilians in the Republican capital and its hinterland.[35] Along with Sir Richard Rees, a fellow ambulanceman and Welsh writer, he planned to bring some children to Wales, at least for a holiday. His idea was that they would attend the National Eisteddfod, to be held in August of that year at Machynlleth.[36] It was reported by Reuters that the Republican government was to form a group of children, apparently selecting them from among many school classes which had been set to making drawings of enemy aviation attacks on their own villages or streets, for use in propaganda projects.[37] The scheme (probably meeting the same fate as Williams-Hughes's projected Welsh-language broadcasts) was never fulfilled. Perhaps it was aborted by the prior arrival of 400 Basque children – at least ostensibly, victims of the bombing of Bilbao – in Wales in July; or perhaps because of the repercussions of a controversial speech made by the eisteddfod committee chairman, Dr Ashton, claiming that Wales's future would be assured if only its young people shared the dedication to their fatherland shown by the Hitler Youth in Germany.[38]

Doubting Thomases?

Whether or not Dr Ashton was partly responsible for the failure of Spanish Republican schoolchildren to sample the eisteddfod, the sentiments he expressed seem almost to be borrowed from a story by Wales's most celebrated student (and teacher) of Spanish, Gwyn Thomas. As a schoolteacher in Barry for some twenty years – and going on other evidence in his autobiography – Thomas would probably have found himself in wry agreement with Ashton about the disciplinary needs of the nation's youth.[39] As a teenager, he had been sent to Oxford University, for a reason which remains mysterious. Perhaps he represented the Valleys' revenge on the institution which had patronizingly inflicted so many over-curious vacation visitors on them. At any rate, strange to record about a sensitive boy from Porth, Rhondda, he remained practically untouched by the emotions of 'Spain', and if anything actually repelled by its effusion of sickly sentiment. According to one authority, he always wanted to write a novel about the Spanish War. The nearest he got was a literally knockabout scene in which a stentorian fascist on a street corner is silenced by the (otherwise feckless) brother of an International Brigader.

'He's one of them, is he?' asked Meirion.
'Them what?'
'Fascists. The sort our Iestyn went to fight against in Spain.'
'That's it.'[40]

In later years Thomas affected to be in cynical reaction against a studentish idealism which he had indulged in 1930s Madrid: 'My arms still ache from the banners I bore and my spirit yawns with disbelief at the incredible scope of my belief in mankind.'[41] His biographer asserts that he was a committed socialist at Oxford – though 'an almost invisible student'.[42] In an essay on modern Spanish literature published in the 1960s, Thomas counted amongst the writers of 'unique wisdom and fluency' not only Unamuno and Ortega y Gasset, figures who reflected a profound scepticism about the Spanish Republic, but also Maeztú and Azorín, who were its outright opponents. Furthermore, Thomas noted that, by the 1960s, Franco's Spain was making an economic as well as a literary recovery from the tragedy of 1936–9: 'The Iberian legs have a new stability, and there is a half-smile on the Iberian face.'[43] Thomas occasionally entered routinely supportive references to the 'last great cause' to which all writers of the 1930s and 1940s were by professional definition/subscription affianced.[44] For all this he remained, at heart, a personality who was apolitical rather than politically disillusioned – and in his home context, which meant so much to him, therefore a heretic.

There was – there usually is – another Thomas. Dylan was a near-exact contemporary of Gwyn's, but where the latter was an amused sceptic, the former was the assured unbeliever, obdurate and contumaceous in the depth of his being. In the mid-1930s, Dylan made the acquaintance of the Romilly brothers, and of John Cornford, Stephen Spender and other communist poets. Indeed, such a conjuncture could hardly be avoided, since he often dossed down in an attic room above a celebrated left-wing bookshop in Bloomsbury which was regularly frequented by the Party literary elite. When Cornford left for Spain and his destiny, he took with him a copy of Dylan's first published collection.[45] Dylan was patronized and cosseted by the *New Left Review* set, and it seems likely that he came under intense moral pressure to reflect the workers' cause – and even 'Spain' – in his writings, if only as a quid pro quo. The latter species of human consideration seems, in general, not to have been one by which the poet was much troubled. His first biographer (and patron) alleged that, despite having no intention of fighting in Spain, Dylan 'was passionately on the side of the Republic'.[46] Building on this unreliable foundation, one 1960s anthologizer, probably driven into error by the ingrained assumption that any major poet of that era was obliged to have entered a token anti-Franco protest, decided to include Thomas's 'The Hand that Signed the Paper' (composed in 1934) in a section of work devoted to the Spanish Civil War.[47] Dylan's authentic comment on the relationship of politics and poetry came in two complex lyrics he wrote in November 1936. Composed at the height of pressure and propaganda about suffering Madrid, they opaquely refer to the harrassment of political acquaintances, and roughly reject any role for poetry as a weapon of political commitment.

> O make me a mask and a wall to shut from your spies
> Of the sharp, enamelled eyes and the spectacled claws
> . . .
> The bayonet tongue in this undefended prayerpiece
> The present mouth, and the sweetly blown trumpet of lies.[48]

Thomas may sometimes have worn 'a very red tie [and] talked bolshie', but his residual attitude (as he told his unofficial tutor in communism) was that 'historically, *poetry* is the social and economic creed that survives'.[49] Thomas's close friend and fellow poet, Vernon Watkins, seems to have nursed a similar view of their trade. In the spring of 1936 Watkins took a holiday in Andalusia. He reacted intensely to what he saw in Seville, 'the beggar woman catching at her black shawl, the scarved man singing, the water-carrier crying pitcher on his shoulder agua agua'. But he saw it only in order to process it as art, not as anthropology, as abstract beauty, not as the human condition. Or was there, perhaps, a hint of a different consciousness in two lines in a draft of a poem . . .?

> Hid in the centre of impending cyclones
> I was caught up by despair's deep music.[50]

By the 1960s, when Jan Morris went to Spain to write a travel book, the *cante jondo* of political despair had faded altogether out of earshot. She was polite almost to the point of praise when dealing with General Franco, recognizing him at least for the fact that he had preserved the 'Old Spain' – a Spain without which her book would have had little artistic or commercial point. On Madrid, she depressingly observed

In the 1930s she had a universal symbolism. In her, as so often in Spain before, the passions of the world were demonstrated, and men everywhere could see themselves and their societies reflected in her agonies. It was this guinea-pig status that brought the young idealists . . . and placed Madrid at the very heart of the world's preoccupations. Today, she offers us no pattern of hope or warning. Her example fires nobody . . . and contributes little to the great issues that inflame us.[51]

In its spicy vocabulary, at least, Morris's reflections on her subject had not travelled too far from the instinctive anti-Spanishness which – as we have seen – lay underneath so many responses to the Civil War in Wales. Yet at the same time, even in the hottest flushes of the Black Legend, she lays down a cool principle of moral equivalence about the war which (in the present writer's opinion) would be difficult to better.

Never was a conflict fought more bitterly. Almost every page of its history reeks with cruelty. Sometimes it is the Army of Africa, Franco's spearhead, whose ghastly revenges still oppress us, as we read of the blood running down the streets of Toledo, or the hundreds of unarmed men slaughtered in the bull-ring of Badajoz. Sometimes it is the frenzied militiamen of the Republican armies, crucifying priests, castrating landowners, cutting off women's breasts or humiliating nuns. Nobody, it seems, was immune to the infection. At one end the mob often tore its victims limb from limb. At the other end the secret courts of the Communists condemned their prisoners first, and tortured them later . . . [Yet] eye-witnesses assure us that even the worst butcheries of the Civil War were generally committed not by sadists or thugs but by men who really thought they were pursuing an honourable purpose.[52]

PART IV: CHAMPIONS

7 Volunteers in Spain I: Soldiers and Heroes

The chairman of the committee appointed by the French and British governments to supervise the operation of the various Non-Intervention Agreements was the earl of Plymouth. As it happened, Lord Other-Windsor-Clive was a public figure in south Wales, with a splendid country home in St Fagans and an impressive collection of business interests. His work on keeping the Italian, German and Russian armed forces out of Spain in the winter of 1936–7 was less impressive, at least as far as observers on the left were concerned. Nonetheless, Cardiff County Council, which enjoyed a Tory majority, thought he was doing a sound job and awarded him the freedom of the city – an honour doubtless long overdue in any case.[1] A few months later, he delivered a speech to the national conference of the British Legion. He disarmingly admitted (on the one hand) that 'the [Non-Intervention] Committee has been criticised from all angles', but modestly claimed (on the other) that 'our work has not been in vain . . . Effective measures have been taken to prevent volunteers going into Spain, and in that we have achieved something concrete.'[2]

Data Analysis[3]

The concrete of Plymouth's claim was in reality no more than sand. Yet, although the reasons for it were little to do with his work, at the time of this speech – seven months into the war – it happened to be true that few Welshmen had managed to get to Spain. As we have seen, a month earlier the British Battalion's chief commissar made an emergency appeal for more Welsh miners to join them in the fight: a fight which was now the cause of 'all freedom-loving peoples of the world' – at least according to Stalin, their self-appointed spokesman.[4] But convincing evidence is lacking that a single representative Welsh warrior took part in any of the campaigns of the war's opening phase – the early exchanges in the Basque Country, the Aragon offensive, the stalemate encounter in the sierras north of Madrid or the chaotic attempts to obstruct the Army of Africa's march towards Madrid from Andalusia. No Welshman can be securely identified in the dozens of militia units which swarmed to the defence of the capital city in the autumn when Franco launched his so-called 'final assault'.[5] The same seems to be true of the two unofficial 'British' units, attached to the XI and XII International Brigades, which were involved in this bitter fighting, groups associated (respectively) with the names of John Cornford and Esmond Romilly. The banks of the River Manzanares, epic locality of heroic last-ditch resistance to fascism, was, I fear, a Taff-free zone – at least on the antifascist side.[6] By the end of the year, however, a trickle of Welsh water had begun to reach the semi-desert province of Albacete, where a new Brigade, the XV, was forming. Even then, only Pat Murphy – actually born in Cumbria of Irish parents – arrived in time to be selected for the expeditionary force sent (as No. 1 Company) to the Córdoba front in late December, an operation which represented the first combat experience of an official British unit in Spain. When the new British Battalion (No. 16) finally entered the line at the battle of Jarama in February – just as Lord Plymouth was addressing the British Legion – there were no more than thirty Welshmen in a corps of nearly 600 men from the British Isles.[7]

Thereafter things altered rapidly. The combat size of the British contingent as a whole was never again to reach the numbers who went into action at Jarama on 12 February 1937. However, in the weeks before the great offensive at Brunete (which opened on 5 July) the Welsh membership of the battalion achieved its highest profile both in terms of sheer numbers and individual importance. Perhaps as many as seventy Welshmen arrived at Albacete – in various parties of a dozen or more – in the spring and early summer of 1937, and the majority of these took part in the battle of Brunete. In the aftermath of that disastrous encounter – in which the Welsh contingent was decimated – recruitment slowed down sharply.[8] For the last three months of the year, hardly a dozen new arrivals were recorded. Enormous efforts by Party agents produced another injection of about forty Welsh recruits in the early months of 1938. Most of these reached the Aragon front just as the decisive Nationalist advance of the war was set in motion (early March 1938) or in subsequent weeks. As the Republican line was shattered, they merely shared in the catastrophic consequences of defeat, many of them becoming casualties or falling into enemy hands during a long sequence of routs and retreats.[9]

Only a handful of fresh Welsh faces were to be seen in the battalion during what remained of its active existence – the painstaking period of reconstruction in May and June, followed by a phase of intense preparation for the major offensive across the Ebro, which began on 25 July. This last battle was still raging when, in the last week of September, the International Brigades were finally taken out of the line. In December 1938, thirty-eight Welsh veterans were amongst the 300 survivors who returned to Britain and to their homeland.[10] A further twenty-two were released from Nationalist POW camps early the following year. The last of all, Tom Jones, a miner from Rhos, Wrexham, who had been reported killed and was certainly (at one stage) under sentence of death, arrived home from his war in April 1940, by which time most men of his age were heading in the reverse direction, towards another war – a war of which Jones and his comrades did not approve.[11]

Based on calculations made for the present book, the total number of Welshmen who were members of the International Brigades was 148, of whom at least 130 served in the British Battalion, and the remainder with other units (administrative, medical, communications, anti-tank battery or artillery) attached to the same Brigade, the XV.[12] This figure represents 6.6 per cent of the total number of volunteers from the British Isles – a higher proportion per capita than with the general population, but (as we have seen) markedly less so than in the case of Scotland and possibly less than that of Ireland.[13] For at least thirty-two of the Welshmen who enlisted in the brigade, no record exists of their ever having returned to Britain. Though it may be regarded as certain that a majority of these were killed in action or subsequently died of wounds, with others dying in hospital of natural causes, relatively few death certificates were issued to relatives. In a handful of cases, the evidence surrounding their deaths is vague and/or inconsistent enough to incur doubt – and even suspicion – as to the relevant circumstances.[14]

In his thesis, completed in 1977, Hywel Francis indicates a very high incidence of Communist Party membership among the Welsh contingent. Of the 104 cases on which he found information of political allegiance, no fewer than 96 were CPGB. To these, in Table C, I have added a further number who joined the party (mostly the PCE) while they were in Spain, as recorded in XV Brigade records in Moscow and London. Nevertheless, the overall density resulting is perhaps not as high as might be expected at just over 70 per cent. But whilst being lower than the British Battalion as a whole (74 per cent) it still exceeded (for example) that recorded in the ranks of French volunteers. It seems, nonetheless, that a high proportion of Welsh volunteers who had no marked connection with the coalfield (that is, around forty) were also – and probably by the same token – not communists.[15]

In any case, being a Party member was no guarantee of any given recruit possessing the political and military virtues required in 'The Comintern Army'.[16] Courage, loyalty, reliability, resilience, determination, initiative –

none of these was more in evidence among the faithful than elsewhere. Two in three of those officially recorded as killed as a result of enemy action were communists – more or less in line with the predicted quantitative average.[17] Indeed, frequent self-examination and attempts at reform within the Party cadres in Spain reveal constant dissatisfaction with levels of performance inside CP ranks. Part of the problem stemmed from the tendency to award furloughs in Madrid and Barcelona – cities from whence desertion was an easier proposition – strictly to Party members, whereas the less trusted infidel minority were allowed to roam only in the less exciting and more carefully supervised streets of Albacete. Leadership concerns also seem justified by the fact that comrades were no more immune than others to acts of indiscipline, ranging from minor infractions to much more serious crimes.

The question of desertion is at once the most sensitive and the most complex that any historian of the International Brigades must deal with. It should be emphasized at the outset that the attitude of the present writer is not one of shock and disappointment that so many volunteers deserted but rather of astonishment and admiration that so many more did not. Moreover, he fully accepts that it was both natural and understandable for men who had deserted to disguise the fact after their return from Spain. Conditions of service for any man who found himself in the war-zones ranged from the intolerable to the impossible. One over-cynical writer has implied that Welsh miners were tempted to Spain with prospects of sunshine, sea, sex and sangria, a package later to become strikingly popular with their descendants. They lusted mightily (she suggests) after an environment which seemed so absolutely in contrast with their normal enslaved existence, *de profundis et in tenebrae*.[18] The unlikely few who followed such illusions received a shock more damaging than can ever be imagined. Even Lance Rogers – certainly not one who fitted this description – later described the experience of Spain as his 'Gethsemane', in the philosophical dimension spiritually elevating, but in that of its daily physical demands often too horrible to bear recollection.[19] For this reason, amongst others, it would be both invidious and gratuitous to publish a list of those who took the desperate and dangerous step of desertion – acting in most cases under a pressure which (I believe) was unique in the annals of twentieth-century warfare.[20] On the other hand, it is much less acceptable for those who deserted to publish claims or allow inferences of infallible loyalty, even sometimes of indomitable heroism.[21] Such claims may be considered to have forfeited the subject's rights to a historian's silence, since silence would involve complicity in the deception. Yet this issue is also not always straightforward. Several Welsh volunteers who deserted in Spain, but were apprehended and (after punishment) rejoined the battalion, later acted with resolution in battle.

So far as I am aware at the time of writing (March 2003) only two Welsh veterans are still alive. One of these – Edwin Greening – came under suspicion of serious disaffection on the part of brigade commissars during the prolonged agony of the Ebro battle (summer, 1938).[22] At least forty of Greening's comrades abandoned their posts at some point during periods of service ranging from one week to twenty months. Furthermore, the records suggest an average rate of desertion amongst the Welsh contingent which is notably higher than the overall battalion figure (27 per cent as against 15 per cent).[23] The greatest haemorrhages came in 1937, during the battles of Jarama (February) and Brunete (July). In the former, men almost totally unprepared for combat were mentally unhinged by what was hardly less than a massacre, a withering fusillade hitting their ranks almost without warning from the guns of a well-trained professional enemy. At the latter, about a dozen Welshmen made unauthorized exits during the dreadful slaughter at Villanueva de la Cañada and Mosquito Ridge. Finally, in March and April 1938, enemy offensives in Aragon caused widespread and sustained panic, leading to another wave of desertions.[24]

In cases where apparently unblemished records are present, not all of the men, even where enlisted in main-line infantry companies, were necessarily present at any fighting.[25] For example, Bill Morrisey, a Cardiff seaman, spent virtually his whole Spanish sojourn in the propaganda and censorship department at base HQ, and was somehow able to avoid the front even in the direst emergencies, when all volunteers short of the halt and the lame were scrambled. On the strength of his loyal Party work he was given an impressive testimonial by the commissariat upon demobilization.[26] On the other hand, William Hopkins, a miner from Aberdare, was arrested on suspicion of desertion and political unreliability before ever going into battle, and spent the rest of his time in prison or labour camps before escaping and arriving home.[27] John Williams from Dowlais was taken seriously ill not long after reaching Spain, spending months in hospital before being allowed to return. He died of his illness a year after reaching home.[28]

One contemporary internal assessment of the British contribution to the defence of the Republic was highly critical of the standards of recruitment adopted, especially by the regional Party committees.

> It seems that certain regions or at least certain localities would have acted sometimes in the wrong spirit: 'He's useless here. So why don't we send him to Spain'. We've seen in Spain some inveterate drunks, specialists in

demoralization and division, who must have enjoyed a negative reputation in their localities. When the occasion offers it might be useful to study the origins of the individuals who have been a scourge as formidable for our comrades as Franco's bullets. Evidently, at the centre, it was difficult if not impossible to verify the volunteers who came recommended by the regions.[29]

This feeling, that unemployed but also politically uncommitted men were the main cause of disruption and poor performance, may well have been aimed primarily at the Scottish record, but it was probably meant to embrace the Welsh also. It was notable that persistent drunkenness, disaffection and desertion from the ranks was more in evidence among older comrades, and the Welsh contingent had a slightly higher than average ratio of the latter. This may have been a matter of 'Party decisions' over which comrades were selected to enlist, but in any case at least a dozen men underestimated their age in order to pass muster. Given that miners who were 40 years old probably *looked* a lot older, even by contemporary standards – not least because many had all their teeth removed at an early age – it seems unlikely that the recruitment officers were genuinely fooled. For some volunteers, this later rebounded on their heads, when after being wounded, they were trapped by a ruling that only injured men over 40 could be allowed to return home to England, and the medical commissions regularly ordered younger men who had recovered from wounds or illness back to the front.[30]

Collective Contribution

Assessment of the positive contribution of Welsh recruits *as a body* to the cause of 'Spain' is not an easy task. The greatest difficulty lies in the fact that their collective experience did not differ in any significant aspect from that of the British Battalion as a whole. In contrast to the Irish, whose nationalist background led to resentments and aspirations ultimately incompatible with the 'international' ideals/objectives of the leadership – and ultimately to outright rejection of its relevant dictates – there was no pervading sense of Welsh alienation from their English colleagues. Perhaps this last word should be amended to 'comrades', for it seems probable that this attitude was not just a matter of the absence of feelings of 'historical oppression' but also a positive indication of class solidarity. In this context, at any rate, it was clearly important that the Welsh differed from the Irish in having a substantial core of comrades who were ideologically sound, and – however paradoxical this may seem – were prepared to accept the middle-class accents and quasi-Sandhurst culture which distinguished the officer corps, at least in the battalion's early stages.[31]

In January 1937, Albacete reluctantly acceded to the demand made by Irish recruits for transferral to the American ('Lincoln') Battalion. Here they were permitted to develop a sense of collective national identity which was – if anything, and virtually by default – anti-British. Even when this arrangement, which was deeply unsatisfactory to André Marty and the commissariat, came to an end after Brunete, the sense of difference and separateness remained strong in Irish ranks. The commissars' awareness of the need to appease Irish sensibilities is reflected in the XV Brigade 'in-house magazine', *The Volunteer for Liberty*, which constantly carried news relating to Irish and Irish-American matters. In stark contrast, the very word 'Wales' only occurs twice in its pages and the word 'Welsh' was never resorted to at all! In other IB publications it was the same story. The official *Book of the XV Brigade* was edited by Frank Ryan, who had been the effective head of the IRA's propaganda machine. Consequently, the book features many dedicated accounts of the Irish contribution to the cause, while their more amenable cousins are accorded little or no recognition.[32] Perhaps Will Paynter (in private a normally patriotic Welshman) had mixed feelings when, in a testamentary epistle, he told readers of the *Volunteer* that: 'in training, in reserve, on rest, in battle, there must be no separation by nationalities. We must see the fight as one of a people for whom national barriers do not exist.'[33]

Yet some compromise measures were allowed in practice: for example, one study prints a photograph of Irish, Welsh and Scottish members 'displaying their own unofficial pennant'.[34] More significantly, when Welshmen first began to arrive in numbers – from April 1937 onwards – the salutory Irish experience, and a confident anticipation of the fighting qualities of the fresh recruits, seems to have persuaded the authorities to allocate most of them to a single company. In a memorandum addressing the nationalities issue, American commissar John Gates argued 'we must be realists', and that for men to be 'put in with a greater number of their own nationality . . . will put new spirit in them'.[35] This nostrum was apparently adopted in the case of Wales. Moreover, in an obvious tribute, it was No. 1 company – regarded as the battalion's elite unit – which was chosen for them.[36] The groups arriving during this phase amounted to a number not far short of half the eventual total of Welshmen destined to serve in Spain. One of the batches was seriously disrupted by the sinking of the steamship *Ciudad de Barcelona* on which many were travelling from France to Valencia in May.[37] Despite this setback, a relatively large number of Welsh recruits spent several weeks at the village of Madrigueras, the battalion's training centre located in remote countryside 20 miles north-west of Albacete, capital town of the province of the same name, and also the base for the whole International Brigade 'army'. At this time, the 16th (later renumbered as 57th) 'British' Battalion itself was stationed in defensive lines above the Jarama valley which had been hastily thrown up during the battle itself.

New arrivals, except for the surviving victims of the *Ciudad de Barcelona*, were filtered through to the front in May and June. Not too many of their pioneer predecessors were there to greet them – most having been casualties of the horrific Jarama fighting, or having deserted the ranks during it and still 'doing time' in consequence. All the same, in a further gesture of recognition to the Welsh, command of No. 1 company was now given to the Rhondda-born communist Alec Cummings, ex-NCO in the Welsh Guards, who had shown promising leadership qualities during the Jarama battle.[38] On 6 July, Cummings led his company into the 'heart of the fire' at Villanueva de la Cañada on the opening day of the Brunete offensive. He himself was badly wounded and only narrowly escaped death. During the next ten days, thirteen other Welshmen were wounded, seventeen fled the danger-zone, and several others simply broke down under the strain. Nine were killed.[39] If anything represents the critical moment for the Welsh in Spain it was these hellish days on the scorching plain west of Madrid. But here, too, the experience was a common one for all nationalities. The consequence of Brunete was that the British Battalion ceased to exist as a fighting force, and for some time there were very serious doubts that it could ever be reconstituted.[40]

A year later, when a number of Welshmen were imprisoned as POWs in the grim circumstances of San Pedro de Cárdena, the uses of adversity produced a keen sense of commonality, which may be taken as a reductio ad absurdum of the prevailing ethnocentric attitude in any Rhondda village or street.[41] In similar fashion, it was only once their compatriots, those who had luckily avoided capture or death during two long campaigns in Aragon, were stood down from the front, that they were allowed officially, for the first time, to express any national difference. In an attempt to maintain morale during the tense period of waiting for full demobilization and repatriation, various interest groups were formed, and the Welsh contingent had their first and only representative meeting in Barcelona. Here was an opportunity for the Welshmen to release all those fiery national resentments, bottled up for so long in the most trying of circumstances. The conjuncture was not spotted – or at least not exploited. According to the liaison officer appointed by the commissars – who was from Feltham – the meeting resolved (first) to pressurize organizations at home to send food ships, along with medical aid and cigarettes, specifically earmarked for their comrades in the Spanish Battalion, and (secondly) 'to petition the MFGB for the use of the Rest Homes for ex-members of the International Brigade in Wales'.[42]

Individual Achievements[43]

It was in the interlude between the major engagements of Jarama and Brunete that Maerdy's 'adoptive son', Will Paynter, took up the post of base commissar, an appointment which further indicated the commitment of Welsh comrades, and was at first seen as reassuring by his compatriots in the trenches.[44] Yet Paynter was under enormous pressure from the start. Resentment and frustration were simmering everywhere in the brigade's ranks. Morale was falling at the front owing to poor weather conditions, inadequate and (for most) inedible food supplies, boredom, drunkenness and general indiscipline. Around a hundred men had deserted in the face of the enemy during the Jarama fighting. Most of these (now in detention of various kinds), along with a large number of wounded (hospitalized or convalescent), made clear their wish to return home. Shortly after reaching Albacete, Paynter told Harry Pollitt that 'repatriation is the big question for us. Every day there are new demands. I am getting as hard-faced as an undertaker.'[45]

Part of Paynter's job was a recognized (if unofficial) role as soldiers' advocate both in this area and in the administration of justice. André Marty, a member of the central committee of the Comintern and administrative head of the brigades, was very reluctant to allow repatriation in general. Marty and Luigi Longo, head of the IB commissariat, were determined to apply the strictest criteria so as not to set evil precedents. Paynter found a similarly hard line amongst senior commissariat colleagues responsible for judicial proceedings, along with others who were in charge of implementing sentences. At first this mostly involved cases of major indiscipline, such as violence against comrades or local people, sexual crimes and serious theft. However, in the wake of the so-called 'uprising' of radical revolutionary organizations in Barcelona (early May 1937) the crime of political subversion was imagined and duly discovered everywhere, the charge often being entered against men who complained once too many times about their material conditions. Will Paynter struggled to make an impression in this perfervid atmosphere. He insisted that the CPGB committee in London support his drive for clear, rational and fair policies about repatriation, home leave and punishment of offences. His letters are full of agonized sympathy with men and their families, though this fell short of accepting the widely held view of both these elements that 'volunteers' (by definition) could not be kept in the ranks against their will. Indeed, if anything, Paynter felt that deserters were being treated too leniently, and was appalled that two such men who had reached home had been allowed to speak at Party-sponsored 'Spanish Aid' meetings.[46] Many years later, Arthur Horner gave a revealing description of Paynter's tense mood as he worked with his mentor, friend and comrade in these difficult days:

> One day I sat by Paynter's side as a pitiful procession of men came before his desk. Men who wanted to go home because their wives were ill, because they themselves were ill . . . but men who mostly just wanted to go home . . . I don't think I could have done his job . . . I said 'You're a bit tough with them, aren't you, Will?' He swept round. 'Arthur', he said, 'you can advise me about politics, you can advise me about Trade Unionism . . . but keep your b— nose out of this business'.[47]

After several weeks' lobbying and negotiation, Paynter reported that 'the situation in the battalion has considerably improved. I put it down to two main reasons. First, an improvement in political work, and second the infiltration of new men, mainly, say I with national pride, of the Welsh variety.'[48]

The consequences of Brunete were to show that this confidence was misplaced. But by this time the flight of Welshmen from the field was relatively low on the list of Paynter's problems.[49] Personal and political divisions inside the battalion leadership were cruelly exposed during the battle, especially by the so-called 'mutiny' staged by some forty unwounded (but hardly 'fit') survivors, who at a late stage in the fighting had refused point-blank an order to go back (for what seemed the umpteenth time) into the front line. Severe criticism on this and other points from Marty and his lieutenant, base commander Vidal, forced the wound open, and British commanders and commissars fell on each other with strident accusations and counter-accusations of responsibility. Paynter, who had visited the battalion at the front during the fighting, was obliged to arbitrate as senior CPGB commissar. He was particularly concerned about the behaviour of Wally Tapsell during the 'mutiny' episode, and recommended that he, Fred Copeman, Bert Williams and several others should be sent home for investigation.[50]

But Tapsell regarded himself as a scapegoat and, on his return to Britain, fought vigorously to reverse Paynter's judgement.[51] Furthermore, Paynter soon came under fire from even closer quarters. In late August 1937, Jack 'Russia' Roberts, acting battalion commissar, was wounded during bitter fighting at Quinto in Aragon, during the Belchite offensive. After treatment, he was sent to the brigade convalescent centre in Benicasim. From this salubrious posting, situated on a Mediterranean beach, Roberts – one miner who certainly never lusted after any 'package' – applied for repatriation in order to defend his Party seat during elections for Caerphilly District Council. When no reply was received from Paynter, the centre's American director took up the case, complaining directly to the chief brigade commissar about dereliction of duty, and adding for good measure that 'the British comrades are pretty burned up about the attitude of Comrade Paynter'.[52] But Paynter had decided that the battalion could ill afford to lose good Welsh Party men, and sent Roberts to train as an officer instead.[53] In the end, however, both Tapsell and Roberts succeeded in their challenges to Paynter's authority. In October, after a rigorous internal investigation, Tapsell was sent back to Spain as battalion commissar along with Copeman, who had been likewise restored as its military commander.[54] Roberts – despite already having been returned unopposed to his council seat – was allowed home 'for political reasons' in February 1938.[55] Paynter's arbitrations had been comprehensively overthrown. But despite mounting criticism, he was unwilling to back down. He assured Pollitt that 'once we can get rid of the deadweight of repatriations with increased volunteers, we shall have a really fine position . . . There is no political strife in our ranks . . . I am personally interested in remaining here until we have built something solid and healthy.'[56] A few weeks later he was on his way home, task unfinished but faith in its significance undimmed.

In the most comprehensive final report on the British effort in Spain which is extant from the hand of a senior member of the commissariat, Paynter's comportment in the crisis received a somewhat reserved assessment.

> At this time, W. Paynter, Welsh miners' union leader and communist, was Base Commissar. The work of the staff under his direction was undertaken by comrades [Bill] Roe and [Alex] Donaldson. It was a time when everyone was learning the ropes, when people had little exact idea about duties and responsibilities, and we still lack the facts to make a full appreciation of that situation. [But] it seems that Paynter should have done more to prevent or limit the crisis in English leadership following Brunete.[57]

Over thirty years later, Will Paynter's own defence of his record failed to throw any clear light on the crux issues he struggled to deal with in Spain.[58] His account was published when many (perhaps most) Welsh veterans of the war were still alive, and its tone reflects a certain consciousness of residual resentment, perhaps expressed with vigour, if in decent privacy. His poor grasp of the political background and context of the war – which he freely admitted for 1937 – seemed to have improved little by 1972. Astonishingly, for example, he recalled that the notorious 'May Events' in Barcelona were part of a *Catalan nationalist* uprising against the government![59] He blamed divisions in the Republican government for 'difficulties in arranging repatriation to Britain, even of wounded men'.[60] Paynter passes lightly over the desperate crisis within the British party leadership over Brunete.[61] *Mutatis mutandis*, his problem was the same as that of many communists caught up in the Spanish War – the agonizing interior conflict between the long-term interests of the Party, inflexible and abstract as they were, and the immediate suffering of the people it (or at least most of its members) wished to serve. Above all, Will Paynter's empathetic feelings for the men in his charge, and particularly for south Wales comrades and their families, are unmistakable. After all, he himself had been 'conscripted' by the party for service in Spain – only a few weeks after his wedding.

The history of another prominent comrade who had to deal with similar problems amongst the rank and file, though impressive on one level, evokes less sympathy. W. J. ('Billy') Griffiths was one of the last sizeable group of Welsh recruits, who arrived in Spain at the worst possible moment, in March 1938, when the whole of the Republican Army of the East was in virtual flight from Aragon to relative safety on the Catalan shores of the mighty Ebro river. Like Paynter, Griffiths was a Party conscript, who had been ordered to raise a platoon of comrades – at almost any cost – to accompany him to Spain.[62] In his own estimation, Griffiths made the most important contribution of any Welshman who went to the Spanish War.[63] Yet scepticism may be misplaced, since a similar assessment was offered at the time by Alonzo Elliott, the Cambridge linguist and Comintern agent, who worked with Griffiths during the ultimate phase of the battalion's existence in Barcelona.

> G. W. Griffiths (sic) is one of the best Welsh comrades. Although he still nurtures a certain spirit of sectarianism, which should be eliminated, he is a very steady influence and a good propagandist . . . He is the most notable among those who have been Party Secretaries in the English Battalion . . . He has shewn himself to be firm, capable and courageous.[64]

The most assiduous historian of the British relationship with 'Spain', James Hopkins, also seems to rate Griffiths highly, at least as an organizer and motivator of others, which are essential criteria of leadership. Griffiths was certainly the political commissar *par excellence*. After his early experience of action during the retreats, he never carried a weapon, although a large proportion of his work was done at the front, among the rank and file, often in dangerous circumstances.[65] His first view of Spain was the sordid spectacle of retreat, men in panic flight, discarding packs, rifles and even uniforms in their blind horror. He saw men whom he had brought to serve the cause of 'Spain' swept away into oblivion – in many cases only days or even hours after setting foot on Spanish soil. All this was profoundly formative for Griffiths, and in subsequent months no one worked harder to restore the battalion's discipline and morale. His first Party appointment was as 'education commissar' to the brigade, but for him, the only relevant education was in the Party catechism, for success in battle depended upon, and was determined by, political purity.[66] Like any chaplain, Griffiths worked by intensive invocation of the higher truth amongst the mundanely apprehensive and the doubtful. When, at the end of July 1938, the Republican Army recrossed the Ebro, prepared to put the fascist enemy to flight, no unit was better equipped for the task, mentally and in terms of training, than the British Battalion. For this, Griffiths was prominent among the responsible leadership.

Yet in practice, on the ground, Griffiths acted more like an informer than a priest, revealing (as it were) the secrets of the confessional to the police department of the organization. This was especially so during the prolonged Ebro campaign when he was Party Secretary for the XV Brigade as a whole. During this period, as chief and coordinator of an internal intelligence system, he systematically betrayed confidences received, both directly and through his agents, from men under intense pressure. As a result, many found themselves being closely watched, while others were reported to the dreaded SIM for action. It was the activities of Griffiths and his assistant commissars which led – for example – to volunteers ending up in the grim prison of Castelldefels, on the Costa Brava, where they were beaten up, tortured and, in some cases, murdered.[67] One wonders, for example, whether Edwin Greening ever knew that comrade Griffiths had reported him as a 'neo-Trotskyist' who had persuaded men to desert – information which might well have led to his arrest and death.[68] On a similar list, noted as a 'dubious individual, being watched', was another Aberdare recruit, William Durston, a quiet young man whom one comrade later remembered as 'very interested in politics and who always bought the *Daily Worker* . . . a cheerful lad of great promise. He was a scout in one of the British companies and he disappeared one night whilst on patrol. It was assumed that he was killed in a skirmish.'[69]

In his written testimony dating from 1964, Griffiths seems wholly undisturbed by the implications of various incidents in which Welsh comrades met their deaths. In June 1938, for example – almost certainly as a result of his surveillance – Tom Howell Jones was arrested and 'tried by a Battalion Tribunal on a charge of spreading rumours with a view to disruption'. Though he was apparently acquitted, Jones's file was marked as 'definitely unreliable'. Two months later he was killed by artillery fire in the Sierra Pandols.[70] Griffiths himself tells of how he denied home leave to his closest battalion butty, Sid James (Treherbert) who had previously taxed him with heartlessness towards others. James 'cursed me bitterly: "You don't want to go home yourself . . . and you are determined to stop everyone else"'. James was killed shortly after his last and fruitless confrontation with Griffiths.[71] Moreover, the latter seems to have developed a deep (and wholly unjustified) personal loathing for one officer, whom he calls 'Captain X' and was in fact Alec Cummings, a Rhondda-born comrade in whose death Griffiths was to some extent implicated.[72] As Hopkins argues, it is precisely (and solely) his fundamentalist belief in the party and its need for control which absolves Griffiths from the charge of being just a nasty little spy.[73] Yet even though – as he himself protested – 'this was no humbug. I was ready to die for it', and despite what seems to have been at the time a self-effacing attitude to his work, Griffiths's exploits cannot but make any modern observer, detached from the iron imperatives of his time, feel uncomfortable, even distressed.

One of the comrades whom Griffiths relied on for advice and information was Harry Dobson. Indeed, Dobson and Griffiths acting together seem at times to have reached decisions (or at least recommendations) upon the fates of fellow volunteers, up to and including that of 'execution'. It could be argued that Dobson had acquired some moral authority for such a role, since he was the most unambiguous example of a Welsh warrior hero produced by 'Spain'. He was already an authentic veteran by the time Griffiths arrived in the battalion. It was Dobson who allegedly posed the resonant question upon release from gaol – after serving a sentence for riotous objection to a fascist meeting in Tonypandy – 'How do I get to Spain?' Whether or not they picked up this announcement, the fascists seemed to know Dobson was coming. Appropriately enough, Harry's war began even before he got to Spain, since he was among the survivors after the troop-ship *Ciudad de Barcelona* was torpedoed by an Italian submarine. Arriving at the battalion in June 1937, Dobson went straight into action at Brunete, where he was wounded. After recovery he succeeded Tapsell as battalion commissar. He took part in the battles on the Aragon front in September–October, and was then sent to the Officers' Training School in Tarazona. Early in 1938 he was promoted sergeant and rejoined the battalion towards the end of the Teruel campaign.[74] During the retreats of March he was captured, along with his whole platoon. Somehow they escaped their captors' clutches and, by travelling at night across country, safely regained the Republican lines. Dobson later – doubtless mainly in obedience to orders – published an account of the exploit which lacks credibility in detail, but may have served its morale-boosting purpose in encouraging the others.[75]

Shortly after the Ebro offensive began, the XV Brigade was engaged in the siege of enemy positions in the hills overlooking the town of Gandesa. Divisional commander, General Walter, estimated that Gandesa's capture was essential to the further progress of the whole offensive; in turn, his staff decided that this success depended on the taking of the nearby summits, in particular the peak numbered 'Hill 481'.[76] Many incidents of the bloody and prolonged encounter between the English-speaking battalions and the 6th Bandera of the Spanish Foreign Legion, an elite Nationalist unit which was well dug in to the key pinnacles, have passed into legend. The hill was attacked repeatedly for four or five days, incurring severe losses, and all in vain. At the first onslaught, Dobson was badly wounded in the upper abdomen and fell alongside Morris Davies (Treharris). Both men sustained their injuries whilst attacking enemy positions without thought of their own safety, an action which deserves to be regarded as heroic.[77] It was an advanced and exposed position and only one stretcher party was in the vicinity. The bearers chose to take Davies, whose wound was more immediately life-threatening.[78] Dobson lay helpless and in agony within the firefield for some time before being rescued.

Eventually he was carried to Brigade HQ, a few kilometres away, in a complex of hillside caves near La Bisbal de Falset. Here a field medical team operated on him. Despite his sedated condition, Dobson later spotted and recognized Leah Manning, ex-MP for the Labour Party and Hon. Sec. of the Spanish Medical Aid Committee, whom he had heard speaking during the very antifascist rally at which he had been arrested. The surgeon, Reg Saxton, told Manning that Dobson could only last a few hours. At some point it was decided to give the patient a blood transfusion, even though his spleen had been destroyed and recovery was impossible. This technique was still a new one, adapted by Saxton from a patent system made famous by the Canadian, Dr Bethune. In a letter to a Welsh comrade, Manning later remarked that 'I may be able to send you a photograph taken of him in bed. We wanted to have a photograph of someone having a transfusion, for propaganda in this country'. In fact, perhaps as a result of this decision, Dobson survived for fourteen hours rather than the two predicted. Manning stayed at his side for most of this period and Dobson asked her to hold his hand. His last words were carefully chosen in order to emphasize the 'Unity' between his own party and that of the Labour MP. 'Comrade' – he said –

'they will never keep back the progressive cause'.[79] For her part, Manning was quite overcome by the occasion, and moved to a lyrically descriptive outburst:

It was a fantastic night, as I sat by this dying comrade, passing along the high winding road on the side opposite the cave, hundreds of camions passed by with singing reserves and loads of material and ammunition on their way to the Ebro, whilst winding down the glen at the bottom, came the ambulances with the dead, dying and wounded men.[80]

Harry Dobson was lionized as martyr and hero in Moscow, in Spain and in Wales. He is the only Welshman whose name appears (with other senior English-speaking dead) on the monument constructed by the Soviet engineer Percy Ludwick on a remote pinnacle of the Ebro battlefield.[81] He was the only Welshman to have a special obituary in the *Volunteer for Liberty* (though the tribute made no mention of his national origin). Uniquely, too, the Spanish Communist Party wrote to the South Wales District Party in appreciation of Dobson's contribution to the cause.[82]

A notable contribution to the life and history of the battalion – if in a manner rather different from Dobson's – was also made by two Rhondda characters who became fast friends on the Jarama front in the spring of 1937. Tom Picton was an ex-miner aged over 50 from Treherbert, who had earned a certain local fame as a 'mountain-fighter'. He and John ('Taffy') Foulkes, a Treorchy volunteer half his age, were fond of a drink and a scrap. Both became notorious for their appalling disciplinary records. The Cardiff student Sid Hamm, who was a rather fastidious young man, still found Tom's company irresistible, and was upset when his behaviour led on one occasion to expulsion from the battalion. On the other hand, he took great exception to Taffy, whose drunken antics earned him time in the calaboose and even in the feared 'punishment battalion' behind the lines.[83] In letters to a friend at home, Picton reported

I have run into Johnny Foulkes on this front . . . all we Welsh boys are going to have our Photos took and we will want you to put it in the [Daily] worker . . . Mrs Pitcairn was up here [and] was interested over my ear I told her it may be a sovernear for Fronca she had a good laugh . . . We are about 40 Welsh boys on this front and Dan Davies, J Williams and Foulkes and a fellow from Merthyr Lance Rogers are on my gun with me [but] a bloody heap more of the boys hanging around the [street] corners should be here with me. I was popular at the Ystrad Police [Station] but I am very much more popular out here because of my Mad Stunts they say here comes Mad Taff . . . We had a hell of a Drive at a place called Brunete I had a crack in the Neck but am OK. Well George I would be pleased if you could see about my Girl, I mean that shes in a good place . . . and explain to her what we are fighting for as she don't understand . . .[84]

On one occasion Picton conspiratorially informed his pal that he had volunteered for 'a very dangerous mission . . . cant tell you what it is but I am going and if I dont come back Jonnie Foulkes will let you know . . . tell the boys at Treherbert about it if things don't work out'. Taffy Foulkes added his own postscript to this cryptic message. 'Today is the first of June and Tom Picton does his stuff [he] has enough bombs in his bag to kill the fucking Italian army on his own I am writing in case anything happens because Pic is as Dull as a fucking bat.'[85] It seems that in reality, Tom had been sentenced to a longer-than-usual spell of detention, or was intending to desert. For all this, Foulkes and Picton both redeemed themselves in the end. The former was officially reported by commissars as 'cowardly, lumpen, a demoralized deserter', having run away during fighting both at Jarama and at Brunete.[86] On one occasion he reached Barcelona and was rescued from a desperate situation by no less a comrade commissar than Jack Jones, later to be General Secretary of the TGWU.

Looking across the dockside I caught sight of 'Taffy' Foulkes a well-known character in the Battalion who had been 'absent' for some time, in fact he was thought to have deserted. I had little doubt that he had been living (and probably sleeping) on the ships and hoped eventually to stow away on one of them. I persuaded him to come back to the Battalion with me . . . I was pleased about this because Taffy was the proverbial jester, and very popular.[87]

During the Ebro campaign, after repeated spells in gaols and a 're-education centre', 'Taffy' the jester acted with such resolution under fire on Hill 481 that he was commended in the pages of the *Volunteer for Liberty*.[88] For his part, Picton reformed to the extent that he was even admitted to the ranks of the Communist Party, before being captured during the retreats of spring 1938. However, the Francoist authorities were less tolerant and understanding of Tom's temper than his commissars had been. In a POW camp near Bilbao, Picton's resistance to bullying led to his last fight. After punching one of the guards he was hauled off and summarily shot.[89] Neither of these men conformed to the template which the party, and the 'cause' generally, would have wished to preserve and polish, yet they are, surely, at least equally representative of the men who went to Spain. Telling us more, and differently, about the ordinary lives of International Brigaders, they were 'Celtic Radicals' of a subversive stripe, who remained to the end in many memories for a variety of reasons, good, bad, and sometimes ugly.

At the same time that Dobson was recovering at Benacasim from his involuntary dip in the Mediterranean, another warrior was on his way home to Wales after 'doing his bit' for the cause. However, Frank Thomas, though born in Pontypridd, 'capital' of the Rhondda coalfield, had fought for the *other* cause – as majority opinion all over the world would still have it, the 'wrong side'. In May 1937, Thomas was acting sergeant in the same Legionary Bandera whose stubborn defence of Hill 481 a year later was to be the occasion of Harry Dobson's death. During a Republican offensive in the Gredos Mountains – an operation which forms the historical background to Hemingway's novel *For Whom the Bell Tolls* – the 6th Bandera was sent to take part in a diversionary attack south of Toledo. Thomas led his *pelotón* forward into an advanced section of the enemy trenches. Shortly afterwards subjected to severe counter-attack, the position became untenable and most of Thomas's comrades were killed around him. After being shot through the jaw and cheek, he attempted to regain his main lines by scrambling up an exposed hillside, and in the process caught another bullet in the leg.[90] After his face was stitched back together in hospital, Thomas was sent for convalescence in the remote town of Cáceres. There he met members of the so-called 'Irish Brigade', the 15th Legionary Bandera, who had been stationed on the Madrid front for four months, but were now preparing (in some disarray) to go home. His new friends suggested that he might like to accompany them as a sort of honorary Irishman. He was 'smuggled' out of Spain with the 'Bandera Católica Irlandesa', and reached Cardiff again via Lisbon and Dublin in late June.[91]

Thomas agonized both then and on many subsequent occasions about his decision to leave the Bandera without permission. To him, desertion was a course of last resort, and left an indelible stain on any soldier's record.[92] Yet, like so many compatriot-enemies of the International Brigades, he felt driven into the decision and ultimately justified in taking it. It must be said that his rationale differed somewhat from many of theirs. No International Brigader from the British Isles had a combat record equal to that of Thomas.[93] He had been in constant battle action since the previous October, with only the occasional brief respite. Trying to cope as a member of a Spanish army unit, desperately picking up survival techniques in a language previously unknown, he was promoted twice in recognition of his personal qualities, while the 6th Bandera collectively accumulated the highest battle decorations. With the exception of one suicidal platoon of Morrocans, his unit penetrated further into the centre of Madrid than any other during the ferocious fighting of November 1936. In Cáceres, despite his record and his injuries, he knew that he was expected to return to the front as soon as the doctors pronounced him fit. All the friends he had made in the Bandera (indeed, some 90 per cent of its original membership) had been killed or rendered permanently *inútil*. Meanwhile, Thomas himself had been increasingly subject to suspicion and even minor harrassment by Spanish officers. This reached a peak during the Basque campaign, when the apparent connivance of the Royal Navy over British supplies to the defenders of Bilbao led to considerable anti-British feeling in the Francoist zone. In an odd coincidence, therefore, Thomas felt a political pressure, not wholly unlike that experienced by volunteers on the other side, and which was frequently a component factor in their desertion.[94]

Thomas's detailed account of campaigns in which he was frequently in harm's way contains few traces of personal boasting or vainglory. It is also disarmingly honest about matters (such as military discipline, shooting of prisoners and plunder of civilian property) on which no veteran of the British Battalion has ever offered more than passing and usually nebulous comment. Unlike many – perhaps a majority – of the latter, he was an authentic volunteer. Like them, however, he remained proud of his service in Spain. Where they lamented the overthrow of a just cause, he was confident in his judgement that he had helped to save the country from communism. In 1940, Thomas offered a similar service to the Finnish Embassy when an appeal for foreign volunteers was made to help that country's defence against Stalin's imperialist aggression. It is noteworthy that on this occasion he cited his Spanish qualifications, and explained 'although a Conservative politically, I joined General Franco's Army for (1) a love of adventure, and (2) through an intense dislike of Communism. I think it only fair to point out that I am also opposed on principle to Fascism.'[95]

8 Volunteers in Spain II: Victims

On the great plaque constructed of Welsh coal, slate and steel which is placed above the entrance to the Miners' Library in Hendrefoilan, Swansea, thirty-three men are commemorated for sacrificing their lives 'in support of the heroic struggle of the Spanish Republic against Fascism'. These are perhaps the 'glorious dead', but also in many senses the 'heroic victims' of Wales's involvement in the Spanish Civil War.[1] In a majority of cases, the deaths of these men is established only by hearsay report. Few death certificates are extant, and in no specific case has any reliable information ever been found regarding the location in Spanish soil of earthly remains. At least three of the soldiers whose names are inscribed at Hendrefoilan can be regarded as 'Welsh' only by the operation of minimalist criteria. For one of these, sources of information about his very presence in Spain have either been lost or were never substantially present in the first place. Most seriously of all, in at least four cases, the evidence for death in action is open to question on circumstantial grounds. I wish to deal with three of these in detail.[2]

The Tragedy of 'Captain X'

The destiny awaiting Alexander ('Alec') Cummings in Spain was the most tragic and the most mysterious. In terms of equal achievement in the military and political-administrative spheres, Cummings's record is (prima facie) the outstanding one of any Welsh member of the International Brigades. Born to working-class Rhondda parents in 1908, he found himself unemployed around the time of the General Strike and entered the Welsh Guards. He seems to have applied himself to the job with determination, as well as using every spare moment in reading 'good' literature and learning French. He left the army – with the rank of sergeant – in the early 1930s, and found work as a furniture salesman. He later became a WEA lecturer in Liverpool, and joined the CPGB in 1935. The next year found him in Cardiff, where the party sent to him to organize 'agitprop' activities, amongst other things liaising with the local YCL group whose fortunes have already been touched upon.[3] As party worker and teacher he was capable of impressing men of his own age and class background, like Bill Coles, a Cardiff steelworker killed in the Jarama battle, and younger, middle-class students like Sid Hamm – and probably influenced both in their decisions to go to Spain.[4] Cummings himself arrived at Albacete in the first week of February 1937, and by the first dreadful day of action at Jarama, only a week later, was in charge of a platoon. He acquitted himself well in those days of panic and carnage, and was subsequently marked for promotion.[5]

Yet even in this period there were ominous signs of febrility in Cummings's behaviour. At quite an early stage of the long and frustrating period of garrison-duty on the Jarama front (February–June 1937) he unsuccessfully applied for transfer to the medical services as an ambulance driver.[6] By the time Sid Hamm arrived at the front in mid-May, Cummings was OC of No. 1 company. But he then got into trouble with a senior colleague and spent a short time under arrest. As a result of this incident, he again applied for transfer – this time within the battalion – to the machine gun company.[7] One report, headed 'Alec Cummings – Coward, Careerist', roundly condemns his over-ambitious and petulant striving for recognition: '[He demanded] that he should be Commander of [the] B[attali]on and when he was turned down said he would not go to [the] front – Has since been made a Co. commander and party sec. There [are] reports that he is very weak showing fear etc.'[8] Despite such opinions, Fred Copeman, the battalion's 'no-nonsense' commander, remained impressed by Cummings, and evidently recommended his appointment as adjutant.[9] As we have seen, he led his company and its forty-odd Welsh members into action at Brunete.[10] On the opening day, the XV Brigade went over the top prematurely because of the unexpected resistance of a strategically crucial village, Villanueva de la Cañada.[11] The fighting was so bitter and costly (especially to the two rifle companies, Nos 1 and 2) that a mood of bloody annihilation swept through the men as the enemy seemed on the point of succumbing. Copeman later recalled that one company commander, Charlie Goodfellow, 'could be relied on not to allow any licence, but I was not so sure about Alec, who had waves of cynical contempt for what he termed "misplaced sentiment" and at the same time an artist's attitude to beautiful things. A curious lad Alec.'[12] During an incident of the siege which later became notorious, Cummings took a bullet in the shoulder, which broke his collar bone cleanly but lodged in a lung. He was to recover from this terrible injury in physical but not in psychological terms. His confidence was terminally destroyed, his mind haunted by the prospect that, one day, he might be ordered back into action. If not already its slave, he certainly now resorted helplessly to the genie of the bottle.[13]

At first, the Party appreciated Cummings's courage at Villanueva. Frank Ryan included a tribute to him in the official *Book of the XV Brigade*.[14] Fred Copeman, twice battalion commander, 'recommended him for personal bravery'. Other colleagues were similarly generous: one commissar reported him as 'a steady and reliable soldier with good sense of responsibility . . . has worked hard and received many disappointments but has faced up to all and shown great courage'.[15] After two months in hospital, Cummings was allocated to the base at Albacete where he occupied a series of important party posts. At first he was in charge of enlistment registration of incoming British volunteers – a light enough task at this stage.[16] For a time he filled in as acting base commissar, when John Mahon, Paynter's succesor, was unwell. Later, however, he was appointed to head up the XV Brigade 'servicio de cadres', a department which vetted Party members for commissariat work.[17] Cummings carried out his work in close liaison with various police and intelligence services, including the newly established International Brigade branch of the SIM.[18] The job involved knowledge of colleagues' personal files up to a very high level of authority, and (moreover) procurement of fresh information in order to keep them up to date. He handled the application for home leave of one future battalion commander, Sam Wild, and the case for promotion of another, Bill Alexander.[19] He almost certainly helped to advance the career of Billy Griffiths. In the process, however, he made enemies. Several later reports speak of his arrogance, aloofness and bureaucratic pettiness. One, more specifically, added

All the time he was in Albacete he did little but criticize the work of others. Moreover, he took it upon himself to proclaim to all and sundry the necessity of having 'informers' in each of the fighting companies, and this view was not put forward discreetly but loudly proclaimed. He often spoke of having 'his spies and advisers' throughout the base.[20]

Cummings's main problem, however, was that he had failed to disclose his British army service to party officials in Spain. Worse, it seems possible that even his British comrades knew nothing about his career in the Guards. Indeed, it was only long after the Spanish War that – it seems – his brother revealed the truth to Hywel Francis.[21] The implications of this deception for Cummings's presence and future in the International Brigade now seem obvious. In April 1938, following the enemy breakthrough in Aragon, the base at Albacete was hurriedly abandoned and the brigades' HQ moved to new quarters in Catalonia. At the same time dozens (if not hundreds) of assorted desk-workers and malingerers were sent to the front in order to bolster critically depleted fighting units – Alec Cummings amongst them.[22]

Not long after rejoining the battalion, Cummings broke down and, pleading exhaustion and illness, was admitted to hospital in the rear. Bill Rust, chief CPGB agent in Spain, told Harry Pollitt frankly that he was avoiding the front. 'He cracked badly when told to rejoin the batt[alio]n and has taken this means of getting out. He has lost his nerve. It would be best to save him by sending him home but that is impossible.'[23] In June, far from being 'saved', he was passed fit again and ordered back to the battalion, now in full training for the forthcoming Ebro offensive, as a section commander in the Spanish company (No. 3).[24] As the prospect of action approached, however, he sought out Billy Griffiths – whom he fondly imagined was a sympathetic Rhondda comrade – and confided his troubles. Griffiths himself takes up the story

> He became quite agitated and threatened to desert if they forced him into action again. He wanted justice . . . I promised to examine the position and have it discussed with the authorities. Secretly I was disgusted. I knew something of the man's record, and as a consequence he should have been the last to act this way. I discussed the matter with Cooney, and a meeting was arranged . . . We met under a tree – Cooney and Capt. Fletcher, who was now in command of the battalion during Wild's absence, myself and Dobson from the Brigade. The man's conduct was most reprehensible. On this we were agreed. On what steps should be taken, there were sharp differences. Dobson held that this was not the case of an ordinary individual who had broken down. One had to take into account his rank and that he was responsible for other men. Then there was his record. He was not new to this kind of business. He had many times been faced, as we were now, with like problems. He had been unduly harsh and was unpopular as a consequence. Even so, this was not our main consideration. Desertion was now being considered – a serious matter. There were a number of unfortunates awaiting trial for this offence. The Army Headquarters were insisting on severe punishment. This man was well known. It was too dangerous to allow him to continue in his command even if he was prepared to do so. If we showed undue leniency, it could affect morale adversely. Dobson was for a Court Martial organised by Brigade with the recommendation that he be shot. I supported Dobson. Neither Fletcher nor Cooney were for this course. So, the matter was referred to the Brigade with no recommendation. Nothing happened.[25]

Claiming sickness, Cummings managed to stay behind the lines during the opening phases of the Ebro campaign, but in mid-August a medical commission again ordered him to rejoin his unit.[26] He wrote to a Cardiff friend of having had to spend time in 'the hottest spot I have ever been in, terrific[ally] high up in the rocky hills with no hope of digging anything like a moderately safe kind of trench or refuge . . . a hell of a place made a thousand times more worse than hell in the night'.[27] On 6 September, during a brief pause in the XV Brigade's frantic defence of a section of the front against massively superior enemy counter-attacks, all commissars were called to a meeting. They were told to assure the men that

> these deserters are not the real representatives of the International Brigades. They are adventurers, criminals and cowards. We have to put such people away from us. We have to pass resolutions demanding the maximum penalty for these deserters and encourage hatred of them among the ranks.[28]

By this time, the XV Brigade had already been ordered back into action on more than one occasion after being relieved with the promise of permanent withdrawal. A week later, Cummings was arrested for being drunk on duty and sent to brigade HQ under escort. He was demoted to sergeant and sent back to the lines.[29] Not long afterwards a vicious and sustained attack developed. On 20 September the 57th (British) Battalion suffered the loss of eleven men in action, including four killed outright, while eight others deserted.[30] During the course of that day, Battalion Commissar Benny Goldman received complaints that Cummings had set up his command post too far to the rear, in a place where communication with his men was impossible. Goldman confronted him with the problem, but Cummings refused to comply with his advice.[31] Three days later the brigade was relieved for the last time. Cummings was not present at the consequent muster. Goldman later noted that he 'was reported killed or captured after the Ebro action'.[32] Even though writing nearly thirty years later, Griffiths was a little more precise, fixing his death at 'the last day in the line, September 22nd', and adding 'I have no doubt that to his family and friends, Captain X was a great loss, but I must say hardly that to the movement [sc: Party].'[33]

In the circumstances related above, an element of uncertainty about Alec Cummings's precise fate seems justified.[34] Perhaps he was indeed killed or captured by the enemy. Perhaps he had deserted *before* being captured and killed. But it seems equally likely that someone in authority on his own side took the law into his own hands. Judging by the wide range of opinions sought, suspicion of Cummings by the SIM on political grounds seems more than likely.[35] A report by Commissar Ollerenshaw noted that at Albacete 'he was regarded by rank and file as sectarian . . . there seemed cause for complaint relating to discrimination shown in some cases where comrades were bad politically'.[36]

Another, by Alex Donaldson, was even more damning. 'Weak politically – obviously petty-bourgeois in outlook – unable to stand criticism . . . not politically active. When wounded cried like a child. Obviously afraid to return to the front.'[37] It seems that rumours about Cummings's past had now begun to circulate. 'If he returns to England [he] should be watched' warned one commissar – *who also did not seem to believe that he was dead*.[38] A few months later, Alonzo Elliott noted that

> Cummings disappeared during the Ebro fighting, but his bad conduct in the summer of 1938 induces the feeling that he had not been a good choice [as senior cadre]. In any case it would be useful to verify the rumours we have heard on the subject of Cummings – that he had been an ex-policeman.[39]

There seems to have been more than one reason for the Party to quietly dispose of the embarrassment represented by Comrade Cummings. In 1996, one of his Cardiff contemporaries and comrades informed the present writer that he had been 'executed for cowardice'. This information originated from an intimate source within the Party. It seems possible that the same source informed Silvia Taylor that her husband had met a similar fate some months earlier.[40] Whatever the truth of his death, however, Cummings's right to a place on the Welsh Roll of Honour can hardly be open to dispute.[41]

The Faint of Heart

This right must be regarded as less clear-cut in the case of Cummings's Cardiff comrade, Gilbert Taylor, and likewise that of the Neath communist Alwyn Skinner. Taylor, as we have seen, went to Spain for all the wrong reasons.[42] But ironically, the particular misdemeanour which lay behind the decision was not his fault. In a very real sense, Taylor was condemned to death before he even left Wales.[43] In effect he was 'sentenced to the International Brigade' by Harry Pollitt, at a time (autumn 1937) when the British Battalion was desperate for new blood, but when the appalling casualty rate in battle was all too well appreciated by the party leadership. Indeed, it seems to the present writer that the relevant circumstances do not preclude use of the word 'blackmail' in describing Pollitt's decision to present Taylor with the choice between explaining his conduct to the police or 'volunteering' for Spain. Skinner on the other hand seems to have been a keen and active antifascist, who (for example) worked hard in mobilizing Swansea to 'resist' a Mosleyite meeting in the town.[44] A member of the Neath CPGB cell, he was friendly with the Abercrave Spaniards, two of whom volunteered later in the year. Skinner himself went out as a member of one of the various groups of Welshmen who left in the spring of 1937.

Even if no doubt existed as to his honourable death in action, Taylor (in any case) had only the flimsiest qualifications for being considered 'Welsh'.[45] He was a product of the expanding semi-professional culture of south-east England – target of snooty satirists like Evelyn Waugh – hailing from the synthetic 'New Town' of Welwyn Garden City, and a printer by trade. He met and married Silvia Shaxby in 1933, and later moved to Cardiff to be nearer her parents, who were Liberal antifascists. Taylor, who was already a party member, joined the local YCL. His Party work introduced him to Alec Cummings and Sid Hamm. For some time he managed the branch of Collett's bookshop in Cardiff, a place which became the main contact location for men desirous of enlisting in the International Brigades.[46] Given the inglorious circumstances of his own recruitment, it is hardly surprising that, once in Spain, he embarked on a determined campaign to avoid being sent to the front. He put his skills to good use in production of so-called 'wall newspapers', a propaganda medium highly valued by commissars, in Albacete and the new British base at nearby Tarazona de la Mancha. His existing personal connection with Cummings, who was then a power in the brigade HQ, proved of great importance to him. Certainly Taylor seems to have been one of the beneficiaries of 'discrimination shown in some cases where comrades were bad politically'.[47] At any rate, he was not dispatched to the battalion at the front until fully three months after his arrival. Even when all available reinforcements were called for during the battle for Teruel, and the training (or reserve) company was moved out en bloc, Taylor was left on his own in Tarazona.[48] His call finally came during the closing stages of the battle, at a time when the Republic was losing more men through the effects of fighting in sub-zero temperatures than to enemy action. Cummings later claimed to have protected Taylor for as long as he could, but that 'suddenly everything was taken out of our hands & G was shipped away to the infantry'.[49] Taylor feigned illness almost immediately on arriving at the front, and was sent to hospital. Writing home from Benicasim, he bemoaned being deprived of action with his comrades, and after two weeks the medical tribunal obligingly prescribed a return to the front. Just before boarding the lorry that was waiting to take men deep into the Aragonese sierra, he wrote to his wife that 'I'm feeling just a bit churned up inside to be quite frank!'[50] By this time, however, the XV Brigade had been pulled out of the Teruel sector, and sent to defend the front around Belchite, 150 kilometres further north, where a major enemy offensive had opened on 8 March. Taylor seems to have caught up with his unit amidst the chaotic circumstances of headlong retreat from a hotly pursuing enemy. According to one muster, he went missing almost at once.[51] Cummings claimed that 'one comrade remembered seeing him wounded and left behind'.[52] But it seems that he managed somehow to rejoin the battalion at a later point. On the first muster drawn up after the brigade (or what was left of it) had reassembled east of the Ebro, Taylor was marked as present. About a month later, however – well into a lengthy period almost clear of enemy action – he was again noted as 'missing', and later still as 'missing, presumed killed'.[53] As already noted, one ex-colleague of Taylor's in the Cardiff YCL has given private evidence that he was executed in Spain. If this is the case, he must have been tried for desertion and shot, 'pour encourager les autres', some time in May 1938.[54]

When the battalion was preparing to leave Spain in the last weeks of 1938, the record of Alwyn Skinner, one of the many volunteers who had gone 'unaccountably' missing, was investigated and found wanting. He was placed on a list of 'Party Members who have deserted or have exceptionally bad records'.[55] Skinner's record was perhaps not 'exceptionally bad', though his desertion was sufficient in itself to attract commissariat condemnation. To start with, like Dobson, he had been one of the survivors of the *Ciudad de Barcelona*. However, he was not cleared for service at the front until some weeks later than his more committed comrade, and was fortunate enough to actually reach it just as the XV Brigade was being pulled out of the Brunete campaign in which Dobson was wounded. During the subsequent rest period he worked hard on the wall newspaper and made himself useful as a clerk – like Taylor, he was well-read and a skilled typist.[56] He was not called upon to take an active part in the Belchite campaign, though apparently able to observe the attack on Quinto at close quarters.[57] However, severe losses during these actions meant that Skinner was (also apparently) pressed into the front-line infantry for the attack on Fuentes de Ebro in mid-October. During the engagement – in true Great War fashion – the battalion advanced on enemy trenches but were repeatedly repulsed.[58] Even before this experience, Skinner's correspondence reveals a mounting anxiety. Stories of wounded veterans he had been regaled with in Albacete were unnerving, and the horrors of Quinto and Belchite confirmed them with interest.[59] At any rate, he applied for leave after only weeks with the battalion, and for repatriation immediately after the fall of Belchite in early September. Though both were refused, he got the job of company quartermaster as some compensation.[60] On one occasion he was sent to the large Catalan town of Lérida for supplies. On a tourist postcard, he told his sister

The Catalans show an indifference to the war and as a member of the IB I am sickened to see so many young men walking aimlessly around . . . I could only get a bed by accompanying a 'whore': strange though it may seem I slept in the truck. War brings many changes – peculiar ones. I've lost all concern for women.[61]

As winter came on, Skinner took sick – being evacuated to hospital on the very day the battalion moved out towards Teruel![62] What remains of his story is practically identical to Taylor's. The hospital (at Tarancón) was bombed, and as a result Skinner was sent further south, to Orihuela in Murcia. From 'this delightful hospital', he told his sister that he had been called before a medical tribunal. 'I suppose . . . I shall be sent back to my battalion . . . not that I regret for one minute my coming here. Not at all. I should never have missed the coming, the risks, the hell. Even altho' when I return I have to start my life all over again – no work – no security.'[63] In the event, Skinner was granted a further five weeks' convalescence, and eventually arrived at the battalion's Teruel positions only days before Taylor. On 20 February he claimed to have taken part in a 'very successful night action' and to be 'working with the Political Commissariat'. Three days later, however, he was just 'leaving for the front'. 'It will be good [he told his sister, Dilys] to be back at this time, in order to help the Brigade at a moment when every available man is needed.'[64] At this point his communications signal, arguably his only reliable attribute, suddenly ceased. Official documents are not forthcoming about the date of his desertion. One muster roll records him as working for the medical services in Barcelona as late as June 1938.[65] At any rate, he never returned from Spain. Many years later he achieved the immortality of recognition as one of Wales's glorious dead.[66]

The Prison-fodder

Among the volunteers who were captured by the advancing enemy during the retreats of March–April 1938 were dozens who had given themselves up – an action which occupies a grey area between surrender and desertion, depending on a level of specific detail to which we can never be privy. After Franco had called an end to his army's advance on the north-eastern front, over 230 British prisoners of the International Brigades were brought together in the 'Campo de Concentración' sited in the monastery of San Pedro de Cárdena, about 10 kilometres from the Nationalist wartime capital of Burgos, in north-central Spain.[67] Conditions in this makeshift, overcrowded prison were grim. Discipline was severely imposed, food and hygiene were basic, heating non-existent – apart from that provided by massed bodies in confined spaces. Official histories of the International Brigades understandably devote extensive space to chapters about San Pedro, based largely on witness descriptions of systematic brutality by the guards.[68] After this lapse of time, it seems there will never be any way of corroborating the large dossier of atrocity stories thus compiled. From the point of view of the guards, who perhaps had relatives or friends killed in action, their charges were foreign 'red barbarians', known to have been among the Republic's fiercest warriors, and who had volunteered gratuitously to come to Spain in order to kill Spaniards. Expectations of more tolerant treatment were (and are) perhaps unrealistic in what was, after all, a war prosecuted with atavistic brutality all over Spain and by both sides. But at least, at the time, the majority of prisoners must have considered that they were now safe from the constant fear of death or crippling injury in battle, and would be able to see their loved ones again, at the latest once the war was over.

One of about twenty Welsh prisoners, Morien Morgan was later to feel that some published treatment of the subject was rather overdrawn.[69] José Larreta, a Cardiff-born Basque who had been captured on the northern front and transferred to San Pedro after his British citizenship was accepted by Burgos, also recalled that conditions, though harsh (and certainly unacceptable by modern standards), were neither unbearable nor inhumane.[70] Vigorous representations by British diplomatic sources persuaded the Franco government to drop initial plans to use foreign prisoners in forced labour gangs.[71] A large group of men were subjected to a sequence of psychological tests devised by a senior Nationalist medical officer, Colonel Antonio Vallejo. These were meant to establish a retardative typology for communists, but although exhausting and irritating, they involved no physical abuse. Vallejo's most intriguing conclusion, from the point of view of the present book, was that all the Welsh prisoners – although only three were actually examined – were alcoholics![72]

A large fraction of the British prisoners had been captured in Aragon not by Franco's soldiers but by Italian units.[73] Although in the first instance they were handed over to the Spanish authorities, the Italians remained mindful of the hundreds of their own soldiers who had been captured by the Republican army during the war. In due course, they applied to Burgos for the relevant British POWs to be transferred to an Italian-run camp, preparatory to an exchange deal with Barcelona.[74] Among a hundred men who left San Pedro for a new site near the town of Palencia was Robert Roberts. He hailed from Bethesda, and had been a slate quarry miner at Penrhyn before joining the army in 1924. From the Italian POW camp he wrote to his uncle that

For some time I had a hard time on different fronts. I was captured at Belchite in March. Since then I have been in camps at Bilbao, Saragossa and Burgos. The present camp is a great improvement on the others. We are allowed to smoke and swim in a nearby river and even drink to a certain extent.[75]

With only a few exceptions, all British prisoners of Franco were released during the winter of 1938–9. At much the same time, several dozen other British volunteers were discharged from confinement in Spain – not from Nationalist gaols, but from those of the government they had come to serve. Moreover, conditions in Republican gaols and prison camps were often little better than those prevailing at San Pedro. Able (but rarely willing) to testify to this were hundreds of International Brigade deserters and other miscreants, some of whom spent lengthy periods incarcerated or impounded, under the care of guards who often showed little respect for their volunteer status.[76] The first of several detention sites, the notorious 'Camp Lucas' (Mahora, Albacete), was at first referred to as a 'correction centre', though André Marty himself called it 'un camp de concentration'.[77] John Angus, commissar to the British prisoners, found that

> although it had some fancy title like 're-education centre' . . . it was in fact a prison camp. The staff consisted . . . of one young Italian who was more or less human, and a considerable number of Germans from the Soviet Union, who were really a pretty grim lot! I expect they've all graduated by now to being Commandants in prison camps somewhere in Siberia.[78]

Persistent malingerers or deserters were often routinely regarded as politically suspect and treated accordingly. An outstanding case concerns a group of men who were still under custody near Valencia when the rest of their comrades were leaving Spain towards the end of 1938.[79] One of these, W. J. Thomas of Aberavon, had been one of the first from Wales to enlist with the newly formed British Battalion in December 1936. He was wounded at Jarama and subsequently saw action at Brunete, where he suffered a nervous collapse. Later, he deserted in company with two other Welshmen, Griffith Jones (Dowlais) and William Hopkins (Aberdare). All three were members of the CPGB. They reached Tarragona, where they looked in vain for a friendly ship. After some time on the run, they were arrested and imprisoned. Thomas claimed to have become ill with a liver complaint soon afterwards, describing his symptoms gruesomely in a letter which reached his parents at Christmas. For a period lasting over a year – approximately between August 1937 and October 1938 – the three men occupied various hospitals and gaols.

The group ended up in a prison at Puig, near the strategic port of Sagunto, in a monastery which – like the infamous San Pedro on the other side – had been adapted as a prison, mainly in order to accommodate recidivist deserters.[80]

At some point in the summer of 1938, while the Ebro campaign was in full swing, Hopkins escaped from Puig and somehow made it back to Wales.[81] Once home, he mobilized sympathetic support for his two mates, and gained the attention of Thomas's union committee in Aberavon. Family members had repeatedly approached Party officials and even – one presumes in desperation, so much of a treason to the class struggle did it represent – the British government, for information and redress.[82] Indeed, it seems that the case was already the subject of rumour amongst comrades in Spain. As early as the previous August, Alwyn Skinner, who had been a friend of Thomas's, alerted his sister with

> a point for your guidance about Thomas from Port Talbot. He left the battalion during the recent big battle, by anti-communist means – without permission. It is true that things were very hard, the shelling intense and bombing terrific, but that does not justify one leaving his post. He has not been heard of since . . . It is possible he will try to get home by some means or other. If this eventuates and he in any way criticises the battalion leadership, just remember that all he is doing is trying to justify his desertion. Don't of course tell his people anything . . . if he ever comes out openly against the Brigade, then you can use the information.[83]

As he himself began to contemplate desertion, Skinner's sympathy for his friend (detectable above in his customary irony) was much less disguised. Hearing on the grapevine that Thomas was still in prison, he confessed 'I am very sorry for him. Everyone says he worked hard at Jarama. His failure to face up to the severe Brunete action mustn't be too highly deplored . . .'[84] This was equally the view of many people in the movement at home, and the matter quickly escalated. Various SWMF lodges had to deal with a groundswell of popular opinion in favour of the men's quick release. At length, Arthur Horner himself agreed to take up the matter with the Spanish Republican authorities during a forthcoming visit. This was all the more remarkable a development, since Horner's reluctance to take such action must have been very firmly rooted in personal as well as political grounds. On his previous trip to Spain he himself had been arrested and spent some hours in a police cell in Valencia as a result of an absurd misunderstanding.[85] Yet, as a man never lacking resolution in the cause of justice, Horner went through with his mission nonetheless, complaining to brigade (or Party) HQ in Barcelona that 'the matter has caused considerable difficulty within the miners' union, since the documents have been circulated to all its branches, and agitation will not cease until the three individuals return home'.[86]

So far from lending a comradely ear, André Marty could hardly restrain his displeasure over these developments, and Harry Pollitt, leader of the CPGB, received an astonishing riposte from Albacete. Marty asserted that all three men were in custody for 'desertion or organisation of desertion'. Though a 'special enquiry' had been launched, in order to appease dissent, he gave little hope that it would ameliorate the situation of the injured parties – rather it seemed to threaten even greater injury, and not merely to the prisoners.

> We very deeply regret that . . . the authors of this document show more faith in deserter who, moreover, escaped from jail, than in the government of the Republic . . . I am sure that the Welsh miners, with their revolutionary trad-itions, would have very well understood the reasons for the arrest of conscious or unconscious agents of Franco who try to break up the People's Army which is holding back the Fascists. What sort of treatment do the miners give one of their number who plays the blackleg in a strike? And why should not the government of Spain have the right to arrest those who provoke desertion and probably organise it in link with the men of the Intelligence Service or in the service of Franco? . . . 20 years experience shows that each time the workers' enemy has wanted to attack the Soviet Union he has always done so with the pretext of prisoners . . . I very much regret that comrade Horner, from whom I had many things to ask, should have spent such a short time in Barcelona that I was unable to meet him.[87]

The prisoners of Puig returned home early in 1939 and thereafter maintained a strict and unflinching decorum.[88] Not even the merest particle of this whole affair seems to have been left in the wind of Wales. Later recollections of dozens of Brigade veterans, published or otherwise, contain no hint of it. An even more striking indication of the profound solidarity of the Party faithful and the whole labour movement in south Wales is that not a word about it ever seeped out to newspapers or was whispered in any risky place. Such people may not have been disfigured by André Marty's political paranoia, but they certainly shared his sense of discipline and obedience to the higher truth, to the ultimate indulgence which justified countless pragmatic injustices.

9   Halls of Fame: Making (and Faking) History

Very truly, I tell you, unless a grain of wheat falls into the earth and dies, it remains just a single grain; but if it dies, it bears much fruit. Those who love their life lose it, and those who hate their life in this world will keep it for eternal life.[1]

All these exact, and get, their fill of martyrs, whose fortitude under duress is extolled in the annals of human deeds. A curious predilection, this, for wanting to see men die 'honourably' for their opinions . . . No less curious is the historian's commendations of heroism on both sides, since it is this . . . in support of merely a contentious opinion, which is to blame for deferring indefinitely the sweetness and the poetry of living in the present.[2]

Placing the Foundations

The work of establishing a deathless list of Wales's glorious dead in the Spanish Civil War began almost as soon as their surviving comrades had returned home and begun to recover from their ordeals. Coming in the wake of those ordeals, and intended to fix them in the collective memory for eternity, it was to prove an appropriately arduous and contentious task. Indeed, the campaign to design and construct the history of Wales's supreme contribution to the antifascist struggle, via a hall of fame or Valhalla of the fallen, was pursued with a single-minded determination almost worthy of the operations of the British Battalion during the war itself. And, similarly, it was doomed to ultimate failure. In the autumn of 1938, the poet T. E. Nicholas wrote to a comrade that 'if we survive the end of the present crisis, I will see to it that a memorial in some form is set up for the gallant Welshmen who fell in Spain . . . the shrouds of the victims of Franco have been glorified into Red Flags in the blood of our class'.[3] But he, and others who strove to apply themselves to the task of making monuments in the literal – not just in the metaphorical – sense, had forgotten Marx's dictum that 'all that is solid melts into air'.

Yet what alternative was there? In many corners of Wales, parents, widows, orphans, sweethearts, families and friends would never rest easy until the deaths of loved ones were explained, justified and (preferably) glorified. It was in the interests of the cause, and of the party, that neither they nor anyone else should harbour any doubt that the missing men were deserving of all honour and emulation. So despite the absence of even a single representative corpus delecti; little evidence of formal burials and almost none of the precise location of earthly remains; serious doubts about the circumstances of many deaths; even (in some cases) actual knowledge of negative and potentially damaging evidence concerning those circumstances, the campaign went ahead. On 7 December 1938, over 7,000 people, led by thirty Welsh veterans, attended a 'National Memorial Meeting' in Mountain Ash. The occasion was honoured by the presence of Paul Robeson, who exactly a year earlier had entertained International Brigade troops behind the lines in Spain, and now spoke of his feelings to an audience which included a contingent of West Indian immigrants from Cardiff. 'I am here because I know that these fellows fought not only for Spain but for me and the whole world. I feel it is my duty to be here.'[4] The meeting was graced by the presence of the dean of Chichester, which must have puzzled some of the faithful. It arose partly because the dean was a Welshman, but perhaps also because, for most of the congregation, only the Church could place a suitably resonant *benedictus* on a ritual act of consecration. Will Paynter read out a 'pledge . . . enthusiastically acclaimed by the audience, to continue the struggle for freedom, democracy and peace until the Spanish people gained victory'. Arthur Horner was rather more businesslike than Robeson, the dean, or even his SWMF colleague. His concern was not the deaths of the men but the cause they sanctified. 'What did they die for? We are not here mourning our dead. We are here to remember what they died for.' The message – perhaps we should say, the instructions – for the bereaved was that it was the cause which mattered; their loved ones were merely its insignificant agents.[5]

Those left to grieve, who were rarely consulted about their actions by the volunteers (or the Party) in the first place, were expected to face stoically a prospect of endless emotional pain, along with the long-term sentence of economic distress imposed upon them by the loss of breadwinners. In September 1938, a cartoon in the *Western Mail* ridiculed the request made by Jack Roberts for the Caerphilly District Council to make a grant 'for widows and orphans of men killed whilst serving in the International Brigade'.[6] The International Brigade Dependents' Fund worked hard to make sporadic ex-gratia payments, and sometimes responded to specific appeals, but there were no pensions, and the word 'counselling' was not yet invented.[7] The desolate landscape of *involuntary* suffering which stands, mostly occluded, behind the figure of every volunteer, hardly ever acknowledged in public, was (*pace* Horner) the authentic monument to the ideals that men had carried to Spain. As Hywel Francis put it in 'revisiting' his subject some years after the appearance of his *Miners Against Fascism*:

> We, as historians, have not asked the right questions about Spain and the 1930s. For example, I was always reluctant to visit widows or close female relatives of volunteers who had been killed in action, often, I should say in my own defence, being warned against some visits by well-meaning Party comrades. One famous survivor of the War, Cardiff seaman Pat Murphy . . . once cautioned me . . . 'it's a bit touchy visiting these relatives as one often gets some nasty remarks instead of compliments. I've had some during my activities as relatives are not always enthusiastic about us.' But not to face the unacceptable, the unpleasant and the unpalatable and only to deal with the convenient is to distort history . . . There was a heroic story to be told but there was also a darker side which unfortunately does not always conveniently fit into our scheme of things.[8]

The collection of minor troubles and private tragedies touched upon here rarely breaks the surface of publicity. In one case, nearly sixty years later, the surviving sister of Cardiff volunteer Bill Coles recalled the family's desolation at his leaving for Spain. They received one letter of reassurance from him, then 'the next thing someone told us he had died fighting at Jarama'. Later still, they heard rumours that he had been seen alive, 'but he never came back and we never heard from him so he must have died there. We still don't know . . . I don't think my mother ever got over it.'[9]

At the time of the Mountain Ash gathering, the first official list of Horner's martyr-drones appeared in print. It contained the names of nineteen Welshmen.[10] Within a year, Bill Rust's official history of the British Battalion had been published, with its 'Roll of Honour' including twenty-one volunteers from Wales.[11] Nearly forty years later, when the 'National Memorial Plaque' was unveiled in Hendrefoilan, Swansea, the number had increased to thirty-three. In between these events lies a stormy and tortuous voyage. Once back at home in their towns and villages, surviving volunteers sought to establish local branches of the International Brigade Association, their main aim being to raise funds with a dual purpose – to alleviate the plight of bereaved families, and to commemorate the Spanish struggle. But matters stagnated during the period of the Nazi–Soviet Pact (August 1939–June 1941) when the official communist anti-war line was seen by the majority as unpatriotic, and by some as actually treasonable. Few, even in south Wales, were inclined to donate to a cause which was so obviously sponsored by communists. Britain had its back to the wall, with not only its armed forces, but soon enough its civilian population too, bloodily engaged against an all-conquering enemy. The Third Reich's ruthless machine of destruction was being supplied with important war-materials by a compliant ally, the Soviet Union. Under the protective shield cover of Hitler's war effort, Stalin swallowed the Baltic States, much of Poland, and tried to crush democratic Finland for good measure. After June 1941, when Hitler invaded the Soviet Union, matters changed. The Popular Front became official policy, smiled on and supported by government. Anglo-Soviet societies sprang up every-where, and Stalin became everybody's benign 'Uncle Joe'.

A recent study of the establishment of the International Brigade Association expresses surprise that complementary activity in Wales was so backward. 'Strangely' – Dr Buchanan notes – 'given the proud record of the region's miners as volunteers in Spain, the association was weak in South Wales and there appears to have been no branch in the Rhondda between 1939–49.'[12] However, by September 1942, Jack Roberts had set up a local group in Treharris, with ten members including two veterans – one of them the redoubtable Morris Davies, felt by some to be the best Welsh soldier in Spain. Ex-lieutenant Ben Davies was struggling to get things moving in Newport, Morien Morgan in Pontypridd, Pat Murphy likewise in Cardiff.[13] These activists liaised with Idris Cox, regional party secretary, and in turn he communicated with the IBA committee in London.[14] Early in 1944, Cox sent T. E. Nicholas a list of twenty-one 'South Wales Comrades who have made the supreme sacrifice . . . as members of the Coal Brigade'.[15] This group-title was an *ex post facto* propaganda invention not dissimilar to – but having even less factual foundation than – the Irish 'Connolly Company'.[16] It was intended to endow the miners, and thereby the Communist Party, with a special elite significance in the historic and ongoing antifascist strug-gle. Within the Ark of the Covenant of Welsh Sacrifice, that holy repository of eternal value, some martyrs were to be more valuable than others.

In 1940, Nicholas and his son Islwyn had served two months in prison having been convicted on a trumped-up charge of sedition, related to their untrammelled support of Comrade Stalin. After their release that autumn, they resumed work in fulfilment of the promise that had been given two years earlier to provide a memorial for the fallen. The father, relying upon his own fame, bardic reputation and eloquent powers of persuasion, took charge of the fund-raising aspect. The son began to collect information on the Welsh Brigaders by circulating letters to hundreds of addresses of family and friends. He uncovered, for example, the story of Arthur Morris from Cardigan, who had emigrated to Canada in the late 1920s, joined the Party there, and was sent to study in the Lenin School in *c*.1934. Morris, like Cambridge graduate Robert Traill, travelled directly to Spain from Moscow; he enlisted in the Lincoln Battalion, and was killed on the Jarama front in the spring of 1937.[17] Partly as a result of this research, by 1944 'Niclas y Glais' felt able to add a number of 'Welsh' names to the lists published in 1938–9. But the main reason for the increase in numbers seems to have been a somewhat simplistic assumption that men endowed with surnames which had ethnically Welsh overtones were indeed Welsh – in some cases, even where Rust had actually indicated cities of origin like Bristol and Glasgow![18] Nicholas's plan was for all the names to be inscribed on a memorial, and in the course of the year he raised £260 from donations to this scheme. Most of the Fed lodges contributed with sums ranging from 10*s*. to £15, while dozens of small private donations helped to swell the total. Mrs K. Aubrey, for example, sent 5*s*. 'in memory of Cardiff comrades who fell in Spain'.[19] However, by this time, the IBA had decided that all relevant activity should be concentrated on a single integrated scheme. The scheme in question, to be supervised by the Joint Committee for Soviet Aid, was to endow a ward in a new hospital in Stalingrad – Stalingrad, Russia, that is, and not some 'little Stalingrad' in the Rhondda – in memory of all the British dead. In this way, a tangible 'thank-you offering' would be made to the people and the city which had, in the CPGB's view, made the greatest of all sacrifices in resistance to fascism. The Welsh element was to be a dedicated hospital bed, along with a page in a memorial album, inscribed with the names of the fallen – 3,000 miles away from Wales and (as it was to prove, for nearly three generations) inaccessible to British non-communists.[20] If ever Nicholas felt a sense of frustration and disappointment with his Party, then this surely must have been the occasion. The soul of the ancient campaigner must have moved in sympathy when one lodge committee secretary wrote to him: 'It should perhaps be stated that some of our committee felt that a memorial to Welshmen who died in Spain should be commemorated either in Spain or in Wales itself. However, we are wholeheartedly in favour of the project – apart from that.'[21]

Even in the first few years of official commemoration, therefore, the hall of fame (under construction) echoed to the sounds of contention. Members' nominations differed, sometimes radically, within the five or six lists drawn up by various interested parties.[22] To give some examples; William Beales, killed at the Ebro, figured on one of them as being from Newport – he was, indeed, from Newport, Isle of Wight. Searches were made in Mountain Ash to locate John Burton, from whence (despite Rust's allocation of him to Bristol) a belief was expressed he had originated. There was evidently a lobby in favour of including J. S. Williams (Dowlais) who died after returning of an existing illness which had seriously deteriorated as a result of his ordeal in Spain. Fred Jones, one-time leader of the British section of the XI International Brigade, *compadre* of John Cornford, Bernard Knox and others, who died in a grotesque accident during the battle for Madrid in November 1936, was twice included and twice removed.[23] It is curious that Sid James (Treherbert), to whose death in action his close friend, Billy Griffiths, could presumably have attested, was omitted from all the early lists.[24]

But it is the posthumous fate of Cummings, Durston, Taylor and Skinner, four volunteers over whose deaths mystery and suspicion continues to hover, which best illustrates the conflicting aims and apprehensions of the (mostly anonymous) doorkeepers of the hall of fame. In the printed programme of the Mountain Ash meeting already described, Cummings and Taylor figured among the honoured dead. But Bill Rust overlooked both. It is almost inconceivable that Rust would have remained unaware of the previous list; so his omission of these two names represented a conscious decision. It seems that Rust was prepared to risk queries and murmurs – political embarrassment – because of his own judgement that the two men were not worthy of inclusion. In turn, such a judgement can only have been based on information to which he (along with others amongst the CPGB leadership) was privy. Equally revealing is that Skinner and Durston *were not even seriously considered as eligible* until a new phase of information-gathering and fund-raising began in the 1970s, as the fortieth anniversary of the Spanish War approached. History's hall of fame – here, as always – had some uncomfortably shifting foundations.

Collateral Damage and Dust

Alongside those who fell amongst the Republic's fighting forces, and the loved ones they left behind, other sacrifices deserve to be remembered. At the grass roots, above all, the nameless thousands who surrendered food, clothing, and even cash to the insistent doorstepping of 'Spanish Aid' groups, giving selflessly to help a people whose deprivation and pain they perceived as greater than their own. In so doing, many amongst them – in order to relieve the suffering felt by the distant objects of their compassion – deliberately imposed part of it upon themselves. The writer Glyn Jones, who helped take up such collections in working-class districts of Cardiff, suffered vicariously even from the action of asking. 'I am deeply wounded somewhere' he noted in his diary (1937). 'This going from door to door hurts me terribly, heaven knows why. Giving out the Food for the Spanish People leaflets pains me.'[25] Jones's invocation of the celestial seems significant. Even today, such bitter-sweet charity conveys a pervading sense of human empathy and identification which remains heart-warming to the observer through the disaster-laden lenses of nearly seventy years and all the intellectual prisms of postmodernism.

Another feature likewise rarely, if ever, brought back to mind by public remembrancers is the casualties incurred by ships' crews manning the maritime supply lines to the republic. At least six Welsh sailors died as a result of airborne attacks on their vessels in Spanish ports. Two of these, J. Mulholland and T. King – both from Newport – lost their lives on board the SS *Stanwell* (skippered by Captain Davies of Cardiff) which was badly damaged when discharging 8,000 tons of Welsh coal at Tarragona in March 1938.[26] A Barry man, A. Perrott, died along with six other crewmen on board the SS *Thorpeness* in Tarragona harbour earlier in the year.[27] Harry Williams, a 59-year-old bosun, was killed when the SS *Stanholm* was bombed in July 1938. Captain John Roberts (who, like Williams, hailed from the tiny fishing village of Borth) died while acting as a non-intervention officer on board a French steamer when a Nationalist plane attacked the ship in June 1938.[28] Another Newport man, Jack Lord, was killed while crewing a supply ship in Spain.[29] No hall of fame records the deaths of over forty British seamen in Spain, and while few would argue that they should carry the same significance as those of volunteers in front-line action, on the other hand, the persistent feeling that (after all) the men were paid well for the risks they took arises from a rather murky ethical compound. In any case, the victims did not have the resources of the Comintern and 'the cause' behind them to perpetuate their memories.[30]

One Welsh non-combatant whose name has run like a thread through the above pages must be mentioned again in the present context. Lewis Jones, a hero whose 'life had the taste of legend', is regarded by some as a martyr of the Spanish Civil War almost as surely as if he had been killed storming Hill 481 alongside Harry Dobson.[31] Indeed, on one level, it seems plausible to regard him as a self-sacrificial martyr, who might stand as a representative symbol of the painful commitment of countless civilians. Lewis ultimately refused the Party's demand to go to Spain; he and his family (but, it seems, not the Party) knew that he was already a sick man. Instead, he embarked on a programme of agitation, organization and inspiration so punishing that it eventually killed him. Shortly after his death it was alleged that he had addressed no less than thirty different audiences in Rhondda streets on the actual day of his collapse.[32] It was as though he deliberately worked himself to death for the cause, like thousands of near-suicidal Stakhanovite workers in the Soviet Union.

One colleague later recalled Jones's fever of activity, recalling that it was undertaken in the spirit of 'I'll show them'. But whereas some assume that this bravado arose from his guilt at failing to 'volunteer' for Spain, there may be an alternative (or perhaps a complementary) explanation. Jones was sexually promiscuous, and consistently exploited his Party work and contacts, along with the frequent absences from home which these involved, in order to lead an energetic private life. Jones's biographer has referred coyly to his 'wilful bohemianism' and less coyly (perhaps) to his 'cockatoo personality'.[33] Jones's liaison with Mavis Llewelyn – charted obliquely in the many visits to Nant-y-moel noted in his diary – was not his only adventure.[34] Indeed, Douglas Hyde later alleged that 'he took it for granted that every girl comrade was his for the asking'. In 1935, Jones's excesses were brought before the Communist Party Regional Committee, by which he was formally reprimanded and suspended.[35] A few days after his death a report of the inquest appeared in the *Western Mail*. The Coroner heard that 'he was found dead in the bedroom of a house at which he was staying in Cardiff after having addressed a number of meetings in the city'. It continued

> Rose Thompson, who also stayed in the house in Clare Road, Cardiff, said that as she was going upstairs she thought she heard something fall. As she passed Lewis Jones's door she called out 'Goodnight' but received no answer. 'Something made me open the door', she said, 'and I saw him lying doubled up on the floor'.[36]

Jones's death seems to have taken place in circumstances hardly less obscure than those of several Welsh International Brigaders – a fact which adds to the mysterious aura of a novelist whose novels had been powerfully influenced (if not co-authored) by a schoolteacher with whom he was having an affair.[37]

Battles in a Welsh Valhalla

Thirty years after the first collection had been taken and Welshmen had gone to Spain a physical memorial to the Welsh dead had still not been constructed.[38] In 1967, however, the Aberdare Labour Party sponsored an appeal, raising funds from miners' lodges and other local organizations, and commissioned a memorial which was installed in the local Labour Rooms. The wooden-carved sculpture incorporates a set of miners' faces, apparently honouring the prone body of one of their fallen, with only two resonant words: 'No Pasaran!'[39] This event, coinciding as it did with the doctoral research of Hywel Francis of University College, Swansea, revived notions and aspirations for a grander project. A Memorial Appeal Committee was established chaired by Dai Francis, general secretary of the SWMF, with ex-brigader Jim Brewer as secretary. Relatives and friends of the fallen volunteers were contacted with the aim of canvassing opinion.

> Wales can be proud of the support it gave to the Republican cause and Welshmen can be proud that it was represented among those who were the first in the field against our late enemies. The Association has resolved that [the] proper form can only be decided upon by you and us and your wishes in the matter will be given due weight and consideration.[40]

The proposal duly emerged 'to erect a memorial near the national shrine at Cathays Park, Cardiff. The names of those Welshmen who made the supreme sacrifice in Spain will be inscribed on the memorial as a permanent tribute.' The appeal was sponsored by all the great and good of Welsh life – from Richard Burton to Dafydd Wigley via such luminaries as James Callaghan, Alexander Cordell, Michael Foot, Jim Griffiths, Sir Archibald Lush, Alun Richards, Professor Brinley Thomas, Gwyn Thomas, Wynford Vaughan Thomas and Lady Eirene White. In addition, the Welsh IBA Committee, which sought the advice and collaboration of the United Nations Association (UNA) in the campaign, was politically broad-based. It included veterans like Jim Brewer and Morien Morgan, Labour Party supporters, ho despite feeling it necessary to join the Party whilst in Spain, had later left its ranks; Tom Glyn Evans, also Labour, who had resisted all pressure to join the PCE; and others such as Tom Stickler and Rowley Williams who were basically non-political.[41] The spirit of 'Unity' had been – it seemed – reborn.

All the same, W. R. Davies, director of the Wales UNA, had misgivings about a possible hidden agenda. He asked Brewer whether the proposed memorial would commemorate an abstract idealism – 'what they [the volunteers] considered right' – or 'whether it might relate more specifically to the political issues in the Spanish Civil War?' He made it clear that 'the Association will not tolerate the using of this appeal as a means of accumulating personal or political capital'.[42] Brewer's attempt at reassurance contained the rather counter-productive observation that 'we held and still hold in contempt those against whom we fought'.[43] Matters were then taken out of his hands, and the Wales UNA was sidelined. Despite the sparkling demonstration of non-partisanship reflected in the appeal publicity – and, we might speculate, despite the opinions of the interested parties canvassed – the relevant decisions were almost certainly taken by Dai Francis, in consultation with Idris Cox, Islwyn Nicholas, Bert Pearce (Welsh Communist Party secretary) and

Bill Alexander (secretary of the national IBA). The plan to place a monument in the War Memorial Gardens in Cardiff city centre was abandoned.[44] Instead the 'permanent tribute' of inscription was engraved on a large plaque, which in 1976 was installed at the internal entrance to the Welsh Miners' Library, itself situated within what had been a country house, Hendrefoilan, acquired by the University College on the outskirts of Swansea.[45] The appeal leaflet had printed the final authorized version of the hall of fame encapsulated in the plaque. The thirty-three names included no fewer than ten newcomers (including Skinner and Durston) who had failed to appear on any previous list, however provisional and optimistic.[46] Today, few people are aware of the plaque's existence and fewer still have ever examined it in person. But at the time at least this meant that the data it recorded were less likely to be the source of future public questionings and possible dispute.

In fact, dispute among the veterans themselves proved difficult to avoid. In the wake of the Hendrefoilan unveiling, the issue of utilizing the residue of the appeal fund – a matter of some £1,100 – came to the fore. Brewer and his non-communist colleagues again approached the Wales UNA with the idea of endowing a Welsh–Spanish exchange scheme which might send young trade unionists to Spain and sponsor return visits from similarly qualified Spaniards. By this time, Franco was dead and the possibility existed for a successful revival of Spanish democracy. However, the condition was made that no money was to be used until a freely elected Spanish government had come into office.[47] The cheque was handed over at a public meeting in Cardiff, which was appropriately held during the week (June 1977) that the Spanish people held their first free general election since 1936. But even – perhaps especially – at what should have been a transcendental moment of satisfaction for the dozen or so veterans present, the occasion was vitiated by irrepressible feelings of personal and party division between them.[48]

Although other memorial committees were set up in order to honour local men, none of them seems to have borne fruit until a further decade had passed, and the significant fiftieth anniversary of the war had come and gone. In 1989, another plaque was unveiled in honour of the Rhondda's International Brigaders. Here, Alec Cummings appears alongside Harry Dobson amongst seven who – in the plaque's carefully chosen words – 'rest in the soil of Spain'.[49] In Penygroes, north Wales, where the death of George Fretwell – like Coles, reported killed in the battle of Jarama – had been taken very badly by some, the villagers united many decades later to support an appeal for a memorial. The official record suggests that time had healed the wounds opened by the war, yet the plaque installed in the village hall in 1991 merely states the fact that Fretwell 'lost his life whilst fighting with the

International Brigade' – firmly avoiding any reference to the nature of the cause once emphasized so firmly by Arthur Horner.[50] By this time the project to establish a memorial in Cardiff's War Memorial Gardens had been revived. With the joint sponsorship of three major local authorities, funds were raised to commission an impressive monument, which took the form of a monolith (as it were) detached from a Gorsedd Circle.[51] Inscribed with suitable sentiments from 'La Pasionaria' and T. E. Nicholas, it may fittingly be regarded (in conjunction with the Hendrefoilan plaque) as a 'national memorial', since it stands in a garden setting with similar monuments close by – to the Welsh dead of two World Wars and to those of the Falklands War.

In the 1990s, further tangible tributes came into being. In 1996, now sixty years on, a Spanish poet and civil war veteran, Marcos Ana, was invited to unveil a memorial in Neath's Victoria Park. MEP David Morris told the *Western Mail* that 'Neath, more than any other area in Britain, provided support for the fight against Franco by providing food, housing refugees and sending men to join the fight.'[52] In recent years the indefatigable zeal of Arnold Owen, brother of Frank Owen (Maerdy) who was killed in action at Brunete, has kept the flame of memory and the vein of tribute bright. Working with veteran Lance Rogers (now deceased) and his brother Garnett, Mr Owen has ceaselessly lobbied politicians, local authorities and a wide range of relevant institutions, efforts which led to a new bridge across the river at Maerdy being named after Frank Owen, and plaques being erected in Burry Port, Llanelli, Ammanford, Porthcawl, Caerphilly, and a second example of the genre in Neath![53] Yet several of these events were the occasion of political infighting and public dissent. In Neath, for example, a councillor caused a furore by opposing the decision to finance a memorial. 'I don't know what the relatives of the fallen who are named on this plaque think about it,' he stated, 'but it is being done whether they like it or not.'[54] In Llanelli, there was resistance to the idea of the public library hosting an exhibition, accompanied by public disagreement about the appropriate siting of a memorial.[55] One objector, the branch secretary of the local Royal Marines' Association, argued that a public monument was inappropriate for 'political recruits' who 'did not go to Spain in defence of Britain'. This position brought an extraordinary concession from the distinguished IB veteran, Dave Marshall, who claimed that 'the people who went to fight were not necessarily left-wing'.[56] At last, perhaps, the legacy of the Popular Front and the honours of antifascism had been prised free of its Stalinist mortmain.

PART V: CONCLUSION

10 Epilogue: The Dragon's Cause Today

In the year of the fiftieth anniversary of the Spanish Civil War, Dr Dai Smith surveyed the condition of Welsh historiography in the pages of *Planet*, the nation's leading intellectual forum. Amongst other things, he lamented that his guild had never been able to 'proceed by examining closely, in their different contexts, the experience of different Welsh peoples, home and abroad, in different wars – from the thirteenth century through to the Zulu Wars, from the World Wars to the Spanish Civil War and the Falklands'.[1] This book has not sought to perform such a task in respect of the penultimate conflict nominated in this list. Prioritizing comprehensive treatment in terms of geography and community has had the effect of simultaneously precluding the kind of in-depth sociological and cultural analysis (presumably) envisaged as the basis of Dai's desiderata. Nonetheless, I hope to have given some fleeting glimpses of 'different contexts' and 'different Welsh peoples'; and, more importantly, to have responded to his even more urgent demand that we 'must openly acknowledge the primacy of historical comprehension over myth'. Indeed, I find myself wholly in agreement with his poetic peroration:

> A society that does not see the purpose of re-imagining its past will prove incapable of cherishing its future. The answer to the question of identity is not to give everyone a uniform but to provide a map for the mind . . . The way forward is not to trace threads of Welshness through our history into the wool-gathering ball in our own hands, but to produce work about that history which attracts others because of its quality.[2]

So, in what significant sense did Dai (and Dame) Wales don the uniform of a Spanish volunteer?

The Dragon's *Distant* Cause?[3]

It must be admitted that for much of the time the idea of an ongoing 'special relationship' – which I set out to analyse and explain – is difficult to maintain at all. In the new century, the good old cause of 'Spain' has lost much of its resonance in Welsh life. One after another, the grizzled champions of socialist Wales have passed away. The Miners' Gala, which often witnessed banners and speeches referring to the International Brigades, has ceased to be. The industry itself is receding into a dim and distant past. Never again, it seems, will a young person feel the call of 'Spain' as the 12-year-old Gwyn Alf Williams, future *maitre à pensée* of Welsh cultural history, felt it at the funeral of volunteer J. S. Williams in 1938, when it entered his soul like a moving spirit.[4] Fifty years later, reminiscing about 'growing up in Dowlais', Williams – in a deadpan, self-deprecatory passage reminiscent of Gwyn Thomas – remembered belonging to a gang of lads who were preparing to join an antifascist demo. There were

> ruins, unemployment everywhere. We hardly saw them. We were burning and bleeding for our martyred comrades in the Vienna flats and Madrid . . . It was the books . . . They dug the banner out of its hiding place. No Passaran it said. They'd argued over how many esses there should be. 'Never mind that', Iorri snapped, 'the Fascists will have gone by the time we get there'.[5]

Thereafter, Williams went on to get adopted by an ex-International Brigader during the Normandy campaign, re-imagining circumstances strikingly akin to those already imagined by another short-story writer, Alun Lewis, in his 'Private Jones' (1943).[6] Gwyn Alf's generation, like so many pickets at a winter pithead, stamped their feet obstinately and blew on the smouldering embers of their obsession with 'Spain'. But in contrast, as early as 1957, Will Paynter confessed that none of his six sons was interested in politics; and that (in a reporter's words) 'young people as a whole aren't really living up to his ideas and ideals . . . Nobody goes on hunger marches as he did. Nobody goes to Spain with an International Brigade.'[7] All the same, there is no doubt that the image of the Rhondda collier as 'volunteer for liberty' in Spain has achieved a certain representative status both inside and outside Wales. So permeating is the stereotype of the mythical 'Coal Brigade' that even Cardiff student Sid Hamm, one of three Welshmen whose experiences figured in a recent Spanish Civil War exhibition in the Imperial War Museum, was automatically mis-described by the curators as 'a Welsh miner'.[8] More-over (as we shall shortly see) the capacity of the Spanish Civil War – or, at any rate, its mythological construct – to inspire feeling and action among young people in Wales is by no means finally extinguished.

This book has shown, on the one hand, that interest in the plight of the Spanish Republic, and even the commitment to do something about it, was widespread in Wales, reaching to most of its geographical areas and affecting many communities. But paradoxically it has also revealed – on the other – that, for the most part, this phenomenon was both superficial and transient. The grip of 'Spain' upon the deprived working-class masses of the southern ports, the rural parishes of west and centre, the small-town societies of west, centre and north, was never strong and only rarely shook anyone to his or her foundations. Even in the southern coalfield, its effect was far from the whirlwind of populist action, restlessly rushing through every valley, street and square, which is sometimes (surely not just in the romantic imagination of the present writer?) summoned up. Indeed, if rather more resonant here than elsewhere, the choral drama was choreographed by a dedicated ideological minority whose fundamental interests often went so far beyond as to be effectively disconnected from the fate of the Spanish (or even the Welsh) people as such. In other parts of Wales, the leadership role of a social elite was underlined by their relative isolation. Small groups of professionals – mostly ministers of religion, teachers, academics or journalists – were complemented by political activists, pacifists and assorted associations of do-gooders, in what was a non-ideological, humanitarian and (above all) low-key campaign. I also found that responses to Spain were more complex and unpredictable in politico-social terms than previously thought. How can one explain (for example) the contrasting experiences of two of the most eminent Welsh historians of their generation, contemporaries and namesakes, who were both born into middle-class households in Dowlais? In their teens, Gwyn Alf Williams became possessed by 'Spain', while Glanmor Williams barely recognized that the Civil War was an important issue.[9] How was it that Reggie Lee, born chronologically between these two, but into a Dowlais working-class family, grew up in the 1930s to be an intelligent and resourceful young man on whom 'Spain' made no impact whatsoever?[10] Finally, if the Welsh working classes were so fired up by a vision of 'Spain' as the critical battlefield of antifascism, why was it that the CPGB had to struggle so grimly even to fulfil volunteer quotas from amongst their own members in the mining valleys?

Though (as we have seen) the volunteer Welsh miner has become almost a stock character amongst the dramatis personae of fictional writing on the Spanish Civil War, his influence on historiography is more patchy. Neither in the pages of general textbooks nor in monographic studies of the International Brigades do the Welsh achieve an impressive level of acknowledgement. 'Ronda' sometimes figures in an index, but 'Rhondda' never. Individual names, notably those of Dobson, Paynter, Horner and Jack 'Russia' Roberts, occasionally crop up *en passant*.[11] In books of American – as well as Spanish and other European countries' – origin, even these worthies are more often than not described as 'English'. In perhaps the most bizarre instance of mistaken national identity, even the already anonymous 'Taffy' suffered an almost terminal ethnic misattribution. One of the earliest general studies of the International Brigades, by the French writer Delperrie de Bayac, mysteriously describes how, at the battle of Jarama, 'The Irish volunteer Taffy, seeing the Fascists attack, launched himself against them with fixed bayonet. He was killed, but the others did not follow him.'[12] In a later Spanish version, evidently derived from this, I read that 'Some brave men distinguished themselves, for example the Irishman, Taffy, who went alone with fixed bayonet, to meet the enemy . . .'[13] I was convinced that this distortion – which, however understandable, remained irritating – represented some kind of oxymoronic nickname to be found in the original documentary source. When I discovered a generous extract from this source in a compilation of contemporary memoirs of the battle made by the Sunderland veteran, Frank Graham, this suspicion seemed to be confirmed. The text – which purported to be a transcript – perfectly justified the attribution made by the two continental historians. 'I particularly remember two incidents. One concerned *an Irishman who we called Taffy*. When he saw the fascists coming he went towards them. I guess he did not go far before being filled with lead.'[14] Yet the editor, strangely, offered no comment or explanation for this peculiar and confusing construction. As later became evident, Graham's editions of all these texts are sadly unreliable, being heavily modified in the interests of the historical reputations of the Party and the battalion. It was only in the last stages of revising this book for publication that I finally tracked down photocopies of the original manuscript in the IBA archive. It was one of several written accounts of the Jarama action collected from Party members who had been in the thick of the fighting. It described an incident on the disastrous second day of the battle. 'There was a Welshman Taffy, who when he saw the fascists advance went over the top to meet them. I suppose that before he got there he was more full of lead than a drain pipe. He was the only man who didn't retreat.'[15]

Of Miners and Media

When the terminal crisis of the Welsh mining industry arrived in 1984, the desperate and often violent struggle of the NUM took place against forces easily portrayed and perceived as 'fascist'. Such rhetoric was especially powerful in south Wales, where the heritage of the 1930s, and inevitably of the blood sacrifice of the International Brigaders, was invoked to stiffen the sinews of the picketing battalions. During the 1984 strike, Raymond Williams and his wife used to visit the coalmining communities situated not far away from their home in the rural borderlands, driving westwards across the Black Mountains. They took tea and sympathy with them to the village halls where the contents of hampers ceaselessly arriving from Hampshire and Hampstead were distributed to the starving children.[16] Not long after the strike's collapse, a collection of essays by sympathetic intellectuals was quickly translated for publication in Spain.[17] Yet on the whole – perhaps because Hywel Francis's book had only just appeared as the strike was getting under way – the left-wing press showed far more interest in making comparisons with the contemporary situation in Nicaragua than in 'Spain' and the 1930s.[18]

Perhaps the closest friend Sid Hamm made in Spain during the few short weeks before his death was Lance Rogers, who actually *was* from a Merthyr mining background.[19] Rogers, who like many others learned public speaking on the streets in his teens, remained active in giving talks to students and fringe leftist parties until the end of his life. On several occasions in the 1990s the present writer was able to witness the inspiring effect of his presence on young people. In stark contrast, Edwin Greening, when approached by a journalist for a comment on the fiftieth anniversary, brusquely responded 'I am sick of the whole subject. The Spanish War has no relevance any more.'[20] Like Rogers, Paddy O'Daire, an Irish veteran and one-time commander of the British Battalion, was a quietly spoken widely read man who was prepared to reflect on the ethical contradictions of his service in Spain in unorthodox ways. He spent the last years of his life in Bangor, and at his funeral service in that city, his coffin was draped with the Red Flag and the banner of the International Brigade.[21]

In the last third of the twentieth century, anniversaries of the war and the obsequies of veterans would constantly bring stories, interviews and archive pictures to the pages of Welsh newspapers. These invariably concentrated on the International Brigaders, reproducing sentimental and heroic tales of mining communities' involvement with 'Spain', in the orthodox political context which had been assiduously worked into our history by the Fed, the CPGB and the evanescent *hiraeth* of the Popular Front 'tradition'.[22] At the same time, some residual memory remains of Welsh support for the Basques. An oral tale is sometimes picked up that for many years during the Franco regime a 'Radio Free Basque' operated from the attic of a department store in Barry, via a transmitter secreted somewhere in rural Pembrokeshire.[23] In recent years a moving exhibition on Wales and the Spanish Civil War, compiled and maintained by Arnold Owen, has travelled all over Wales and further afield in the British Isles and beyond, being seen by thousands of schoolchildren, many of whom respond with interest and emotion. Teachers of history in the principality are still keen to acquire and deploy materials which enable pupils to learn about the Spanish War from a local perspective.

Much recent interest, however, has been stimulated as part of the fall-out from a major event in Welsh cultural life. In 1998, the rock group the Manic Street Preachers wrote and recorded a number entitled 'If You Tolerate This Your Children Will Be Next'. The song quickly occupied the No. 1 place in the charts and sat there for several weeks.[24] Its title was taken from a propaganda poster issued by the Republican government in 1936, graphically illustrating the young victim of an alleged bombing raid by the Nazi Condor Legion on a small town near Madrid. The poster, sometimes recalled by International Brigade veterans in the context of their decisions to go to Spain, was displayed in a Cardiff exhibition devoted to the cultural world of the Manic Street Preachers in 1999, and also illustrated in its brochure.[25] The Manics are from Blackwood, Gwent. They were already regarded by many as the most significant 'political' band to make an impact in Britain since the 1960s. The band's strident socialism avowedly arose from the socio-cultural background of its members, deriving from a consuming interest in the history of south Wales, and in particular from the complementary legacies of Aneurin Bevan and the Spanish Civil War.[26] The lyrics of 'If You Tolerate This' – accompanied in the CD insert by a group photograph of Welsh International Brigaders taken just before the Ebro offensive – incorporated a remark made by a brigader from the 'red' village of Bedlinog upon his volunteering: 'If I can shoot rabbits, then I can shoot Fascists.'[27] The group also strongly identified with the example of Paul Robeson, the great American Black singer who sang in both Wales and Spain for the International Brigaders, and who was persecuted by the FBI in the 1950s. In media interviews following a celebrated visit to Cuba, the Manics spoke of the emotional effects of the 1984 miners' strike, and what the historic legacy of the people's struggle meant for their emergent political consciousness as teenagers. Nicky Wire, main inspiration for the 'Spanish' element in all this, confessed his inadequacy compared to the idealism of the International Brigaders, and of not having the courage to join a similar outfit in contemporary Bosnia.[28] The band's drummer, Sean Moore, has been heard quoting La Pasionaria's dictum, 'It is better to die on your feet than live on your knees'.[29]

This salient and Manic episode, for all its glitzy uniqueness, was nevertheless firmly in the mainstream of Welsh artistic feeling. Wire's brother, Patrick Jones, is the author of a stage play *Everything Must Go* (1999) in which a foul-mouthed self-mutilating gang of oppressed teenagers is led by

'Dai Cunt', a sort of cunning-punning lingual descendant of Dic Penderyn, 'the first Welsh working-class martyr'. Dai takes revenge on the manager of a Korean-owned electronics factory – who has just sacked his father – by shooting him dead with the revolver that his grandfather had carried as an International Brigader.[30] Another recent play features a putative Welsh Messiah who claims to be 'Franco's Bastard'. This antihero is perhaps based loosely on a leader of the late and unlamented Free Wales Army, and behaves like a narcoleptic anarchist gangster.[31] A generation earlier, when Welsh drama was not quite so indiscriminately resentful (or histrionic), Roger Stennet presented a play set in a Barcelona bar, where demobbed Welsh Brigaders discuss their feelings about 'Spain' while the farewell celebrations and La Pasionaria's famous speech ('You are History. You are Legend') is heard from the square outside.[32] A recent cultish novel, written by a Cardiffian 'born to an Irish family', is located in the sunset years of the Welsh capital's legendarily notorious 'Tiger Bay'. Given all the circumstances of genre and *mise-en-scène*, it comes as no surprise to find, as central characters, members of a family descended from 'a Trinidadian woman who arrived in Cardiff in 1936, only to entwine her destiny with a braggard refugee from the Spanish Civil War'.[33]

The irregular irruption of these artefacts seem to indicate, if only obscurely, subliminal traces of a 'special relationship' between Wales and 'Spain' in our genetic memory. Perhaps these are, indeed, inextinguishable organic cells, all matter, after all, being ultimately imperishable. Yet if so, an element of more conscious reflection has also emerged in a parallel mode and temperament. For example, in 1975 – year of Franco's death – *Planet* published two relevant items in the same issue.[34] John Tripp's story 'The Reds are Coming' presented a reasoned debate between a Nationalist field officer and an American journalist, in which the former's cause and motives were given a sympathetic (if not exactly empathetic) hearing. Alan Perry's poem 'Spain (1975)' paid homage to the recently visited ex-revolutionary city of Barcelona:

> I will look for the Ramblas' twin observatories
> where Orwell sat guard with a pocketful of Penguins,
> tired, ravenous and bored – for a cause.[35]

More notably, another Welsh poet, and one who has been emotionally involved with 'Spain' for all his creative life, is now concerned to take a wider perspective on the question of artistic antifascism, including Stalin's victims from the 1930s (Mayakovsky and Mandelstam) alongside Franco's (Lorca and Hernández) amongst his 'Beautiful Dead Poets'.[36]

Resistir es Vencer! Pasarémos!

Of all the tributes given by Welsh writers to the struggles chronicled in this book, that of Gwyn Alf Williams still has the most seductive resonance. Himself now suitably metempsychosized into one of the legendary and fiery dragons who stand guard over our mountain-buried monumental hoard, Williams completed his 'history of the Welsh' just as the miners' strike was taking hold of south Wales in the summer of 1984. With the Welsh people having (in his view) finally capitulated to populist imperialism and reactionary Thatcherism, with his own political and emotional world in agonized turmoil, he reached for the steady, solid signal of the sacrosanct cause.

> The greatest moment of glory was the Spanish Civil War. In a country which had plenty of working-class Spaniards and established links with Bilbao, the Civil War struck an even deeper chord than it did elsewhere . . . To serve in Spain became as much a mark of honour as to have gone to jail for the cause. Lodges raised money; a poverty-stricken people gave milk, money and goods to the Spanish Republic and took children from the Basque Republic into sanctuary even as Cardiff ship captains tried to run the Franco blockade. Lewis Jones the writer spent his energies on the cause; he dropped dead from exhaustion after addressing over thirty street meetings on Spain. His novel *We Live* reaches a climax with the departure of his hero (Communist, of course) for Spain. He had intended to complete the trilogy with the returned volunteers leading a revolution.[37]

This last sentence hints at the ultimate lost fulfilment of Williams's intellectual generation, greater even than the phantasm of worker–student solidarity, which moved them to a desperate and terminal sense of *hiraeth* – resistance, in arms, against a sea of troubles, even if it means Sartre's hard road to death.[38] The turnip-ghost army marching, banners bright for the cause, out from Merthyr and Maerdy to inevitable but exemplary defeat.

It was no mere coincidence that on the same page as the words quoted above, Williams referred to 'regular battles' in 1930s Merthyr, to 'some drilling around Tredegar', and recalled Aneurin Bevan's project for 'the formation of defence militias' against the fascists.[39] In Gwyn Thomas's writings, this feeling (or something similar) is transmuted into metaphorical divagations on the children's 'Jazz Bands' which are still a curious feature of Rhondda life. 'We were like an army that had nothing left to cheer about or cry about, not sure whether it was advancing or retreating and not caring. We had lost . . . [But] imagine' – Thomas later mused – 'if, instead of gazookas, they had carried rifles'.[40] A lineally descended, if attenuated, version of this sublime vision perhaps explains Plaid Cymru's recent tendency to adopt the cause of the Welsh Brigaders, a child which the demise of its parents, the Communist Party, and the altered circumstances of its guardians-by-default, Welsh Labour, has effectively orphaned. The move is strikingly reminiscent of the breathtaking opportunism of the Irish Labour Party and its union allies, who stridently took up the cause of the so-called 'Connolly Column' in the 1970s, having with almost equal vigour supported the Francoist cause in the 1930s! In both cases, the point is that, in the logic of cultural politics, resistance predicates oppression.

No one doubts the existence of oppression, either today in the wider world, or in 1930s Wales. Nor that the anonymous Rhondda housewife who saved the odd ha'penny from her housekeeping for 'Spain' and Augustus John who offered to paint the portrait of any patron who would donate 500 guineas to 'the cause' were, at least in this effort, united in one communion.[41] But in the cases of Ireland (and arguably Scotland) there was no need to manufacture a history of popular struggle and armed resistance, whether in the 1930s or the 1960s. As we have seen, both countries sent men to Spain in greater numbers than did Wales, even when calculated pro rata. In the Irish Free State, the Catholic clergy and some key lay organizations played a role analogous to that of the CPGB in Wales in mobilizing men and resources – but for the 'other side'! All the sums collected from the people across Wales by all the Spanish Aid agencies put together in three years of war, in total came nowhere near the more than £43,000 contributed by Irish Catholics – most of them poor by any standards – *on one day* in October 1936, to defend the rights of their Spanish co-religionists to worship in freedom.[42] From these differing perspectives, a conventional leftish vision of 'Celtic Radicals' which equates the histories of these nations in service to 'Spain' seems a somewhat myopic one.[43]

Moreover, as this book has amply illustrated, the cause supported by a huge majority of the population of Ireland – the 'other side' – was also 'the other' in a more current critical discourse. Ireland's cause was Franco's and the Catholic Church's, and thus utterly alien and suspect to the huge majority of the population of Wales. In many parts of Wales, expatriate Irish Catholics were often seen as something akin to the enemy within. Here and there, a few idiosyncratic Catholic aristocrats or dissident Welsh intellectuals played a similar role (if in miniature) to their 'Anglo' Church of Ireland equivalents across the Irish Sea. Whether their background was traditional Baptist or modern Bolshevik, the Welsh people agreed on anathematizing such papistical and retrogressive persuasions, a majority consensus which was frequently expressed as support for 'Spain'.[44]

In the end, therefore, it is not surprising that the Welsh role in Spain's civil war has hardly ever been singled out for specific mention by any relevant Spanish writing or media presentation. Apart from Franco's psychologist, Colonel Vallejo,[45] no one in Spain has ever noticed any special quality, ethnic or otherwise, neither fighting nor singing, contributed by Welsh members of the International Brigades. As already noted, few history textbooks or scholarly studies in English have detected anything specially different, noteworthy or substantial in the role played by Wales in the war's international dimension.[46] But there is one exception to this dictum, all the more startling for being both fervent and recent. The American scholar, James Hopkins, produced his outstanding interpretative study of the British Battalion in 1998. The book was greeted with dismay by many loyal 'insiders', including some academics, who considered it to be unjustly critical in detail, and negative in its general tone. Wherever else in Hopkins's book this dirt might stick, it certainly slides smoothly off the impeccably gleaming surface of his treatment of the Welsh involvement. With an admirable sense of the importance of place to any historian's analytical processes, as part of his fieldwork Hopkins spent some time in south Wales.

> I attended a gala in Swansea after the end of the miners' bitter year-long strike in 1984–85, and along with many others was deeply affected by the sad eclipse of what had long been a principal public and civic ritual of the Rhondda. During previous weeks I had spent a good deal of time in the company of several veterans of Spain, and was struck by the iconic status they possessed in their communities. This sense was reinforced when Neil Kinnock, the Labour leader, unveiled a memorial to the Welshmen who had fought in Spain, and in a few words, offered them the benediction of a new generation.[47]

The emotional rites of initiation made their mark on Hopkins, with the result that his book contains several glowing encomia to the Welsh volunteers, including the *summa cum laude* award, that they were produced by 'an unusually, perhaps uniquely literate population'.[48] He corroborates all the other qualities proposed by Francis, Smith, and other experts, and finds other collective distinctions where the present writer has often failed to do so – in their profound class solidarity and empathy, their informed and concerned internationalism, above all a 'unique political development' and sense of historical mission which set them apart as a 'working-class elite in Spain'.[49]

My scepticism on this and other points does not involve a failure to acknowledge the real substance of Wales's part in the Spanish Civil War.

Testaments to this (dear reader) are present on most of the pages of the book you have just (nearly) read.[50] As in some other relevant writings, my problems are not with the realities, insofar as I can assure myself of them, as with the myths, insofar as they were assuredly made in Wales. But rather than fall back existentially on the atheistic attitudes to 'grand narrative' espoused by Jean-Jacques Lyotard (his own adjective is 'pagan', but I'd as lief worship one god as many) we may adopt a middle way of limited and provisional belief. Estimating the historical impact of Wales's 'overseas' dimension upon the home communities, Gwyn Alf Williams remarked that 'the truth registers so powerfully on the Welsh imagination precisely because the Welsh, even the 2,600,000 Welsh of 1921, remained in objective terms a small people'.[51] Personally – though this is merely a matter of fundamentals – I would not be so cavalier about the truth. Nevertheless, Gwyn Alf's formulation is close enough to that which I essayed when setting out on this journey to encourage the feeling that a similar rationale may explain the impact of 'Spain' – or at any rate, the impression of the response to the impact – on Wales's historical memory. The Red Dragon, though appearing at first glance to be rampant, is in fact permanently suspended between our soiled green land and its pure grey air.

Appendix

Table A. Welsh Companies and Ships Trading with the Republic, 1936–1939

Name(s)[a]	No. of ships[b]
1. Melrose Abbey Shipping Co. [The Abbey Line]	4
2. F. Jones & Co.	4
3. Angel, Son & Co.	8
[Dillwyn Steamship Co.]	5
[Angel-Dalling Co.]	
4. Walter Vaughan (Cardiff) [Good Hope Steamship Co. Rising Sun Navigation Co. Anglo-Canadian Shipping Co. Seven Seas Shipping Co.]	5
5. Veronica Steamship Co.	3
6. Mooringwell Steamship Co.	2
7. S & R Steamships	3
8. Ridge Steamship Co.	1
9. Mordey, Son & Co.	1
10. African & Continental Steamship Co. [Atlantic & Mediterranean Trading Co. Continental Transit Co.]	14
11. Tatem Steamship Co.	2
12. Guardian Line Ltd.	4
13. Barry Shipping Co.	?
Total ships	56 plus

[a] Associate company names in brackets. Only holding companies are listed here, but several other firms were engaged in ancillary operations – management, contracts, etc.

[b] Some vessels changed hands during the period of the war – in certain cases, more than once.

Source: Heaton (1985).

Table B. Welsh Coal Exports to the Spanish Republic, 1938 (in tonnes)

Sailed	Vessel	Cargo	From/To	Category
April	Parklaan	5,998	Newport–Almeria–Barcelona	
	Clonlara	1,100	Cardiff–Almeria–Barcelona	
	Sheaf Water	3,800	Cardiff–Valencia	
	Willodale	2,455	Newport–Almeria–Barcelona	R Cardiff
	Farnham	7,525	Newport–Almeria–Barcelona	
	Lanchrome	1,020	Port Talbot–Almeria–Barcelona	
	Clintonia	4,968	Port Talbot–Almeria–Barcelona	
		26,866		
May	Stanburn	3,968	Cardiff–Almeria–Barcelona	
	Candleston Castle	3,531	Cardiff–Barcelona	R Cardiff
	Meopham	6,622	Newport–Almeria–Barcelona	
	McBrae	2,933	Newport–Almeria–Barcelona	O 12
	St Winifred	7,989	Newport–Almeria–Barcelona	
	MacLaren	3,398	Newport–Almeria–Barcelona	O 12 + R Cardiff
	Jeanne M	2,774	Port Talbot–Almeria–Barcelona	O 6 + R Cardiff
	Gothic	3,428	Newport–Almeria–Barcelona	
	Nailsea Lass	6,368	Newport–Almeria–Barcelona	O ? + R Cardiff
	Stanforth	2,303	Port Talbot–Almeria–Barcelona	
	Mortlake	2,327	Port Talbot–Almeria–Barcelona	
	Transit	4,750	Cardiff–Almeria–Barcelona	O 10
	Emerald Wings	2,750	Cardiff–Almeria–Barcelona	O 10
	Clintonia	4,999	Cardiff–Almeria–Barcelona	
		58,140		
June	McGregor	3,326	Cardiff–Almeria–Barcelona	O 12
	African Explorer	6,958	Newport–Almeria–Barcelona	O 10
	Houstone	5,697	Cardiff–Almeria–Barcelona	
	Stanhope	2,873	Cardiff–Almeria–Barcelona	
	Meopham	3,788[a]	Barry–Valencia	
	Peckham	3,788[a]	Cardiff–?	do
	McBrae	3,788[a]	Barry–Gibraltar[b]	do
		18,854		
July	Gothic	3,567	Cardiff–Almeria–Barcelona	
	Jeanne M	2,593	Port Talbot–Almeria–Barcelona	
		6,160		

Table B. *(Contd.)*

Sailed	Vessel	Cargo	From/To	Category
Aug.	Porthcarrick	403	Port Talbot–Almeria–Barcelona	
	Dover Abbey	1,250	Cardiff–Almeria–Barcelona	
	Gothic	2,912C	Newport–Barcelona	
	Toussika	2,698	Cardiff–Gibraltar[b]	
		7,263		
Sept.	Yorkbrook	1,259C	Newport–Barcelona	O 3
	Seabank Spray	3,450	Cardiff–Gibraltar[b]	O 5
		4,709		
Oct.	Luimneach	1,221	Swansea–Valencia	
	Essex Lance	9,628	Cardiff–Cartagena–Barcelona	
	Clare Lilley	6,364	Cardiff–Gibraltar[b]	
		17,213		
Nov.	Stanwold	**1,200**	Port Talbot–Valencia	
Dec.	Stanhope	**2,800**		
	plus	721[a]	Newport–Valencia	

Recorded Total **143,926 tonnes of coal fuel (incl. 4,892 coke)**, based on 38 voyages at an average of 3,788 tonnes per delivery. Total allowing for coefficients (41 voyages): 155,308 tonnes.

[a] These cargoes have been recorded at a coefficient derived from existing data.
[b] Nationalist intelligence indicated these sailings as having 'probable destino rojo'.

O = Owned by (nos refer to list in Table A)
R = Registered
C = Coke

Unless otherwise indicated, the source is MAE/R894. The last four sailings for June were reported to Burgos via its legation in Bucharest; report of 3 July 1938, MAE/R1058/1.

It seems possible: (i) that the Barry departures represent Cardiff sailings which loaded extra cargo in Barry before proceeding and (ii) that this information originated from the FET cell operating in Cardiff. It seems more than coincidence that this was established in the spring of 1938.

The quantity of Nationalist intelligence probably declined in the middle of 1938, since monthly totals must have been at least as great as earlier, given the *Western Mail* figures of 518,697 tons (NOT tonnes) for Jan.–Nov. 1938 inclusive, which indicate over 47,000 tons per month. In the same period, the same source gives 103,437 tonnes delivered from other British ports. Thus Welsh deliveries accounted for 58.2% of the total British contribution.

Table C. International Brigade volunteers giving home addresses or contact locations in Wales and/or with convincing evidence of recent Welsh connections (not a list of 'Welsh Volunteers')

1. Adlam, Thomas	Pentre	28	CP	Multiple
2. Baker, George	Rhondda	35	CP	Multiple
3. Barrett, David	Blackwood	23	CP	4, 5, 13
4. Bevan, Kenneth	Gorseinon	28		2, 3, 4
5. Bevan, William	Penycraig	21	CP	1, 14, 15, 19
6. Boddy, Henry	Cardiff	23		1, 8, 19
7. Brewer, Jim	Rhymney	24	CP/LP	2, 3, 16, 17
8. Brickell, Leslie J.	Tredegar	24		2, 3, 9, 11, 17
9. Brown, Ronald	Aberaman	21	CP	2, 3, 5, 20
10. Bush, Arthur	Port Talbot	30	CP	1, 20
11. Coles, William	Cardiff	25	CP	1, 10, 20
12. Condon, Robert	Aberaman	24	CP	Multiple
13. Cook, Archibald	Ystrad Rhondda	29	CP	Multiple
14. Cox, Robert	Tredegar	38	CP	1, 14, 20
15. Cummings, Alec	Dinas	28	CP	Multiple
16. David, Reginald	Ton Pentre/Canada	29		20 (2)
17. Davies, Ben	Newport	34	CP	1, 2, 3, 13, 14
18. Davies, Dan D.	Pentre	26	LP	1, 2, 3, 14, 15
19. Davies, D. R.	Crumlin	23	CP	1, 20 (2)
20. Davies, Harold	Neath	35	LP	1, 8, 20
21. Davies, Ivor	Neath	23	CP	2, 3, 4, 13
22. Davies, Morris	Treharris	32	CP	Multiple
23. Davies, Thomas E.	Penygraig	38	CP	1
24. Davies, Thomas R.	Bedlinog	39	CP	Multiple
25. Davies, William J.	Tonypandy	26	CP	1, 10, 16, 17
26. Davies, William J.	Pantyffynon, Carms	36	CP	1, 17
27. Dimitriou, Euripedes aka James Peters	Cardiff [Cypriot]			2, 3
28. Dobson, Harry	Blaenclydach	29	CP	Multiple
29. Donoghue, Michael	Merthyr	34	CP	Multiple
30. Durston, William	Aberaman	18	CP	3, 10, 12, 13
31. Ellis, Evan	Caerphilly	29	CP	Multiple
32. Esteban, Victoriano	Abercrave	40	CP	Multiple
33. Evans, Thomas G.	Bridgend	27	LP	1, 2, 3, 20
34. Faraday, William	Goodwick, Pembs			20
35. Foulkes, John	Treherbert	25		Multiple
36. Fretwell, George	Penygroes	20	LP	1, 10
37. Gale, I. J.	Abertillery			17, 18
38. Ginsberg, Reuben aka Gainsborough	Carmarthen	20		5, 11, 16, 17

Table C. *(Contd.)*

39. Greening, Edwin	Aberdare	27	CP	Multiple
40. Griffiths, Emrys	Pontypridd	29		16, 20
41. Griffiths, William	Llwynypia	30	CP	2, 3, 13
42. Hamm, Sidney	Cardiff	21	CP	Multiple
43. Harrington, Tim	Merthyr	40	CP	1, 6
44. Harris, Jack	Llanelli	34	CP	1, 10
45. Hausmann, Carl	Conwy/San Francisco	19		4, 20 (2)
46. Havard, Morgan	Craig-Cefn-Parc	23	CP	2, 3, 16, 17
47. Hooper, David	Porth/Kilburn		CP	3, 11, 12, 20
48. Hopkins, William	Aberdare	37	CP	Multiple
49. Horridge, Richard	Swansea	30		10, 20
50. Howells, D. J.	Rhondda	42	CP	1
51. Howells, Glyn	Blaengarw/London	18		3, 5
52. Howells, John D.	Blaengarw/London		CP	2, 3
53. Humphreys, Charles	Tremadoc			2, 3, 20
54. Hurley, Thomas J.	Treharris	18		2, 16, 17, 20
55. Hyndman, Tony	Cardiff/London	25	CP	Multiple
56. James, Percy M.	Crymwch/Vancouver	35		4, 20
57. James, Sidney	Treherbert	33		Multiple
58. Jenkins, Brynley	Swansea	22		2, 3, 5, 20
59. Jenkins, H. R.	Barry	39		1, 8
60. Jenkins, Joseph	Pontardawe	49	LP	1, 14, 15, 20
61. John, Leonard	Cardiff	24	CP	Multiple
62. Jones, Bedlington	Tredegar	35	CP	Multiple
63. Jones, David A.	Ammanford	29	CP	1, 20
64. Jones, D. Howell	Maesteg	35	CP	1, 16, 20
65. Jones, Joseph	Penygraig	39	CP	1, 16, 17, 20
66. Jones, David M.	Maerdy		CP	2, 3, 10, 20
67. Jones, Emrys	Tonypandy	30	CP	Multiple
68. Jones, Evan J.	Llanelli	25	CP	2, 3, 5, 20, 21
69. Jones, Griffith	Dowlais	31	CP	Multiple
70. Jones, Jack	Tonypandy	40	CP	Multiple
71. Jones, Richard	Cardiff	45		4, 9, 8
72. Jones, Thomas C.	Wrexham	29	CP	Multiple
73. Jones, Thomas	Tonypandy	29	CP	Multiple
74. Jones, Thomas H.	Aberdare	36	CP	Multiple
75. Jorro, José	Cardiff/Slough			2, 3, 20
76. Ledbury, Archie	Swansea	29	CP	Multiple
77. Levin, Matthew	Caerphilly	23		2, 8, 16, 19, 20
78. Llewelyn D. R.	Blaengarw	29	CP	16, 17, 20
79. Lloyd, Emlyn	Llanelli	29	CP	Multiple

Table C. *(Contd.)*

80. Lloyd, Evan	Bedlinog	21	CP	3, 5
81. Lloyd, Harold	Cwmtillery	38	CP	Multiple
82. Magner, Charles C.	Cardiff	30	CP	5, 8
83. Manning, Hector	Dinas	22	YCL	Multiple
84. Middleton, Frank	Trealaw	56	CP	Multiple
85. Morgan, Morien	Ynysybwl	21	CP	2, 4, 9, 20
86. Morris, Arthur	Cardigan/Canada	30	CP	10, 20
87. Morris, Alfred J.	Maerdy	40	CP	Multiple
88. Morris, W.	Llanelli	38		1, 10, 20
89. Morris, Sam	Ammanford	30	CP	1, 10, 14, 20
90. Morrisey, William	Cardiff	29	CP	Multiple
91. Morrison, William	Maerdy	27		2, 11, 12, 20
92. Murphy, Daniel	Cardiff			2, 3, 10, 20
93. Murphy, Pat	Cardiff	40	CP	Multiple
94. Murray, John	Maesteg	34	CP	1, 2, 3, 14, 20
95. Nash, William	Nantyglo	56	CP	1, 20
96. Nicholls, M. Gwilym	Cardiff	27	CP	Multiple
97. Oliver, John	Blackwood	27		2, 5, 16, 17
98. Owen, Frank	Maerdy	34	CP	Multiple
99. Palmer, Charles E.	Llandudno	27		Multiple
100. Parfitt, Cyril	Llangynwyd	25		1, 2, 4, 20
101. Patterson, Harold	Penarth	29	CP	1, 8, 20
102. Paynter, Will	Tonypandy	33	CP	Multiple
103. Peters, Evan	Merthyr	30	CP	1, 14, 15, 20
104. Peters, Robert	Penarth/Canada	23	CP	5, 8, 9
105. Picton, Thomas	Treherbert	40	CP	Multiple
106. Powell, Edwin J.	Treorchy	30	CP	3, 13
107. Price, Evan G.	Onllwyn	25	CP	Multiple
108. Price, Godfrey J.	Cardiff	36	CP	2, 3, 5, 8
109. Price, Leo	Abertregwen	32	CP	2, 3, 4, 12, 20
110. Price, Reg George	Bedlinog	22	CP	2, 3, 5, 16, 17
111. Price, William	Ton Pentre	35	CP	7, 16
112. Rees, William J.	Glanaman	23	LP	1, 2, 7, 14
113. Reynolds, Thomas W.	Swansea		CP	17, 18, 20
114. Roberts, Jack	Abertridwr	35	CP	2, 3, 7, 20
115. Roberts, Jack C.	Trealaw	32	CP	2, 3, 5, 13, 20
116. Roberts, Penry	Caernarfon	24		3, 4
117. Roberts, Robert	Anglesey	29		2, 3, 4, 20
118. Roberts, Thomas	Bedlinog	31	LP	Multiple
119. Rodriguez, Roman	Dowlais	37	CP	Multiple
120. Rogers, Lance	Merthyr	20	CP	Multiple

Table C. *(Contd.)*

121. Rogers, William	Wrexham	23	CP	5, 13, 20
122. Scott, James	Swansea			2, 3, 10
123. Skinner, Alwyn M.	Neath	27	CP	Multiple
124. Skinner, Baden A.	Tredegar/Vancouver	37	CP	10, 20 (3)
125. Stickler, Thomas	Cardiff	29		5, 8, 19, 20
126. Strangward, James	Onllwyn	24	CP	2, 3, 16, 17
127. Stratton, Harry	Swansea	32	CP	6, 14, 20
128. Taylor, Gilbert	Cardiff		CP	2, 3, 10, 20
129. Thomas, Brazell	Llanelli	26	CP	2, 3, 10
130. Thomas, Thomas J.	Bedlinog	35	CP	1, 20 (3)
131. Thomas, William J.	Aberavon		CP	Multiple
132. Traill, Robert	Cardiff	23	CP	1, 10, 20 (2)
133. Vranch, Bertram	Abertillery	32	CP	Multiple
134. Ward, William H.	Barry	34		8, 17
135. Watkins, Wyndham	Abertridwr	35	CP	Multiple
136. Watts, James	Swansea		CP	2, 10, 16, 17
137. Watts, Robert	Swansea	33	CP	2, 3, 4, 16, 17
138. White, Fred	Ogmore Vale	33	CP	1, 10, 14
139. Widdess, J. K.	Cardiff			3, 5, 9
140. Williams, Alun M.	Penygraig	24	CP	Multiple
141. Williams, Edwin F.	Newport	24	CP	3, 11
142. Williams, Frank	Newport/Calgary			2, 3, 5
143. Williams, Henry	Penygraig	29	CP	Multiple
144. Williams, John S.	Dowlais	40	CP	1, 14, 20
145. Williams, John E.	Ammanford	29	CP	Multiple
146. Williams, Rowland	Trelewis	33	CP	Multiple
147. Yemm, Archibald aka Bartlett	Pontypridd			20 (3)
148. Zamora, Frank	Abercrave	22	CP	2, 3, 10

Also served with the Republican forces
Amador Aristegui, Dulais/Baracaldo (Vizcaya) (?Basque Militia)
James Cope, Cardiff (?POUM Militia)
Uriah Jones, Tumble (POUM Militia)
Parry Thomas, Anglesey (POUM Militia)
Robert Williams, (?POUM Militia)

Served with the Nationalist Army
Frank Thomas, Cardiff (Spanish Foreign Legion)

Sources:
  1. Full Battalion Roll, [May/June 1937] IBA Box D7-A2
  2. Full Battalion Roll, [June/July 1938] IBA Box D7-A1

3. Full Battalion Roll, [Sept. 1938] RGASPI 545/6/39/65–99
4. POW Lists [April 1938, San Pedro] AHM Avila Leg CGG 58
5. Lists of Repatriated British Brigaders [Dec. 1938] PRO FO 369/2514
6. Medical Commission Reports [Aug.–Nov. 1937] ANGC Salamanca SM 4763
7. Individual Brigaders' Index Cards, ANGC Salamanca PS Aragon Leg. 127
8. J. Carmody, List of Cardiff & District Volunteers based on IBA Archive.
9. POW lists and Diplomatic Inquiries, MAE Madrid R1051 & 1069
10. Memorial Plaque, Miners' Library, Hendrefoilan
11. 'Bad Elements', c.May 1938, RGASPI 545/3/451/156
12. 'Elementos sospechosos de Tarazona', 17 March 1938, RGASPI 545/6/39/9–25
13. 'Party Comrades in Spain or Repatriated', 19 September 1938, RGASPI
   545/6/99–104
14. 16th Battalion Roll, c.25 June 1937 RGASPI 545/6/47/17–9
15. List of 'English Comrades at Madrigueras', 5 May 1937, RGASPI/545/6/53/5
16. Francis, Ph.D. thesis (1977), vol. ii, appendix list
17. Francis (1984)
18. Stradling (1998)
19. Stradling (1996)
20. Scattered/random corraborative sources

Cases which have more than five independent corroborations are recorded as 'Multiple'.

Table C has been reduced from an original list of 181 names for whom some reference exists for having been to Spain. My procedure was:
A. to include all names with a Welsh connection attributed in the official documentation of the British Battalion (mainly to be found in the IBA Archive or in RGASPI, Moscow), or in contemporary archival sources of other organizations, or in contemporary newspapers, even where such reference was uncorroborated elsewhere;
B. to exclude all names where a Welsh connection was not evident, either directly or circumstantially (thus I discounted volunteers born outside Wales to emigrant parents, and who had never returned to live in Wales; those whose (putative) claim resided merely in 'Welsh' surnames; those who came to live in Wales after serving in Spain; and – of course – all whose attribution rested on hearsay alone).
C. to exclude any who volunteered, but never actually arrived in Spain;

However, the following anomalies may be noted. First, Carl Hausmann was born in Colwyn Bay (?c.1910) of German (Sudeten?) parents who later re-emigrated to the USA (presumably in 1914). He went to Spain from San Francisco, travelling with a British passport, and on arrival joined the British Training Battalion in Tarazona (July 1937). He was later transferred to the (American) Lincoln Battalion, but after being wounded during the Teruel campaign he rejoined the British. He was captured at Belchite on 10 March 1938, imprisoned in San Pedro de Cárdena, and released with the main body of British POWs in late 1938; see IBA Box 21/J/H, memo. probably by M. Economides. In March 1939, a correspondent signing himself 'Carel Hautmann' wrote to the *South Wales Echo* on the subject of the war in Spain.

Secondly, the only relevant piece of evidence about Robert Traill is the contact address in Radyr, Cardiff, which he gave to Albacete officials on arriving in Spain from Moscow and is found in several subsequent documents. Since he had married in Moscow, this address probably indicated a parent or close parental relative. However, Kelly's *Directory* for 1937 fails to confirm any Cardiff resident with this surname. [Possibly his mother had remarried.] I have given some weight to the fact that Traill's was amongst the bundle of death certificates specifically relevant to Welsh volunteers which Bert Williams brought home to Britain in the summer of 1937; RGASPI 545/6/51/107. In 2001 the present writer was in contact with Traill's daughter, who knew little about her father's background, and was unable to confirm any Welsh connection. Nevertheless, I have included his name on the strength of rule A above added to the descriptive title of this Appendix; for further information and sources, see Stradling (1996), 122–3.

Notes

Chapter 1:   Prologue: Castles in Wales

[1] Howells (1975), 97.

[2] *Tenby Observer*, 31 July 1936.

[3] See Kollar (1995).

[4] In 1913, south Pembrokeshire boasted no fewer than twenty places of worship belonging to the Calvinistic-Methodist Church alone: Evans and Symond (1913). The Cistercians – it may be noted – are not a missionary order.

[5] Howells (1975), 82–3. One is not sure of the manner in which brethren could have obeyed their superior's advice. However, on more than one occasion that summer, local police officers visited the abbey and interviewed some foreign inmates. At the outbreak of war in 1939, several of the younger monks who had thus adopted 'England' were to be called up by the Belgian and French governments: ibid., 83, 223.

[6] See, for example, Morris (1986), 325, who goes so far as to indict it as 'the most absolutely un-Welsh of all the towns of Wales'.

[7] *Tenby Observer*, 28 August 1936.

[8] *Tenby Observer*, 11 September 1936.

[9] *Tenby Observer*, 18 September 1936.

[10] *Tenby Observer*, 27 November 1936.

[11] *Tenby Observer*, 23 July 1937.

[12] Griffiths (2002), 23.

[13] For some time in the 1580s, Jesuits operated a secret recusant propaganda press from a cave poised above the sea on a promontory near Llandudno: Morris (1984/1986), 100. One wonders if Mrs Horner was privy to this information as well as Sir Francis Walsingham.

[14] The topics touched on in these two paragraphs receive more detailed attention (and source-referencing) below, in Chapters 9 and 10.

[15] Apparently, the irate man had been deeply moved by relevant local memorials during a recent holiday in Pyrenean France. Many refugee veterans of the Republican armies defeated by Franco were still in France at the time of the German invasion in 1940. Their consequent further struggles and sufferings are the subject of Pike (1969).

[16] Stradling (1999).

[17] *El Pais*, 20 September 1997.

[18] G. A. Williams (1985), *passim*; Morris (1984), 334, 394; Morgan (1981), 9.

[19] Davies (1994), 595; Morgan (1981), 290–1 and (1995), 193–4; Jenkins (1992).

[20] Morris (1984), 410.

[21] Buchanan (1997), 66 and 96.

[22] Smith (1993), 339–40.

[23] Francis (1984). The doctoral thesis on which this study was based was, however, completed in 1977 and carried the title 'The south Wales miners and the Spanish Civil War: a study in internationalism'.

[24] Ibid., 68–74 and 80.

[25] Lyne (1996), 1–2 and 10–11.

[26] Francis (1984), 157. See also the advance summary of his book, published as a chapter of Francis and Smith (1980), 350–75, where this point emerges strongly.

[27] Gli antifascisti (1976), esp. 35–48.

[28] Francis (1991), 69–76. A friendly reviewer of Miners Against Fascism complained that 'there is no need for Hywel to tell us on every possible occasion that a particular "goodie" is a communist': Radical Wales, 3 (Summer 1984), 24.

[29] Perhaps more usefully defined, this refers to the area which today lies between the M4 motorway to the south and the road-sequence which run along the heads of the valleys to the north.

[30] Williams J, (1985), 62–5.

[31] Evans (2000), 95.

[32] Francis (1984), 115.

[33] Welsh Review, 1, 3 (May 1939), 180–1.

[34] Caernarvon and Denbigh Herald, 20 January 1939. We may safely assume that the garages were not named in celebration of their owner's ideological affiliation.

[35] Caernarvon and Denbigh Herald, 10 February 1939.

Chapter 2:   Bible and Babel: Rural and Industrial Wales

[1] G. A. Williams (1985), 211.

[2] Wrexham was more akin to the anthracite valleys of the south-west than to the Rhondda: see Matthews (1992), 96–104. Pontypool was set exactly on a geological divide. It had been the site of early industrial development, and by the 1930s boasted railway marshalling yards and the Hanbury mineral works – with pitheads not too far away: see, for example G. A. Williams (1985), 143. Interestingly, there is no record of any International Brigade volunteer hailing from the town.

[3] See Williams (1996), passim.

[4] Francis (1984), 31–4. For further exposition of this theme, see below, Ch. 5.

[5] However, another consequence of this – as Bill Jones pointed out to me – was that the phenomenon of intra-migration in the previous century (above all from north and mid to south) had by the 1930s woven greater and tighter connections than ever before between the peoples of the different areas of Wales subsumed in the present chapter. See also Evans (1989).

[6] 'Rhyfel Cartrefol Spaen', Seren Cymru, 24 July 1936. For the Western Mail, see below, Chapter 4, esp. pp. 93–4.

[7] *Seren Cymru*, 18 December 1936 (printed in English).

[8] Though the role of the press is directly considered elsewhere (see Ch. 4), the varied mix of local reports, editorial comment and readers' correspondence provide a valuable source of information which cannot be overlooked at any stage of this study.

[9] See Bebbington (1983), 76ff. (However, the writer fails to include the Spanish Civil War amongst the issues which concerned Baptists in the 1930s.)

[10] 'Trafferth Spaen', *Seren Cymru*, 31 July 1936.

[11] *Miners Against Fascism* fails to acknowledge that coalfield internationalism owed any debt to older organizations, except in pointing out that Welsh International Brigaders acted in conformity with their compatriots' opinion (70 per cent in the Peace Ballot of 1935) that military measures may be legitimately utilized to counter international aggression; Francis (1984), 31–2. It goes on to suggest that the internationalist spirit of the coalfield was unique and indigenous, partly because inspired by the cosmopolitanism endowed by its many immigrants, including Spanish and Italian antifascist families.

[12] He adds that 'Baptist Churches commonly affiliated to the [League of Nations] Union as corporate members': Bebbington (1983), 83–4.

[13] Jones (1969), 97–140, *passim*, esp. 131, 140.

[14] I am indebted to Meirion Hughes for this suggestion.

[15] In the early 1930s this proposal was stimulated by stories about the *Schützbunde* in socialist Vienna and was popular within the Aneurin Bevan–Archie Lush (Central Labour College) circle; see Francis (1984), 62–3.

[16] *Caernarvon and Denbigh Herald*, 24 February 1939.

[17] I failed to find any recorded expression of *explicit support* for the Spanish Nationalist cause deriving from within the regions covered by this chapter. Though absence of evidence is not evidence of absence, this fact tends to support the chapter separation resolved upon.

[18] Indeed, Franco's personal *bêtes noires* were not the Reds but the Freemasons, traditionally denounced as enemies of the Church, to be found in many areas of Spanish business life, and (to the *Caudillo*'s extreme disapproval) even amongst the army top brass: see Ashford-Hodges (2000), 150–2.

[19] Above, n. 6. The word 'tenants' ('deiliaid') was carefully selected to remind many rural-based readers of the ancestral bondage maintained by vicar and squire from which they themselves had all-too-recently escaped.

[20] G. Williams (2002), 14.

[21] The original diagnosis was made by Julián Juderías in 1912. On the singularity of Wales's subscription to this cultural construction, see G. A. Williams (1985), 123ff. Though spawning a considerable literature, little study has been made of its function in northern Europe subsequent to the Reformation epoch. For comment on its US dimension in the Franco period, see Powell (1971), esp. 155–6.

[22] *West Wales Observer*, 31 July 1936. The athletes had been carefully briefed by the CPGB in an attempt to counter (or 'explain') press accounts of anticlerical atrocities in Barcelona and elsewhere. Their version was not wholly convincing.

Readers may have been surprised, for example, that they were fluent enough in Spanish (or Catalan) to have interviewed so many witnesses.

23   *South Wales Weekly Argus*, 10 April 1937. It was resolved that material issued by the Council should also warn against atheistic communism. It has been noted that 'the sufferings of Baptists in Russia, though acute after 1929, were very little known' to their co-religionists in Britain: Bebbington (1983), 84.

24   Francis (1984), 117.

25   Davies (1961), esp. 164–6 and 170–1. The author states that he 'co-operated closely' with the Communist Party on the issue of Spain, a euphemistic formulation, often encountered, of fellow-travelling and even actual membership. The mission to which Davies belonged published a *Report of a recent Religious Delegation to Spain, April 1937, by the Dean of Canterbury (et al.)* (Gollancz, 1937).

26   As claimed in the marvellous Channel 4 programme *Voice of the People* (No. 6 in the series 'Cracking Up' (1989) directed by C. Thomas, scripted and presented by G. A. Williams).

27   Francis (1984), 49. Cf. the accounts of Nicholas's loyalties given in Peate and Hughes (1948) and Anon. (1981).

28   Letters printed in Francis (1984), 269, 274.

29   Stratton (1984), 33. The key words here are 'They told us that . . .' Jack Roberts of Abertridwr claimed to have heard the same story from village schoolchildren who 'revelled in the macabre details': Felstead (1981), 60. Around the same time these accounts appeared, one of the witnesses in the BBC Wales TV series *Collier's Crusade* (episode 2), told viewers that the said priest had slaughtered women and children; when captured he was thrown out of the tower with a rope around his neck and hit the ground in two pieces. Sincere as witnesses may have been in retelling them, little credence can be placed in any of these tales: cf. Stradling (1999), 193–7 and (2003), 134–5.

30   Inglis (1985), 117; see also (for example) 106, 122, 164, 183. Edmunds lived in England for eight months in 1936–7, but never seems to have strayed across Offa's Dyke.

31   Ibid., 182.

32   Francis (1984), 117, 123, 183–4, 187.

33   Morgan (1981), 55, 149, 151, 174.

34   Glanmor Williams – however – asserts that 'relatively few of the Spaniards were fervently Catholic'; Williams (2002), 10.

35   Llewellyn and Watkins (2001); Macho (1976). See also Eaton (1980), 78–9.

36   Quoted in Lewis (1990), 58. (The reference is to Arthur Horner.)

37   Llewellyn and Watkins (2001, publication unpaginated); Macho (1976), 20–1. The issues raised here are treated more expansively below, Ch. 3. As a child the present writer spent holidays in Abercrave, and remembers it as the place where he heard both Welsh and Spanish spoken for the first time – a veritable Babel!

38   Pugh (1988), 72–3.

39   *Manchester Guardian*, 5 April 1940: cutting in IBA/Box 50/Jo/10. International Brigade POWs were indeed for a time forced to attend Sunday Mass, but to

administer the Eucharist in the manner suggested would have constituted a flagrant act of blasphemy, allegedly performed in front of the invited Francoist press.

[40] *North Wales Observer*, 19 November 1936.

[41] *North Wales Observer*, 17 September 1937. In this context, many must have drawn certain conclusions from McGrath's visit – in full canonical regalia – to Saunders Lewis in his cells at Wormwood Scrubs; see Hughes (1999), 183.

[42] Quoted ibid., 68.

[43] *Wrexham Leader*, 21 May 1937. If made about the PCE itself, W. Maldwyn Jones's point would have been strictly correct, but by 'communism' McGrath meant (and his critic understood) all the forces on the left who challenged the power of the Church.

[44] *Wrexham Leader*, esp. various contributions by the vicar in July and August. For Cosmo Lang's remarks, see *Caernarvon and Denbigh Herald*, 8 January 1937.

[45] *Wrexham Leader*, 13 August 1937.

[46] *Caernarvon and Denbigh Herald*, 5 March 1937. The reference was to the execution of around a dozen priests who had acted as chaplains to the forces of the autonomous Basque government – an office which, of course, was commonplace throughout the ranks of Nationalist Army itself.

[47] *Wrexham Leader*, 9 April 1937.

[48] After the electricity supply failed in one local venue, a local minister ran a line from his private generator and salvaged the meeting; see Fyrth (1986), 205.

[49] Hyde (1952), 58. Hyde later converted to Catholicism. The present writer was introduced to his book as a sixth former in his Catholic grammar school. It had, of course, an equally propagandist purpose to the earlier communist mission it relates.

[50] *Caernarvon and Denbigh Herald*, 5 March 1937. See also *North Wales Observer*, 11 March 1937. Revd Davies announced that the Free Church Council for Wales would organize a house-to-house collection for 'Spain' in Holyhead.

[51] *North Wales Observer*, 18 March 1937. On other aspects of this campaign, centred around the slogan of 'A Welsh Ambulance for Spain', see below p. 35ff.

[52] B. Davies to Dr R. Jones, 4 September 1937, NLW/Ben Davies Collection/Box 18/1.

[53] *North Wales Observer*, 20 August 1936. Though perhaps exaggerated, the letter (written from Marseilles) seems too early an artefact to be the result of deliberate Francoist attempts to influence British opinion. After being disabled from flying, the writer was seconded to the Irish Legionary Bandera (the 15th) as a liaison officer; see Stradling (1999), 264 and sources cited.

[54] See the tribute to him in the memoir of one of Franco's aviation 'aces', José Larios (1966: 46), who also comments on his inappropriate surname – given that many of the Nationalists' best regiments were Moroccan.

[55] For this and other reasons it seems less than fully correct to assert that Plaid's policies in this era were 'essentially an extension of Lewis's personal views'; Davies, in Jenkins (1998), x.

[56] Meils (1977). (Despite his intellectual obsessions, Bebb 'remained a Welsh Presbyterian all his life': D. G. Jones (1973), 44.)

[57] It seems likely that the 'spiritual ancestor' of the group was Robert Ambrose

Jones ('Emrys ap Iwan'), an advocate of Welsh home rule during the Gladstone era, Jones was 'an eccentric figure . . . sympathetic to Roman Catholicism and an ardent admirer of French culture, who felt distaste for the narrow horizons of Calvinist Wales'; Morgan (1981), 113; see also Jones (1973), 52–4.

[58] See Griffiths (2002).

[59] Humphreys (1986), 124ff., 150ff.; quotation from p. 93.

[60] Jenkins (1998). The Plaid leadership's inspiration was, of course, rooted in indigenous and even spiritual considerations – the fact that the site chosen was sacrosanct in the heritage of both language and religion. But also influenced by the tactical reckoning that the party needed its 'martyrs' and would benefit from the publicity that such a protest would inevitably bring in its train.

[61] For the dampening influence of the 'hunger march' campaign on awareness of the Spanish War, see Francis (1984), 107–8. Of course, the marches had begun some two years before the crisis of 'Spain', and as a recent scholar observes, provided a groundswell to the drive for 'Unity': Evans (1999), 187–9. He also points out the strong links of ministers of religion with anti-Means Test campaigns in Wales (190–1).

[62] See my forthcoming study 'Imagined atrocity: the Getafe incident and Republican propaganda in the Spanish Civil War'.

[63] Thomas and Witts (1975/1991).

[64] *Welsh Nationalist*, February 1936. These leader column comments may be fairly attributed to the editor, Saunders Lewis.

[65] *Welsh Nationalist*, July 1938.

[66] See Stradling (2003), 125–6. Because of its role as part-instigator of 'non-intervention', many regarded (and some still regard) Britain as an accessory to the 'baby-murdering'.

[67] *Welsh Nationalist*, February 1936.

[68] Q. in Jenkins (1998), pp. ix–x.

[69] 'Esbonio Helynt Spaen', *Y Ddraig Goch*, September 1936. 'Pronounces' refers to the origins of the Castilian word for a *coup d'état*, that is, 'pronunciamiento'. The quotation is from S. de Madariaga's *Spain* (Routledge and Kegan Paul, 1930) – but it should be noted that the exiled author adopted a carefully neutral stance on the war.

[70] *Welsh Nationalist*, September 1936. Neither Daniel nor Lewis mentioned General Franco. In allowing the inference that Portugal was genuinely neutral, Lewis wrote in complete ignorance of the true situation. On Portugal's role see Rosas (1998) and Wharton (2000).

[71] 'Y Sefyllfa yn Sbaen', *Y Ddraig Goch*, November 1936.

[72] *Welsh Nationalist*, October 1936.

[73] See *Y Ddraig Goch*, December 1936, *et seq*. Lewis was obliged to relinquish the editorial chair of *The Welsh Nationalist* on his committal to Wormwood Scrubs in early 1937. Further exploration of *Plaid*'s (and other party) policies over Spain will be found below, Ch. 4.

[74] *North Wales Observer*, 1 October 1936. (I have assumed that this newspaper was

not singled out for attention.) The apparent lack of response to this appeal may have been due to its emphasis that 'relief given, will, of course, be administered without regard to creed or politics or race'.

75 Hyde (1952), 45.

76 Lewis (1970), 22ff.

77 The author confessed to have been a devout communist, even down to the practice of free love – a remarkable achievement for the time and place. Some readers may be relieved to discover that 'recruits to the party came thick and fast' not for this reason but as a result of the outbreak of the Spanish War. Like George Orwell in Hertfordshire, Hyde ran a smallholding as well as writing profusely, and was on good terms with the squire and the vicar.

78 Ibid., 58–9. At one of these meetings, at the 'slate' village of Penygroes, Hyde recruited the unemployed quarryman George Fretwell, who was to be killed on the first day of the British Battalion's campaign, at the battle of Jarama (12 February 1937); Williams *et al.* (1996), 66.

79 In autumn 1936, for example, he was contributing an occasional column to the *North Wales Observer* covering such topics as social events, countryside issues, gardens and the theatre.

80 He himself attributed it to 'humanitarian motives' in an article he wrote for *Peace News*, 20 November 1937. But in addition to this essay ('To bomb or not to bomb? – That is *not* the question') Williams-Hughes contributed over a dozen other pieces to various English- and Welsh-language papers after his return from Spain, including the *News Chronicle*, the *Western Mail* (in Welsh), the *South Wales Echo* and *Tir Newydd*; see the collection in SUCC/SC 324.

81 *Wrexham Leader*, 12 March 1937.

82 See Hyde (1952), 59–61.

83 Fyrth (1986), esp. 181–7.

84 *Wrexham Leader*, 5 March 1937.

85 Brief treatment of the campaign described below can be found in Francis (1984), 99–100 and 122–3, and Fyrth (1986), 204–6.

86 *North Wales Observer*, 11 March 1937; see also *Caernarvon and Denbigh Herald*, 12 March 1937. The bullet, which was passed from hand to hand, was a brilliantly chosen artefact, since it put across three powerful propaganda notions in one pocket-sized item. First, the idea that the enemy was operating ruthlessly and outside the Geneva Convention on the conduct of war; second, that the enemy included German infantry units; third, that the British medical staff treated all wounded irrespective of their affiliation. Only the last of these points was valid; the second was untrue (there are very few recorded cases of capture of German personnel by republican forces); the first was true of both sides.

87 *Wrexham Leader*, 12 March 1937.

88 *North Wales Observer*, 18 March 1937.

89 *North Wales Observer*, 1 April 1937. This item appeared the newspaper's final issue – before it merged with a competitor. Yet, in 35 issues which appeared after war had broken out in Spain, neither editorial comment nor readers' correspondence

on the subject had been printed. It seems that no sign of any 'widespread sympathy' in Bangor was evident before its report on the Caernarfon meeting (above, n. 74)!

90   Few or none of these events – at one time running, Hyde claimed, at two or three per day – were reported in the press: Hyde (1952), 58.

91   *Wrexham Leader*, 9 April 1937.

92   Williams-Hughes to Hyde, 3 April 1937, SUCC/SC753.

93   *Western Mail*, ?5 April 1937. See also Jones (1991), 116 and 125.

94   *Caernarvon and Denbigh Herald*, 9 April 1937. (£20 would be the equivalent of nearly £1,000 today.)

95   Francis (1984), esp. 86–95.

96   *Wrexham Leader*, 25 September 1936.

97   *Wrexham Leader*, 13 October 1936. (In fact this report contains no mention of Spain.)

98   *Wrexham Leader*, 18 September 1936. Only eleven delegates supported Monslow's call for active British intervention on behalf of the Republic.

99   *Caernarvon and Denbigh Herald*, 19 March 1937.

100 *Welsh Gazette* (Aberystwyth), 31 March 1938.

101 For closer attention to the 'Unity Campaign', see below, p. 66ff.

102 I refer to the 'civil war within the civil war' which broke out in Barcelona in May, terminally poisoning relations between the government and the PCE on the one hand, and the 'revolutionary' elements of the Popular Front on the other.

103 *Proceedings of Cardiff City Council* (1936–7), 308. A 'flag day' was agreed for 27 March 1937.

104 *Caernarvon and Denbigh Herald*, 23 April 1937.

105 Ibid.

106 For detailed general treatment of the evacuation, see Legarreta (1984). Bell (1996) concentrates on the British aspect, on which see also the dedicated chapter in Fyrth (1986), 220–42, and Buchanan (1997), esp. 109–16. However, none of these has anything of substance to say about the Welsh dimension, a lacuna which places an even greater premium on the excellent section in Francis (1984), 125–8.

107 *South Wales Weekly Argus*, 29 May 1937. The novelist, Richard Hughes, observed that the Basques deserved every hospitality in Wales because they were 'brothers of blood'; quoted by Francis (1984), 126.

108 Ibid., 125–6. In Cardiff, over £500 was collected by the end of July, including £11 from Cardiff High School for (middle class) Girls and 10s. from the Infants' School in working-class Grangetown; *Western Mail*, 30 July 1937.

109 'Orphans of the Storm', BBC Radio Wales (?1987). I am most grateful to Mrs L. Savens of Caerleon who kindly sent me a recording of this programme.

110 *Caernarvon and Denbigh Herald*, 14 June 1937; *Cambrian Times*, 14 August 1937.

111 A certain number (perhaps 50 to 100) of the 1,200 children taken care of by the Catholic Church also came to Wales, mainly for shelter with comfortably off Catholic families. In addition a party of fifteen or more was accommodated for

a time by the nuns of Cardiff's Nazareth House; *Welsh Catholic Times*, 25 June 1937, and letter to author from Mrs E. Gispert, 18 March 2002.

[112] Only one passing mention of the Old Conwy centre can be found in the relevant literature. I am grateful for information to Mrs E. Hughes, whose family were active in its support. She is still in touch with some of those who returned to Spain but continue to appreciate the kindness of her community.

[113] *South Wales Weekly Argus*, 17 July 1937; on Esteban, SUCC SC 712.

[114] Jones was later replaced by Mrs Fernandez, perhaps because of her lack of Spanish. On Cambria House see also Stradling (1996), 51–4; *Cambrian Times*, 14 August 1937.

[115] As n. 113. For evidence of popular disapproval, see the press correspondence studied in Lewis (1992), 43–5 and *passim*.

[116] Phillips (1987).

[117] L. Abse to author, 4 March 1997; see also Abse (1973), 42–3. On Henson, see below, p. 69ff.

[118] For example, fifteen children took part in such a performance at Felinfoel Public Hall under local Labour Party auspices in March 1938; names on the autographed programme indicates that as many hailed from the Cantabria region as from Basque-speaking communities; NLW James Griffiths Collection, B1/36.

[119] The late Christopher Hill, with whom the present writer talked and corresponded during research for an earlier book, always remained proud of his association with Cambria House.

[120] *Western Mail*, 9 January 1939; letter by south Wales Organiser for the National Joint Committee (D. L. Wickes), August 1939, SUCC/SC257. The NJCSR was planning to hold its General Meeting in Cardiff in September 1939. Though the event was cancelled because of the (World) War, it indicates the influence of the Cambrian House venture.

Chapter 3:   Armadas and Alcázars: Urban and Maritime Wales

[1] Correspondence of F. H. Thomas with J. Ormond (1982–5), Thomas Collection. Ormond went ahead with the interview – doubtless he felt it added a touch of exotica to the programmes – but Thomas was bitterly dissatisfied with the broadcast, which played up his desertion from the Legion after being seriously wounded in May 1937. See also Stradling (1998), esp. 118–23. The analogy used here may be put in proper perspective by the fact that Thomas was again badly wounded when fighting against the Afrika Korps in 1942.

[2] The equivocation here arises from my research on the Irish volunteers, which strongly indicated that veterans of the Francoist side have generally been reluctant to seek publicity.

[3] Above, p. 16.

[4] P. Lewis (1990), 82. (This studies the *Western Mail* and the *South Wales Echo*, both printed in Cardiff; the *South Wales Evening Post* (Swansea) and the *South*

Wales Argus (Newport); and also the Welsh edition of the weekly *Catholic Times*. With the exception of the *Argus*, all these were – at least to begin with – unfavourable to the Republic.)

5   'Men of Ethiopia – in our midst', *Western Mail*, 28 September 1935.

6   *South Wales Echo*, 1 August 1936. Thomas used the pseudonym 'Spartacus' – ironically a *nom-de-guerre* later adopted by several members of the International Brigade. One reply to this letter told him 'Spartacus, there is no middle course. Choose your side': *South Wales Echo*, 11 August 1936.

7   See various reports in the business pages of the *Western Mail* during 1935–6.

8   On the Welsh–Irish background, Hickey (1967); O'Leary (1999); and Price (1992). With more specific reference to the 1930s and the Spanish War, see Fielding (1993), esp. 109, 118ff., 125.

9   The following section is indebted to the richly detailed study by P. M. Heaton (1985). See also relevant chapters in the same author's separate studies of south Wales shipping companies, (1983: 93–104), and (1987: 33–6). The account given in the present writer's *Cardiff and the Spanish Civil War* (1996: esp. 65–77) provides a different perspective and some fresh materials.

10   See Alpert (1984).

11   On the maritime history of the Spanish Civil War, see Alpert (1987); Gretton (1984); Cable (1979). González Echegaray (1977) – the only monograph devoted to strictly commercial aspects – deals mainly with the role of the Spanish merchant fleet. In his treatment of 'Welsh shipping', Heaton never precisely defines his criteria for the description. Being underqualified to venture my own, I have followed his actual practice here.

12   Edgell Rickword, 'To the wife of any non-intervention statesman', Cunningham (1981), 374. The poet's confusion worse confounded over the 'brave lass' will become apparent directly.

13   The press corps settled in nearby Biarritz and Bayonne comprised those who were awaiting permission to work within the Francoist zone, others whose applications had been rejected and others still who had already been ejected from it.

14   Quoted by Heaton (1985), 39.

15   Romaña Arteaga (1984), v, 1249–61. The official banquet on 21 April lasted until 5 a.m. the next morning – very little was surely left of Captain Roberts's cargo! In the 1980s, one veteran Basque administrator still recalled that 'John Potatoes' had been in command of the *Seven Seas Spray*. A photograph of the crew printed here shows that nine out of its seventeen members were Black or Asian. Ibid., 1253 and 1261.

16   For more details and source references relevant to foregoing paragraphs, see Stradling (1996), 69–73.

17   See, for example, Moradiellos (2000), esp. 152–65.

18   Cable (1979), 26, 48, 75.

19   T. Buchanan's indispensable survey (1992) corrects some imbalances in previous accounts of the comportment of government and business interests, but makes only passing reference to British shipping. A wider discussion in Fyrth (1986),

250–6, implies that profit, if not always exploitation, was the only motive of relevant decision-makers. Less predictably, Admiral Cable also excoriates 'the one undoubted achievement of British policy . . . the fat profits made by block-ade-running British shipowners – the effect that no-one defended' (1979), 179. However, it should be noted that CPGB and other left-wing sources made much pro-'Spain' propaganda over Nationalist attacks on British vessels. Although a large body of Spanish work now exists on the war's international character, none of it allows any positive recognition of the contribution discussed in this section. Indeed, grateful memories were short-lived even amongst Basque exiles: see, for example, Lizarra (1944). More surprising is the virtually complete absence of reference to the subject in more recent English-language writing, such as Kurlansky (1999).

[20] Basque war-industries were starved of fuel. In the first six months of 1937, production of iron and steel fell to 5 per cent of 1929 levels, mostly through short-age of coal supplies: González Portilla and Garmendía (1988), 85–7. Attempts to exchange iron ore for British coal met with constant obstruction on the part of Basque industrialists; ibid., 85–92 and Romaña Arteaga (1984), iii, 619–47; see also ibid, iv, 884. Over 45,000 tonnes of ore arrived in Cardiff and Port Talbot in the last quarter of 1936, but Basque steamers faced a wall of red tape before returning with coal; ibid, iii, 626–7.

[21] Alcofar Nassaes (1975), 295–302 – a list of contraband vessels, including 26 'Welsh', in which some of the supporting evidence seems sketchy.

[22] See, for example, H. Thomas, *The Spanish Civil War*, where differences between the original edition (1961; Penguin reprint, Harmondsworth, 1965: 525) and the 3rd (Harmondsworth, 1977: 622) are explained by the intervening demise of its subject.

[23] See also J. G. Jenkins, 'Cardiff shipowners', *Maritime Wales/Cymru a'r Môr*, 5 (1981) 115–31, who states that 47 firms were still active on the outbreak of the Second World War. (The fact that this journal has flourished since 1976 to date is evocative of the powerful maritime element in the history of Wales as a whole.)

[24] See Table A, p. 180.

[25] Romaña Arteaga (1984), v, 1301–31.

[26] Heaton (1985), 55–71.

[27] The Cardiff-registered *McGregor* was fired on by a Nationalist cruiser when leaving Santander with 1,500 refugees; *South Wales Echo*, 23 July 1937. The *Candlestone Castle*, also registered in Cardiff, along with the *Molton* and – a sat-isfying prize for Franco – the *Seven Seas Spray* were amongst a total of eight Welsh steamers captured by the enemy; *South Wales Echo*, 14 and 18 July 1937; *Western Mail*, 15 July 1937; see also Heaton (1985), 101–2.

[28] One mariner on board Lord Glanely's steamer *Pilton* compiled a detailed account of a 'mercy' trip to Santander which he later included in his published memoirs; see the lengthy extract from W. Patton's *The Scrap Log of an Engineer*, printed ibid., 59–65.

[29] See O. Muñiz (1976), 112–13.

[30]   The Republican campaigns were those of Brunete (Madrid front, July), northern Aragon (August–October) and the arguably decisive failure of Teruel (December 1937–February 1938).

[31]   For narrative treatment which complements the account given below, see Heaton (1985), 73–7 and 85–96; and see also González Huix (1995).

[32]   *Western Mail*, 25 January 1939. The figures given were: 1937, 366,969 tons; 1938, 518,697 tons.

[33]   See Table B, p. 181.

[34]   It was not, perhaps, surprising that when a scholar produced a study of feature films set during the Spanish War, she mistakenly assumed that 'Benditch' – the mining village of Graham Greene's *The Confidential Agent* – was in the South Wales Coalfield: Valleau (1982), 51.

[35]   The Cardiff seaman Bob Anderson helped to bring war materials to Barcelona from Marseilles in autumn 1938. He was recruited via political channels to work for the Republic, as were other veterans of this trade, such as Emanuel Drakakis, a Greek communist who later settled in Cardiff, and Dafydd Davies (Swansea) who sailed on the *Dellwyn*. Anderson's ship, SS *Foynes*, was officered by antifascists from Limerick. They threw Nationalist intelligence off the scent by exporting pyrites from Franco-held Huelva to France before heading back to Barcelona with munitions. (However, on its third run, the *Foynes* was bombed and sunk by enemy aviation in Barcelona dockyard.) The fact that the non-intervention agent on board turned a blind eye to the payload points to a Comintern hand in the operation; interviews with Messrs Anderson and Davies, November 1997; see also Stradling (1996), 65–9.

[36]   Fearing that the USSR itself might be threatened, Stalin curtailed supplies to the Republic during the prolonged international crisis over Czechoslovakia in the summer of 1938. Traffic was resumed in the wake of the Munich Agreement (October 1938).

[37]   Letter from B. W. Roberts to author, 22 March 2002.

[38]   Interview with R. Anderson (see note 35).

[39]   *Caernarvon and Denbigh Herald*, 11 November 1938.

[40]   The story – which continued in this fuel-injected vein for several columns – was reprinted in *Caernarvon and Denbigh Herald* (20 January 1939) with no source details. It seems the story originated in the American *Daily Worker* and was brought to the editor's attention by a local left-wing seaman.

[41]   *Western Mail*, 12 December 1938.

[42]   Report summarized by H. Avgherinos, 15 May 1938, RGASPI/545/6/87/6 and memo. by A. Marty, 9 September 1938, ibid. 3/451. David Hooper, originally from Porth, was shipped to Algeria in the SS *Stanhope* after deserting at Brunete; see his *No Pasaran* (1997), 44 – one of few credible incidents in an otherwise fanciful and inconsequential account.

[43]   Skinner to (his sister) Dilys, Orihuela, 20 January 1938, SUCC/1995/14.

[44]   For a useful summary of British business interests in Spain, see Edwards (1979), 65–70.

[45] Alpert (1987), 177ff.; Avilés Farré (1994), 54–5.

[46] Howson (1998), 192–3, who shows that the exercise was not as exciting as first appeared.

[47] Ibid., 195; see also Romaña Arteaga (1984), iii, 633–8. The consequences of this scam were all the more dreadful since two armed trawlers sent to escort the *Yorkbrook* were sunk by a Nationalist warship with great loss of life. It must be asked whether it could have taken place without the connivance of the officers and management. Yet despite it, the Angel-Dalling company went on to become one of the Republic's chief suppliers.

[48] Heaton (1985), 19. Franco's decision also recognized the firm's established experience and their links with Rio Tinto, the major British-owned mineral company of western Andalusia: Harvey (1981), esp. Ch. 10.

[49] Private information of a contemporary, and see Stradling (1996), 117–18. The Spanish–Portuguese borderlands are where the *roble de corcho*, the cork-oak, is traditionally farmed.

[50] Letter of James Barnett (grandson) to author, 16 May 2001; see also Heaton (1985), *passim*.

[51] Ibid., 92 (my quotation incorporates a slight emendation of the closing phrase).

[52] Spender (1937/1978), 64–5; see also Worsley (1967/1985), 13–16.

[53] *Western Mail*, 25 August 1938 (originally published in *Spain*, a magazine circulating in the USA).

[54] *Western Mail*, 7 September 1938. Of six replies, only one was sympathetic to Lady Bute's position.

[55] *Western Mail*, 26 September 1938.

[56] MS memoir by Murphy enclosed in letter to Klugmann, 17 May 1971, NMLH/-CP/IND/KLUG/11/01. See also Hughes (1999), 218.

[57] F. Keeling to W. Roberts (Foreign Office), 5 July 1938, PRO/FO/371/22694/130. In 1938, as the penultimate act in a sequence of 'abdications' from their position as uncrowned monarchs of south-east Wales, the Butes liquidated their entire urban landed estate in Glamorgan for a total of £5 million: Davies (1981), 78 and 187.

[58] Edwards (1979), 9.

[59] Keeling to Roberts, as n. 57. Of course, 'Communist Party' here may have meant the same, *per contra*, as 'fascist' did when used by Spender: that is, someone recognized as sympathetic to the other side.

[60] Other than via charitable work, the Bute family and its chaplains had little or no contact with Cardiff Catholics and their clergy. In any case they only spent a few weeks in the city each year. Much of the material presented here about working-class Irish communities derives from the author's own experience and casual conversations with relatives and friends over many years.

[61] Sanchez (1987).

[62] Buchanan (1992), esp. 167ff.

[63] *Welsh Catholic Times*, 31 July 1936.

[64] *The Universe* (Welsh edn) 21 August 1936.

[65] *The Universe*, 28 August 1936.

66 *Welsh Catholic Times*, 28 August 1936.

67 E. G. Coffey to Franco, 19 November 1936, MAE/R593. It may be surmised that Coffey's father owned the hotel. The son's fate is unknown.

68 *Welsh Catholic Times*, 25 September 1936.

69 *Welsh Catholic Times*, 2 October 1936.

70 Cf. Fielding (1993), 79ff. In certain circumstances, Welsh persons of Irish descent were also quite capable of turning their backs upon the faith of their fathers – or, at least, of setting aside the advice of the clergy, in favour of more powerful feelings of working-class solidarity.

71 Denning (1974), 53.

72 Fielding (1993), 125.

73 Francis (1984), 107ff.

74 See Cole (1937), esp. 332ff. addressing those who aspired to collaboration, both practical and idealistic, irrespective of Comintern policy.

75 *Daily Worker*, 1 February 1937. (I have not found any reports of 'Unity Campaign' meetings in Wales outside the south-east.)

76 Executive Committee Minutes, 16 November 1937 and 3 January and 22 February 1938, NLW, Labour Party (Wales) Archive, 1985 Deposit, vol. 1, pp. 83, 97 and 101.

77 Cox (1937), 11–14, claimed that it was the SWMF, inspired by the communists, that was showing the whole country the way to left unity. See also Jeffries (1937), 15–17.

78 In fact both the CPSU and the CPGB had for some time disavowed and discouraged these ideas. This was part of a campaign to assuage subliminal fears within the middle classes of the social dissolution which sexual libertarianism might bring in its train.

79 L. Abse to author, 4 March 1997. Several of Taylor's letters from Spain to his wife Silvia comment on the 'mess' and frankly acknowledge his own responsibility for it (collection in private possession). My treatment of it draws on private information from a number of individuals.

80 *Proceedings of Cardiff City Council, 1936–37*, 787.

81 Interview with L. Abse (1997) and other private information. See also Stradling (1998), 7–15 and sources cited. The 'memorial meeting' – like many others of its kind – was, of course, not so much in memory of the deceased as an agitprop exercise intended to arouse feeling and action on behalf of 'Spain'. It made Dannie Abse, aged 14, want to volunteer: 'maybe if I got killed they'd have a memorial meeting for me' (1971), 78.

82 Q in Buchanan (1992), 165.

83 Stradling (1996), 44 and sources cited.

84 See Eisenwein and Shubert (1995), 144–64 and 217ff.

85 Executive Committee Minutes, 14 December 1937, NLW Labour Party (Wales) Archive, 1985 Deposit, vol. 1 p. 88.

86 S. Robinson's diary, 13 December 1936, SRC. Details given in the following paragraph, unless otherwise referenced, are based upon this source and interviews with Mr Robinson held in 2002–3. Sidney Robinson was a trainee in the office of

a local ship-repair company, a business in which he was to spend a long and rewarding career in the maritime world of Severnside.

[87] The exception was the Co-operative Society, which insisted on managing its own fund-raising effort for 'Spain'; L. M. Squire to S. Robinson, 20 January 1937; SRC.

[88] See file of letters from Morrisey to E. Thomas, SUCC/SC606–14. The writer worked in the propaganda and censorship office of the International Brigades' base throughout his time in Spain.

[89] P. Lewis (1990), 11–12, 20, 79.

[90] *South Wales Weekly Argus*, 23 January 1937.

[91] F. Morrice to Robinson, 6 and 28 March, 1937, SRC. *The Defence of Madrid* was a documentary film made by Ivor Montagu for the CPGB. See above, pp. 36–7.

[92] Robinson blamed 'a good deal of apathy' for the fact that that his group 'has not been functioning for some time'; letters of 25 November and 7 December 1938, SRC.

[93] Robinson to Morrice, 7 December 1938, SRC.

[94] *Daily Worker*, 1 February 1937. The Socialist League was a group founded by Stafford Cripps dedicated to finding a strategy for 'unity'.

[95] F. Coles (Secretary, Cardiff and District Unemployed Workers' Association); letter published in the *Volunteer for Liberty*, 15 November 1937.

[96] L. Jones, MS diary for 1937, entries for 6 September and 23–4 November, SUCC/SC553.

[97] 'Cardiff' – recalls Leo Abse – 'was enveloped at that time in a terrible apathy, [and] substantial sections of the working class [were] extraordinarily acquiescent to the Bute and Church hierarchies'; letter to author, 4 March 1997.

[98] On 9 December 1937, Jones recorded having a 'seizure' at his home; thus he knew something of the risks he was running. For further discussion of his work and significance, see below, pp. 164–5.

[99] Annual Report, 11 June 1938, NLW, Labour Party (Wales), vol. 1, p. 133.

[100] Executive Committee Minutes, 12 July 1938, NLW, Labour Party (Wales), vol. 1, 163, see also 191 and 203.

[101] E. Rawden (secretary) to S. Robinson, 12 March 1937, SRC.

[102] For more expansive treatment of issues discussed in this section, see my *Cardiff and the Spanish Civil War* (1996), 16–64, where additional source references appear *passim*.

[103] Ibid., 44–5 and source cited. Norwegian mariners in Cardiff were numerous enough to have their own place of worship, a characteristic structure which was recklessly destroyed during the redevelopment of the docklands in the 1990s and subsequently replaced by a shameless impostor.

[104] Twamley (1980), 52.

[105] Though I gave some account of Danís's work in my *Cardiff and the Spanish Civil War*, the existence of a local Falange group was discovered on a subsequent visit to the Madrid archive; MAE/R1057/4. The branch leader, Señor Ormaza – who described himself as the 'delegado nacional marítimo para Inglaterra de F.E.T y J.O.N.S.' – had caused a crisis inside the pro-Franco lobby in Britain by demanding public commitment from ship's officers to 'the cause'. Part of Danís's

mission was to replace Ormaza in line with Franco's own incorporation of the Falange into the unified 'movimiento' in April; see copies of letters by H. Ormaza and I. Muguiro, December 1937.

[106]   See Danís to Foreign Minister, Burgos, 19 July 1938.

[107]   These ships later operated clandestinely out of Milford Haven under British flags.

[108]   *Tenby Observer*, 23 July 1937.

[109]   Reeve-Jones 'has long insisted that an international communist organization exists to promote desertions from our country and protect those who flee'; Danís to Foreign Minister, Madrid, 21 June and 12 July 1939; MAE/R1057/4.

[110]   See *Western Mail*, 16 and 30 July 1937. At least one non-Spanish businessman, R. G. Parsley, was a member – later acting secretary – of the Falange branch. After returning from Spain, Frank Thomas encountered Parsley at his father's business premises. He borrowed a copy of the Nationalist propaganda book, *Red Terror in Madrid* (which still bears Parsley's signature over the stamped seal of the 'Jefatura Local Cardiff' of the FET), but declined his invitation to join the party.

[111]   Similar incidents took place in several other British ports, including Londonderry and Hull. Only one attempt seems to have been successful; see Buchanan (1997), 91.

[112]   However, violence was never far away, at least amongst Spanish seamen. Two were arrested when their ship docked at Cardiff for making death threats to compatriots in the city, apparently via radio messages; Stradling (1996), 58 and source cited. In August 1937, the body of a 21-year-old cook from the Spanish steamer *San Sebastian* was fished out of the East dock, 'drowned whilst swimming . . . apparently seized with cramp': *Western Mail*, 2 August 1937.

[113]   Note of 13 April 1938, MAE/R1057/4.

[114]   Intercepted circular by Cebada, 6 September 1938, MAE/R1057/2.

[115]   See, for example, Danís to Foreign Minister (Madrid), 20 July 1939, enclosing *South Wales Echo* clipping, 19 July; MAE/R1057/4.

[116]   See Table B in Appendix below. In addition to Parsley and Munitiz ('persona de gran influencia entre marineros'), Messrs Formoso, Zamacona and Campos were named in this file as strong supporters of the cause; these and most of the sea-captains were present at a celebration of the second anniversary of the uprising in the 'Sub-Agency of Cardiff'; J. Yzaguirre to A. de Olano (London Office), 11 June 1937; Danís to Foreign Minister, 19 July 1938, MAE/R1057/4.

Chapter 4:   The Academy: Education and the Press

[1]   Jim Brewer to Ben B. Thomas (Mondéjar, October 1937), Francis (1984), 282.

[2]   I am indebted for this point to Paddy Kitson, a Harlech alumnus who describes the college as performing the function of a 'safety valve'.

[3]   Brewer to Thomas, 20 June 1937, Francis (1984), 275–6.

4   *Ninth Annual Report of Coleg Harlech* (1936), T. J. Jones Papers, NLW/K9/104. The college's historian confirms that only thirty-five north Walians from a total of 239 students were enrolled for its first ten sessions (1927–37); Stead (1977), 73.

5   Thomas to T. J. Jones, 25 November 1936, NLW/K9/106.

6   Same to same, 13 April 1937, NLW/K9/106, fo. 18.

7   *Tenth Annual Report of Coleg Harlech* (1937), NLW/K9/106, fo. 72.

8   'These ten years', in *Eleventh Annual Report of Coleg Harlech* (1938), NLW/K10/151 (my emphasis). Here, a notorious characteristic of the Spanish 'Black Legend' is ascribed to those who were *supporters of* the Republic. The writer and International Brigade Commissar, Ralph Bates, had made a similar attribution at the Madrid Congress of Antifascist Writers, organized by the Spanish Communist Party, the previous year; see Stradling (2003), 179–80.

9   In 1969, Hywel Francis was told about 'a verbal tradition in the College that at the time of the Spanish Civil War the students passed a resolution that they should all leave college and go to Spain but were dissuaded from this by Mr. James Jones'; I. Hughes to H. Francis, 30 July 1969, SUCC/SC 181.

10   Brewer to W. Davies, 23 May 1979, WCIA/IBF File. The others were Alun Menai Williams (Penygraig) and Dan Davies (Pentre).

11   See below, p. 154.

12   Private information. The subsequent career of Leo Abse is too well known to require comment. Ted Edwards later became a university teacher, and was appointed by Harold Wilson as the inaugural Vice-Chancellor of the University of Bradford in 1966.

13   Dykes (1992), 123; see also Williams (1997), 293, where the date is wrongly given as 1937. (No history of any constituent institution of the national university that I have consulted has any sections devoted to student matters.)

14   *North Wales Observer*, 20 August 1936. The affair was one of several propaganda exercises masterminded by Ribbentrop, Hitler's ambassador.

15   Stansky and Abrahams (1994), 199, 243. The authors print a love-poem apparently composed in Cardiff's Angel Hotel; ibid., 244. See also Stradling (2003), 43–7.

16   Toynbee (1976), 171. See also Heinemann's novel *The Adventurers* (1960).

17   M. Morgan, transcript of interview with H. Francis, 15 October 1969, SUCC/SC 180.

18   'There was thick snow at the summit and we had to carry a comrade, a University student from Cardiff, the rest of the way. He was completely exhausted.' 'The Spanish Civil War 1936–1939', typescript memoir by Syd Booth (Working Man's Library, Salford), 24.

19   See above, pp. 23–4.

20   *Wrexham Leader*, 31 July 1936.

21   *Wrexham Leader*, 28 August 1936 (Evans's letter home was dated 30 July).

22   'The Spanish Civil War – a personal viewpoint', SUCC/SC158. This unpublished memoir, dating from 1975, was compiled from various speeches and broadcasts made by Cule in the late 1930s.

[23] I can only record what (by Cule's own account) a Spanish friend expostulated to him at this point. 'Haven't you read the papers?'; ibid., 4.

[24] See also above, p. 35.

[25] I quote from autobiographical notes apparently made by Thomas in the 1950s; NLW/E32.

[26] Draft MS of a BBC Radio talk from [?] the 1960s, NLW/E 46G. See also Thomas (1968/1994), 65–81.

[27] See also below, p. 122–3.

[28] In the present context, it must be borne in mind that in the 1930s the colleges of the University of Wales were home to a privileged academic elite – only a small fraction of today's numbers, both in terms of teaching staff and students.

[29] *Welsh Gazette*, 24 February 1938.

[30] *Welsh Gazette*, 16 June 1938.

[31] Printed circular, 17 August 1936, NLW (Ben Davies Collection) Box 18/1. However, the UDC's secretary, Dorothy Woodman, and several other key members, were covert communists.

[32] Davies to D. Woodman, 21 August; to Dr Rhys Jones, 4 September; and list enclosed with letter to Woodman, 25 September (all 1936), ibid. The committee included Dr Gwenan Jones, Lloyd H. Jones, J. Pryse Howell and Daisy Grindley – all linked to University College – and two reverends. However, to judge by the large amounts of undistributed UCD propaganda material left in the Davies Collection, it was not specially energetic; ibid., Box 25/7.

[33] *North Wales Observer*, 18 March and 1 April 1937. See also above, pp. 29–31 and 35ff.

[34] Dr Hill's correspondence with author, 1996. See also Williams (1997), 293.

[35] *Western Mail*, 26 January 1939. Dr Shaxby's son-in-law, Gilbert Taylor, was a member of the International Brigade and died in Spain (see above pp. 68–9, and below, pp. 150–2).

[36] *Caernarvon and Denbigh Herald*, 23 April 1937. It is not clear who or what is referred to by the reporter as 'them' (i.e. the object of the third sentence quoted).

[37] Jones (1969), 112–13.

[38] Williams (1997), 244–6. (The author intimates that politics played no part in Davies's opposition.)

[39] This outcome and Christopher Hill's appointment demonstrates that communists were not banned from academic jobs in Wales any more than in England; see also Dykes (1992), 118. But in 1936, the controversial sacking of Saunders Lewis from his Swansea post threw the academic community back into chaos. Carr later became Britain's most celebrated historian of Soviet Russia, spending a lifetime in chronicling and eulogizing its alleged socio-economic achievements. He was also author of *The Comintern and the Spanish Civil War* (first published 1983), a somewhat bleached account which has little credibility today. While teaching at Cardiff, Christopher Hill – later the century's outstanding historian of seventeenth-century England – worked on his dual hagiography of *Lenin and the Russian Revolution*, which appeared in 1947.

[40]   *Cambrian Times*, 30 January 1937.

[41]   Jones (1969), 112–13.

[42]   Hyde (1952), 60–1; Buchanan (1997), 149, 158.

[43]   Lewis (1970), esp. 76ff. The Club's part in creating the groundswell of feeling for 'Unity' in 1937, for example, is incalculable: see Cole (1937). Instances on which veteran International Brigaders and many others involved in aiding 'Spain' have referred to its influence are too numerous to cite here.

[44]   For background information and discussion of party personalities, policies and internal pluralities, see Davies (1983).

[45]   See, for example, Hermet (1989), 238–40.

[46]   Meils (1977), 71–4; Griffiths (2002).

[47]   Williams (1985), esp. 278–84.

[48]   *Y Cymro*, 10 February 1937.

[49]   R. C. Richards, 'Peryglon Gau Newyddion', *Y Ddraig Goch*, February 1937. (Cf. *The Welsh Nationalist*, March 1938, where Saunders Lewis exhorts readers to 'study the press reports of Spain [for] examples galore of news fabrication'.) Richards concluded, in line with editorial opinion, that 'the main intention of Communist Russia at this time is to precipitate a general war'. Certainly, the particular operation, like many others of its kind, was the brainchild of Willi Muenzenberg, Stalin's master propagandist based in Paris; and its purpose was to frighten France and Britain into abandoning 'non-intervention' and backing the republic: see Pike (1968), 35, 57, 79.

[50]   'Esbonio Helynt Spaen', *Y Ddraig Goch*, September 1936. See also above, pp. 34–5.

[51]   'Y Sefyllfa yn Sbaen', *Y Ddraig Goch*, November 1936. Despite Daniel's protest, his failure to mention the role of indigenous fascism in the war's origins, to deplore the atrocities of the right wing, and to acknowledge the military intervention of Germany and Italy, all conduced to the impression reacted against by Cule and others.

[52]   'Y Sefyllfa Heddiw yn Ewrop', *Y Ddraig Goch*, October 1936.

[53]   'Sbaen', December 1936, passage underlined in the original. Bebb added explicitly that 'it will neither be profitable to announce that Fascism is the enemy of Europe nor that Communism is the destroyer of civilization'.

[54]   Here I beg to differ with the party historian for whom 'the analyses published in *Y Ddraig Goch* and *The Welsh Nationalist* were inevitably amateur, arm-chair exercises': Davies (1983), 112.

[55]   For example: 'From Spain's hell we must now turn to the purgatory which is Europe': *Y Ddraig Goch*, December 1936.

[56]   'Cip Olwg ar Helyntion Ewrop', *Y Ddraig Goch*, July 1937: 'to *explain* – explain, I say, and not justify'.

[57]   A slightly clearer image can be observed in the pages of *Y Ddraig Goch*'s English-language companion monthly, *The Welsh Nationalist*. Once Saunders Lewis (by, as it were, His Majesty's pleasure) relinquished its editorship, leader comment took a distinctly leftward turn. After his release, Lewis was allowed to contribute a column, but wisely kept off the subject of Spain; see esp. issues of October and December 1937.

[58]   Quoted from *Y Ddraig Goch*, August 1937, by Meils (1976), 75.

[59]   *Y Ddraig Goch*, July 1937.

[60]   Quoted from *Y Ddraig Goch*, April 1938, by Davies (1983), 113. Cf. T. C. Edwards in *The Welsh Nationalist*, January 1937: 'Whatever else is today at stake in Spain, it is not the cause of parliamentary democracy.' However, Lewis needed not to deter the working-class element – especially the quarrymen of North Wales, some of whom had recently joined 'the National Party . . . a movement of the workers and the defenceless rural poor of all Wales' as he put it in a congratulatory letter written from his prison cell and printed in *Y Ddraig Goch*, March 1937.

[61]   *Y Ddraig Goch*, September 1938.

[62]   Davies (1983), 105ff.

[63]   *Y Ddraig Goch*, July 1937.

[64]   D. J. Davies, 'Ychydig Nodiadau ar Gatalonia', *Y Ddraig Goch*, May 1937 – published at exactly the time that anarchist rule in Catalonia was challenged and broken by the Spanish Communist Party.

[65]   See above, pp. 18–19.

[66]   'Rhyfel Cartrefol Spaen', *Seren Cymru*, 7 August 1936.

[67]   'Creulonderau yn Spaen', *Seren Cymru*, 25 December 1936.

[68]   'Eglwys Spaen', *Seren Cymru*, 1 January 1937.

[69]   *Seren Cymru*, 4 December 1936 and 19 February 1937. See also 21 August ('Franco and his kind excelling even Lenin in their barbarism') and 9 October 1936 ('both sides . . . have behaved barbarously, but this will pale into insignificance once Franco gets the upper hand'). At the same time, however, the Nationalists' courage during the siege of the Toledo Alcázar also made an undeniable impression; 'Toledo', *Seren Cymru*, 25 September 1936.

[70]   'Safle'r Gwledydd a Spaen', *Seren Cymru*, 15 January 1937. This acute general observation was accompanied by the following detailed estimation: 'The Russians are better in the air than the Germans and their weapons both in the air and on land are superior' – surprising to find as the subject matter of a Christian-pacifist organ and (at least for the precise time of writing) so surprisingly accurate!

[71]   'Achos Gwrthryfel Sbaen', *Y Cymro*, 8 August, and 'Sbaen Yn Wers i'r Pleidiau', 26 December 1936. (The paper had been carrying Cule's reports from Spain before the start of the war; see *Y Cymro*, 25 July 1936.)

[72]   'Helynt Sbaen' – two letters with the same by-line – *Y Cymro*, 1 August and 3 October 1936.

[73]   'Mwy o Olau ar helynt Sbaen', *Y Cymro*, 9 January 1937.

[74]   'Porth Neigwl a Guernica', *Y Cymro*, 8 May 1937.

[75]   'Chwilio am Gymry yn Sbaen', *Y Cymro*, 26 June 1937; see also *Y Cymro*, 17 July 1937, where schedules and waveband details are announced.

[76]   *Western Mail*, 14 and 28 July 1937. On the putative broadcasts, see also Davies (1999). (I am grateful to Mr Davies for further information on this subject.)

[77]   *Y Cymro*, 26 March 1938.

[78] 'Crefydd o Wlad y Soviets', *Y Cymro*, 29 January 1938.

[79] 'Ateb dau Ohebydd', *Y Cymro*, 5 February 1938.

[80] *Y Cymro*, 12 and 19 February 1938. McGovern's pamphlet *Why the Bishops Back Franco* was published in 1936 (National Labour Press).

[81] 'Ein Barn Ni', *Y Cymro*, 3 December 1938.

[82] It is interesting, however, that the *South Wales Echo* allowed its foreign correspondent, Harry Greenwall, to adopt a pro-Republican line which tended to cut across editorial comment: P. Lewis (1990), 32–3.

[83] *South Wales Argus*, 17 January 1939, quoted Lewis (1990), 21.

[84] Ibid., esp. 82–3.

[85] Both in the *South Wales Echo* – quoted ibid., 23–4. (Though correspondence columns are quoted from *passim*, the author's research was limited to four English-language secular dailies and one Catholic weekly – all published in Cardiff, Swansea or Newport – and provided no statistical data for its conclusions.)

[86] Ibid., 28–9.

[87] Even the *Western Mail* turned angrily against Franco and by the summer of 1937 had achieved a complete *volte-face* in its attitudes; ibid., 40–1, 70–1; see also Francis (1984), 125–6.

[88] For example, in a book review, 25 August 1938.

[89] These conclusions are drawn from the whole range of press sources researched in the preparation of this book.

Chapter 5:   The Miners: Little Moscows, Big Moscow

[1] In these opening paragraphs I rely heavily on material presented by Francis and Smith in their comprehensive survey of *The Fed* (1980), from which quotations are also taken unless otherwise noted. On Maerdy itself, see also S. Macintyre (1980), esp. 23–47.

[2] Francis and Smith (1980), 161–2, where the authors (however) also point out that this 'counter-community' never quite succeeded in asphixiating the old established 'christian-respectable' culture of the village.

[3] Macintyre (1980), 30ff.

[4] Morris (1986), 276–7 (my emphasis).

[5] Cf. also Smith (1993), 121–2. In much writing about the south Wales valleys it seems – to quote Trotsky – that 'the worse things are, the better they are'.

[6] Francis (1984), 249.

[7] 'Understanding Nationalism', repr. in Hannan (1988), 133–5.

[8] See Francis and Smith (1980), esp. 350–75, and Francis (1984), *passim*. Non-Welsh historians, whilst acknowledging the sterling work carried out in Wales, have usually failed to resonate in sympathy with these grander claims; see, for example, Buchanan (1997), 66 and *passim*; Fyrth (1986), 204–5, 269–70.

[9] No specialist studies of the Asturias revolution exist in English. For starkly contrasting views, see Grossi Mier (1935/1978), an account by one of its leaders, and

Barco Teruel (1984), esp. 209–92, by a right-wing journalist. Shubert (1987) has only a short concluding sketch of the event.

10 See witnesses interviewed in BBC Wales TV, *The Colliers' Crusade*, (1983), episode 1. If in somewhat less concrete terms, such parallels are endorsed by Francis (1984), see esp. 75.

11 Ibid., 68ff. Most of D. Hooper's alleged adventures in Spain were shared with an equally dubious 'Ramos Jones' from Maerdy, whose family hailed from Almería – probably Hooper's error for Asturias; (1997), 3 *et seq.*

12 Francis and Smith (1980), 13.

13 Davies (1993), 44.

14 Francis (1984), 139–40; see also Francis and Smith (1980), 352–6, and Hopkins (1998), 388–9. Spanish presence in the Neath–Swansea valleys perhaps led to some awareness of a socio-economic correspondence between Asturian colliers and the Welsh anthracite communities. (This was evident, for example, in the working of hillside smallholdings which formed part of family economies.) However, the Cambrian Lodge's protest concerned a Greek communist and had nothing to do with Spain.

15 *Daily Worker*, 11 July 1936. Largo – main driving force behind the attempted coup – had recently been released from prison under the terms of the amnesty granted by the Popular Front government elected in February. A matter of days later, his remarks were endowed with booming resonance.

16 *Daily Worker*, 13 October 1934.

17 See Manning's pamphlet *What I Saw in Spain* (TUC, 1935). However, the author noted that 'as we ran into the mining area, I was irresistibly reminded of the South Wales coalfield'. (I am indebted for material and references in the above paragraph to a fascinating section in Lyne (1996), 224–44.) More Romantic resemblances between Wales and Asturias were noted at the time by the Irish writer, Kate O'Brien; see her *Farewell Spain* (Heinemann, 1937), 67.

18 *Caernarvon and Denbigh Herald*, 19 November and 3 December 1937. Ernest Ffendall, author of the second letter, was apparently a civilian domiciled in Spain who had returned to Wales after being freed by the Valencia government on the instance of the Foreign Office in August that year; MAE/R1784/6.

19 *Western Mail*, 26 and 30 January 1939.

20 Francis (1984), 266 (my emphasis).

21 Francis and Smith (1980), 370; the leader, Lance Rogers, took a copy of Hywel Francis's thesis to present to their hosts; author's interview with L. Rogers, March 1998. Because of the strategic isolation of the northern provinces, and the lack of Comintern influence, International Brigade units were never engaged there. But a lone Welshman, Amador Arostegui Ezquerra – whose family were from Vizcaya but who was born in Dulais on 25 October 1903 – fought in Asturias, and was captured in the autumn of 1937; see MAE/R1051/24 and IBA/Box 28/A/6b.

22 Francis (1984), 33–4. In terms of 'popular front' allegiances, it is true that Asturias was the only part of Spain where all the workers' parties and unions had

managed to collaborate successfully under the rubric of the 'alianzas obreras' patented by the PSOE in the early days of the Republic: see Alba (1978). But if some Welsh International Brigaders privately professed a fellow feeling for 'anarchism', few had more than a vague notion of the ideology, history and programme of the CNT/FAI.

[23] See Buchanan (2001).

[24] See Morgan (1981), 148.

[25] *Western Mail*, 16, 20 and 21 November 1936 (my emphasis). The first example headed a front-page story and was evidently expropriated by the palace for the monarch's personal use. The two latter were headlines which appeared after the royal visit to the Valleys on 18 November.

[26] Moreover, many miners who were unemployed for long enough not to afford SWMF dues joined the NUWM – a communist organization; see, Evans (1999), 180.

[27] Rees and Thorpe (1998), esp. 67–86 and 143–67.

[28] See Hopkins (1998), 99–103. B. McLoughlin's work in the Comintern Archive, Moscow, has shewn that the three Welshmen named above were among nine British Battalion commissars to have attended the Lenin School; unpublished paper cited in Baxell (2004). Francis (1984), 198, confirms Dobson but not Roberts as an alumnus. The latter's biographer makes no of mention his going to Moscow, explaining his nickname of 'Jack Russia' somewhat differently: Felstead (1981), 15ff.

[29] W. Paynter, 1973 interview, quoted Hopkins (1998), 100.

[30] Williams (1996), 191ff.; Smith (1982), 7.

[31] Williams (1998), 55, which regards Labour Party commitment to 'self-help' schemes as being sporadic at best. The Quakers filled this gap with characteristic energy: see Naylor (1986).

[32] Paynter (1972), Stratton (1984), 26–7.

[33] Naylor (1986), 58–9; see also Jones (1983), 82.

[34] Notably – in view of the students' vacation schemes noted above (see p. 80) – there was also a distinctly Oxford flavour to the Friends' initiative, two of its main sponsors being A. D. Lindsay, master of Balliol, and his wife; Naylor (1986), 30 *et seq.*

[35] Ibid., 27, 47–8. See also Williams (1996), 198–9, and Evans (1999), 177–8. Perhaps most frustrating for any CP activist was the story that one client of Maes-y-haf told visitors that he had 'given up communism and taken to culture': Naylor (1986), 36.

[36] Ibid., 42–54.

[37] It is worth noting that the Albacete authorities were suspicious of the Quaker programme of medical and material relief in Spain, mainly because the Friends insisted upon carrying out work on both sides; Fyrth (1986) 158–80. On one occasion, Quaker medical staff were shadowed by agents of the SIM who believed they might be involved in assisting deserters or even in military espionage; C. Bloom interview, IWM/992/3.

[38] This issue is discussed below, p. 131ff.

[39] Based on Baxell (2004), ch. 1 and figs 4 and 9. Even more telling is that for British volunteers as a whole, those from professional backgrounds (including publishing) registered a higher percentage than miners – 12 as against 9 per cent.

[40] See Stradling (1999).

[41] Records of SIS 'Operation Mask' (interception of Comintern radio messages), PRO/HW17/22 (Moscow–London), nos 7736–7 and 7752 (December 1936) where dispatches of men to Spain were encoded as 'copies of Dickens and pamphlets' sent to 'Switzerland'. Pollitt reported that production of the *Daily Worker* was facing a crisis since 'our staff is seriously depleted through comrades going to Spain'; ibid., 7739.

[42] Ibid., HW17/14/83–4.

[43] Quoted Francis (1984), 160. Springhall's desperation was partly motivated by the large numbers of unruly Scots from the Gorbals present in Albacete. These were often refugees from gang vendettas whose violently drunken behaviour threatened the very existence of the Battalion even before it went into battle.

[44] Tom Glyn Evans (Kenfig Hill) was one of these few – a Labour Party member, ex-miner and ex-soldier who made his own way to London in order to volunteer in December 1936; autograph MS 'biography' (April 1937) in Evans's file, RGASPI/545/6/130/43–4.

[45] Data based on taped interviews made by Hywel Francis in the SWML (for example, T. Adlam (TA/178–9), G. Baker (GB/178/1–7), and J. Brewer (JB/57)); and a wide selection of sources referenced in Table C in the Appendix below. The above paragraphs hardly bear out Francis's reference to a 'host of Welshmen' coming forward in response to the initial CPGB effort in 1936: (1984), 162.

[46] 'Spain – memories of the Spanish Civil War, 1936–1939' written as a course-work dissertation, now in SUCC/SC161. (I have mainly used an unpaginated transcription made by S. Davies, dated August 1997.) The American scholar, James Hopkins, based an entire chapter of his book about the British Battalion on this document, apostrophizing Griffiths as 'The True Believer': (1998), 219–313.

[47] Francis (1984), 169. On Paynter's work in Spain, below pp. 134–7.

[48] Among Francis's total of 174 Welsh brigaders are no fewer than 19 who set out for but never made it to Spain; see (1984), 179.

[49] Stradling (1998), 155, 171–2; Lance Rogers interview (1998).

[50] Haldane (1948), 112–4.

[51] 'Miners help the workers of Spain', *Y Cymro*, 3 October 1936.

[52] Ibid. It seems likely that the speaker was already known to Cule from his time in Barcelona (SUCC SC158). His insistence that volunteers were not needed indicates a non-communist allegiance, for it directly cut across the message now coming from Moscow.

[53] This mundane yet seemingly all-pervasive aspect of the 'Welsh response' to the Spanish War is one which (like the experiences of the families left behind by volunteers) has still not yielded much information to the researcher; see, however, Francis (1975), 79–80.

[54] Interview transcript, J. Roberts, SWML/AUD/73–4.

[55] V. Alvarez-Buylla (Spanish Embassy, London) to Foreign Ministry, Barcelona, 9 June 1938, MAE/R894/37. The joint choirs sang (*inter alia*) the Republican anthem, 'El Himno de Riego'.

[56] From Jones's holograph diary for 1937, SUCC/SC553. See also Francis (1984), 168–9 and Smith (1982), esp. 22–3. Jones wrote to Paynter in Spain shortly before his return – here I am surmising circumstantially that he was thinking of succeeding Paynter in the non-combatant role of base commissar at Albacete. (No composer named Field appears in the 1937 edn. of *Who's Who in Music* (Shaw Publishing).)

[57] 'The war diary of a Welsh miner', in Jones and Williams (1999), 156. The donations mentioned were official levies for 'Spain' paid by employed miners to the Fed.

[58] Brome (1953), 103.

[59] For narrative details of Bevan's antifascist odyssey, see Foot (1962), 195–299. Whilst this biography has itself become part of the legend of its subject, there is another side to the story, more apprehensively hinted at than seriously explored by D. Tanner, 'The pattern of Labour politics, 1918–39', in Tanner *et al.* (2000), 113–39.

[60] Alexander (1982/1987), 160. For the significance Attlee attached to his visit, see Williams (1961), 10, 13–5.

[61] J. Griffiths to Mrs Griffiths, 15 January 1938, James Griffiths Collection NLW/B1/30.

[62] Same to same, 19 January 1938, NLW/B1/34.

[63] It is notable that Bevan does not figure in Griffiths's letters, nor in the collection of photographs and other memorabilia he brought back from Spain; NLW/B1/3–26. It may be noted that Llanelli was the only town in Wales which was host to a pro-Franco meeting; see the enigmatic reference in Francis (1984), 128. As we have seen, other Welsh Labour MPs (such as D. Richards) made valuable contributions to the Aid Spain movement, while D. Grenfell (Labour, Gower) was a member of a very influential all-party group of MPs who visited Madrid during the rebel assault on the city in October 1936.

[64] Francis and Smith (1980), 366–7.

[65] 'Wales miners threaten general strike for Spain', *Volunteer for Liberty*, 13 April 1938; see above, p. 55ff.

Chapter 6:   The Word was God: Writers and Heretics

[1] F. H. Thomas, 'Spanish Legionario: a professional soldier in Spain', in Stradling (1998), 35–131; see also Thomas to his mother, 1 February, and to his brother and family, 13 February 1937; F. Thomas Collection. Thomas's memoir, written immediately on his return home, was devoted exclusively to the war. The only (partial) exceptions to the point made above are Harry Stratton, whose autobiography (1984) includes two short chapters on Spain, and Will Paynter, in a chapter of his autobiography (1972). Other veterans – such as Morien Morgan

and Edwin Greening – expressed intentions to write memoirs, but apparently never fulfilled them. A substantial memoir by W. D. Griffiths (see above, pp. 105–6), although of surpassing interest from both military and political points of view, remains unpublished. Only two veterans have attracted biographers: R. Felstead – the subject's' grandson – on Jack 'Russia' Roberts (1981), and J. Pugh on Tom Jones (1988), see esp. 59–76. Only two Welshmen – the London expatriate, Sir Richard Rees, and Lewis Jones – rate a mention in a chapter devoted to 'Intellectuals' in T. Buchanan's study (1997), though the latter would surely have rejected the title.

2   Murphy to W. Rust, 26 July 1940, MML Box D3/F-1; same to Klugman (and enclosures), 17 May 1971, NMLH/CP/IND/KLUG/11/01. Despite the encouragement of Hywel Francis, Murphy never managed to construct a sustained or coherent narrative of his experiences in Spain. See, however, Macmillan (1980).

3   See the range of unpublished primary sources from Britain, Spain and Russia itemized in my book, *History and Legend* (2003). This absence puts an even greater premium upon the value of the recorded interviews carried out by H. Francis in the 1960s and 1970s. It should be noted that the selection of letters home published in Francis's monograph are a mere fraction of the total now held in the SUCC.

4   Jones (1937/1978) and (1939/1978). In the reissues, original forewords by D. Garman are supplemented by new introductions from D. Smith. See also the latter author's monograph study (1982). The hero of the novels is obviously a version of Jones himself, just as the fictional village title is based on Maerdy and its *cwm*.

5   Meyn (2000), 125–7. Jones's work was originally inspired by Arthur Horner, and is seen by a Spanish scholar as 'pouring from his pen as an integral part of his working-class, trade union struggle': López Ortega (1974), 52.

6   See Francis (1984), 280. One reader apparently attempted to emulate Jones by beginning a short story set in a mining village (but written as a children's 'escapist' adventure tale). Four holograph pages of this text were found by the present writer amongst a file of personal effects of the British Battalion captured by the enemy during the Aragon retreats of March 1938. Scraps of letters from home located in close proximity in the file suggest that the writer may have been from the Penygraig area; ANGC/PS/ARAGON/7.

7   Francis (1984), 73.

8   Francis (1991), 69–76.

9   Jones (1939/1978), 318. For further discussion of this theme, below p. 158ff.

10   Spender and Lehmann (1939), 31.

11   Ibid., 40.

12   Nicholas (1948), 69; first published in the *Daily Worker*, 8 February 1938.

13   Francis (1984), 284. Roberts's poem was not posted home – it would never have escaped the censor. See Stradling (2003), 147–8, 241.

14   Jones (1939/1978), 333.

15   Ibid., 324, 331–2.

[16]   Humphreys (1986), 210–1.
[17]   Thomas (1986/1987).
[18]   Ibid., 511. Thus (also) a further example of this peculiar epistolatory-testamental technique. In reality (for what *that* is worth) the censorship office in Albacete would never have allowed such a letter to leave Spain. In contrast, the letters of Len and Pen are very similar to 'real' examples printed in an appendix by Francis (1984) – whose monograph appeared, it seems, when both novels were at an early stage of writing.
[19]   Ibid., 589. It almost goes without saying that the basic instincts of both Humphreys and Thomas are pro-Republican, but time and the higher requirements of 'art' seem together to have worked them free of the unblinking intensity of Lewis Jones's propaganda vision.
[20]   Williams (1985).
[21]   My reading of *Loyalties* is (in part) an extension of ideas advanced in Pinkney (1991), 110–17. So many are the interlacing 'correspondences' between these three novels (on the one hand) and between them and the person and writings of Lewis Jones (on the other) that one can imagine them being the products of some creative writing seminar attended by all three novelists during the miners' strike of 1984.
[22]   Burton (1999).
[23]   Ibid., 47–50. See also p. 296, where Robeson figures in his own right. The author's thinking seems to have revolved around *Proud Valley*, the 1940 feature film starring Paul Robeson about a black collier's adventures in a Welsh mining village.
[24]   Gregory (1986), 69. On the evidence provided by the author, the victim may have been any one of Frank Owen (Maerdy), Sam Morris and J. E. Williams (both Ammanford), W. J. Davies (Tonypandy) or Fred White (Ogmore Vale).
[25]   Burton (1999), 85–6, 283. For Lloyd Edmunds, see Inglis (1985) and above, p. 26.
[26]   Goddard (1992), 89, 97–8. Christopher Hill (who died at 91 while this chapter was being written) figures in the present book as history as well as historian and as fiction.
[27]   Jordan (1994), 65. The character bears some resemblance to Tom Picton, the veteran mountain fighter from Treherbert, 'executed' in a Bilbao gaol in 1938.
[28]   McLean (1957/1970); film screenplay by C. Foreman (Columbia Pictures, 1961). The original character is a Clydesider with no Spanish War background. Yet ironically, in the actual membership of the Brigade, Scots outnumbered Welshmen by more than three to one. Equally curious is that another star of the film, the Scots actor James Robertson Justice, was for a remarkably brief period an officer in the British Battalion.
[29]   See above, n. 12.
[30]   Burton (1999), 240. This character is a version of Ivor Montagu, who compiled *The Defence of Madrid* for the CPGB.
[31]   See, for example, the selection printed by Francis (1984), 269–93.
[32]   'Madrid' by R. Price, *Seren Cymru*, December 1936.

[33] NLW/20759/E81. The scrapbook volume which contains numerous drafts of unpublished novels and stories is entitled 'A writer I would be', and begins 'This is the story of my struggle to become a writer'. Glynne-Jones subsequently lived through the London Blitz, writing even in the air-raid shelter, ignoring the plight of his family in his obsessive search for literary glory.

[34] Maseras (1938/1991), in MML/Box 40/E3. The foreword, apparently by Mr Hughes, acknowledges his Spanish teacher's 'constructive criticism'. It seems possible that the agency of contact between Pontypridd and Barcelona was Cyril Cule. *A Europa* was originally published by Editorial Forja (Barcelona, 1938).

[35] He ended a letter to an Aberystwyth literary acquaintance 'The air raid alarm has just sounded . . . We had our last raid a week ago tonight, they are very unwelcome visitors.' Williams-Hughes to M. Humphreys, Valencia, 22 May 1937, NLW/A1398.

[36] *South Wales Weekly Argus*, 3 July 1937, referring to 'two well-known Welshmen doing relief work in Spain'. On Rees, editor of the literary magazine the *Adelphi*, see Fyrth (1986), 73–4 and *passim*.

[37] Williams-Hughes brought a collection of originals from this genre back to Wales, which were later donated to the Bangor Museum (Box 1425, Accession No. 73/16). Others were published in book-postcard form, many copies being sold to foreign visitors in the Mediterranean ports.

[38] *Caernarvon and Denbigh Herald*, 15 January 1937.

[39] Thomas (1968/1994), esp. 107ff.

[40] Quoted by Smith (1993), 149–50, from *The Alone to the Alone* (1947).

[41] 'GT and Spain – his experiences there: 2nd Part. Man of action', MS in Thomas Collection NLW/E46.

[42] This seems to be extrapolated from the fact that 'few came out of the Rhondda with its despoliation and exploitation without being so': Parnell (1988), 33–4.

[43] 'The Spanish Flavour', MS in NLW/E217, published in *The Teacher*. On the relationship of Spain's intellectuals to the Republic, see Stradling (2003), ch. 1 and *passim*.

[44] See, for example, his unfinished account of a visit to Spain in 1947, when at the border 'we were asked whether we had any contraband. We had some ideas about freedom that would have wrung the Caudillo's withers, but, as we wanted to see what went on to the south of those tall, castellated mountains, we said nothing': NLW/E92.

[45] Stansky and Abrahams (1964/1994), 190–1. See also 'No. 4 Parton Street', typescript memoir by B. Weinreb, NMLH/CP/HIST/1/14.

[46] Fitzgibbon (1965), quoted by Weintraub (1968), 80–1.

[47] Skelton (1964), 153–4; cf. Davies (1974), 97.

[48] Ibid., 48, 110–11; cf. also Davies (1998), 165.

[49] Fitzgibbon (1965), 89–90, 267 (my emphasis in the phrase quoted). Neither Fitzgibbon's book nor its replacement as the standard biography, Ferris (1999), has any index reference for 'Spain'. If hardly in the same category as Frank (or

even Rose) these two Doubting Thomases clearly did not regard support for the Spanish Republic as a deeply personal mission.

[50] 'Impressions – street in Seville', NLW (V. Watkins Collection), 22453B/11–12.

[51] Morris (1964/1982), 138, see also 145.

[52] Ibid., 97.

Chapter 7:   Volunteers in Spain I: Soldiers and Heroes

[1] Stradling (1996), 42.

[2] *South Wales Weekly Argus*, 27 February 1937.

[3] The following section is based on Table C in the Appendix below, and other information contained in the sources used in its compilation.

[4] See above, p. 105.

[5] The term 'Welshman' is used here in the sense defined in Table C. I have discounted information contained in the unpublished diary of James Albrighton, a brigader from Salisbury who settled in Swansea after the war. Transcripts of extracts from this text were sent by Albrighton to Bill Alexander, IBA secretary and effective controller of its archive, in the 1980s. They claim that their author fought with a Spanish militia company in all the Madrid battles of autumn 1936; and met one Sidney Lloyd Jones, a Welshman later killed at Chapinería, near Talavera, that September. However, evidence from both the IBA and Moscow archives suggests that Albrighton did not arrive in Spain until July 1937. At present the diary also lacks any independent corroboration whatsoever; see IBA/Box 50/A1/1–12.

[6] However, Frank Thomas was in the thick of all these battles with the 6th Bandera of Franco's Foreign Legion; see Stradling (1998), 67–78.

[7] See Battalion Rolls cited as sources 1–3 for Table C. These indicate that 26 Welsh volunteers took part in the Jarama battle. In addition, Pat Murphy was in hospital with wounds incurred at Las Rozas, Madrid, the previous month.

[8] Table C, sources 1 and 2, indicate that the numbers of Welshmen present with the battalion rose from 59 to 84 during June. Nine of this total were killed at Brunete.

[9] Table C, source 3.

[10] This figure does not include those in Table C who gave addresses in England.

[11] Pugh (1988), 71–6. See also memo of 12 June 1939 (in Spanish) Burgos Ministry of Foreign Affairs; MAE/R1069/57.

[12] See Table C, where the criteria utilized for inclusion are set out.

[13] My calculations differ only slightly from those made by Baxell (2004), ch. 1.

[14] These issues are discussed in detail below, Chapters 8–10 passim.

[15] Skoutelsky (1998), 154, 225; British Battalion figure calculated from Baxell (2004), ch. 1, fig. 1. These totals may be misleading. No recorded affiliation has been found for 39 of the Welsh volunteers, whilst a mere seven were Labour Party members. If only one in four of the former were in fact CP – which seems

more than likely – the percentage would reach over 75, i.e. around the general British figure.

16 General context and comments in this section are based on intensive research on the XV Brigade (by the author, Richard Baxell and others) in the Moscow and London IB Archives. To cite specific documents would render these references umanageably dense and top-heavy.

17 Based on the list of names engraved on the so-called 'national memorial' – the plaque in the Miners' Library at Hendrefoilan, see Williams (1996), 60–1, and Francis (1984), 268.

18 Lyne (1996), 283–5.

19 Francis (1984), 252, and author's interview, March 1998.

20 I would be prepared (in principle, and privately) to supply details and sources in respect of specific individuals to any bona-fide enquirer.

21 Prominent amongst the latter is David Hooper, originally of Porth, whose stories, ranging from the ridiculous to the outrageous, were published by one alleged expert and mysteriously endorsed by the doyen of Spanish Civil War studies in Britain: Hooper (1997).

22 See below, p. 138.

23 Any explanation for the discrepancy would at present rely on mere surmise. My figures are based on a list (presently withheld from publication) of nearly 360 deserters from the battalion, drawn from a wide range of primary sources. Five Welshmen repeatedly attempted desertion. Of the overall total, at least four were successful – that is, they returned home from Spain as a result. By definition these figures can only be provisional.

24 For the 16th Battalion's experience at Jarama, see Stradling (1999), 162–8. For a close study of the circumstances of the Brunete casualties, based on much Welsh testimony, see Stradling (2003), 123–44.

25 I have traced only two women of Welsh origins who went to Spain: Thora Craig from Abertillery and Margaret Powell (? also Gwent) both worked as nurses: 'They kept the Red Flag flying', Sunday Independent, 21 July 1996, and (unidentified) south Wales newspaper extract (c. 1970) in IBA/Box D1/F/6. For this reason I have not felt it necessary to observe gender inclusiveness in my present discourse.

26 See Morrisey's pro-forma 'Biography' and appended commendation by Base Commissar A. Donaldson, RGASPI/545/6/175/66–70.

27 See below, pp. 155–7.

28 Francis (1984), 251.

29 'Les volontaires anglais', report by A. Elliott (for the Comintern Committee, Moscow 1939), RGASPI/545/6/22/15.

30 See, for example, Medical Tribunal Judgements for summer/autumn 1937, ANGC/SM F4763 and F1688. The average age of Welsh brigaders was 30 (based on 115 cases where given).

31 On the matter of Irish independence and the British Battalion, see Stradling (1999), 152–62 and 171–3. One American writer on the brigades questions Francis's assessment of the Welsh volunteers as 'an army of comrades': Jackson

(1996), 126 and see Francis (1984), 223ff. But whilst not always to be assessed as 'comradely' in the general sense, the latter's specific meaning is surely unexceptionable.

[32] Ryan's book first appeared in English and French in 1938. It was republished in 1975 (the edition used here) and again in 2003. In it 'The Irish Unit' – which never officially existed – is recorded with the same status as other *battalions* of the brigade! (28). Other specific sections celebrate 'Irish fighters for freedom' (63); 'How Kit Conway died' (64); 'Charles Donnelly, Irish revolutionary' accompanied by one of Donnelly's poems (117–18); 'Captain Paddy O'Daire' (194); 'Robbie' (J. Robinson) (195–6); 'Battalion Commander Peter Daly' (287); and finally, a large group photograph (73). In contrast, the Welsh are recorded in a smaller group picture, another of Will Paynter, and passing mentions of a few individuals. See also Acier (1937) – addressed to an American audience – which dedicates a chapter to the letters home of Irish comrades.

[33] 'To the British Battalion – a message from Bill Paynter on his departure from Spain', *Volunteer for Liberty*, 25 October 1937. For 'Irish' material see, for example, 15 November, 20 and 27 December 1937, 3 January, 12 and 23 February 1938.

[34] However, the pennant itself lacks any distinguishing logo. The picture evidently dates from the period when the 'Irish Mutiny' was still an open wound. If anything relevant *was* happening in what it portrays, it was certainly intended as a prophylactic balm: Bradley and Chappell (1994), 20.

[35] J. Gates to W. Rust, 23 June 1937, RGASPI/545/6/141/107.

[36] 'English comrades at Madrigueras', 5 May 1937, ibid., 53/4, and 'Battalion Roll June 1937', 47/17–9.

[37] E. Lloyd, H. Dobson, R. Brown and A. Skinner were among 17 British survivors; untitled lists, ibid., 53/47.

[38] A. Cummings, personal file, ibid., 121/20–1. Cummings had previously been in charge of No. 2 company. He was also appointed battalion adjutant – that, is second-in-command to Fred Copeman – shortly before Brunete; List of Officers, June 1937, ibid., 47/21.

[39] Figures compiled from XV Brigade archive; 'List of death certificates [of Welsh volunteers] taken by Bert Williams', c.August 1937, ibid., 51/107, includes D. Jones (Penygraig), P. Murphy (Cardiff, in error), S. Morris, W. Morris, S. Hamm, F. Owen, R. Rodriguez, R. Traill and J. E. Williams. A 'List of men lost during the retreat', ibid., 3/426/249 mistakenly gives P. Murphy as killed, while noting H. Dobson, R. Horridge and E. Lloyd as wounded and one other Welshman as missing; a round-robin request from the base for information on missing men, 8 August 1937, ibid., 427/4, nominates eight Welsh volunteers, including Rodriguez and Hamm.

[40] Total casualties were 79 dead, with 201 wounded and missing, out of 330 British soldiers mustered, ibid., 3/486/184.

[41] M. Morgan interview (1987), IWM/9856/3, cited in Baxell (2004), ch. 6.

[42] Notebook of J. Johnstone, November 1938, IBA/Box 50/Je/2. All the same, about a dozen brigaders from Wales described themselves as 'Welsh' rather than as

'British' on the questionnaires which they were required to complete during an intense 'de-briefing' exercise carried out before they left Spain; personal files scattered in RGASPI/545/6/101–21. Moreover, some candidates who seemed unlikely at first dash even claimed to be Welsh-speaking; see, for example, the files on twelve brigaders with the surname 'Jones' in ibid/p. 155.

43 In this section I have largely eschewed personal anecdotes of battle experiences, as tending to fall into the category of 'the "just fancy that" school of history' recently identified by Keith Jefferey and drawn to my attention by Bill Jones; see Aled Jones and Bill Jones (2003), 59–60.

44 See Paynter (1972), 38 (on Maerdy) and 61–81, chapter titled 'The war in Spain'.

45 Paynter to Pollitt, 20 May 1937, IBA/Box C/13/8.

46 Same to same, 30 May 1937, ibid. One of the men Paynter probably had in mind was Harold Patterson of Penarth who reported sick at the battle of Jarama and then absconded, later publishing newspaper articles claiming to have been wounded in the thick of the fighting. Around this time it was agreed that wounded men over 40 years of age should be allowed home: see Stradling (2003), 39.

47 'This man Will Paynter by Arthur Horner, As told to Ron Evans', third episode of a series published in the *Empire News*, 5 April 1959. The occasion seems to be that recalled by Paynter himself: (1972), 71. See also Stratton (1984), 41–3, and Hopkins (1998), 254–7.

48 Paynter to Pollitt, 9 June 1937, IBA/Box C/14/5.

49 See, however, the notebook of Battalion Commissar Bert Williams (a 'Birmingham Welshman') who drew the large numbers of Welsh offenders to Paynter's notice shortly after the battle: RGASPI/545/3/437/192–5.

50 See the extensive correspondence in IBA/Box C/16–17.

51 See his angry letter to Paynter, accusing him of 'political jobbery', 9 August 1937, IBA/Box C/16/2.

52 T. Maynard to K. Bender, 29 September 1937, RGASPI/545/6/39/2. See also Felstead (1981), 99, 107.

53 Roberts's name appears on a list of Brigade Staff (*Estado Mayor*) as a lieutenant in the 'Training Battalion' at Tarazona, 27 November 1937, ANGC/SM1061/79.

54 Baxell (2004), 'Conclusion'; cf. Alexander (1982/1987), 131–2.

55 Roberts's card-index, RGASPI/545/6/193/15a–16, where he is described as 'propagandist and local councillor'; see also Felstead (1981), 112.

56 Paynter to Pollitt, *c*.16 September 1937, IBA/Box C/17/6.

57 Elliott Report (1939), RGASPI/545/6/22/16–17. Cf. the detailed and positive assessment of Paynter's work in Spain by the American scholar, J. Hopkins (1998), 255–7.

58 He laments the fact that he failed to keep any personal records: Paynter (1972), 67. But in fact even the specific correspondence he refers to (with Wally Tapsell) was available to him at the time of writing in the custody of the IBA in London.

59 Ibid., seemingly not a disingenuous remark.

60 Ibid., 69. This was probably the excuse given Paynter at the time by André Marty

and Luigo Longo who were guiding Comintern policy on the issue. It may be doubted that it calmed the troubled feelings of surviving Welsh Brigaders who were involved in the unfortunate events Paynter described.

61 'It is fair to say, too, that at this time problems of battalion leadership contributed to this situation. It became my task to deal with the reorganization of the battalion': ibid., 70–1.

62 See above, pp. 106 and 113.

63 Griffiths (1964) SUCC/161 (my citations are from an unpaginated word-processed copy of 1997).

64 Report on British Battalion (1939), RGASPI/545/6/22/7 and 47. Elliott goes on to name Griffiths among a magnificent seven comrades whose work in Spain was beyond criticism; ibid., 48. The work in Barcelona on which they were jointly engaged is often described as 'preparing the men for their return home' or words to that effect. In fact, the priority task was a rigorous investigation of individuals' combat records, political contributions, feelings about their experiences and other matters relevant to the future interests of the Comintern. It involved personal interviews as well as interminable form-filling, the results of which are now in the International Brigade section of the Comintern Archive in Moscow; ibid., 46.

65 At least according to his detailed reminiscences of the battles of the Ebro campaign.

66 See his cadre report on B. Goldman, RGASPI/545/6/141/21. Griffiths's trust in political solutions even bred a contingent *distrust* of the military leadership, as in the case of Battalion Commander Sam Wild, who was impeccably working-class and communist as well as an outstanding soldier.

67 M. González Moreno-Navarro, 'Brigadistas Internacionales al Castell de Castelldefels, (1938–39)', in González (1996), 19–24. Two (doubtless disillusioned) Welshmen – William Rees (Glanaman) and Gwilym Nicholls (Cardiff) – were lucky to survive sentences in this hell-hole, situated in what is now a Costa Brava beach resort.

68 Report on W. Thompson, 8 September 1938, RGASPI/545/6/207/98. The entry is initialled by John Bourne but is certain to have emanated from Griffiths as Brigade Party Secretary. See also the 'List of suspicious individuals' (summer 1938) printed in Klehr *et al.* (1998), 166, 171. (I was unable to locate the original of this document when investigating the cited file in Moscow in September 2000.)

69 Anonymous note (possibly by Greening), SUCC/SC/184. Some time before 1996, it was officially decided that he had been killed on the same day as Tom Howell Jones, also from Aberdare district – that is, 25 August 1938. However, the Roll of Honour printed in the same volume oddly records him as having died in September; see Williams (1996), 62 and 147.

70 T. H. Jones file, RGASPI 545/6/155/70-v. Francis's 'Prologue' is in effect an extended tribute to this exemplary volunteer (1984: 27–8). His death and burial was one of the most poignant moments in the experience of his Welsh comrades: see Greening's account, ibid., 290.

71 Only days before his death, James had been recommended for promotion by

Commander Sam Wild, on the grounds that 'he was capable of handling men, especially bad elements': IBA/Box C25/3.

72 See below for investigation of this case, p. 145ff.

73 Hopkins (1998), 307–10.

74 Dobson's 'Livre militaire', IBA/Box D4/Do; see also RGASPI/545/3/426/249 and 6/53/47.

75 'Behind their Lines', *Volunteer For Liberty*, 15 June 1938. The title and content suggest *Boys' Own* style commando operations rather than inglorious retreat. The story falls short of self-glorification (perhaps it was at least edited by Dobson himself) but is at times simply nonsensical. For example, 'We realized almost too late that the town was occupied by the fascists. Our replies to the questioning of sentries being unsatisfactory they ordered us to proceed.'

76 An excellent introduction to the Ebro campaign can be found in Henry (1999).

77 What seems to be Dobson's only surviving letter to his family convincingly reflects his stoical and selfless attitude – its contents being the exact antithesis of the human foibles extensively illustrated by the correspondence of many other comrades; to Irene, 26 December 1937, SUCC/SC182/1. Many years later a copy of a photograph of Harry Pollitt which Dobson carried into his last action was sent to the IBA archive; R. F. Bill to A. Atienza, 16 January 1991, IBA/Box D4/Do.

78 Bert Hartwell, one of the bearers, states that both had stomach wounds from machine-gun fire; Hartwell and Hartwell (1988), 23. Davies survived. Other accounts attribute Dobson's death to aircraft bombing, but I am disinclined to this view since (a) terrestrial fire was later corroborated by Bob Cooney, see IBA/Box A12/Do/4; (b) the two men's wounds were similar and consistent with local enemy weaponry; and (c) no other reports of this day's fighting mention aviation. Indeed it seems unlikely that Nationalist aircraft would have been involved in such action at all only two days into the offensive, leave alone bombing or strafing with such accuracy lines which were highly indistinct and only yards apart.

79 Manning to 'Gwen' [?Gwen Jones], 20 September 1938, IBA/Box A12/Do/2. It is to be hoped that no other soldier died that day because of plasma shortage.

80 Quoted ibid., 129.

81 This artefact, constructed in the last weeks of the XV Brigade's Ebro campaign, was recently restored by a team of Spanish experts. (Percy Ludwick became a Soviet citizen in the 1920s, and died in Moscow in 2001.) In addition, A. Jackson is working on a history of the 'Cave Hospital' near La Bisbal in which Dobson and many others were treated.

82 Obituary by Bob Cooney, *Volunteer for Liberty*, 17 September 1938. Cooney had been a room-mate of Dobson's in the Lenin School. See also Francis (1984), 235. Dobson's was the only portrait of a Welshman to be featured in the IWM Exhibition of 2001–2.

83 'The diary of Sid Hamm', in Stradling (1998), esp. 164 ff. However, Hamm attended card schools in Picton's dug-out, and regularly registered hefty winnings, in which his comrades' tippling doubtless played a part. See also RGASPI/545/3/451/106.

84 Quotation compiled from various letters of Picton to George Thomas, May–September 1937, SUCC/163. After treatment for his wound, Tom enjoyed a spell at Benacasim, where he entertained his fellow patient and ex-commanding officer, Lt. Alec Cummings: Cummings to F. Crabbe, 29 August 1937, IBA/Box A15/11.

85 Picton and Foulkes to Thomas, 1 June 1937, SUCC/163. By 'bombs', Foulkes meant the crude hand-grenades of regular infantry issue – pull-top cans capable of refreshing many parts which other beers could not reach. The Albacete censors must have been asleep when this particular item crossed their desks. (Men were regularly misinformed that enemy facing them were Italian or German, and thus infallibly 'fascists'. Confronting the fact that so many Spaniards were fighting against them was politically awkward for the commissars, while it was useful to disseminate as much 'evidence' as possible about the 'invasion of democratic Spain' by the fascist powers. Consequently, few letters home (or subsequent memoirs) refer to the presence of an indigenous enemy at all! Dr Lyne is one of few experts ever to have commented on this point: see (1996), 351ff.)

86 Various lists of offenders, RGASPI/545/3/451/99, 111 and 156. See also 'Elementos sospechosos de Tarazona', 17 March 1938, ibid., 6/39/9–25 – which features both these particular suspects.

87 Jones (1986), 69.

88 '"Hill 481" by Morris L. Miller, Adjutant Commissar, 57th Battalion', *Volunteer for Liberty*, 17 September 1938.

89 Alexander (1987), 187.

90 Thomas in Stradling (1998), 112–17. Physical signs of these injuries – along with a cricket-ball-sized hole in his back made by a German shell at the siege of Tobruk in 1942 – were still discernible when the present writer first met Frank Thomas in 1995.

91 See Stradling (1999), 102–5.

92 Hywel Francis (1984), 138, 175, neglects Thomas's fighting record and concentrates on his desertion. In contrast great care is taken never to name any Welsh International Brigader in the same context.

93 The dubious reader might care to note the corroborative sources cited by the present author in his edition of Thomas's memoir; consulted in addition to personal inspections of several battle sites. Thomas died in 2002 without ever returning to Spain.

94 See, for example, Thomas to his brother, 11 March 1937, FHT Collection, and in Stradling (1998), 120. In fact, Thomas had become aware of the Irish Bandera a month earlier, and thereafter, as a sense of isolation and (eventually) alienation grew, unsuccessfully applied for transfer to it; see letters of 19 February and 5 May 1937, FHT Collection. From hospital at Talavera he wrote disparaging remarks about the inadequate fighting record of the Irishmen – 'farcical' to his mind – in a letter to his parents; 25 May 1937, ibid. It was sharply ironical that only two days later, to his own great good fortune, he was to meet the objects of his scorn in person.

95 Thomas to Finnish Military Attaché, 16 February 1940, ibid.

Chapter 8:   Volunteers in Spain II: Victims

1   For the most horrific account of the repressive regime inside the brigades, see Romerstein (1994). Another recent account, emphasizing the miserable predicament of the rank and file produced by intrusive political surveillance, is given by Mackenzie (1997), 116–217. Although reaching a more empathetic conclusion, Durgan (1999) – who addresses the issue from a socialist-revolutionary perspective – also illustrates the grim effects of Stalinist exploitation on the ideals of the volunteers. All these experts, and others listed in the Bibliography, pay tribute to the military contribution of the brigades to the Republican war-effort. The present writer shares this opinion. Moreover, there is no intention in this chapter to deny that all those whose idealism drove them to serve in the International Brigades are deserving of honour, in many cases even admiration.

2   The other, W. Durston, is touched on above, p. 138.

3   See above, p. 68–9.

4   On Coles, see Stradling (1996), 88–91.

5   Biographical details are compiled from various documents in Cummings's personal file, RGASPI/545/6/121/3–31, hereafter referenced as 'AC File'. For his coolness under fire, see Stratton (1984), 40.

6   Cummings to J. Cunningham, Battalion O/C, 5 March 1937, AC File 25, endorsed 'Military Commander and Political Commissar [of] Brigade must recommend this'.

7   Hamm, in Stradling (1998), 161 and 164.

8   AC File 28.

9   Copeman (1948), 109ff.

10   XV Brigade Command Structure, Albacete 7 July 1937, ANGC Salamanca SM 1061/110.

11   For analysis of this action, see the dedicated chapter in Stradling (2003), 123–44.

12   Copeman (1948), 132.

13   'Being wounded had spoiled my nerve for the time being – I believe this usually happens – and the prospect of being under fire frightened me horribly': Orwell, *Homage to Catalonia* (Harmondsworth, Penguin, 1966), 192.

14   'Lieutenant Alex Cummings, who had become Company Commander through sheer ability': Ryan (1938/1986), 189.

15   Unsigned reports, former dated 7 January 1938, AC File 23, 26.

16   See, for example, his report on Dan Trainor, a sailor who jumped ship at Alicante in order to join up but had no idea of what he was doing, other than 'qu'a la fin de la guerre il espere pouvoir trouver un place commode'. Cummings recommended rejection: RGASPI/545/6/208/72.

17   General Lists of IB Estado Mayor, 27 November 1937, ANGC/SM1061/72.

18   Huber (1997).

19   Cummings to Pollitt, 21 September 1937, IBA/Box C/17/6; RGASPI/545/6/101/22. See also 47/29 and 162/107.

20   Undated, anonymous report (in Spanish); AC File 24.

21   I had assumed that Cummings's rapid promotion after Jarama was partly

explained by his military experience, but found that no official document in Moscow or elsewhere made reference to it. Even when interviewed by a German SIM officer during a later spell in hospital (summer 1938) he stayed *stumm* on the subject; AC File 29 (report in German). See also Francis (1984), 233 and 245. When completing his thesis (1977) Hywel Francis believed that Cummings was a policeman at the time he volunteered.

22 Cummings was at a training camp in Catalonia when Malcolm Dunbar, Brigade chief of operations, ordered him to provide 'as many details as possible on all the cadres and soldiers there' and to bring to the front 'all the ex-fighters of the XV Brigade who are under his command': (instructions in Spanish), 23 and 26 April 1938, RGASPI/545/3/434/159, 162.

23 Rust to Pollitt, 26 May 1938, IBA/Box C/22/6. The German intelligence officer added that 'he probably felt degraded when sent back to join the brigade' ['wird wahrscheinlich degradiert werden wenn er zurück an die Brigada geht'], AC File 29.

24 At the end of June, Cummings told a correspondent 'I am better now with only the stupid danger that my nerves may let me down occasionally. This can happen quite involuntarily': letter of 29 June 1937, IBA/Box A15/11. It was a clear message (via the censors) to brigade command, and without compromising himself, that his employment in action might have negative consequences for others.

25 Griffiths, 1964, original typescript, SUCC/SC161/38–9.

26 AC File 30.

27 Cummings to S. Taylor, 27 and 29 August 1938, GTC. By this time enemy artillery and air superiority was total and the Republican army was bombarded by day and night. Damage caused by shrapnel was multiplied tenfold by the explosive disintegration of the rocky terrain.

28 Minutes of Commissars' Meeting, 6 September 1938 (in Spanish), RGASPI/545/3/435/145.

29 *Parte del Dia* (Daily Report), XV Brigade Command, 14 September 1938, ibid., 157.

30 *Parte del Dia*, XV Brigade, 20 September 1938, ibid., 169.

31 Unsigned report in Spanish, AC File 32. Cummings argued that he was under the command of the 58th (Lincoln) Battalion at the time.

32 AC File 31.

33 Griffiths (1964/1997).

34 Indeed, this uncertainty was present at the time, since another contemporary document stated that he was reported as 'missing' on 23 September; Cummings's index card, AC File 3.

35 In Cummings's Moscow file there are a further three cadre reports – by Finkelstein, Wild and Cooney – not cited here. See also, 'List of suspicious individuals and deserters' (*c.* July 1938), Klehr *et al.* (1998), 166, 171. (At around the same time and place, the commander of the Lincoln Battalion, Milton Woolf, took it upon himself to 'execute' a comrade whose cowardice put the lives of others in danger.)

36 AC File 31.

37 AC File 14. By any standards these comments, by an office wallah who never fired a rifle in earnest, about a comrade, a seriously wounded veteran who had

(ostensibly) been killed in action defending Spanish democracy against the fascist invader, seem despicable.

38 AC File 27.

39 Elliott Report (1939), RGASPI/545/6/22/76. This section of the typescript has – uniquely – been marked in the margin with a double tick. One wonders which reader in the Kremlin had some interest in the case.

40 The same source further stated that she had confronted Will Paynter with these facts in the 1970s. The details were substantially repeated to another enquirer in 2003.

41 Especially so, perhaps, since Cummings's name is conspicuously absent from the list of officers and commissars killed at the Ebro inscribed at the time on the Ludwick Monument (see above, p. 141).

42 See above, p. 68.

43 Of course, if Cummings was a SIS (=MI6) agent then a similar consideration applies to him. (I remind the reader that letters home were read by the censorship and suspect remarks reported – if important enough, to security services.)

44 See general source-reference in n. 56 below.

45 This remark is not meant to imply that such a categorization would have necessarily meant anything to Taylor himself.

46 Stradling (1996), 101.

47 After Taylor's disappearance, Cummings was overcome by a sense of personal responsibility and remorse, which dominates his correspondence and (if exacerbated by alcohol) seems genuine.

48 Taylor to S. Taylor, 27 December 1937, GTC. Around this time a censor drew Bill Rust's attention to some sentences which Taylor used in a letter home (to M. Shaxby, 28 December 1937, GTC) and which were later quoted in Rust's official history of the British Battalion (1939) 130.

49 Cummings to S. Taylor, 15 July 1938, GTC. Even before going to the front, Taylor had criticized Cummings for being too cynical about the cause; after that event, he turned on him bitterly; to same, 9 January and 12 March, 1938, GTC.

50 Taylor to S. Taylor, 13 March 1938 (see also same to same 28 February 1938), GTC.

51 'Relacion de los Bajos en el Frente de Belchite-Caspe desde 10–17 de Marzo', 25 March 1938, IBA/Box 21/B/6a. Some of the 49 missing men are also marked as proven or suspected deserters, but these do not include Taylor.

52 Lt. Tom Glyn Evans went to see Taylor's widow, Silvia, after being repatriated in August 1938. He told her that Cummings had reported a different story to him – perhaps the full story – which was vehemently denied by the latter; to S. Taylor, 27 August 1938, GTC.

53 Battalion Roll, 27 April 1938, IBA/Box 21/A/3; undated Roll [?May 1938], IBA/Box D7/A1; Roll (c.15 September 1938), RGASPI/545/6/39/95. Matters are obfuscated by the presence in the ranks in this period of several other men with this surname – no fewer than six in the latter two lists referenced here (two of whom had deserted!). This degree of superogation may have confused battalion commissars.

54 Though I found no details of the case in the Moscow archive, survivors of the

retreats were later interrogated by intelligence personnel about their own experiences and their observation of others. Unsatisfactory performances were noted. Taylor's performance was perhaps more unsatisfactory than most.

[55] RGASPI/545/6/39/151–2.

[56] Skinner to Thelma, 9 August 1937, SUCC/1995/14. A further comment in this letter, that Jack Roberts, company commissar, was 'a typical Welshman complete with accent and mannerisms', suggests that Skinner too was not born in Wales. (Skinner's correspondence from Spain was addressed to two married sisters, one of whom was resident in England.)

[57] Same to same, 25 August 1937, ibid.

[58] Skinner did not report this action (which took place 13–18 October) until a letter of 9 November, a month after it had taken place; to Dilys, ibid. Moreover, despite this ostensibly first-hand account, the fact that he was made company QM on c.9 October, and was 100 km away at Lérida on 21 October, inspires doubt as to his actual involvement.

[59] 'They recount in vivid terms the experiences on this hellish front, the remorseless test of endurance that the conditions call for': to Thelma, 27 July 1937, ibid.

[60] Same to Dilys, 7 September and 9 October 1937, ibid.

[61] Same to same, 21 October 1937, ibid. This item, posted in a civilian box, may have escaped the censors – but, in any case, the contents of Skinner's correspondence had already compromised him.

[62] Same to Thelma, 25 November 1937, ibid.

[63] Same to Dilys, 20 and 29 December 1937, ibid. The bitterly ironical tone utilized here might also be detected in Skinner's habit of pouring torrents of praise on the Party and its champions in Spain. A local historian has noted another ominous phrase from this correspondence, in which Skinner expressed an intention to 'write about things in Spain if it was desired', Eaton (1980), 83.

[64] Same to same, 20 and 23 February 1938, ibid. Letters contain what may be coded euphemisms – which I will leave to the reader's surmise. Skinner appears (along with Picton, G. Baker and G. Price) on a payroll of the reserve company, used as brigade HQ guards, for the period 21–8 February 1938, ANGC/PS/AR 7.

[65] Rolls of June and September, 1938, see above n. 53. Skinner's family later made representations to the Foreign Office to ascertain his circumstances. The British ambassador duly contacted Burgos to enquire whether he was a POW – with negative results; MAE/R 1051/63.

[66] Alwyn Skinner does not, however, appear on any official IBA list of British killed in action in Spain. For further comment on the Roll of Honour, see below, p. 158ff.

[67] Coronel Inspector (L. Pinillos) to Asesor Jurídico, 22 April 1938, AGM Avila, CGG 56/58/2.

[68] See, for example, Alexander (1982/1987), 187 ff.; Geiser (1986), 100 ff. The Welsh POW Morgan Havard confirmed many details of brutal treatment, but also illustrated how the inmates were allowed to enjoy communal and individual recreation, often of a self-improving and morale-building kind: 'Concentration camp', *Our Time* (1943), 10–12 (copy in IBA/Box 28/A14).

69   He wrote to Bill Alexander, official historian of the British Battalion, 'I do not think that the San Pedro de Cardena that I was in was the same place that is described in the book. Some time in the future I shall send you a different account': 9 August 1986, IBA/Box A12/Mor/1a. For corroborative detail, see typescript of Morgan's interview with H. Francis (15 October 1969), SUCC/SC180.

70   Interviews with author, 1995; see Stradling (1996), 86.

71   See various documents in MAE/R1051/24.

72   Feature Report by G. Tremlett, *Guardian*, 1 November 2002, based on research by R. Vinyes.

73   See IBA/Box C/3/1a.

74   'Elenco di Miliziani di Nazionalità Irlandese e Inglese', MAE R1051/75.

75   *Caernarvon and Denbigh Herald*, 30 September 1938. It seems the Italians must have recognized the particular needs of Welsh prisoners as established (but doubtless not satisfied) by Col. Vallejo. The story had a sad ending, for Roberts's uncle, who brought him up after he was orphaned, died before he returned home a month later: *Caernarvon and Denbigh Herald*, 28 October 1938.

76   Serious offenders spent time in 'punishment battalions' doing hard labour tasks, and often working dangerously near the front. Veterans who experienced such punishments invariably avoid the subject in subsequent recollections. Claims of ill-treatment made by contemporaries are customarily dismissed as pro-Franco propaganda; see, for example, Moroney (1938), 86–7, and Anon. (J. Alexander) (1938), esp. 21–30 and 50–2.

77   A Marty to J. Weissman, 23 March 1937, RGASPI/545/3/541/11–13.

78   Angus (1983), 7. See also 'List of camp personnel', 7 December 1937, ANGC/SM1061.

79   The documentary kernel of the case in contained in a sequence of documents in RGASPI/545/6/87/11–20, cited here as 'Dossier'.

80   All three men were arrested together in Tarragona on 20 August 1937; see the postcard written in Spanish in the Valencia gaol and signed by Thomas, 17 September 1937: PRO/FO/889/2.

81   The following (not unusual) scenario may be conjecturally reconstructed. Thomas feigned a willingness to rejoin the battalion to commissars who were themselves under great pressure to get men to the front. Taking the opportunity of looser supervision en route to the war-zone, he escaped and was able to get on board a British steamer.

82   G. Owen (Aberavon) to ?, 23 August 1938, statement by W. Hopkins, 20 August 1938, and extended explication of the case, Dossier 11–5.

83   Skinner to Thelma, 14 August 1937, SUCC/1995/14.

84   Same to ? [first page missing] *c*.January 1938, ibid.

85   See Horner (1960), 159. What is more, in the perfervid atmosphere then prevailing, the incident described had potentially serious political implications for Horner.

86   Unsigned report (in Spanish), Dossier 17.

[87] Marty to Pollitt, 4 October 1938, ibid. 20.

[88] Thomas was released in early 1939; see PRO/FO/369/2514/K15325/230. He later emigrated to Australia. Jones also reached home safely, and remained a supporter of the USSR into the 1970s. He attended a reunion of veterans in Manchester in 1975. On Hopkins no further information is available: see Francis (1977), ii, 40.

Chapter 9:   Halls of Fame: Making (and Faking) History

[1] John 12. 24–5 (New Revised Standard Edition, Oxford, OUP, 1995), 103.

[2] Gerhardie (1990), 304.

[3] Nicholas to ?, c.October 1938, SUCC/SC248/1. The crisis referred to is that associated with the Munich Agreement.

[4] Francis et al. (2001), 39–44.

[5] See Francis (1984), 249–50, for quotations and factual material in this paragraph.

[6] Western Mail, 9 September 1938. However, as I write, a commemorative plaque has recently been unveiled in the town.

[7] For the Dependents Aid Committee, see Haldane (1948); N. Suart of De Montfort University is near to completing a doctoral study based on perceptions of the International Brigades within the families of the British volunteers.

[8] Francis (1991), 72. This admirably courageous statement did not inspire any other writer – historian or journalist, in Wales or out of it – to 'ask the right questions'.

[9] 'The "Little Bolshie" who broke his mother's heart', South Wales Echo, 18 July 1996. See also Stradling (1996), 88.

[10] British Battalion XV International Brigade – Roll of Honour (?1938, Marston Printing for TUC), SUCC/SC29.

[11] Rust (1939), 189–99.

[12] Buchanan (2001), 297.

[13] See assorted correspondence, 1940–5, IBA/Box D3/F1–9. On Morris Davies, see above, p. 140, Francis (1984), 235; Castells (1974), 356; and an English translation ('The plaque on the wall') of an extract from E. Downing's memoirs (1985) which has recently disappeared from its posting on the internet.

[14] IBA/D3/F11, 15, 18.

[15] Cox to Nicholas, ? March 1944, SUCC/SC187/39. See also same to same, 28 March 1944, SUCC/SC190/2, stating that a room in the Cardiff Party offices was being decorated with the roll of honour.

[16] On the dubious history of the 'Connolly Column', see Stradling (1999), esp. 171–3.

[17] On Arthur Morris, see, for example, L. Morris to T. E. Nicholas, 19 May; letter to I. Nicholas from Canada, 10 July 1944, SUCC/SC185; extract from Weekly Bulletin of Information (Valencia), 28 June 1937, IBA/Box 8/B/3, which claims him as a member of the 'Connolly Unit'. His parents told a reporter that he was 'employed by a New York firm on whose behalf he had recently toured Europe': Caernarvon and Denbigh Herald, 28 May 1937. The firm was in fact the CPUSA. On Traill, see Stradling (1996), 122–3.

[18]   See Nicholas's list, August 1944, IBA/D3/F13. Seven names in this category were later dropped.

[19]   Aubrey to Nicholas, 22 May 1944, SUCC/SC186/8.

[20]   Cox to A. Digges, ? April 1944, IBA/D3/F11.

[21]   J. E. Morgan (Lady Windsor Lodge) to Nicholas, ? May 1944, IBA/D3/F19.

[22]   See the correspondence in SUCC/SC186-7/190, 252.

[23]   Sloan (1938), 237. Information was evidently received that Jones hailed from Cardiff – in fact he was a Londoner.

[24]   See above, p. 139.

[25]   Jones (1999), pp. xi–xii.

[26]   *Welsh Gazette* (Aberystwyth), 17 March 1938; Heaton (1985), 75.

[27]   *The Seaman*, 2 February 1938; *Volunteer for Liberty*, 5 February 1938.

[28]   *Welsh Gazette*, 14 July 1938. At least a dozen others were killed or injured on board Welsh-owned or registered steamers in the course of this year. It is not known how many of them were Welsh; see Heaton (1985), 103–5.

[29]   Private information.

[30]   Britain's only memorial to the merchant seamen killed in the two World Wars is set near the Welsh Assembly Building in Cardiff Bay.

[31]   Smith (1982), 2, with a reference to his 'final sacrifice', 5. However the same author had sought to contradict the legend of martyrdom in his (unpaginated) 'Introduction' to Jones's novels (1978); see also Jenkins (1992), 361. Cf. Francis, who deliberately mentions Jones's death in the context of the Spanish heroes' sacrifices (1984), 251. See also Meyn (2000), 128.

[32]   This (mis)information was first supplied by D. Garman (who originally edited Jones's novels for Lawrence & Wishart) in an obituary appreciation 'A revolutionary writer', *Welsh Review* (May 1939), 263–7.

[33]   Smith in Jones (1937/1978); see also the euphemistic treatment in idem (1982), 6–8. In *We Live*, the hero's wife is wary of walking their dog, Bonzo, because 'fearful of the many fights he engaged in and also shy because in practically every street there were dogs hardly distinguishable from him'; ibid., 326.

[34]   Jones's diary for 1937, SUCC/SC553, *passim*; see also Stratton (1984), 23–4.

[35]   Hyde (1950), 40–1; Smith (1982), 22. Hyde evidently disliked and/or was envious of Jones (whom he refrains from naming). His diluted version of the Garman legend was that Jones once addressed 'forty meetings in a single week', a figure which reduces the Titan to slightly more human dimensions. By the 1990s, D. Smith was also implicitly critical of Jones's behaviour, contrasting it with the 'respectability' culture prevailing amongst other Party leaders; see Smith (1993), 82–4.

[36]   *Western Mail*, 1 February 1939.

[37]   Stratton (1984), 24; Francis (1991), 74.

[38]   Nobody knows what happened to the Stalingrad hospital memorial ward. Bill Alexander (*inter alia*) presumably had opportunities to visit it during post-war trips to the Soviet Union. Yet no mention of the artefact can be found in the official IBA record of such memorials (Williams, 1996).

[39] Ibid., 62–3. No names or any further details are inscribed on the sculpture, which carries a representation of the Red (Soviet) Star rather than its three-pointed International Brigade version, and is clearly intended as a tribute to 'The Coal Brigade'. The local committee evidently acted without CPGB support. The sculpture was unveiled by Labour MP Bob Edwards, who had been a leading ILP activist in the 1930s, and was 'political delegate' of Orwell's company in the POUM militia. In the Spanish context, such men were regarded as 'objectively fascist' by the CPGB.

[40] Circular letter signed by J. Brewer, June 1971, WCIA/IB File. Note the text's careful renewal of the propaganda trope that the volunteers fought against Germans and Italians and not against Spaniards. I have been unable to locate any record of responses received by the committee.

[41] See, for example, T. G. Evans File, RGASPI/545/6/130/39–71.

[42] Davies to Brewer, 9 February 1971 (see also same to same, 17 May 1971); WCIA/IB File.

[43] Brewer to Davies, 22 March 1971, ibid.

[44] Cardiff City Council, Conservative-led at the time, rejected an appeal to contribute to the fund; see *South Wales Echo*, 7 July 1971.

[45] Williams (1998), 60–1. However, the plaque was first unveiled by Will Paynter at 50 Sketty Rd, Swansea, on 24 January 1976: IBA Box 21/G.

[46] Appeal Leaflet, SUCC/SC175. The present writer has not been able to ascertain how these new claims were originated, nor any evidence adduced by their advocates, nor the criteria on which final selection was based. Only one name seems to lack any independent corroboration. There seems to be no extant record of the presence in Spain of R. Jamadeesis (Cardiff); however, see Stradling (1996), 122.

[47] Brewer to Davies, 2 February 1976, WCIA/IB File.

[48] The quarrel, in which T. G. Evans and Jack Roberts were chief protagonists, was precipitated by some unfortunately slanted publicity in the local press about R. Felstead's (then forthcoming) biography of the latter. See note and annotated cuttings enclosed in Brewer to Davies, 23 June 1977, WCIA/IB File.

[49] Williams (1998), 64–5. All this time, Dobson's name slowly weathered away, along with those of thirty-five other Party dead in the Ebro campaign, on the great concrete catafalque built as a micro-model of the Moscow Lenin mausoleum in the Sierra Pandols; see illustration ibid., 135. Now that the monument has been restored, those who so wish can read it, carved with pride as 'Harry Dobson (England)'.

[50] Ibid., 66–7.

[51] Ibid., 58–9. In the last century it became the practice to erect a Gorsedd Ring or Circle in every town where the annual National Eisteddfod was held.

[52] *Western Mail*, ? August 1996. Mr Morris's claim seems over-enthusiastic.

[53] Author's correspondence with A. Owen. In 1995, the Spanish government offered to bestow Spanish nationality upon surviving veterans of the International Brigade. Three Welsh veterans (Alun M. Williams, Lance Rogers and Thora Craig) initiated the complex proceedings established to verify eligibility.

The project ultimately proved unfeasible on legal grounds; see records in APA/10/120/3/11.

[54] 'Battle waged over £500 Spanish Civil War memorial plan', *Western Mail*, 30 January 1997. (I owe this reference to Jonathan Osmond.)

[55] *Llanelli Star*, 8 June and 20 July 2000.

[56] *Western Mail* cutting (?summer 2000) in WCIA/IB File. Marshall, who became head of the Friends of the British Battalion, set up after the death of Bill Alexander, was one of the earliest British volunteers who joined the original 'Tom Mann' centuria raised in Barcelona in August 1936.

Chapter 10:   Epilogue: The Dragon's Cause Today

[1] Smith (1986), 20.

[2] Ibid., 25.

[3] A sceptical variation on my subtitle, suggested by Meirion Hughes.

[4] See G. A. Williams's TV biography of T. E. Nicholas, one of HTV's series *Cracking Up*, broadcast in 1986.

[5] Williams (1987), 45–6.

[6] See Williams (1988). In Lewis's story, set in the Second World War, a naive conscript from rural Cardiganshire is taught to adapt to army life by a hard-bitten ex-International Brigader from the coalfield, 'Dai Spain': Lewis (?1990), 27–42. Williams's character was further modelled on George Nathan, a British Battalion officer who had previously been a Black-and-Tan hit man in Ireland.

[7] *Empire News*, 8 December 1957.

[8] 'Dreams and Nightmares', IWM Exhibition, 2001–2.

[9] G. Williams (2002), 37, 55.

[10] In Lee's affectionate memoir of Dowlais, *The Town that Died* (London, self-published, 1975), politics, Spanish or otherwise, hardly ever happen. Equally notable is the failure of 'Spain' to make any impression on George Thomas, already a strong pacifist and Labour Party activist in 1936; at least to judge by the biography of Robertson (1993).

[11] Jackson (1996), who pays serious attention to *Miners Against Fascism*, also contrives to render Arthur Horner's name as 'Antony Harner' (86).

[12] Delperrie de Bayac (1968), 228.

[13] Castells (1974), 167.

[14] Graham (1987), 20 (my emphasis).

[15] IBA/Box D7/E. The 16-page MS begins 'I was a member of the 2nd Company . . . ' and relates the circumstances of the capture of most of its members on the second day of fighting. Yet another version, written by 'O.R.', appears in Ryan (1938/1975), 56–7, beginning 'I heard afterwards of a Welsh comrade, known to most of us only by his national nickname'.

[16] Inglis (1995), 289. Williams worked his feelings about these events into his current novel *Loyalties* (see above, p. 117).

17 Francis and Houdmont (1985), 8.
18 See, for example, the content of *Radical Wales* for five consecutive issues in 1984–5.
19 Stradling (1998), 162ff.
20 *Western Mail*, 17 July 1986.
21 Monks (1985), 50.
22 To give examples from the *South Wales Echo*; a three-part series 'Crusade to Spain: Welsh memories of the Spanish Civil War' by D. O'Neill, July 1976; 'Valley crusaders to war', 25 July 1989; 'Why the Welsh stood up to Franco', 17 July 1996; and various similar features and stories in earlier decades.
23 Details differ with the source.
24 After I played the number during a lecture and explained its background, student interest in the Spanish Civil War module registered a dramatic revival. The song was later voted onto a list of the best pop numbers of all time (at number twenty) in a survey carried out for Channel Four TV; *South Wales Echo*, 8 January 2001.
25 'Unconvention' (1999–2000) by Jeremy Deller. The exhibition included a section devoted to Wales and the Spanish Civil War.
26 Middles (1999), 47, 180.
27 Insert to CD *This Is My Truth Tell Me Yours* (Sony Music 1998). See also Francis (1984), 215. Sad to relate, when the hunter in question, Tom Thomas, was given an opportunity to shoot fascists at the battle of Brunete, he reacted more like a rabbit: RGASPI 545/3/451/65 and IBA/Box 21/B/3e.
28 *Design for Life* (produced by Darren Broome), BBC Radio 2, 12 October 2002. As it happened, in the mid-1990s, a representative Manics' fan, 'Mark Casnewydd', served as a volunteer with Muslim freedom fighters in Kossovo: BBC Wales TV, *The Slate* (broadcast 12 January 2000).
29 *Close Up*, BBC2 TV, 23 September 1998.
30 Presented at the Sherman Theatre, Cardiff, in 1999. If tangentially, it might be remarked here that there were probably some parallels in real life for the lead character in a TV play by Alan Plater, in which a Rhondda miner invents a past as a volunteer for liberty in Spain, and as a result never has to pay for his own beer in the local clubs.
31 *Franco's Bastard* by Dic Edwards (no relation). I read the text online at playwright30.freeserve.co.uk/franco_text.htm
32 R Stennet, *The Blood that Sings*, Sherman Theatre, 1979.
33 Burke (2002), 63.
34 *Planet* (1975), 37–40.
35 At the time recalled, of course, Orwell was acting in rebellion against the Republican government he had come to serve – a fact which (I am assuming) the poet recognized.
36 Abse (1994), 20.
37 Williams (1985), 270–1.
38 The central character of Sartre's *Roads to Freedom* is said to be modelled on a Spanish Republican exile who died fighting with the French Resistance.

[39] See above, p. 101 *et seq.*

[40] Quoted and commented by D. Smith (1993), 121–2.

[41] Artists International Association, 'Portraits for Spain', fly-leaf (1937) to illustrate T. Buchanan's lecture 'Mobilising art: British artists and the Spanish Civil War', Oxford, January 2003.

[42] McGarry (1999), 161. Something in the region of £250,000–300,000 was raised for the Republic from public appeals in Great Britain as a whole; rough estimate based on material in Buchanan (1997), ch. 4.

[43] See, for example, *Drawing a Line in the Sand*, programme in the series *Celtic Radicals* (made by Concordia for S4C and Irish Television, broadcast 17 December 1998).

[44] Cf. Morris (1984/1986), 322–3, 389.

[45] See above p. 154.

[46] In my own library of some 600 items, references amount to a mere handful. Individuals who rate a mention in one or two prominent textbooks are Paynter, Horner, Dobson; and (in a curious irony) Captain Cecil Bebb, the Welsh mercenary who piloted Franco's Dragon Rapide, without which the Spanish Civil War may never have got off the ground.

[47] Hopkins (1998), 15–6.

[48] Ibid., for example, 99, 147, 291–313 *passim*, 388–9.

[49] Ibid., 147.

[50] In any case, and by definition, the mere existence of this book attests to my belief in the significance and interest of its subject.

[51] Williams (1985), 180. (Gwyn Alf was in fact speaking in very subjective terms here, but his actual subject was Welsh 'colonies' in North and South America.)

Bibliography

Primary MS Collections

Public Domain
(For analytical descriptions of several sources listed below, see my books *The Irish and the Spanish Civil War*, 272–3, and *History and Legend*, 255–6).

AGM   Archivo General Militar, Avila
         CGG – Sección Cuartel General del Generalísimo
ANGC   Archivo Nacional de la Guerra Civil, Salamanca
         PS – Sección Político-Social
         SM – Sección Militar
APA   Archivo Provincial de Albacete, Albacete
         Mainly copies of materials sent by veterans to the Spanish pressure-group Amigos de las Brigadas Internacionales in 1995–6
IBA   International Brigade Association Archive, Marx Memorial Library, London
MAE   Archivo del Ministerio de Asuntos Exteriores, Madrid
NLW   National Library of Wales, MSS Dept., Aberystwyth
         Mainly personal archives of Welsh public figures
NMLH National Museum of Labour History, Manchester
         Assorted records and memorabilia of the CPGB
PRO   Public Record Office, London
         FO 371 Embassy and Diplomatic papers
         FO 369 Consular papers
         FO 889 War Office papers
         HW17 Operation Mask (Comintern Surveillance Intercepts)
RGASPI Russian Centre for the Study of Modern History, Moscow
SUCC   Swansea University Coalfield Collection
         A major repository of original Spanish Civil War material relevant mainly to Wales
SWML South Wales Miners' Library, Hendrefoilan, Swansea
         Tape-recorded interviews with volunteers (and some transcripts) made by Hywel Francis
WCIA   Welsh Centre for International Affairs, Temple of Peace, Cardiff
         International Brigade Fund File
WML   Working Man's Library, Salford
         Various unpublished memoirs of volunteers, mainly from the north-west of England

Private Collections

FHT   Frank Thomas Collection
GTC   Gilbert Taylor Collection
SRC   Sidney Robinson Collection

Newspapers and Journals

Caernarvon and Denbigh Herald
Cambrian Times
Y Cymro
Y Ddraig Goch
Empire News
North Wales Observer
Seren Cymru
South Wales Echo
South Wales Weekly Argus
Tenby Observer
The Universe (Welsh edn.)
Volunteer for Liberty
Welsh Catholic Times
Welsh Gazette
The Welsh Nationalist
Welsh Review
Wrexham Leader

Secondary Works

(Place of publication is London unless otherwise stated.)

Abse, D. (1953/71), *Ash on a Young Man's Sleeve* (Vallentine, Mitchell).
—— (1974/1984), *A Poet in the Family* (Robson Books).
—— (1994), *On the Evening Road* (Hutchinson).
Abse, L. (1973), *Private Member* (MacDonald).
Acier, M. (ed.) (1937), *From Spanish Trenches: Recent Letters from Spain* (New York, Modern Age Books).
Alba, V. (1978), *La Alianza Obrera: Historia y análisis de una táctica de unidad en España* (Madrid, Ediciones Júcar).
Alcofar Nassaes, J. (1975), *La Marina Italiana y la Guerra de España* (Barcelona, Editorial Euros).
Alexander, B. (1982/1987), *British Volunteers for Liberty: Spain, 1936–39* (Lawrence & Wishart).
Alpert, M. (1984), 'Humanitarianism and politics in the British response to the Spanish Civil War', *European History Quarterly*, 14(4), 423–40.
—— (1987), *La Guerra Española en el mar* (Madrid, Ediciones Siglo XXI).
Alvarez, S. and Cabra, D. (1996), *Historia Política y Militar de las Brigadas Internacionales* (Madrid, Compañía Literaria).

Angus, J. (1983), *With the International Brigade in Spain* (Loughborough, Dept. of Economics, Loughborough University).

Anon. [Alexander, J.] (1938), *In Spain with the International Brigade: A Personal Narrative* (Burns, Oates & Washbourne).

Anon. (ed.) (1981), *'Tros Ryddid Daear': T. E. Nicholas, Political Verse* (Mountain Ash, Niclas Books).

Ashford-Hodges, G. (2000), *Franco: A Concise Biography* (Weidenfeld & Nicolson).

Avilés Farré, J. (1994), *Pasión y Farsa: Franceses y Británicos ante la Guerra Civil Española* (Madrid, Eudema).

Barco Teruel, E. (1984), *El 'Golpe' Socialista; Octubre 1934* (Madrid, Ediciones Dyrsa).

Baxell, R. (2004), *British Volunteers in the Spanish Civil War: The British Battalion in the International Brigade, 1936–1939* (Routledge).

Bebbington, D. (1983), 'Baptists and politics since 1914', in K. W. Clements (ed.), *Baptists in the Twentieth Century: Papers Presented at a Summer School, 1982* (Baptist Historical Society).

Beevor, A. (1982/2001), *The Spanish Civil War* (Cassell).

Bell, A. (1996), *Only for Three Months: The Basque Children in Exile* (Norwich, Mousehold Press).

Bradley, K. and Chappell, M. (1994), *International Brigades in Spain* (Osprey Publishing).

Brome, V. (1953), *Aneurin Bevan: A Biography* (Longmans Green).

—— (1965), *The International Brigades: Spain, 1936–1939* (Heinemann).

Buchanan, T. (1992), *The British Labour Movement and the Spanish Civil War* (Cambridge, Cambridge University Press).

—— (1997), *Britain and the Spanish Civil War* (Cambridge, Cambridge University Press).

—— (2001), 'Holding the line: the political strategy of the International Brigade Association, 1939–1977', *Labour History Review*, 66(3), 294–312.

Burke, S. (2002), *Deadwater* (Serpent's Tail).

Burton, B. (1999), *Not Just a Soldier's War* (Grafton Books).

Cable, J. (1979), *The Royal Navy and the Siege of Bilbao* (Cambridge, Cambridge University Press).

Castells, A. (1974), *Las Brigadas Internacionales de la Guerra de España* (Barcelona, Ariel).

Cole, G. D. H. (1937), *The People's Front* (Gollancz).

Cook, J. (1979), *Apprentices of Freedom* (Quartet Books).

Copeman, F. (1948), *Reason in Revolt* (Blandford).

Cordell, A. (1980), *To Slay the Dreamer* (Wembley, The Leisure Circle).

Corkill, D. and Rawnsley, S. (1981), *The Road to Spain: Antifascists at War 1936–1939* (Dunfermline, Borderline Press).

Cox, I. (1937), 'South Wales shows the way', *Discussion*, 14, 11–14.

Cunningham, V. (ed.) (1981), *The Penguin Book of Spanish Civil War Verse* (Harmondsworth, Penguin).

Davies, A. (1999), 'The first radio war: broadcasting in the Spanish Civil War, 1936–1939', *Historical Journal of Film, Radio and Television*, 19(4), 473–515.

Davies, D. H. (1983), *The Welsh Nationalist Party, 1925–1945: A Call to Nationhood* (Cardiff, University of Wales Press).

Davies, D. R. (1961), *In Search of Myself* (Geoffrey Bles).

Davies, I. (1993), *The Angry Summer: A Poem of 1926* (Cardiff, University of Wales Press).

Davies, J. (1981), *Cardiff and the Marquesses of Bute* (Cardiff, University of Wales Press).

—— (1994), *A History of Wales* (Harmondsworth, Penguin).

Davies, J. A. (1998), *A Reference Companion to Dylan Thomas* (Cardiff, University of Wales Press).

Davies, W. (1974), *Dylan Thomas, Selected Poems* (Dent).

Delperrie de Bayac, J. (1968), *Les Brigades Internationales* (Paris, Fayard).

Denning, R. (1974), in S. Williams (ed.), *The Cardiff Book*, vol. 2 (Barry, Stewart Williams).

Downing, E. (1985), *La Niña Bonita, agus an Roisin Dubh* (Dublin, An Clochombar Tta).

Durgan, A. (1999), 'Freedom fighters or Comintern army? The International Brigades in Spain', *International Socialism Journal*, 84 (Autumn).

Dykes, D. (1992), *University College of South Wales, Swansea* (Stroud, Alan Sutton).

Eaton, G. (1980), *Neath and the Spanish Civil War: Catalyst of the Angry Thirties* (Neath, privately printed).

Edwards, J. (1979), *The British Government and the Spanish Civil War, 1936–1939* (Macmillan).

Eisenwein, G. and Shubert, A. (1995), *Spain at War: The Spanish Civil War in Context* (Longman).

Evans, D. G. (2000), *A History of Wales 1906–2000* (Cardiff, University of Wales Press).

Evans, N. (1989), 'Gogs, cardis and hwntws: region, nation and state in Wales, 1840–1940', in idem (ed.), *National Identity in the British Isles* (Harlech, Coleg Harlech).

—— (1999), ' "South Wales has been Roused as Never Before": marching against the Means Test, 1934–36', in D. Howell and K. O. Morgan (eds), *Crime, Protest and Police in Modern British Society: Essays in Memory of David J. V. Jones* (Cardiff, University of Wales Press).

Evans, W. and Symond, O. (1913) *The History of South Pembrokeshire Calvinistic Methodist Churches* (Wrexham, Hughes & Son).

Felstead, R. (1981), *No Other Way: Jack Russia and the Spanish Civil War* (Port Talbot, Alun Books).

Ferris, P. (1999), *Dylan Thomas: The Biography* (Phoenix).

Fielding, S. (1993), *Class and Ethnicity: Irish Catholics in England, 1890–1939* (Buckingham, Open University).

Fitzgibbon, C. (1965), *Dylan Thomas: A Life* (Dent).

Foot, M. (1962), *Aneurin Bevan: A Biography*, vol. 1 (Macgibbon & Kee).

Francis, H. (1975), 'Rhondda and the Spanish Civil War', in K. S. Hopkins (ed.), *Rhondda Past and Future* (Rhondda Borough Council).

—— (1977), 'The South Wales miners and the Spanish Civil War: a study in internationalism' (2 vols, University of Wales Ph.D. Swansea).

—— (1984), *Miners Against Fascism: Wales and the Spanish Civil War* (Lawrence & Wishart).

—— (1991), ' "Say Nothing and Leave in the Middle of the Night": the Spanish Civil War revisited', *History Workshop Journal*, 32, 69–76.

—— and Houdmont, R. (1985), *Striking Back* (Welsh Campaign for Civil and Political Liberties with the NUM, 1984).

—— and Smith, D. (1980), *The Fed: A History of the South Wales Miners in the Twentieth Century* (Lawrence & Wishart).

—— et al. (2001), *Let Paul Robeson Sing! A celebration of the Life of Paul Robeson and his Relationship with Wales* (Paul Robeson Cymru Committee/Bevan Foundation).

Fyrth, J. (ed.) (1985), *Britain, Fascism and the Popular Front* (Lawrence & Wishart).

—— (1986), *The Signal was Spain: The Aid Spain Movement in Britain, 1936–39* (Lawrence & Wishart).

García Volta, G. (1975), *La Campaña del Norte* (Barcelona, Ediciones Bruguera).

Geiser, C. (1986), *Prisoners of the Good Fight: The Spanish Civil War, 1936–1939* (Westport, CT, Lawrence Hill).

Gerhardie, W. (1981/1990), *God's Fifth Column: A Biography of the Age 1890–1940* (Hogarth Press).

Gli antifascisti (1976), *Gli antifascisti Lombardi alla Guerra di Spagna (1936–1939): celebrazione del quarantesimo anniversario* (Turin, Consiglio Regionale della Lombardia 1976).

Goddard, R. (1992), *Hand in Glove* (Bantam Press).

González, A., González, M. and Pinos, N. (eds) (1996), *Los Grafitos de las BBII de la Iglesia del Castillo de Castelldefels (1938–1939)* (Barcelona, Diputació de Barcelona).

González Echegaray, R. (1977), *La marina mercante y el tráfico marítimo en la guerra civil* (Madrid, Ediciones San Martín).

González Huix, F. (1995), *El puerto y la mar de Tarragona en la Guerra Civil, 1936–1939* (Tarragona, Ediciones Tarraconeses).

González Portilla, M. and Garmendía, J. M. (1988), *La guerra civil en el País Vasco: política y economía* (Leioa, Universidad del País Vasco).

Graham, F. (1987), *Battle of Jarama, 1937: The Story of the British Battalion of the International Brigade in Spain* (Newcastle upon Tyne, Graham).

—— (1999), *The Spanish Civil War: Battles of Brunete and the Aragon* (Newcastle upon Tyne, Graham).

Gregory, W. (1986), *The Shallow Grave: A Memoir of the Spanish Civil War* (Gollancz).

Gretton, P. (1984), *El factor olvidado: La marina británica y la guerra civil española* (Madrid, Ediciones San Martín).

Griffiths, R. (2002), 'Another form of fascism: the cultural impact of the French "radical right" in Britain', (forthcoming)

Grossi Mier, M. (1935/1978), *La Insurrección de Asturias* (Madrid, Ediciones Júcar).

Haldane, C. (1948), *Truth will out* (Right Book Club).

Hannan, P. (1988), *Wales on the Wireless: A Broadcasting Anthology* (Llandysul, Gomer Press/BBC Wales).

Hartwell, H. and Hartwell, E. (1988), *The Long Weekend* (Derby, Postmill Press).

Harvey, C. (1981), *The Rio Tinto Company: An Economic History of a Leading International Mining Concern 1873–1954* (Penzance, Alison Hodge).

Heaton, P. M. (1983), *The Abbey Line: History of a Cardiff Shipping Venture* (Newport, Starling Press).

—— (1985), *Welsh Blockade Runners in the Spanish Civil War* (Newport, Starling Press).

—— (1987), *Tatems of Cardiff* (Newport, Starling Press).

Heinemann, M. (1960), *The Adventurers* (Lawrence & Wishart).

Henry, C. (1999), *The Ebro 1938: Death Knell of the Republic* (Oxford, Osprey).

Hermet, G. (1989), *La Guerre d'Espagne* (Paris, Éditions de Seuil).

Hickey, J. (1967), *Urban Catholics: Urban Catholicism in England and Wales from 1829 to the Present Day* (Catholic Book Club).

Hooper, D. (1997), *No Pasaran: A Memoir of the Spanish Civil War* (Avon Books).

Hopkins, J. (1998), *Into the Heart of the Fire: The British in the Spanish Civil War* (Stanford, CA, Stanford University Press).

Horner, A. (1960), *Incorrigible Rebel* (MacGibbon & Kee).

Howells, R. (1975), *Total Community: The Monks of Caldey Island* (Tenby, H. G. Walters).

Howson, G. (1998), *Arms for Spain: The Untold Story of the Spanish Civil War* (Murray).

Huber, P. (1997), 'Surveillance et repression politique dans les Brigades Internationales' (unpublished paper given at International Brigade Conference, Lausanne).

Hughes, T. O. (1999), *Winds of Change: The Roman Catholic Church and Society in Wales, 1916–62* (Cardiff, University of Wales Press).

—— (2002), 'Anti-Catholicism in Wales, 1900–1960', *Journal of Ecclesiastical History*, 53(2), 312–25.

Humphreys, E. (1986), *An Absolute Hero* (Dent).

Hyde, D. (1952), *I Believed: The Autobiography of a Former British Communist* (The Reprint Society).

Inglis, A. (ed.) (1985), *Lloyd Edmunds: Letters from Spain* (Sydney, Allen & Unwin).

Inglis, F. (1995), *Raymond Williams* (Routledge).

Jackson, M. (1996), *Fallen Sparrows: The International Brigade in the Spanish Civil War* (Philadelphia, American Philosophical Society).

Jeffries, L. (1937), 'Cardiff campaigns for Spain', *Discussion*, 15, 15–17.

Jenkins, D. (1998), *A Nation on Trial: Penyberth 1936*, ed. J. Davies (Cardiff, Welsh Academic Press).

Jenkins, J. G. (1981), 'Cardiff shipowners', *Maritime Wales/Cymru a'r Mor*, 5, 115–31.

Jenkins, P. (1992), *A History of Modern Wales, 1536–1990* (Longman).

Johnston, V. B. (1967), *Legions of Babel: The International Brigades in the Spanish Civil War* (Pennsylvania State University Press).

Jones, Aled and Jones, Bill (2003), 'The Welsh world and the British Empire, *c*.1851–1939: an exploration', *Journal of Imperial and Commonwealth History*, 31 (2), 57–81.

Jones, D. G. (1973), 'His politics', in A. R. Jones and G. Thomas (eds), *Presenting Saunders Lewis* (Cardiff, University of Wales Press).

Jones, G. (1969), *Wales and the Quest for Peace: From the Close of the Napoleonic Wars to the Outbreak of the Second World War* (Cardiff, University of Wales Press).

Jones, G. (1999), *The Collected Stories of Glyn Jones*, ed. T. Brown (Cardiff, University of Wales Press).

Jones, H. C. (1983), 'W. R. Hearst and St. Donat's', in R. Denning (ed.), *The Story of St. Donat's Castle and Atlantic College* (Cowbridge and Barry, D. Brown & Sons with Stewart Williams Publishers).

Jones, J. (1986), *Union Man: An Autobiography* (Collins).

Jones, L. (1937/1978), *Cwmardy* (Lawrence & Wishart).

—— (1939/1978), *We Live* (Lawrence & Wishart).

Jones, M. (1991), *A Radical Life: The Biography of Megan Lloyd George, 1902–66* (Hutchinson).

Jones, W. and Williams, C. (eds) (1999), *A B. L. Coombes Anthology* (Cardiff, University of Wales Press).

Jordan, N. (1994), *Sunrise with Sea Monster* (Chatto & Windus).

Keene, J. (2001), *Fighting for Franco: International Volunteers in Nationalist Spain during the Spanish Civil War, 1936–39* (Leicester University Press).

Klaus, H. G. and Knight, S. (eds) (2000), *British Industrial Fictions* (Cardiff, University of Wales Press).

Klehr, H., Haynes, J. E. and Anderson, K. (1998), *The Soviet World of American Communism* (Yale University Press).

Kollar, K. (1995), *Abbot Aelred Carlyle, Caldey Island and the Anglo-Catholic Revival in England* (New York, Peter Lang).

Kurlansky, M. (1999), *The Basque History of the World* (Cape).

Lagerreta, D. (1984), *The Guernica Generation: Basque Refugee Children of the Spanish Civil War* (Reno, Nevada University Press).

Larios, J. (1966), *Combat over Spain: Memoirs of a Nationalist Fighter Pilot, 1936–1939* (New York, Macmillan).

Lewis, A. (n.d. ?1990), *The Collected Stories*, ed. C. Archard (Bridgend, Seren Books).

Lewis, J. (1970), *The Left Book Club: An Historical Record* (Gollancz).

Lewis, P. (1990), 'The Anglo-Welsh press response to the Spanish Civil War 1936–1939' (unpublished MA dissertation, University of Wales, Cardiff).

Lizarra, A. de (1944) [M. de Irujo], *Los vascos y la República Española: Contribución a la historia de la Guerra Civil* (Buenos Aires, Editorial Vasca Ekin).

Llewellyn, C. and Watkins, H. (2001), *Los desconocidos a l'extranjero/Strangers in a Foreign Land: The Spanish Immigration to Dowlais* (Merthyr Tydfil Historical Society in conjunction with Merthyr Tydfil Central Library).

López Ortega, R. (1974), *La crisis económica y la novelística de tema obrero en Gran Bretaña en los años treinta: Resúmen de la tésis doctoral* (Salamanca, Gráficas Europa).

Lyne, K. (1996), 'Perceptions of Spain and the Spanish and their effect on public opinion in Britain at the outbreak of the Spanish Civil War' (unpublished Ph.D., University of Wales Lampeter).

MacDougall, I. (1986), *Voices from the Spanish Civil War: Personal Recollections of Scottish Volunteers in Republican Spain 1936–39* (Edinburgh, Polygon).

McGarry, F. (1999), *Irish Politics and the Spanish Civil War* (Cork, Cork University Press).

Macho, L. (1976), 'Growing up in Spanish Abercrave in the 1930s', lecture transcript, SUCC/SC179.

Macintyre, S. (1980), *Little Moscows: Communism and Working-Class Militancy in Inter-War Britain* (Croom Helm).

Mackenzie, S. P. (1997), 'The International Brigades in the Spanish Civil War: No Pasaran?', in *Mackenzie, Revolutionary Armies in the Modern Era: A Revisionist Approach* (Routledge).

McLean, A. (1957/1970), *The Guns of Navarone* (Fontana).

Macmillan, R. (1980), 'Pat Murphy (1898–1974): the making of a revolutionary' (unpublished diploma dissertation, Gwent College of Education, copy in SWML).

Martínez Bande, J. M. (1972), *Las Brigadas Internacionales* (Barcelona, Caralt).

Maseras, A. (1938/1991), *A Europa (To Europe)*, tr. from Catalan by H. G. A. Hughes (Mold, Gwasg Gwenffwrd).

Matthews, I. (1992), 'The world of the anthracite miner', *Llafur*, 6(1), 96–104.

Meils, G. (1977), 'Ambrose Bebb', *Planet*, 37/38, 70–9.

Meyn, R. (2000), 'Lewis Jones's *Cwmardy* and *We Live*: two Welsh proletarian novels in Transatlantic perspective', in H. G. Klaus and S. Knight (eds), *British Industrial Fictions* (Cardiff, University of Wales Press).

Middles, M. (1999), *Manic Street Preachers* (Omnibus Press).

Monks, J. (1985), *With the Reds in Andalusia* (Authors' Publication).

Moradiellos, E. (2000), *La perfidia de Albión: El Gobierno británico y la guerra civil española* (Madrid, Ediciones Siglo XXI).

Morgan, K. O. (1981), *Rebirth of a Nation: A History of Modern Wales* (Oxford, Oxford University Press).

—— (1995), *Modern Wales: Politics, Places and People* (Cardiff, University of Wales Press).

Moroney, B. (1938), 'Twenty months in the International Brigade', *Spain*, 45, 86–7.

Morris, J. (1984/1986), *The Matter of Wales: Epic Views of a Small Country* (Harmondsworth, Penguin).

—— (1964/1982), *Spain* (Harmondsworth, Penguin).

Muñiz, O. (1976), *Asturias en la Guerra Civil* (Salinas, Ayalga Ediciones).

Naylor, B. (1986), *Quakers in the Rhondda, 1926–1986* (Chepstow, Maes-y-Haf Educational Trust).

Nestorenko. I. *et al.* (1975), *International Solidarity with the Spanish Republic 1936–1939* (Moscow, Progress Publishers).

Nicholas, T. E. (1948), *Prison Sonnets* (Griffiths & Co.).

Norman, T. (2002), 'Ammanford and the Spanish Civil War: Ammanford miners die in Spain', terrynorm.ic.24.net/ Spain%20Rightframe.htm (4 March 2003).

O'Leary, P. (1999), *Immigration and Integration: The Irish in Wales, 1798–1922* (Cardiff, University of Wales Press).

Parnell, M. (1988), *Laughter from the Dark: A Life of Gwyn Thomas* (Murray).

Paynter, W. (1972), *My Generation* (Allen & Unwin).

Phillips, B. (1987), 'When Brechfa village was terrified by the Basques', *Western Mail* (15 December).

Pike, D. W. (1968), *Conjecture, Propaganda and Deceit and the Spanish Civil War: The International Crisis over Spain, 1936–1939, as Seen in the French Press* (Stanford, CA, California Institute of International Studies).

——— (1969), *Vae Victis! Los republicanos espanoles refugiados en Francia, 1939–44* (Paris, Ruedo Ibérico).

Pinkney, R. (1991), *Raymond Williams* (Bridgend, Seren Books).

Powell, P. W. (1971), *Tree of Hate: Propaganda and Prejudices Affecting United States Relations with the Hispanic World* (Basic Books).

Price, R. T. (1992), *Little Ireland: Aspects of the Irish and Greenhill, Swansea* (Swansea, Swansea City Council).

Pugh, J. (1988), *A Most Expensive Prisoner: Tom Jones, Rhosllannerchrugog's Biography* (Llanrwst, Gwasg Carreg Gwalch).

Rees, G. (2001), *Sketches in Autobiography*, ed. J. Harris (Cardiff, University of Wales Press).

Rees, T. and Thorpe, A. (eds) (1998), *International Communism and the Communist International, 1919–43* (Manchester, Manchester University Press).

Richardson, R. D. (1982), *Comintern Army: The International Brigades in the Spanish Civil War* (Lexington, Kentucky University Press).

Robbins, K. (1976), *The Abolition of War: The 'Peace Movement' in Britain, 1914–19* (Cardiff, University of Wales Press).

Robertson, E. H. (1993), *George: A Biography of Viscount Tonypandy* (Marshall Pickering).

Romaña Arteaga, J. M. (1984), *Historia de la Guerra Naval en Euskadi* (6 vols, Echevarri, Amigos del Libro Vasco).

Romerstein, H. (1994), *Heroic Victims: Stalin's Foreign Legion in the Spanish Civil War* (Washington, DC, Council for the Defense of Freedom).

Rosas, F. (ed.) (1998), *Portugal e a Guerra Civil de Espanha* (Lisbon, Edicoes Colibri).

Rust, W. (1939), *Britons in Spain* (Lawrence & Wishart).

Ryan, F. (ed.) (1938/1986), *The Book of the XV Brigade* (Sunderland, Frank Graham).

Sanchez, J. M. (1987), *The Spanish Civil War as a Religious Tragedy* (Notre Dame, Notre Dame University Press).

Shubert, A. (1987), *The Road to Revolution in Spain: The Coal Miners of Asturias, 1860–1934* (Urbana and Chicago, University of Illinois Press).

Skelton, R. (ed.) (1964), *Poetry of the Thirties* (Harmondsworth, Penguin).

Skoutelsky, R. (1998), *L'espoir guidait leurs pas: Les voluntaires francaises dans les Brigades internationales* (Paris, Grasset).

Sloan, P. (ed.) (1938), *John Cornford: A Memorial Volume* (Jonathan Cape).

Smith, D. (1982), *Lewis Jones* (Cardiff, University of Wales Press).

——— (1986), 'Back to the Future', *Planet*, 56 (April/May), 14–25.

——— (1993), *Aneurin Bevan and the World of South Wales* (Cardiff, University of Wales Press).

Spender, S. (1937/1978), 'Tangiers and Gibraltar now', *Left Review*, repr. in Spender, *The Thirties and After: Poetry, Politics and People* (Fontana), 62–5.

——— and Lehmann, J. (1939), *Poems for Spain* (Hogarth Press).

Stansky, P. and Abrahams, W. (1964/1994), *Journey to the Frontier: Two Roads to the Spanish Civil War* (Constable).

Stead, P. (1977), *Coleg Harlech: The First Fifty Years* (Cardiff, University of Wales Press).

Stradling, R. (1996), *Cardiff and the Spanish Civil War* (Cardiff, Butetown History and Arts Centre).

—— (ed.) (1998), *Brother against Brother: Experiences of a British Volunteer in the Spanish Civil War* (Stroud, Sutton Publishing).

—— (1999), *The Irish and the Spanish Civil War, 1936–1939: Crusades in Conflict* (Manchester, Manchester University Press).

—— (2003), *History and Legend: Writing the International Brigades* (Cardiff, University of Wales Press).

Stratton, H. (1984), *To Antifascism by Taxi* (Port Talbot, Alun Books).

Tanner, D., Williams, C. and Hopkin, D. (eds) (2000), *The Labour Party in Wales, 1900–2000* (Cardiff, University of Wales Press).

Thomas, G. (1968/1994), *A Few Selected Exits* (Bridgend, Seren Books).

Thomas, G. and Witts, M. (1975/1991), *Guernica: The Crucible of World War II* (Chelsea, MN, Scarborough House Publishers).

Thomas, H. (1961/1977), *The Spanish Civil War* (Harmondsworth, Penguin).

Thomas, R. (1986/1987), *The White Dove* (Bantam).

Toynbee, P. (1976), 'Journal of a Naïve Revolutionary', in Toynbee (ed.), *The Distant Drum: Reflections on the Spanish Civil War* (Sidgwick & Jackson).

Twamley, B. (1980), *Cardiff and Me Sixty Years Ago* (Newport, Starling Press).

Valleau, M. (1982), *The Spanish Civil War in American and European Films* (Ann Arbor, MI, UMI Research Press).

Vidal, C. (1998), *Las Brigadas Internacionales* (Madrid, Espasa Calpe).

Watkins, K. W. (1963), *Britain Divided: The Effect of the Spanish Civil War on British Public Opinion* (Nelson).

Weintraub, S. (1968), *The Last Great Cause: The Intellectuals and the Spanish Civil War* (New York, Weybright & Talley).

Wharton, B. (2000), 'La Sexta Columna: un análisis del papel portugués en la Guerra Civil Española (1936–1939)' (Salamanca, Archivo Nacional de la Guerra Civil).

Williams, C. (1996), *Democratic Rhondda: Politics and Society, 1885–1951* (Cardiff, University of Wales Press).

—— (1998), *Capitalism, Community and Conflict: The South Wales Coalfield, 1898–1947* (Cardiff, University of Wales Press).

—— Alexander, B. and Gorman, J. (eds) (1996), *Memorials of the Spanish Civil War* (Stroud, Alan Sutton).

Williams, F. (1961), *A Prime Minister Remembers: The War and Post-War Papers of the Rt Hon. Earl Attlee* (Heinemann).

Williams, G. (2002), *Glanmor Williams: A Life* (Cardiff, University of Wales Press).

Williams, G. A. (1985/1991), *When was Wales? A History of the Welsh* (Harmondsworth, Penguin).

—— (1987), 'Defending the USSR', *Planet*, 62, 37–47.

—— (1988), 'Are Welsh historians putting on the style?', *Planet*, 66, 23–31.

Williams, J. (1985), *Digest of Welsh Historical Statistics* Vol. I (Welsh Office and Government Statistical Service).

Williams, J. G. A. (1997), *The University of Wales, 1839–1939* (Cardiff, University of Wales Press).

Williams, R. (1985), *Loyalties* (Chatto & Windus).

Worsley, T. C. (1967/1985), *Flannelled Fool: A Slice of a Life in the Thirties* (Hogarth Press).

INDEX

NB   The index covers all textual references, content of end-notes which is not strictly related to source materials, and the commentary section of Table C. It does not include listings to be found in the Tables themselves.